The Data Recovery Bible, Preventing and Surviving Computer Crashes

The Data Recovery Bible, Preventing and Surviving Computer Crashes

Pamela Kane
with
Andy Hopkins

New York   London   Toronto   Sydney   Tokyo   Singapore

Brady Publishing

A Division of Prentice Hall Computer Publishing
15 Columbus Circle
New York, NY 10023

ISBN: 1-56686-080-6

Library of Congress Catalog No.: 93-16645

Printing Code: The rightmost double-digit number is the year of the book's printing; the rightmost single-digit number is the number of the book's printing. For example, 93-1 shows that the first printing of the book occurred in 1993.

96 95 94 93   4 3 2 1

Manufactured in the United States of America

Dedication

For Dr. Harold Joseph Highland, FICS

... honored mentor, eager student, treasured friend, *eminence gris*.
With sincere admiration and deep affection.

Credits

Publisher
Michael Violano

Acquisition Director
Jono Hardjowirogo

Managing Editor
Kelly D. Dobbs

Production Editor
Bettina A. Versaci

Developmental Editor
Michael Sprague

Technical Editor
Padgett Peterson

Copy Editor
Kathy Murray Sabotin

Editorial Assistant
Lisa Rose

Book Designer
Michele Laseau
Kevin Spear

Cover Designer
HUB Graphics

Production Team
Diana Bigham, Danielle Bird, Katy Bodenmiller, Jeanne Clark, Scott Cook, Tim Cox, Mark Enochs, Linda Koopman, Tom Loveman, Joe Ramon, Caroline Roop, Carrie Roth, Greg Simsic

About the Authors

Pamela Kane and Andy Hopkins have both been involved in the world of personal computers since Day One—right after the silicon in the chip cooled sufficiently to be put in the first IBM PCs.

Hopkins began his career as a "talented amateur programmer" (*LOTUS* magazine, October, 1985) writing small utilities. He soon achieved international prominence with the first two anti-Trojan horse programs CHK4BOMB and BOMBSQUAD. Kane's early work was in the area of system design. Andy credits Pam with development of the "Beach Boys Method of Program Design." Many of the programs they have developed together began with Pam saying, "Wouldn't it be nice if ..." To which Andy reliably responded, "Can't be done." Obviously, it could.

They began working together in the mid-1980s, developing the DISKJOCKEY series of programs, document and billing management systems for lawfirms, and the WRITEGUARD series of data protection utilities.

In 1987, after the first computer virus strike at Lehigh University, they were called on to create a software routine that would "find" the virus. With a gentle nudge from Gus Venditto, then Editor of *PC Magazine*, PANDA Systems and the DR. PANDA Utilities were born. The PANDA utilities share with Ross Greenberg's Flu_Shot in the distinction of being the first true anti-virus programs in the marketplace.

In 1989, after testing the waters of the computer publishing world by co-authoring COMPUTE!'s *Computer Security*, Kane wrote *V.I.R.U.S.— Vital Information Resources Under Siege* (Bantam, 1989). *V.I.R.U.S.* included the DR. PANDA Utilities and was a main selection of the Small Computer Book Club. Since then, she has written *PRODIGY Made Easy*, now in its second edition. In each book, Hopkins has contributed the technical chapters. Kane is also widely published in computer magazines and is Senior Contributing Editor of *Portable Computing magazine*. She was featured for her "data detective" activities in the November, 1992 issue of *CompuServe magazine*.

Andy attempts to maintain his amateur standing. He is the mid-day voice, Monday through Friday, of Philadelphia's WPEN (950 AM) radio. Pam is a Founding Member and officer of the Virus Security Institute, an international organization of virus and security specialists.

They live noisily in Wilmington, Delaware, with their four children, four cats, one dog, seven computers, and two sailboats.

Acknowledgments

The place to start is logical—Jono Hardjowirogo, Acquisitions Director of Brady Books, who made a phone call. "Pam, what do you know about data recovery?"

After twelve years of losing data and getting most of it back, the easy answer was, "A lot."

From that first phone call and the initiative to get this monster book and its associated software written and in your hands as quickly as possible, an incredible supporting cast at Brady was assembled: Michael Sprague, Developmental Editor, who kept the project on its ballistic track; Kelly Dobbs, Managing Editor, who always had time to explain that it was <Shift><CTRL><BT> to get us out of trouble with the style sheet; Bettina Versaci, Production Editor, who coordinated the various editing processes; and Kathy Murray Sabotin, a well-known computer writer who took time to copyedit this book while awaiting the arrival of a new baby, and whose skills added immeasurably to the finished product. Sincere thanks.

Thanks, next, to Padgett Peterson for his technical edit. There are few people in this world to whom Andy Hopkins would entrust his work for criticism. Padgett's #1 among them; Bill Gates may be a distant second.

Thanks to the other founding members of the Virus Security Institute for being on hand with quick answers when they were needed: Harold Highland, Klaus Brunnstein, Ross Greenberg, Jon David, Padgett Peterson, Frisk Skulason, Alan Solomon, Chris Fischer, Vesselin Bontchev, Yisrael Radai, and Bill Caelli.

There are a number of thank-yous to be spread around various locations on the PRODIGY Service. Thanks to the folks in PC Club for coming up with your own questions that, often, helped us to figure out the right way to address a problem. Thanks, too, to those of you who contributed Stupid Human Tricks. The public domain and shareware offerings on ZiffNet led us to several of the utilities on the disk in the back of the book. And then there are the HWs. Thanks for the chocolate, the frog spit, the ceremonial dances, and proper respect for the aqua chenille concept of writing.

At Patri-Soft, thanks to Norm Patriquin and Doug Nasluchacz.

Special thanks to Ed Ross for rewriting HOWBAD to our specifications—literally overnight.

Thanks to Jack Bologna for being sufficiently paranoid to come up with the disaster recovery planning material in Chapter Six.

Rob Rosenberger and Ross Greenberg rushed an update of their famous Virus Myths treatise so it could be included. Thanks, guys.

We're grateful to Microsoft Corporation for providing DOS 6.0 in advance of release so that both the book itself and the PANDA Utilities included are as up to date as possible. Thanks also to Fifth Generation Software, Symantec Corporation, and Central Point Software for being on the spot with the latest releases.

Thanks, as always, to the kids ... Rob, Max, Liz, and JT ... and to their grandmother, who's still waiting for a book she can understand.

TOC-At-A-Glance

Introduction xxxi

PART I EDUCATION

1 In the Beginning 3

2 A PC Primer 11

3 Bits and Pieces: The Hard(ware) Way 33

4 Software 43

5 Computer Viruses and Malware 57

6 Disaster Recovery Plans 73

7 Stupid Human Tricks 87

PART II PREVENTION

8 The Backup Bible 107

9 Backup II 123

PART III THE DATA RECOVERY COOKBOOK

10 Troubleshooting 137

11 Disk Errors and Failures System 153

12 The Operating System (OS) 163

13 DOS Error Messages 187

14 Let's Get Technical 215

15 Tips, Tricks, Traps 273

PART IV THE DISK IN BACK

16 The Disk Bank **305**

A Virus Facts and Fun **337**

B The Virus List **353**

C-1 MegaBack **363**

C-2 PCOPY Version 9.2B **417**

C-3 Stowaway: True Archival **455**
System for PC Systems

D Glossary **509**

Index **527**

Contents

Introduction xxxi

PART I Education

1 In the Beginning... 3
    Data Basics 4
    The Hardware Store 5
    The Software Stop: DOS 1.0 - 6.0 6
    Applications Accepted Here 8
    Environmental Concerns 8
    The Best Defense... 9

2 A PC Primer 11
    Number, Please: Computer Math 12
        Decimal versus Binary 12
        Hexidecimal Notation 13
    The ASCII Letter Sweater 14
    The Chips Are Down: How They Work 24
    Thanks for the Memories: RAM and ROM 27
    CPU Stuff 27
    Boot Camp: How It All Works Together 28
    COMMAND.COM-Base Commander 30
    Formatting 31
    WONK Cum Laude 32

3 Bits and Pieces: The Hard(ware) Way 33
    Your Keyboard: The Key to the City 33
    Your Monitor: Time for a Screen Test 35
    Floppy Drives: The Discus Throw 36
    Hard Facts about the Hard Drive 38
    The Power Supply and Your Power Monopoly:
      Power to the PC 40
    Laptops and Notebooks: Little Machines,
      Big Problems 41
    The Spare Parts Department: A Shopping List 41

4 Software 43

Creation versus Evolution 43
Import Duties: Moving Data between Programs 45
Missing, Presumed Lost 46
Stupid Software Tricks 47
   Death by Disk Swap 47
   The Installation from Hell 48
   AUTOEXEC.BATty 51
   TSRs at War 52
   TSR Tweaking 53
Don't Do Windows? 54
Write On/Over 55
SoftSell 55
SoftWarning 56

5 Computer Viruses and Malware 57

The First Virus? 58
Viruses Defined 59
Early Malware 62
What to Call Them? 63
Viruses Sorted Out 64
   Boot Infectors: Disk-Based 64
   Program Infectors: Execution-Based 65
   Direct and Indirect Infectors 66
   Stealth 67
   Stealth Techniques and Targeting 67
Anti-Virus Solutions 68
   Scanners 68
   Integrity Checkers 69
   Behavior Blockers 70
   Point-Counterpoint 70
   Clean-Up Caution 71
Keep Your Fingers Crossed 72

6 Disaster Recovery Plans 73

How Much Planning Is Enough? 74
Management Considerations 75
Vulnerability Assessment 77
Hardware 79
Software 79

Working with DOS 80
%$#@& Software 81
RTB: Documentation 82
Media Blitz: Your Storage Media 83
Let's Get Physical: Site Security 85

7 Stupid Human Tricks 87

FORMAT Me! 88
Auto-Pilot 88
Don't Leave through the Back Door 89
Know the Question before You Answer 90
Software Piracy 91
Know Your Software 92
Error (Message) Prone 92
Trust Me! 93
Outsmarting INSTALL 93
Ray-Ban 94
DELDOT 94
Stupid Pet Tricks 94
Keyboard Bashing 96
Real-Life Experiences 96
  Stupid Human Trick #1: The Clobbered Keyboard ... 96
  Stupid Human Trick #2: The Invisible Update 97
  Stupid Human Trick #3: The Backup School
    of Hard Knocks 97
  Stupid Human Trick #4: Copy Gone Wrong 97
  Stupid Human Trick #5: Stewed Story Searching 98
  Stupid Human Trick #6: File Hide-and-Seek 98
  Stupid Human Trick #7: The Scenic Route
    to No Backup Canyon 98
  Stupid Human Trick #8: That Freebie's a Keeper 99
  Stupid Human Trick #9: DELETE Can Be
    Hazardous to Your Health 99
  Stupid Human Trick #10: Low Memory Laser
    Show 99
  Stupid Human Trick #11: When It Rains, It Pours ... 99
  Stupid Human Trick #12: A Little Goes a Long
    Way? Not Far Enough… 100
  Stupid Human Trick #13: Consumer Training 100

Stupid Human Trick #14: Not a Boot Disk
in Sight 101
Stupid Human Trick #15: Eh? Can't Hear You! 101
Stupid Human Trick #16: Hat-in-Hand DOS
Retrieval 101
Stupid Human Trick #17: Look before You Leap! .. 101
Stupid Human Trick #18: You Speakin' My
Language? 102
Stupid Human Trick #19: Curiosity *Scared*
the Cat 102
Stupid Human Trick #20: The Forgotten Files 102
Stupid Human Trick #21: AUTOEXEC.BAT
by Any Other Name… 102
Your Turn 103

PART II Prevention

8 The Backup Bible 107

Silent Screams 107
Me and My Data 108
What Should You Back Up? 110
How To Back Up 110
File Management—Naming Conventions 112
An EXTended Example 112
More Nomenclature 113
Backup Basics: DOS 113
Using BACKUP and RESTORE 114
Using COPY 115
Using XCOPY 116
Using DISKCOPY 117
Plain Vanilla Backup (hold the jimmies) 118
Other Backup Methods 121

9 Backup II 123

What Should You Back Up? 123
When Should You Back Up? 125
Ways to Back Up 126
Backup Software 126
Backup Hardware 127
Off-Site Backups 128

Dial 1-800-BACKUPS 129
Remote Control 130
    MDR (Minimum Design Requirement) 130
    Homebase 131
The Rational Archives 132
    Single Project Archives 132
    Rolling Thunder Archives 132
Fort (Hard) Knox 133

PART III The Data Recovery Cookbook

10 Troubleshooting 137

My Computer Won't Start! 137
    Is It Plugged in? 137
    Is There Power in the Wall Socket? 137
    Does the Computer Make Any Noise at All? 138
The Fan Makes Noise, but Nothing Happens 138
    Do You See Any Messages on the Screen at All? 138
    Does the Speaker Beep? 138
    Does Drive A: Begin To Spin? 139
    Does Drive A: Stop Spinning? 139
    I Got this Far and It Still Won't Work 139
...That Rhymes with "V" and Stands for Virus 140
    Double-Check the Monitor 140
    Try a New Disk 140
    The New Disk Doesn't Work, Either 140
I Get a Number on the Screen and It Won't Work 141
    xxxx 201 141
    301 141
    601 142
    1701 142
    The Screen Says "Parity Check 1" or
      "Parity Check 2" 142
I Type a Command and the Screen Starts Scrolling... 143
Sometimes It Runs the Wrong Program 144
I Know the File Is There, but I Can't Find It 145
    I Saved the File, but When I Turned
      the Computer on, It Was Gone 145
    My Disks Won't Work in another Computer 146

I Get a Message That Says… 148
S.O.L. (Stopped Or Locked Out) 149
   So What's to Lose? 149
   The CAD Method 149
   The Big Red Switch...150
   What's Different? 150
   What Did I Do Differently? 151
   Aunt PANDA's Best Advice 152

11 Disk Errors and Failures System 153

Operating on Disks...153
Let's Get Physical 154
Not All Codes Are Area.......................................154
Protect Me from Myself 155
Head 'em Up (Move 'em Out) 155
Fondly Fondling Floppies.....................................156
How Much Wood Could a Woodchuck Chuck? 158
Getting Harder 159
Faster Than a Speeding Bullet 161
Let's Get Logical 162

12 The Operating System (OS) 163

The History of DOS 163
Upgrade (I think I can, I think I can)........................164
Don't Cry for Me…As We Peel the OS Onion 166
   Basic Input Output System 166
   Basic Input Output...166
   Disk Operating System 167
   The Outer Shell 167
Is That Device Logical?.......................................168
Logical Sectors 170
The 32-Megabyte Barrier 170
How DOS Does It 170
The Inside Story 171
The BIOS Parameter Block....................................172
Keeping the FAT Slim 172
Direct(ory) Me to the Proper Cluster 174
   OFFSET 00h: FILENAME (Eight Bytes)
      EXTENSION (Three Bytes) 175
   OFFSET 0Bh: Attribute (One Byte) 176

OFFSET 0Ch: Reserved (0A Bytes) 177
OFFSET 16h: File Time (Two Bytes) 177
OFFSET 18h: File Date (Two Bytes) 177
OFFSET 1Ah: Starting Cluster Number
  (Two Bytes)...177
OFFSET 1Ch: File Size (Four Bytes) 178
Data Area 178
Storing and Retrieving Files 178
Creating Files...178
Opening Files 179
Writing to Files..180
Reading from Files..181
Closing Files 182
Erasing Files 182
Un-erasing Files 182
Other Problems 185
Abnormal Termination of Programs 186

13 DOS Error Messages 187

Disk Problems..187
Your Computer Won't Boot from the Hard Disk ...187
Your Computer Won't Start from the Hard Disk
  ("Starting MS-DOS" Message) 190
Deleted File..190
Removed Subdirectory 191
Bad File Allocation Table (FAT)...............................191
Accidental Floppy Disk Format 192
Accidental Hard Disk Format 192
Lost or Damaged Subdirectories 193
Missing File(s)...194
Overwritten Files 195
Bad Root Directory 195
DOS Error Messages (COMMAND.COM) 195
Abort, Retry, Ignore, Fail? 196
Access denied 197
Bad command or filename...197
Bad or missing command interpreter 197
Cannot find system files 198
Cannot load COMMAND, system halted 199
Data error reading/writing drive x 199

Disk boot failure 200
Divide overflow 200
Drive not ready error reading/writing drive x 201
Error in EXE file 201
Error loading operating system 201
Error writing fixed disk 201
Error writing directory 202
Error writing FAT 202
Error writing partition table 203
File allocation table bad, drive x 203
File creation error 203
File not found 204
General failure reading/writing drive x 204
Incorrect DOS version 205
Insert disk with \COMMAND.COM in drive x 205
Insufficient disk space 206
Invalid drive specification 206
Invalid partition table 207
Invalid path, not directory, dir not empty 207
Memory allocation error 209
Missing operating system 209
Non-DOS disk error reading/writing drive x 209
Non-system disk or disk error 210
Not ready error reading/writing drive x 210
No room for system on destination disk 210
Path not found 211
Read fault error reading drive x 211
Sector not found error reading/writing drive x 212
Seek error reading/writing drive x 212
Top level process aborted, cannot continue 212
Write protect error writing drive x 212

14 Let's Get Technical **215**
WARNING LABEL 215
Pocket Protectors Optional 216
Diagnosis and Repair with CHKDSK 217
Using CHKDSK to correct errors 219
Lost Clusters (Allocation Units) 219
Cross Linked Files (Directory Entry) 222
Cross-Linked Files (FAT Entry) 224

Allocation error (size adjusted) 227
Invalid subdirectory entry 228
Using DEBUG.COM (DEBUG.EXE) 232
STUPID MATH TRICKS (Hex on you) 235
Repairing the DOS BOOT SECTOR 238
Booting Up 240
Virus in the Boot Sector 241
REPLACING THE BOOT SECTOR (Diskettes) 242
REPLACING THE BOOT SECTOR (Hard disks) 243
The Master Boot Record Explained 246
Replacing the MBR start up code. 249
RECONSTRUCTING PARTITION DATA
  (The Harder Way) 259
COMPLETING THE MBR 266
Conclusions 266
Repairing The FAT 267
Repairing the Root Directory 268
What to Look for 269
Repairing Subdirectories 270
Deciphering the FAT 270
<EOF> 272

15 Tips, Tricks, and Traps **273**
There's Safety in Shrinkwrap 273
Beyond Repair(shops) 274
Beware the Jabberwock 275
Beware the Jabberwock II 276
Beware the Jabberwock III 277
The Bleeding Edge of Technology 277
Vaporware 278
Weirdware 279
Adopt-A-Wonk 280
(Black) Mail Order 281
Flee Markets 281
The Dangers of Defrag 282
BATs in the Belfry: BATch Files 283
Can You EXE(cute) a COM(mand)? 284
What's in a Name? An EXE by Any Other
  Name Would Load as Sweet 284
The COM before the Workhorse 285

Go To… 286
TSRs: A Hitchhiker's Guide to the Memory 286
   Rules? We Don't Need No Stinking Rules! 287
   DOS Memory Allocation 287
   Getting Control of the Situation 288
   We Don't Do DOS (Again) 288
   Let Me Outta' Here 288
Devices and Files…What's in a Name Revisited 289
   Workin' on the Chain Gang 289
   A Device Is Not a File 289
Supporting Cast 290
At Last It Can Be Told 290
EOF Marker 301

PART IV The Disk In Back

16 The Disk Bank 305

   PANDA UTILITIES 305
   PATRI-SOFT UTILITIES 306
   FROM THE PUBLIC DOMAIN 307
The Disk 307
The INSTALL Batch File 308
The PANDA Programs 308
PANDA Programs 309
   BOOTINFO.EXE 309
   BROWSE.COM 310
   DISKINFO.EXE 311
   DRHOOK.EXE 312
   PARTINFO.EXE 313
   WHEREIS.EXE 314
   MONITOR.EXE 315
   NODEL.EXE 317
   DELALL.EXE 319
   FINDPART.EXE 319
MegaBack 320
   MegaBack Features 321
   Backing up with MegaBack 322
Stowaway 324
   Stowaway Features 325
   Archiving with Stowaway 327

PCOPY and PMOVE 327
   The PMOVE Option of PCOPY 329
   PCOPY Features 330
LHARC 332
CMOS.EXE 333
DELBUT.COM 334
CHKDIR 334
HOWBAD 335
PANDA Programs Not On This Disk 336
Technical Support 336

A Virus Facts and Fun 337

Virus Myths Explained 337
   All purposely destructive code spreads
     like a virus. 339
   Viruses and Trojan horses are a recent
     phenomenon. 340
   Viruses are written by teenage hackers. 340
   Viruses infect 25 percent of all IBM PCs
     every month. 340
   Only 500 different viruses? But most experts
     talk about them in the thousands. 341
   A virus could destroy all the files on my disks. 341
   Viruses have been documented on over
     300,000 computers {1988}. 341
   Viruses have been documented on over
     400,000 computers {1989}. 341
   The Michelangelo virus alone was estimated
     to be on over 5,000,000 computers {1992}...........341
   Viruses can hide inside a data file..........................342
   Some viruses can completely hide themselves
     from all antivirus software, making them
     truly undetectable. 342
   BBSs and shareware programs spread viruses. 343
   So-called boot-sector viruses travel primarily
     in software downloaded from BBSs. 344
   My files are damaged, so it must have been
     a virus attack. 344
   Donald Burleson was convicted of releasing
     a virus. 344

Robert Morris Jr. released a benign virus
on a defense network. 345
The U.S. government planted a virus in Iraqi
military computers during the Gulf War. 346
Viruses can spread to all sorts of computers. 347
My backups will be worthless if I back up
a virus. 347
Antivirus software will protect me from viruses. 347
Read-only files are safe from virus infections. 347
Viruses can infect files on write-protected
floppy disks. 348
Virus Prevention Guidelines 348
Virus Fun 349
Moving Right Along… 352

B The Virus List **353**

C-1 MegaBack **363**
IMPORTANT WARRANTY INFORMATION 363
TRIAL USE (SHAREWARE EVALUATION
VERSION) WARRANTY: 363
REGISTERED VERSION ONLY WARRANTY: 363
About MegaBack 364
MegaBack Features 364
Backing up with MegaBack 365
The compressed size of the backup file 367
Full/Incremental Backup 367
Multiple Hard Disks 368
Complements Tape Backup 369
Select/Exclude 369
Reliability 370
System Setup/Installation 371
Setting system options 372
Quick Start Guide 375
Starting MegaBack 376
Backing up files 376
Restoring files 378
How MegaBack works 380
Backup Volumes 380
Backup Sets 380

Backup File Index 381
The Backup Volume Index 381
MegaBack reference 381
MegaBack's Main Menus 382
Backup Processing 383
    Backup Type Selection Display 383
    Full Backup <F> 384
    Incremental Backup <I> 384
    List Files <L> 385
    Backup Status Display 385
    Disk Statistics 386
    Request for Backup Volumes 386
    Recovering from Disk Write Errors 387
Restore 389
    Entering Restore Criteria 390
    Selection criteria specification 390
    Listing Files to Restore 392
    Restore File Select List Processing 393
    Starting Restore 395
    Restore Processing 396
    Overlaying Files with duplicate Names 397
Restoring to an Empty System 398
Making a System Recovery Boot Diskette 398
Utility Functions 399
    Selection/Exclusion Processing 401
    Backup File Selection Operation 402
    Marking a full directory 403
    Verify Backup Volume Data 404
    Build Index from Backup Volume 405
    Reinitialize Backup Indexes 406
    Set Alternate Display Colors 407
    Synchronize Indexes with Hard Disk 408
Command Line Operation 409
Specifying Options through DOS Environment
    Variables 410
Backup Maintenance 411
    Making Copies of Backup Volumes 412
The Context-Sensitive Help System 412
System Requirements 413

Troubleshooting 414

    I/O errors on disks 414

    Error Messages 414

Technical Support 414

C-2 PCOPY Version 9.2B 417

DISCLAIMER 417

LICENSE.. 418

REGISTRATION 418

PCOPY 420

The PMOVE Option of PCOPY 421

    PCOPY Features 421

PCOPY Command and Parameters 423

    Example of /CD Parameter 425

IMPORTANT!! 428

Activating Exclude 430

PCOPY Menu Operation 437

PCOPY MENU (1 of 3)... 437

    Copy Profile 437

    From Path 438

    Drives 438

    To Path 438

    Process Options? 438

    Multiple Directories? 439

    Directory Actions? 439

    File Filtering? 440

The second menu of PCOPY options 440

    LIST FILES NOT PROCESSED 440

    SET DOS FILE CHANGED INDICATOR
      AFTER COPY 440

    SET DOS FILE DATE TO TODAY AFTER COPY 441

    FILL OUTPUT DISKS EFFICIENTLY
      WITH BEST FIT 441

    ERASE OUTPUT DISKS BEFORE USING ERASE
      ON ALL BUT FIRST 441

    APPEND COPIED FILES TOGETHER IN ONE
      OUTPUT FILE 441

    FILES MAY BE DIVIDED INTO PARTS
      ACROSS DISKS 441

ASK FOR MULTIPLE INPUT DISKETTES 441
DISABLE SOUNDS DURING PROCESSING 442
The third and last PCOPY menu 442
Select files by size ===> 442
Select by date From Date: to Date: 442
Stop when Source Drives freespace > 442
Stop when Target Drives freespace < 442
Duplicate Files: 442
Networks 443
Process files in date sequence 443
WAYS TO USE PCOPY 443
Site licensing plans for one or more
  Patriquin utilities: 453

C-3 Stowaway: True Archival System for PC Systems 455
Stowaway User's Guide 455
IMPORTANT WARRANTY INFORMATION 455
REGISTERED VERSION ONLY WARRANTY: 456
Important Information About This Manual 456
About Stowaway 457
Stowaway Features 458
Archiving with Stowaway 458
System Setup 459
Setting system options 460
C> STOW<Enter> 460
Drive to archive to/from? 461
Level of compression desired? 461
Disk capacity? 461
Enter descriptions when archiving (Y/N/Ask) 461
Perform a group archive? (Y/N/Ask) 462
Enter an expiration date for files archived?
  (Y/N) 462
Verify archive data after it is written? (Y/N) 463
Use DOS Verify feature? (Y/N) 463
Sound speaker tones when action needed?
  (Y/N) 463
Action to perform on archived files? 463
Overlay files when restoring? (Y/N/Ask) 464

Test to verify installation 465
SET STOW=/ID:TMP 465
Quick Start guide 465
Starting Stowaway 465
Archiving files 466
Restoring files 468
Archival Concepts 470
Archival vs Compression Systems 472
How Stowaway works 472
Archive Volumes 472
Archive Sets 473
Archive File Index 473
Archive File Expiration Dates 474
Other Archive Indexes 474
Stowaway reference 475
Preparing archive volume sets 475
Stowaway's Main Menus 475
Manual Archive Processing 476
Entering archive file descriptions 476
Request window for file description 477
The Archive File Selection Display 477
Selecting Groups of Files for Archival 478
Archive File Selection Operation 478
Archiving a full directory 480
Completing file selection 480
Automatic Archive Processing 480
Pattern to archive: 481
Select only files needing backup? 482
Reset ARCHIVE attribute after archival? 482
Specifying Archive Groups 482
Archive groups... 482
Adding an archive group 483
Archive Processing 483
Recovering from disk write errors 484
QuitStop archiving immediately. 485
Force new disk and try again 485
Completing archive 485
Saving Archive index backup to disk.
Please wait 485

Restore 486
    Entering Restore Criteria (level 1) 487
    Listing Files to Restore (level 3) 489
    Restore File Select List Processing 489
    Contents of archive list views 489
Starting Restore 491
Overlaying Files with duplicate Names 491
    Yes/No/Update/Continuous update/continuous
        Replace 492
Completing Restore 492
    Utility Functions 493
Command Line operation 498
    Specifying options through DOS environment
        variables 501
Archive Maintenance 501
    Multiple Archive sets 501
Backing up the indexes 503
Making copies of archive data 503
The Context Sensitive Help System 504
    System Requirements 505
Troubleshooting 505
    I/O errors on disks 505
    Error Messages 506
Technical Support 506

D Glossary 509

Index 527

Introduction

This is a big, whomping book. Because you were not scared off by either the size or the price, we can draw two logical conclusions:

1. You think you have just lost all the data on your computer and you're desperate; or

2. You're really serious about not losing your data.

We hope it's number 2.

Word One...
Backup! Backup! Backup!

This is The Word for data recovery. Period. If you have your data, you can't lose it. You'll see this message repeated, in one way or another, countless times in this book. Just to show how serious we are about this, stop reading and remove the disk from the back of the book now. Put it in your A drive, type the following command, and press Enter:

```
HOWBAD
```

We're that serious. And so should you be.

Is This Book for You?

Yes. If you can create data, you can lose data. And if you can create data, you can learn how to keep it safe from harm. Sooner or later, though, each of us *will* lose data.

Yes. This book *is* for you, regardless of the level of your computer literacy. Every concept you need to know is explained simply and clearly, from the origin of the term *bug* (that, no doubt, every computer user has heard) through the use of the DOS DEBUG program.

All Procedures in This Book Can Be Performed with Simple Tools Found around the Home or Office

You only need a few things:

➤ A PC running PC-DOS or MS-DOS, from version 2.0 through version 6.0

➤ This book

➤ Extra disks for backups

➤ A screwdriver (optional)

How This Book Is Organized

Part I, "Education," includes seven chapters that serve as a short course on the hows and whys of PCs and those who use them. These chapters deal with the basics of hardware and software, computer viruses, planning for disaster, and provide a wry look at the Stupid Human Tricks we've all performed.

Part II, "Prevention," will show you the ins and outs of various ways to manage, preserve, and protect your data.

Part III, "The Data Recovery Cookbook," explains what can happen and what to do about it using commercial utilities, DOS functions, and the utilities included with this book. You'll also find a chapter on tips, tricks, and traps.

Part IV, "The Disk Bank," includes the utilities provided on the disk in the back of this book. Many of them were written by PANDA staff particularly for this book. Others are fine shareware and public domain programs selected especially to form a fine toolkit. This section contains the documentation for these programs.

NOTE

If you bought this book for reason number 1 (because you think you've lost your data), you may want to proceed directly to Chapter 13 ("Troubleshooting") and possibly beyond, to at least diagnose your problem.

Underknowledged?

A favorite third-grader, long ago, once defended a poor test score by saying "It's not that I'm stupid or didn't try—I was just *under-knowledged.*" In the world of personal computers, we *all* start out underknowledged. Some just start sooner than others.

As you read through the early sections of the book, you may run across an unfamiliar term set in boldfaced type that's not explained at that point. Look to the margin for an icon directing you to the chapter where that term or concept is explained in detail. If the term isn't defined and you see the icon, it's not essential for you to understand fully the term or concept at that particular moment in time.

Here's an example:

If the **frobotz** isn't properly connected to a settled connector, the wimwams may...

There's also a glossary of terms at the back of the book.

If Extra Help Is What You Crave, Then Check the Icons. Burma Shave.

Throughout this book, you'll see special icons directing your attention to information that is so important it needs to be set apart from the regular text. You'll see the following icons:

NOTE

Think about this.

TIP

Useful information.

CAUTION

Be careful.

WARNING

Read it and believe it.

 The disk in the back of the book has a program for this function.

In addition, we've used the following conventions for setting out commands you enter from the keyboard, messages returned to you on the screen, and other miscellaneous extras:

Words that are defined appear in *italic* type.

On-screen messages are placed in `monospace` type.

DOS commands are shown in uppercase type (although you can enter them in either upper- or lowercase characters).

Tables are used, where appropriate, to display information in a columnar format.

Numbered and bulleted lists are included to help set off steps and items in a series.

PART

Education

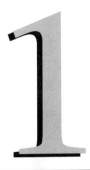

In the Beginning...

IBM created the PC. Before creating the PC, however, IBM created a marketing study. This marketing study, quoted years later across the country at various 1987 roll-out parties for the PS/2 line, showed that about 500,000 of these little computers would be sold. That was not the first—or last—time IBM would be wrong about something in the personal computer arena.

Today, over 80 million personal computers are used around the world. It is tempting to wonder where the people who did that study are today.

Along with the PC came the disk operating system, DOS. Given the marketing studies, no one was surprised when IBM purchased the operating system from outside. Given what's happened over the past twelve plus years, no one is surprised that Bill Gates, who sold his DOS to IBM, is one of the richest men in the world.

If IBM could have known or predicted the incredible success of the PC, they would probably still be writing an operating system and there would be no PCs at all!

At PANDA, we still have—and sometimes use—one of the earliest IBM PCs. The system is a PC1, and originally, it came with 64K on the motherboard and one floppy drive. The computer has been enhanced since then. Also in inventory, we have a later model PC1—state of the art at the moment of purchase in late 1984—with 128Kb on the motherboard and two floppy drives. Nobody can remember what happened to the AT, but several hard drives from that particular model are sleeping with the fishes.

Today, you can purchase two 486s with huge hard drives, incredibly crisp VGA monitors, and more memory than the entire cast of Cats could sing about for the same price as one of those early PC1s.

Enter the user. The very first PCs were purchased by computer hobbyists who were greeted with DOS and a PC version of BASIC. If you wanted your PC to do something, you pretty much had to make it happen by writing a program in BASIC. You could toy with the BASIC sample programs that played music, calculated mortgages, and did a few other things long since forgotten. Three software programs were available at the outset, all from IBM: VisiCalc (a spreadsheet), MASM (Microsoft Assembler), and a rudimentary word processor.

Before long, third-party software, developed in garages and basements across the country, began to make an appearance. Lotus 1-2-3, dBASE II, and WordStar quickly leapt to industry standard status.

And data began to be created. And lost.

Nothing is particularly mysterious about creating data or recovering data that's been lost. The biggest question when data is lost is usually "How'd that happen?" In order to dispel the mystery, it's important to have some understanding of how things happen in the PC world. This chapter is dedicated to the absolute basics.

Data Basics

Computers in general—and PCs in particular—are rather simple-minded machines. They only know two states: off and on. Not surprisingly, this is called the *binary* system.

A computer sees everything stored on it as *data*. This technically correct definition of data means that data is anything the computer can read and anything that can be lost. For the purpose of this book, breaking data down a bit further—into *programs* and *data*—simplifies things.

NOTE

In the arcane world of data modeling, the two sorts of data are called process data (programs) and semantic data (what they create).

Programs, often called *applications*, are the software packages you install on your PC such as spreadsheets, word processors, communications programs, and database managers. DOS is made up of a set of programs. Program files are identified by the extensions .COM or .EXE. COM is short for COMMAND, and EXE is an abbreviation of EXECUTABLE.

Some programs do just what they are told to do, simply, with no fuss and without really creating data. The DOS COPY command (part of COMMAND.COM) does just that. The following command simply copies a file from drive A to drive B:

```
COPY A:FILENAME.EXT B:
```

And that's all. No data is created in the process, although the data *is* replicated by the copying process.

Using another DOS program—either EDLIN or EDIT—to type and save a batch file does create data. Some applications also create data in response to your instructions. Good examples are spreadsheets that do all sorts of fancy math upon command, word processing programs that create tables of contents or indexes from codes you imbed in the documents themselves, or relational databases that can draw information from several sources to create a new set of data after you've defined the form in which the data is to appear.

The Hardware Store

Hardware consists of the components of your physical system and the peripherals you attach to it. A PC has three major components: the system unit, the monitor, and the keyboard.

The *system unit*, often incorrectly called the CPU, is the box that either sits on your desk or, if you have what's called a *tower configuration*, stands on the floor under your desk. (These definitions don't fit if you're using a portable of some sort.) The *CPU*—central processing unit—is a chunk of silicon inside the system unit. You probably call that chunk a *chip*.

Inside the system unit is a *power supply* that provides electricity to the components. The constant noise your PC makes is the power supply's fan. The floor of the system unit is the *motherboard*, made up of chips and circuitry. Usually, you will find a *hard drive* inside the box as well as one or more *disk drives*.

The *keyboard* and *monitor* are connected to the system unit through cables, both for input (from the keyboard) and output (to the monitor) and for electrical power. Monitors are sometimes called *CRTs* (for Cathode Ray Tube) or *VDTs* (for Visual Display Terminal).

NOTE

In the newer notebook and laptop computers, the separateness of the components is not as obvious as in a desktop configuration, but separate they are.

Obvious peripherals are printers, modems, mice, and external backup devices such as tape drives, CD-ROM drives, and floptical drives. Peripherals are any pieces of hardware that you attach to your PC. These devices connect to the system unit through a *data port*. Data ports come in two flavors: *serial* and *parallel*.

The Software Stop: DOS 1.0 - 6.0

Software is to a computer what gasoline is to a Ferrari. Without software (or gasoline), all you have is an expensive piece of machinery that's going nowhere fast.

The basic software on any computer is DOS, the disk operating system. The master DOS program, COMMAND.COM, made its debut on August 4, 1981. Everything on the very first PC-DOS disk, including 23 sample BASIC programs and BASIC itself, took up 136,405 bytes. Here's a DIR listing of those very first DOS programs:

```
COMMAND  COM     3231 08-04-81  12:00a

FORMAT   COM     2560 08-04-81  12:00a

CHKDSK   COM     1395 08-04-81  12:00a

SYS      COM      896 08-04-81  12:00a

DISKCOPY COM     1216 08-04-81  12:00a

DISKCOMP COM     1124 08-04-81  12:00a

COMP     COM     1620 08-04-81  12:00a

DATE     COM      252 08-04-81  12:00a

TIME     COM      250 08-04-81  12:00a

MODE     COM      860 08-04-81  12:00a

EDLIN    COM     2392 08-04-81  12:00a

DEBUG    COM     6049 08-04-81  12:00a

LINK     EXE    43264 08-04-81  12:00a
```

Of those listed, TIME and DATE have become internal commands. EDLIN has, by and large, been supplemented with a far superior text editor, EDIT.

TIP

If you plan to have more than a passing relationship with your PC, you should learn to use either of the DOS editing programs. In the case of serious DATA loss, being able to create files like CONFIG.SYS and AUTOEXEC.BAT with these simple editing programs can save your skin.

COMMAND.COM for DOS 5.0 takes up 47,845 bytes, and COMMAND.COM of Beta 5 of DOS 6.0 weighs in at 52,841 bytes. That's an increase of 1,635 percent from DOS 1.0 to DOS 6.0.

The *hidden files*—the ones that run before you're even aware of any activity—have increased, too. IBMBIO.COM has gone from 1,920 bytes to 40,454. IBMDOS.COM's increase is a bit smaller: from 6,400 bytes to 37,480. IBMDOS.COM and IBMBIO.COM are the file names used by PC-DOS. If you're using MS-DOS, the file names will be MSDOS.SYS and IO.SYS.

Applications Accepted Here

Once DOS is up and running, applications (programs) come next. These applications are spreadsheets, database managers, word processors, communications packages, utilities—including data recovery and security utilities—and games. Some omnibus packages such as Symphony, combine almost every type of application.

Environmental Concerns

Many PCs now run within particular environments created by additional software, such as a DOS shell or Microsoft Windows. Part of the charm of environments is that they allow you to bypass learning about or understanding DOS and can enable you, with mouse in hand, to skate through the most elementary level of PC use.

Today, it is possible that a significant percentage of PC users have never seen this:

```
C:>
```

The days of an almost empty screen with the cursor's hostile blink challenging you to do something—*anything*—are almost gone. GUI, short for *Graphical User Interface* and pronounced *gooey*, is hot now. Some people say GUI stands for *Guess—U are In it* because more guessing goes on in GUI than in a room full of high school seniors taking SATs. When using a GUI, you're often tempted to think "Hmm, let me click on this and see what happens..."

> *"Easy to use is easy to say."* —Jeff Garbers

Not knowing what a particular command means or what it is going to do is one of the greatest dangers of GUI. It's too tempting—and too easy—not to do your homework.

The Best Defense...

The best defense, as they say, is a good offense (except maybe in football). If the first parts of this book can keep you from losing DATA, everyone will be happy. There is only one absolute rule in the world of computing:

BACK UP! BACK UP! BACK UP!

The motto of the ladies who practice the world's oldest profession is "You got it; you sell it; you still got it!" This motto can be applied, with a small change, to DATA: "You back it up; you lose it; you still got it!"

There is nothing on or in your PC that's irreplaceable—except your data. And that's what this book is about.

CHAPTER

A PC Primer

In the early days of PCs, there were *gurus*—people who had either learned through trial and error, or understood through intuition and logic, just how PCs worked. Whenever more than four or five PCs were clustered together, a guru emerged from the ranks of users.

Back in the day when PCs were new, gurus tended to wear plaid shirts and pocket protectors. They were easy to spot. As PC use proliferated in corporate America, the idea of appointing PC managers seemed like a good one. Most companies did not require that their employees have PC experience, and if you attended management seminars and had good performance reviews in your previous position, those considerations carried more weight than your PC experience or lack of it. You could recognize a good PC manager by his or her ability to find and rely on a resident guru.

As managers built empires by requesting budgets for more and more PCs, more and more software, and more and more training sessions and consulting services, the gurus went around cleaning up after them. The gurus, individually but almost as a cohesive whole, soon figured out two important things: (1) they weren't management material; and (2) they weren't getting paid adequately for their work and knowledge. Thus, lots of gurus struck out on their own.

Many of yesterday's gurus now consult with their previous employers at rates that are many times higher than their former salaries. A few have been featured in national magazines as extremely successful businesspeople. Some are delivering pizza.

Today, the nomenclature has changed—possibly due to the fact that American culture is now influenced more by Dana Carvey than by John Lennon—and the people who "get" PCs are called *wonks*.

In this chapter, you'll learn enough to pass yourself off as a wonk should the need arise. You'll look inside that box sitting on your desk or your lap, peek behind the fancy interface that greets you when you power up, and see beyond your PC as a very smart typewriter, adding machine, or telephone connection.

And if you really get hooked (or you already *are* a wonk), proceed to Chapter 14 where a former guru holds forth in far greater detail.

Number, Please: Computer Math

If people were porpoises, we would all understand binary math. We'd count on our flippers instead of on our fingers. Even if we counted by things we have in twos—eyes, ears, nostrils, arms, legs, hands, feet—we'd be ahead in understanding the binary system. As it is, someone somewhere set up a school in a cave and began using *fingers* as measures for counting. That's the decimal system, and we're stuck with it.

Decimal versus Binary

The decimal system uses ten digits: 1, 2, 3, 4 , 5, 6, 7, 8, 9, and (gotcha!) 0. The **binary** system uses only two digits: 1 and 0 (zero). In the decimal system, each "place" represents a power of 10; in binary, each place is a power of 2.

One of the reasons that porpoises travel in pods instead of schools is that their math is so easy. There are only a few rules:

> ➤ In binary multiplication, zero times anything is zero. One times one is one.

> In binary addition, you have three rules: zero plus zero equals zero; one plus zero equals one; and one plus one is zero, carry the one.

The decimal multiplication tables you so painfully committed to memory in third grade require a 10-by-10 grid (100 spaces) to show the values 0 through 9. The **binary multiplication table** is a 2-by-2 grid with four values.

NOTE

Division in binary is the opposite of multiplication and there isn't any subtraction, because subtraction is nothing more than adding negative numbers.

A BInary digiT (**bit**) cannot contain a lot of information, so many bits are needed to express large quantities. In a convention established by IBM long before the birth of the personal computer, eight bits is referred to as a **byte**. Half a byte is called a **nibble**. Really. A byte can hold the decimal equivalent of 256 different values from 0 to 255. In binary, this is expressed 0000 0000 to 1111 1111.

Hexidecimal Notation

Both decimal and binary numbers can be difficult to use. In binary, a huge number of bits is required to express large quantities. For example, the one-megabyte address space of a PC would be represented by 10000000000000000000 (a one and 20 zeros). In decimal, each byte can contain the values from 0 to 255. Two bytes (16 bits) can express 0 to 65,535. Thus, the one-megabyte address would be 1,048,576 in decimal. There is no real correlation between the two systems. As luck would have it, each group of four bits (the nibble, remember?) can represent the 16 values 0 through 15. This makes a numbering scheme based on powers of 16—rather than 2 or 10—a tidy fit.

You already know how to show the symbols for 0 through 9, but you need to come up with six more symbols to get to 16. Anything on a keyboard would work, but it would be hard to remember symbols like !, @, #, $, %, and ^. For that reason, the letters A through F were chosen to follow the number 9.

Of course, calling the system *Sweet Little Sixteen* would be too easy, so it's called *hexidecimal* from the Greek *hex* for six and the Latin *deci* for ten.

TIP

Don't even think about trying to do arithmetic in hex. There are dandy calculators that do it just fine.

The only other thing you *really* need to know is that a *kilobyte* (2 to the 10th power)—usually shortened to *K*—is 1024 bytes, not 1000. Computers offer a free 24 bytes for each K.

A *megabyte* (Mb or meg) is 1024 kilobytes and a *gigabyte* is 1024 megabytes. Purists pronounce gigabyte with the *gi* sounding like the first sound in "giant" rather than the *gig* in "giggle." Other purists insist that a megabyte is 1000 kilobytes and a gigabyte is 1000 megabytes. Just say "meg" and "gig," and you'll be fine.

But hold on. Half of sixteen is *eight*. Wouldn't a system based on eight be easier? Yes and no. There is a system based on eight, called *octal*. Octal's counting goes zero to seven; then 10 to 17; then 20 to 27; and so on. The advantage of learning and using octal is that you don't have to be troubled with the A through F symbols hex uses, but it takes more spaces to indicate the state of a byte of memory—and it doesn't work out evenly. If a byte were set with all bits on, it would be represented as 377 in octal, 255 in decimal, or OxFF in hex.

The ASCII Letter Sweater

ASCII (pronounced "askie") is an acronym for the *American Standard Code for Information Interchange*. Because computers store numbers, not letters or punctuation marks, some standard is needed to define which numbers represent which characters. The American National Standards Institute (ANSI) defined 128 codes that would be used to represent alphabetic characters and punctuation marks. IBM extended the ASCII character set another 128 characters with the introduction of the PC in 1981. The extended ASCII characters are often referred to as "high bit" characters because they are all defined with the highest bit of a byte set to one.

The standard ASCII character set includes 128 characters. The ones you see most frequently on the keyboard and on the screen are ASCII characters 32 through 126. They are the letters (upper- and lowercase), numbers, punctuation marks, and other symbols that you can type on a standard keyboard.

The characters from 1 through 31 are *control characters*. You enter these most often from the keyboard by pressing and holding the Ctrl key while typing a letter. The control character character code is determined by the position of the letter in the alphabet. Control A is 1, Control 2 is 26. The symbol ♀ (which many of us wore around our necks in the days of the gurus) is called Control L and is ASCII character 12, universally recognized as an end-of-page or form feed marker.

^L is the 12th character in the set. In hexidecimal, the character is 0C, count to nine, then A, B, and C to get to 12.

NOTE

Control codes are an essential part of programming, primarily giving instructions on format.

The higher-numbered ASCII characters can appear on your screen but must be "asked for" either by number or by a change in the setup of your keyboard. Characters 129 to 175 are foreign letters and punctuation, 176 to 223 support ASCII's limited graphics capabilities, and 224 through 255 represent scientific and mathematical symbols. Table 2.1 shows all of the characters in the ASCII character set.

TABLE 2.1. ASCII TABLE FOR ROMAN-8 CHARACTER CONVERSIONS

Graphic	Hex	Dec	Oct	Description
	00	0	000	NUL (null)
	01	1	001	SOH (start of heading)
	02	2	002	STX (start of text)
	03	3	003	ETX (end of text)
	04	4	004	EOT (end of transmission)
	05	5	005	ENQ (enquiry)
	06	6	006	ACK (acknowledge)
	07	7	007	BEL (bell)
	08	8	010	BS (backspace)
	09	9	011	HT (horizontal tabulation)
	0A	10	012	LF (line feed)
	0B	11	013	VT (vertical tabulation)
	0C	12	014	FF (form feed)
	0D	13	015	CR (carriage return)
	0E	14	016	SO (shift out)
	0F	15	017	SI (shift in)
	10	16	020	DLE (data link escape)
	11	17	021	DC1 (device control 1 or X-ON)
	12	18	022	DC2 (device control 2)
	13	19	023	DC3 (device control 3 or X-OFF)
	14	20	024	DC4 (device control 4)
	15	21	025	NAK (negative acknowledge)
	16	22	026	SYN (synchronous idle)
	17	23	027	ETB (end of transmission block)
	18	24	030	CAN (cancel)
	19	25	031	EM (end of medium)
	1A	26	032	SUB (substitute)
	1B	27	033	ESC (escape)
	1C	28	034	FS (file separator)

Graphic	Hex	Dec	Oct	Description
	1D	29	035	GS (group separator)
	1E	30	036	RS (record separator)
	1F	31	037	US (unit separator)
	20	32	040	Space
!	21	33	041	Exclamation point
" "	22	34	042	Quotation mark
#	23	35	043	Number sign (hash mark)
$	24	36	044	Dollar sign
%	25	37	045	Percent sign
&	26	38	046	Ampersand
'	27	39	047	Apostrophe (closing single quote)
(	28	40	050	Opening parenthesis
)	29	41	051	Closing parenthesis
*	2A	42	052	Asterisk
+	2B	43	053	Plus
,	2C	44	054	Comma
–	2D	45	055	Hyphen (minus)
.	2E	46	056	Period (point)
/	2F	47	057	Slant (solidus)
0	30	48	060	Zero
1	31	49	061	One
2	32	50	062	Two
3	33	51	063	Three
4	34	52	064	Four
5	35	53	065	Five
6	36	54	066	Six
7	37	55	067	Seven
8	38	56	070	Eight
9	39	57	071	Nine
:	3A	58	072	Colon
;	3B	59	073	Semicolon
<	3C	60	074	Less than sign

continues

TABLE 2.1. CONTINUED

Graphic	Hex	Dec	Oct	Description
=	3D	61	075	Equal sign
>	3E	62	076	Greater than sign
?	3F	63	077	Question mark
@	40	64	100	Commercial at sign
A	41	65	101	Uppercase A
B	42	66	102	Uppercase B
C	43	67	103	Uppercase C
D	44	68	104	Uppercase D
E	45	69	105	Uppercase E
F	46	70	106	Uppercase F
G	47	71	107	Uppercase G
H	48	72	110	Uppercase H
I	49	73	111	Uppercase I
J	4A	74	112	Uppercase J
K	4B	75	113	Uppercase K
L	4C	76	114	Uppercase L
M	4D	77	115	Uppercase M
N	4E	78	116	Uppercase N
O	4F	79	117	Uppercase O
P	50	80	120	Uppercase P
Q	51	81	121	Uppercase Q
R	52	82	122	Uppercase R
S	53	83	123	Uppercase S
T	54	84	124	Uppercase T
U	55	85	125	Uppercase U
V	56	86	126	Uppercase V
W	57	87	127	Uppercase W
X	58	88	130	Uppercase X
Y	59	89	131	Uppercase Y
Z	5A	90	132	Uppercase Z
[	5B	91	133	Opening square bracket
\	5C	92	134	Reverse slant

Graphic	Hex	Dec	Oct	Description
]	5D	93	135	Closing square bracket
^	5E	94	136	Caret (circumflex)
_	5F	95	137	Underscore (low line)
"	60	96	140	Opening single quote
a	61	97	141	Lowercase a
b	62	98	142	Lowercase b
c	63	99	143	Lowercase c
d	64	100	144	Lowercase d
e	65	101	145	Lowercase e
f	66	102	146	Lowercase f
g	67	103	147	Lowercase g
h	68	104	150	Lowercase h
i	69	105	151	Lowercase i
j	6A	106	152	Lowercase j
k	6B	107	153	Lowercase k
l	6C	108	154	Lowercase l
m	6D	109	155	Lowercase m
n	6E	110	156	Lowercase n
o	6F	111	157	Lowercase o
p	70	112	160	Lowercase p
q	71	113	161	Lowercase q
r	72	114	162	Lowercase r
s	73	115	163	Lowercase s
t	74	116	164	Lowercase t
u	75	117	165	Lowercase u
v	76	118	166	Lowercase v
w	77	119	167	Lowercase w
x	78	120	170	Lowercase x
y	79	121	171	Lowercase y
z	7A	122	172	Lowercase z
{	7B	123	173	Opening brace (curly bracket)
|	7C	124	174	Vertical line
}	7D	125	175	Closing brace (curly bracket)

continues

TABLE 2.1. CONTINUED

Graphic	Hex	Dec	Oct	Description
~	7E	126	176	Tilde
□	7F	127	177	Delete (rubout)
	80	128	200	—undefined control code—
	81	129	201	—undefined control code—
	82	130	202	—undefined control code—
	83	131	203	—undefined control code—
	84	132	204	—undefined control code—
	85	133	205	—undefined control code—
	86	134	206	—undefined control code—
	87	135	207	—undefined control code—
	88	136	210	—undefined control code—
	89	137	211	—undefined control code—
	8A	138	212	—undefined control code—
	8B	139	213	—undefined control code—
	8C	140	214	—undefined control code—
	8D	141	215	—undefined control code—
	8E	142	216	—undefined control code—
	8F	143	217	—undefined control code—
	90	144	220	—undefined control code—
	91	145	221	—undefined control code—
	92	146	222	—undefined control code—
	93	147	223	—undefined control code—
	94	148	224	—undefined control code—
	95	149	225	—undefined control code—
	96	150	226	—undefined control code—
	97	151	227	—undefined control code—
	98	152	230	—undefined control code—
	99	153	231	—undefined control code—
	9A	154	232	—undefined control code—
	9B	155	233	—undefined control code—
	9C	156	234	—undefined control code—
	9D	157	235	—undefined control code—

Graphic	Hex	Dec	Oct	Description
	9E	158	236	—undefined control code—
	9F	159	237	—undefined control code—
	A0	160	240	—undefined—
À	A1	161	241	Uppercase A grave accent
Â	A2	162	242	Uppercase A circumflex
È	A3	163	243	Uppercase E grave accent
Ê	A4	164	244	Uppercase E circumflex
Ë	A5	165	245	Uppercase E umlaut or diaeresis
Î	A6	166	246	Uppercase I circumflex
Ï	A7	167	247	Uppercase I umlaut or diaeresis
´	A8	168	250	Acute accent
`	A9	169	251	Grave accent
^	AA	170	252	Circumflex accent
¨	AB	171	253	Umlaut (diaeresis) accent
~	AC	172	254	Tilde accent
Ù	AD	173	255	Uppercase U grave accent
Û	AE	174	256	Uppercase U circumflex
£	AF	175	257	Italian Lira symbol
‾	B0	176	260	Over line (high line)
	B1	177	261	—undefined—
	B2	178	262	—undefined—
°	B3	179	263	Degree (ring)
Ç	B4	180	264	Uppercase C cedilla
ç	B5	181	265	Lowercase c cedilla
Ñ	B6	182	266	Uppercase N tilde
ñ	B7	183	267	Lowercase n tilde
¡	B8	184	270	Inverse exclamation mark
¿	B9	185	271	Inverse question mark
¤	BA	186	272	General currency symbol
£	BB	187	273	British pound sign
¥	BC	188	274	Japanese yen symbol
§	BD	189	275	Section sign

continues

TABLE 2.1. CONTINUED

Graphic	Hex	Dec	Oct	Description
f	BE	190	276	Dutch guilder symbol
¢	BF	191	277	U.S. cent symbol
â	C0	192	300	Lowercase a circumflex
ê	C1	193	301	Lowercase e circumflex
ô	C2	194	302	Lowercase o circumflex
û	C3	195	303	Lowercase u circumflex
á	C4	196	304	Lowercase a acute accent
é	C5	197	305	Lowercase e acute accent
ó	C6	198	306	Lowercase o acute accent
ú	C7	199	307	Lowercase u acute accent
à	C8	200	310	Lowercase a grave accent
è	C9	201	311	Lowercase e grave accent
ò	CA	202	312	Lowercase o grave accent
ù	CB	203	313	Lowercase u grave accent
ä	CC	204	314	Lowercase a umlaut or diaeresis
ë	CD	205	315	Lowercase e umlaut or diaeresis
ö	CE	206	316	Lowercase o umlaut or diaeresis
ü	CF	207	317	Lowercase u umlaut or diaeresis
Å	D0	208	320	Uppercase A degree
î	D1	209	321	Lowercase i circumflex
Ø	D2	210	322	Uppercase O crossbar
Æ	D3	211	323	Uppercase Æ ligature
å	D4	212	324	Lowercase a degree
í	D5	213	325	Lowercase i acute accent
ø	D6	214	326	Lowercase o crossbar
æ	D7	215	327	Lowercase ae ligature
Ä	D8	216	330	Uppercase A umlaut or diaeresis
ì	D9	217	331	Lowercase i grave accent
Ö	DA	218	332	Uppercase O umlaut or diaeresis
Ü	DB	219	333	Uppercase U umlaut or diaeresis
É	DC	220	334	Uppercase E acute accent

Graphic	Hex	Dec	Oct	Description
ï	DD	221	335	Lowercase i umlaut or diaeresis
ß	DE	222	336	Sharp s
Ô	DF	223	337	Uppercase O circumflex
Á	E0	224	340	Uppercase A acute accent
Ã	E1	225	341	Uppercase A tilde
ã	E2	226	342	Lowercase a tilde
Đ	E3	227	343	Uppercase D with stroke
đ	E4	228	344	Lowercase d with stroke
Í	E5	229	345	Uppercase I acute accent
Ì	E6	230	346	Uppercase I grave accent
Ó	E7	231	347	Uppercase O acute accent
Ò	E8	232	350	Uppercase O grave accent
Õ	E9	233	351	Uppercase O tilde
õ	EA	234	352	Lowercase o tilde
Š	EB	235	353	Uppercase S with caron
š	EC	236	354	Lowercase s with caron
Ú	ED	237	355	Uppercase U acute accent
Ÿ	EE	238	356	Uppercase Y umlaut or diaeresis
ÿ	EF	239	357	Lowercase y umlaut or diaeresis
Þ	F0	240	360	Uppercase thorn
þ	F1	241	361	Lowercase thorn
	F2	242	362	—undefined—
	F3	243	363	—undefined—
	F4	244	364	—undefined—
	F5	245	365	—undefined—
—	F6	246	366	Long dash (horizontal bar)
¼	F7	247	367	One fourth (one quarter)
½	F8	248	370	One half
ª	F9	249	371	Feminine ordinal indicator
º	FA	250	372	Masculine ordinal indicator
«	FB	251	373	Opening guillemets (angle quotes)
■	FC	252	374	Solid

continues

TABLE 2.1. CONTINUED

Graphic	Hex	Dec	Oct	Description
»	FD	253	375	Closing guillemets (angle quotes)
±	FE	254	376	Plus/minus sign
	FF	255	377	—undefined—

The Chips Are Down: How They Work

Without electricity to make a computer work, of course, there would be no need for octal, hex, ASCII, or anything else. Ditto for the chips. If you slept through high school physics (or skipped it entirely), a brief refresher on electricity is in order. Although general knowledge of physics has grown in recent years, we'll leave the truly small stuff, like *quarks*, out of this discussion.

Atoms consist of a *nucleus* of positively charged *protons* and uncharged *neutrons*. A ring of negatively charged *electrons* orbits the nucleus. Like charges repel each other (similar to two like poles of magnets) and unlike charges attract each other. This keeps the electrons from hitting each other in their orbits (they are repelling each other). This also means that electrons that are farther away from the nucleus are less bound to that nucleus by the positive attraction of the protons.

If you remember the periodic table of the elements that was always rolled up like a window shade during exams, each element is unique because of the number of protons in the nucleus. Everything we sense through sight and touch—and some things we don't—is made up of one or more elements.

In some elements, the outer electrons are so loosely bonded to the nucleus that they can become free. These free electrons are the basis for the flow of electricity.

NOTE

You probably will not get far with your local power monopoly if you refuse to pay your bill based on the argument that they are selling you free electrons.

Any good *conductor* contains many free electrons. Gold and silver are excellent conductors, but they also make great jewelry. Copper, then, has become the element of choice for moving electrons around. There are other elements that contain almost no free (or expensive) electrons. They are called *non-conductors*.

Although it's hard to imagine electrons flowing along a copper wire, you can easily imagine water flowing through a garden hose. Put a pump on one end of the hose, a nozzle on the other, and you have an instant analogy.

With electricity, a generator or battery takes the place of the pump and supplies the pressure, called *electromotive force* (EMF), which is measured in units called *volts*. If the nozzle of the hose is turned off (no flow, just pressure) you have resistance. With electricity, resistance is measured in *ohms*.

If you turn the nozzle of the hose on and water begins to flow, you have the equivalent of *current*. With electricity, current is measured in *amperes* and is proportional to the resistance in the circuit.

The relationship of volts, ohms, and amperes is such that one volt flowing with an ohm of resistance produces one ampere of current.

This is the point in the lecture where some kid in the class (a wonk?) has been reading ahead. "What about *electrons*?" Aha!

Electrons are incredibly small, negatively charged atomic particles that can flow freely through a conductor. Back in the 1940s, the scientists at Bell Labs in New Jersey—possibly after a weekend at the shore, certainly after an infusion of several million dollars—made an amazing discovery. They could make electrons flow through a supposed non-conductor, silicon. Because all of New Jersey south of Trenton seems to be composed of sand, it was an ideal location for these experiments.

Sand is composed mostly of the element *silicon*. In its pure state, silicon is a non-conductor. A few impurities in silicon allow it to become not a great conductor but a *semiconductor*. With a semiconductor, you can build a *transistor*.

A transistor is composed of three layers of silicon with a trace amount of impurities thrown in. The junction where two types of impure silicon meet makes electricity flow through the transistor in a strange and wonderful way: electrons flow in one end, the *emitter*, and out the other end, the *collector*. They won't flow in the other direction.

Between the emitter and the collector is a third layer, the *base*. Current flowing through the base will cause a current to flow through the collector. If no current flows from emitter to base, no current flows from emitter to collector. The whole thing acts like an electronic switch with no moving parts. Under most circumstances, the current flows only in one direction. If too high a voltage (power spike or surge) is placed on the transistor in the opposite direction, the junction breaks down, the current flows the wrong way, and the transistor is destroyed.

TIP

One of the corollaries to Murphy's Law states that if a fast-acting fuse is placed in the circuit to protect the transistor from overload, the transistor will burn out first, protecting the fuse. Always try to prove Murphy wrong with a high-quality surge suppressor.

Given the time and inclination, you could wire several transistors together so that once a circuit is turned on, it stays on and once turned off, it stays off. This type of circuit—called a *flip-flop*—is the basis of computer logic. The circuit has only two states: on and off. Thus, digital computers can have only two digits: 1 and 0. (Remember the porpoises?)

You then could wire different combinations of transistors together to form not only flip-flops but *logic gates* as well. A logic gate accepts two inputs and gives one output. Logic gates have strange names like NAND, NOR, AND, and OR. Wire a few thousand of these together, add some timing circuits to flip them at high speed, and you've got a computer. Of course, if you did this all by hand, the computer would be the size of a room, and its cost would equal the GNP of many Third World nations. Looking back, the first computers *did* take up entire rooms and were *very* expensive to build.

What makes today's PCs possible (and ever smaller) is the use of *integrated circuits* (ICs). Because an electron is incredibly small, a transistor does not have to be very big in order to work with a small current capacity. Millions of transistors and their connecting circuits can be etched on a silicon wafer smaller than a fingernail.

Thanks for the Memories: RAM and ROM

Ask almost anyone who has more than a passing acquaintance with computers, and you'll be told that **RAM** means **random-access memory**. Not exactly. If you've plowed this far into the discussion, you know that there is nothing random about computers. All memory must be accessed by a unique numeric address in order for the computer to work. Groups of eight bits (a byte) must be accessed individually at their own addresses.

Some bytes are set by the manufacturer and can't be changed by the user. That's called **ROM** or **read-only memory**. Other memory can be changed (setting on to off, or vice-versa) by a *write* to that byte. After the write, the bits in the byte remain in their new state and can be *read* until they're changed by another write. The write/read memory is what's commonly called RAM.

CPU Stuff

The central processing unit (CPU) is what makes the computer work. You have probably seen "Intel Inside" commercials that zoom through the inside of a computer to the chip with the spinning whirlpool and the sparks flying from exposed electrodes. Although this makes nice TV graphics, the chip itself is not nearly so dramatic. It sits in a dark gray ceramic (or plastic) case that is much larger than the actual chip itself. The size of the chip depends on the number. The 80386 is about half the size of a pinkie fingernail, and the 80486 is about the size of a thumbnail.

These integrated circuits are all based on the Intel 80x86 series and all are upwardly compatible. That means that instructions for the 8086 will operate on the 80186, 80286, 80386, and 80486. The same instructions don't always work the other way, however. Not all 80486 instructions will operate on the 8086. Each increasing number in the series added new features and carried out more instructions, but they all operate in the same basic manner. The 80486 is apparently the end of the numeric series. The next chip in the series is known as the Pentium.

Located inside the chip are dedicated memory locations called *registers*. Instructions are sent to the CPU indicating what to do to the registers. Some instructions tell the CPU to copy the contents of a register to memory or copy memory to a register. Other instructions add the contents of one register to another or manipulate the bits in one way or another. Each instruction does a very small task, but does it very quickly. Most computers can carry out over a million instructions every second. Computer people often talk about the number of *MIPS* (short for *million instructions per second*). Newer high-speed mainframe computers are rated in *BIPS* (or *billion instructions per second*).

The instructions come from an area of memory pointed to by two of the CPU registers: the *Instruction Pointer* (IP) and the *Code Segment* (CS). These instructions are the basis of .EXE and .COM files. To us, the contents of these files look like gibberish, but the CPU interprets them as instructions that tell it how to react to any given situation. These instructions are just another form of DATA. If the DATA is corrupted, the CPU blindly follows the wrong instructions.

Boot Camp: How It All Works Together

The CPU is always busy. Even if you aren't telling it to do anything through keyboard input or program operation, the CPU is running another program that tells it to sit there and wait patiently for the next instruction.

Before the CPU can get busy, it has to start somewhere. When the power to a PC is turned on, the CPU figuratively pulls the computer up by its bootstraps (that's where the term *boot* comes from—*bootstrap loader program*). Because computers can't do anything randomly, the

CPU chip is designed so that when the power is turned on, the Code Segment (CS) is all ones and the Instruction Pointer (IP) is all zeros. Binary. On or off. Flip-flop.

Next, the CS and IP registers are loaded, and the CPU begins fetching instructions. The first instructions are in the *Power On Self Test* (POST) which tests the CPU itself and the memory. Next, the CPU searches for system components like a hard drive controller and the video controller for the monitor. These instructions are in what's called *device ROM* and can't be changed by the user.

Error messages can pop up during this process, most notably 301, which indicates that no connection has been made with the keyboard, and 1701, which says the hard disk isn't home. Error messages vary depending on the type of ROM installed in the computer. Some ROMs contain helpful messages, and others contain just numbers.

After the POST is complete and device ROM has run whatever setup routines it needs, the bootstrap program has a decision to make. This decision—where you will be landing within the system—is carefully coded into the instructions. First, the disk drive called A: starts to spin and the CPU tries to read into memory the first sector on the disk. If no disk is in drive A: or the latch to the drive is open, the read is unsuccessful, and the CPU goes for Alternate Plan B.

If there is a disk in drive A that does not contain the essential system files for bootup, you may see this message or something similar:

```
Non-system disk. Replace and press any key.
```

Alternate Plan B does not mean that the CPU looks for a disk in a closed B: drive. Rather, the CPU searches for the presence of a hard drive. If the hard disk is present, the first sector of the hard drive is read into memory, and you're in business on the hard drive.

CAUTION

Allowing a system to boot with a disk in drive A is (1) a time-waster, and (2) a good way to transfer a bootsector virus to the hard drive. Always make sure that the disk drive door is open and any disks are removed before you boot the system.

If the CPU finds neither a disk drive nor a hard drive (trouble), control stays in ROM, and IBM users will find themselves in the Cassette Basic program. Owners of clones (which don't include Cassette Basic) might find themselves in Never-Never Land with no clue as to how to get home. Most often, clone-owners will see this message:

```
Non-system disk. Replace and press any key.
```

Few people have another hard disk sitting on the shelf, waiting to replace the one in the system unit.

NOTE

Failure to boot from the hard drive does not necessarily mean that you have lost data, although it does mean that DOS is temporarily unable to get to your data.

Assuming your PC gets this far, the CPU will begin to read the *boot track/sector*. The boot sector is very small—only 512 bytes long—and contains both data and instructions. The data contains information about the disk (number of sides, number of tracks, number of sectors per track, etc.) and a few error messages that will print to the screen if something goes wrong.

The instructions are fairly brief; just enough to search for a file called IBMBIO.COM (IO.SYS in clone systems) and load it into memory. At this point, IBMBIO gets active and begins to load the disk operating system (DOS) contained in the file IBMDOS.COM (MSDOS.SYS).

The last part of the bootup procedure is loading the file CONFIG.SYS. CONFIG.SYS is computer shorthand for *CONFIGure this SYStem, please*. Unless a *shell* other than COMMAND.COM is called in CONFIG.SYS, COMMAND.COM is loaded and takes control. IBMBIO and IBMDOS remain in read-write memory (RAM), COMMAND.COM takes control, and the bootstrap procedure is almost over.

COMMAND.COM-Base Commander

You know that *some* program is running all the time when others aren't. That's usually COMMAND.COM and for a good reason. Of all the DOS programs supplied, COMMAND.COM is the only one that will exit to itself.

Once COMMAND.COM is loaded, it goes to work and looks, first, for a file called AUTOEXEC.BAT. This is the only AUTOmatically EXECuted BATch file on a PC. AUTOEXEC.BAT can contain commands that designate which subdirectories should be searched to find a program file, how the prompt appears on your screen, whether to load memory-resident utilities, and, as TV ads for Ginsu knives, workout equipment, or cheap vacations say, "Much, *much* more."

Finally, it's your turn. Once AUTOEXEC.BAT has been completed, unless AUTOEXEC.BAT contains a line to run a program like WIN-DOWS or DOSSHELL, COMMAND.COM loops into a *keyboard input routine* and waits. At this point, you can finally tell the PC to *do* something, such as loading your word processing program (WP).

When you type *WP* and press Enter to start your word processing program, COMMAND.COM starts to look in the current directory for files called WP with the extension .COM, .EXE, and .BAT, respectively. If you're working in the root directory, COMMAND.COM probably won't find the files it's looking for. Next, COMMAND.COM looks at the **PATH** statement in AUTOEXEC.BAT and continues to search through the defined path for the files.

TIP

Put all .BAT files used to call programs in a subdirectory called BATS (or something similar) that appears in the PATH statement immediately after the subdirectory where your DOS programs are stored. For example:

```
PATH=C:\;C:\DOS;C:\BATS
```

Formatting

Fresh out of the package, most disks and tapes used to be unformatted. These days, more and more types of preformatted media are available. Preformatting is particularly attractive for folks who use tape backup systems. Formatting a 120 Mb tape ties up an entire system for well over an hour. Formatting a disk or, worse, not having a formatted disk when you need one can be a minor pain.

CAUTION

There have been too many instances where a preformatted disk was not only ready to receive data but was quite prepared to pass some along—a bootsector virus—as well.

The process of *formatting* organizes the magnetic media so that it will accept the data being sent to it from the PC.

Hard drives must also be formatted before you can use them. This is usually done at the factory or at your local computer store. There is little reason, short of a total DATA disaster, that you would ever need to format a hard drive. The following dangerous keystrokes should *not* be in your fingers' keyboard vocabulary:

```
FORMAT C:
```

If a disk or tape already has DATA on it, formatting destroys the DATA. Period. Under some circumstances, it can be recovered.

TIP

Always label your diskettes as soon as they are formatted. An unlabeled diskette shouts "FORMAT ME!" Always do a DIR on an unlabeled diskette before typing the fatal FORMAT command.

WONK Cum Laude

Congratulations. You can now hold your own in almost any discussion on the inner workings of PCs, including those that will take place later in this book.

CHAPTER

Bits and Pieces:
The Hard(ware) Way

Now that you know what happens *inside* your PC, it's time to consider the *outside*—the parts you see every day, the parts that let you work with your PC. Hardware failures (head crashes, for example) can destroy DATA, but it's more likely that a hardware failure will make your data difficult, if not impossible, to access—at least in the short term.

This chapter concentrates on the various parts of PCs and helps you build your own spare parts department. You discover what can happen, what it can happen to, how to keep it from happening, and what to do if it does.

Your Keyboard: The Key to the City

You may never actually *lose* data because of a keyboard going on the fritz, but when your keyboard goes out, your data may as well be floating off in Never-Never Land. Without a working keyboard, you simply can't get to your data. You can't move to another machine and keep working because you can't even close the file you were working on when the keyboard went out.

If you have another PC close by, you can play cannibal by borrowing the keyboard for a few minutes, closing the open file, and copying it to a disk. If the computer is being used, however, you're out of luck—at least until you can repair or replace the keyboard.

TIP

The best strategy is to get your hands on either a new or reconditioned keyboard and store it in a cool, dry place. The cost should be less than $25 for a good reconditioned keyboard. If you find it hard to justify the purchase when your keyboard is working fine, balance the static cost against the number of hours of work you'll lose if you have to stop now and go out in search of a repair facility.

You should be aware that there is always a risk associated with connecting or disconnecting electrical components. If you decide to borrow another keyboard to close out a work session, understand that you may be causing more problems than you're solving.

Many keyboard problems can be repaired with simple household implements. A sturdy nailfile or a small screwdriver can remedy the most common of keyboard ills: a stuck key. You'll know you have a stuck key when your PC starts screeching and characters you know you didn't type start filling up the screen. If you see 100 replications of the letter P, it's a good guess that you've got a stuck P. If an applications program starts acting strangely, one of the keys that activates functions is probably the culprit.

The stuck key is usually caused by a particle (or chunk) of something underneath the key. With your screwdriver or nail file, pop the key off (practice this in advance!) and then blow gently on the area around the key. Whatever's there should release. A foam-tipped swab (*not* cotton) and "canned air" can also be used to clean out the substance causing the problem.

CAUTION

Every now and then—once a month should do—turn your keyboard upside down and whap it against your lap. This should prevent whatever's precipitated into your keyboard from taking up permanent residence.

TIP

If the keyboard is not recognized during the POST (Power On Self Test), a 301 error displays on the screen. Turn the PC off, disconnect the keyboard, and then reconnect it securely. Try again.

Your Monitor: Time for a Screen Test

Monitors generally are fairly good sports about warning you of their impending demise, giving you a chance to get them in for repair or diagnosis of terminal illness. Look for shimmying, shrinking of display size, or anything that is not as it should be. Of course, you're not going to lose any data if your monitor goes south (unless it somehow sends a power blast back to your system unit on its way), but losing video makes it impossible to see your data.

Monitor failure rates are so low that stocking one as a spare part may seem impractical. If the extra monitor could serve a number of machines in a single location, or if you simply cannot afford to lose the time it would take to get a replacement for your daily monitor, having a spare monitor may be a good idea.

On the plus side, if you do decide to keep a monitor in stock, the likelihood of it dropping off the trailing edge of technology is very slim. You can always use the monitor as part of a new machine you build from components, so it's not a bad investment.

TIP

If the monitor isn't found on the POST, nothing will be visible. Check your computer's manual for the function key that will allow the boot to continue. Then use PRINT SCREEN to dump what would have been seen on the monitor to the printer. You may find more than you counted on.

If at all possible, swap the misbehaving monitor with one known to work. The problem could be your video ROMs on the motherboard. If the replacement monitor acts the same way, move the problem component to another PC. If the problem is *not* the monitor, a little panic—at least in the direction of your wallet—is warranted.

WARNING

Make sure that it's your monitor that is bad before racing out to the computer store or ordering a replacement from your vendor's spare parts department. If you're working with a new application, close it out, reboot your PC, and access a known program to make sure the problem isn't caused by the new program's configuration.

CAUTION

Keep the air vents of your monitor at least marginally clean at all times. Keep a good distance between all components and heat traps such as walls, stacks of paper, or anything that could interrupt a constant air flow.

Floppy Drives: The Discus Throw

The floppy drives are the toxic waste dumps of your PC. Ambient air is constantly being pulled through the floppy drive openings (and the small vents on the front of your system unit) to maintain a constant air flow over the very expensive silicon of your motherboard.

Two technical terms are used for the stuff that can collect inside your drives: *glarnge* and *gradoo*. You don't want this stuff, but you can't avoid it. Doubtful? Find a black floppy, stick it in the drive, and leave it there for a few weeks. You won't need the White Glove Test to find the dust.

TIP

Even if you rarely use your disk drives, keep a disk in the slot at all times. The disk serves as a block for incoming flotsam and jetsam that can grime the drive. When you leave a disk in the drive, however, don't close the drive door.

Floppy drives also have moving parts and moving parts can break.

5.25-inch drives are fairly simple mechanically. You slide in a disk, close the latch, and the PC will tell that drive when to spin. Sometimes the PC doesn't tell the drive when to spin. That's a problem, but it's not too bad a problem.

What *is* bad is when, somehow, the drive has been knocked out of alignment. In that case, when the system says Spin!, the disk is damaged or destroyed.

A more common problem is not looking before shoving and slipping a second disk into the slot when one is already there. It happens. And you'll have more trouble getting both out than you had getting the last one in. Here's a time when data can be destroyed through pure physical damage. Everyone has probably heard a story, apocryphal or not, about the extremely enthusiastic computerist who has actually bent a floppy trying to jam it in the drive.

3.5-inch drives and their associated disks are more complex than the 5.25-inch models. Look closely at how a 3.5-inch drive works and you will see that the disk doesn't just slide in, it seats at a slightly lower level. This requires a more sophisticated mechanism, which gives the drive more moving parts to break.

Sometimes, even though the ejection mechanisms on some drives could do double-duty as jet fighters' pilots' seats, the disk stays put.

This is another time for handy household tools. A good pair of tweezers can be helpful here, as can a pair of small needle-nosed pliers. Go gently. Usually, the problem is a slightly warped or misshapen 3.5-inch diskette, not the drive itself.

A dead disk drive is no immediate big deal if you keep all your work on the hard drive. The time it takes to locate and swap out a dead drive usually is minimal. Whether you should keep a spare or spares on-hand probably depends on your distance from a reliable replacement source. One day (to almost anywhere in the U.S., at least) is probably tolerable.

CAUTION

Purchase a cleaning disk and run it through, according to the manufacturer's directions, at the specified intervals.

Hard Facts about the Hard Drive

The temptation to wax nostalgic about my first hard drive is almost overwhelming. The year was 1984; and the hard drive was external, held 10 *huge* megabytes of data, required its own interface card and startup software, and, like the Energizer bunny, is still working. Those were the days. The only downside is that the hard drive—in 1984, remember—cost almost $4,000.

With the advent of the PC-XT, hard drives took over the computer world. The days of floppy swapping in mid-application and digging through stacks of disks to find that one project disk were over. The programs and the data were all `right there` on the hard disk. And, when the hard disk died, the data was `all gone`.

Today, with 120 Mb hard drives serving as standard and 270s, forty-leventy-millions, and other astronomical storage capabilities not unusual, the *all gone* is a lot more *all gone* than it was just a few short years ago.

A variety of things can happen to make a hard drive fail. Many people use the term *crash*, but that's not always accurate. A crash occurs when the reading heads, which normally float above the hard drive's data-recording platter(s), literally crash into the platter, destroying data. And, after a crash, the disk usually still works, but the data is gone. (So, take the word *crash* out of your vocabulary as a synonym for *dead disk*.)

TIP

The moving parts, in particular the stepper motor, tend to fail first on a hard drive. PCs are energy efficient; keeping one turned on all the time isn't much different in energy costs than leaving on a bathroom light. Further, there's a dramatic shot of power from the power supply to all that circuitry every time you turn on a PC. If you use your PC daily, leave it on to save wear and tear on the moving parts.

Indications that your hard drive is dead, together with EMT techniques and autopsy methods, are covered in Chapter 11. The goal here is to get you back up and running as quickly as possible.

Of course you have the original installation disks for all of your application programs and your operating system. Of *course* you have a good and current backup of your data. But on what are you going to put the programs and data? Unless a dead hard drive will, finally, provide the rationalization you need to buy a new PC, you need a new hard drive.

How long will it take to get a new hard drive, format it, reinstall all your applications, and restore the backed up data? What is it worth to you to be able to get out your screwdriver, remove the dead disk, install a new one that's already been formatted and set up the way you want it, and then need only to copy your backed up data? The answer is up to you.

TIP

Don't think in terms of "What if your hard drive goes down," think in terms of when. All hard drives are rated for a certain number of hours of use (check this when making a purchase) and today's hard drives are much more reliable than those of just a few short years ago. (The CMI drives that were part of the early ATs had a dramatic failure rate of above 200 percent, according to one national PC publication!)

The Power Supply and Your Power Monopoly: Power to the PC

One of the most expensive parts of your PC—in terms of purchase price and destructive potential—is the power supply. Not only does the power supply provide power to the various components of a PC, it also drives a fan that cools the interior of the PC's case. The fan can easily become clogged with particles from the ambient air.

CAUTION

A pass over the external housing with an old, soft toothbrush every week or so can help prolong its life. Also, make sure that you don't put the case of the PC right up against a wall or anything else that might block air flow.

Your local power monopoly can also play hob with your power supply. Your in-line surge suppressor won't do much good for a serious surge.

TIP

If you turn your PC on and don't immediately hear the hum of the fan, turn it off quickly. In the event of a power supply failure, it's unlikely that the machine would even begin to boot, but better safe than sorry.

Power supplies don't often fail, but when they do it can be dramatic. In one well-remembered event, the power supply went, taking with it all the video ROMs on the motherboard. The cheaper route was to buy a new PC (replacing a 286 with a 386) than to replace the motherboard and power supply. Troubleshooting the problem was, in this case, lengthy and painful. Fortunately, a replacement system unit was close at hand and the hard drive from the fried machine was swapped into the replacement so work could continue.

The only amusement in that particular circumstance was a serious wagering pool covering just how long the old case, placed on top of a trashcan next to a busy street, would last before some enterprising soul collected it. (Less than two minutes.)

CAUTION

Experienced repair people caution against amateurs mucking about with power supplies.

Laptops and Notebooks: Little Machines, Big Problems

The main difference between these little wonders and their desktop siblings is size. If you're using a laptop or a notebook computer, parts can be swapped out, but design considerations play a much larger role than in cabled components. A service manager at IBM, when asked about amateur surgery on laptops, warned against it unless you have two important prerequisites: experience and very small hands.

WARNING

Dangerous waters: Because of the design of these small computers, not only your data but you can be in danger from electrical accidents. A lightning strike to an RJ-11 phone jack to which your PC's internal modem is connected might not kill you, but it would certainly rearrange the axes of your dental work.

The Spare Parts Department: A Shopping List

As part of your decision-making in assembling a spare parts shelf, you need to use what MBAs like to call *Cost Benefit Analysis*. If you can't afford to lose an hour of productive time, you'll probably want what the computer security professionals call *complete redundancy*. If you are a more casual user, enjoy hanging around repair shops and computer stores, and have time to burn, you may not want to go to the expense of keeping spares around. It's up to you.

Use the following shopping list, with prices obtained from two major top-of-the-line manufacturers and one street price vendor, to give you a starting point for your calculations.

Part	Source 1	Source 2	Source 3
Monitor			
Keyboard			
Power Supply			
5.25-inch Drive			
3.5-inch Drive			
120 Mb Hard Drive			

You might conclude that it is cheaper to buy another computer than to take the spare parts approach, which is almost like building a computer from the ground up. Obviously, if one spare parts closet can serve many machines, the cost per PC is shared among them. For a single machine? Your call.

Software

Without software, your hardware is just that...hard, if not impossible, to use. Beginning with DOS, everything that makes something happen on your PC is *software*. Alternately, you can call software *applications* or *programs*.

In general, programs can be sorted neatly into categories: database managers, spreadsheets, word processors, utilities, communications, and games. A number of omnibus programs combine several functions, a trend started by Lotus Development Corporation with its Symphony package in the mid-80s. In a symphony orchestra, only one player can be musician; similarly, do-it-all packages are likely to have one part that is considerably stronger than the rest.

Programs, by definition, execute a set of instructions. You can recognize program files easily by looking for a file extension of either .EXE or .COM. Whenever you come across an .EXE or .COM extension, you can run the program by simply typing the filename.

Creation versus Evolution

Everyone is familiar with the task of putting fingers to keyboard and seeing letters or numbers pop up on the screen. That's data input in its simplest form. The data, however, has to be in some kind of *format*;

that's what software provides. This book is written using Microsoft Word version 5.5 with the addition of a *style sheet* developed by the publisher which provides still further formatting capabilities. Wherever you see a heading, an illustration, a tip or caution, or any other special formatting in this book, a unique code was inserted to "tell" the production department—more often another computer than a human being—how to handle a particular section of text.

Both the codes and the typed words in the word processing document are considered data. Without the codes, there would be nothing to print—either to the screen or a printer—except an endless string of letters, numbers, punctuation marks, and spaces. Losing formatting codes can be as much of a disaster to a writer as losing an entire chapter of a book. A finished word processing document is evolved data.

Formatting, data entry, and the evolution of data is probably clearest in spreadsheet applications. You type numbers that the program enters into the spreadsheet's cells; then you tell the spreadsheet program what to do with the numbers.

With database managers, most of which can also handle math these days, data is stored in *fields*, similar to the cells in spreadsheets. As part of database design, fields are defined for length and type of data in the field—alphanumeric, numeric, date, time, and so on. A group of fields is called a *record*. The main function of databases is to sort data according to criteria, or *arguments*. A list of names and addresses, for example, could be sorted alphabetically by last name, numerically by ZIP code, or, through a date field, from oldest to newest entry.

Simple databases, composed of sets of records with the same fields, are called *flat databases*. *Relational databases* are more sophisticated and can sort and combine several sets of records by using *key fields* that are the same in all the sets of records. A business's customer number is a good example of a key field. One set of records might hold address information, another the customer's order history, and a third would contain payment history. Data evolves from database programs when reporting parameters are defined, but the customer number (key field) would be included in all of these databases so that you could find additional information about particular business easily.

Import Duties: Moving Data between Programs

Importing data from other places can be as simple as snagging an ASCII text file into a word processing program or as complex as taking database records created with one program and plugging them into an omnibus package from another developer.

The sort of data created by spreadsheets and database managers can be dumped into what's called a *delimited file*, with each chunk of data separated from the next by a delimiting character like a semicolon (;) or a front slash (/). This makes importing easier, as long as you make sure that the format of the file into which you are importing is *exactly the same* as the one you are importing. Trying to cram alphanumeric data into a field formatted as Date or Currency just will not work—or, if it does work, the data will be useless.

Most high-powered programs sold today include conversion utilities to make sure that the data comes across as cleanly as possible. But mistakes happen. Some possible glitches occur because:

➤ The software doesn't quite understand what you're trying to do

➤ The program doesn't recognize the sort of data you're trying to convert

➤ You manage to send the wrong instructions to the software

Regardless of the why, your data can end up looking like cream of wheat.

TIP

If possible, run a test of your import/conversion with a small data sample to make sure everything works before you attempt importing or converting an important file.

Even the simplest ASCII file, worked over by the tender mercies of a big-time word processing program, can make tired users wish they had typed the text from the keyboard rather than trying to "save time" by importing data with a conversion program.

CAUTION

Importing or converting data is one time when an ounce of prevention is worth ten pounds of cure. Always make a copy of your data file before attempting this sort of machination.

Missing, Presumed Lost

You know it's there. Somewhere. You might even remember the name of the file. LETTER.TOM, maybe. And you only have 17,421 files on your disk in 23 subdirectories. How to find LETTER.TOM?

You could use the DOS command DIR LETTER.TOM, subdirectory by subdirectory, bringing a new definition to the word *tedium*. To increase the pain, you can't even use the F3 key to repeat the DIR command because you have to change to a new directory (by using the CD command) every time you enter the command. And you probably have to print out a list of the subdirectories on the disk before you start. Not a recommended approach.

Beginning with DOS version 5, several additions to the DIR command made searching much easier. To search subdirectories, use the /s switch. To search an entire drive for LETTER.TOM, you could change to the root directory (by entering CD\) and type

```
DIR LETTER.TOM /s
```

If your hard disk is partitioned into several logical drives, you must repeat the DIR search for each of the drives.

What's needed is a simple utility that calmly leaps the walls between subdirectories and partitions and looks all over the disk for LETTER.TOM—and then tells you where it is. Guess what? You've got it on the disk in the back of the book.

 The WHEREIS.EXE program on the accompanying disk is the PANDA version of one of the old war-horses of PC utilities. The utility displays the file match, complete with the path to the file, the size of the file, and the date and time stamp.

If WHEREIS comes up with several matches, it's up to you to search your memory for the right one or access each of the files until you find the one you seek. Full instructions for using WHEREIS are given in Chapter 16, but it's comforting to know that wildcard characters can be used as well. For example, in this case, you could enter either of the following command lines:

```
WHEREIS *.TOM

WHEREIS LETTER.*
```

TIP

If you are clueless as to the actual filename but have a dim recollection of when you created the file, try a utility like Norton's Directory Sort (DS) and sort on date. DOS version 5 (and later) will let you order the directory listing by using the /o:[sortorder] *switch. To order by date, use* DIR /o:d*.*

Stupid Software Tricks

More stupid software tricks were around in the ancient days (the early to mid-80s) than are around today. Microsoft has worked hard to solve problems with succeeding releases of DOS, and software vendors, responding to the screams of customers, have eliminated most of the real problems. Not everyone can afford all the latest releases—both of DOS and all the applications programs they use—so there's still a significant installed base of software that plays tricks.

Commercial packages tend to provide margins of safety from stupid software tricks, but don't count on it.

Death by Disk Swap

The space a data file uses on a disk is marked in the disk's directory and *file allocation table* (FAT). If you open a file on one disk, swap the disk for another (to import data from another file into the file you're working on, perhaps?), and then forget to put your original disk back where it belongs, funeral arrangements for both disks may be in order.

Here's what could happen if the software does not close the first file before reading the second. When the first file is finally closed, the disk's directory and FAT are rewritten to update the disk storage space. But the *second* disk is still in the drive. DOS writes the directory and FAT information from the first disk to the second disk. Unfortunately, the directory information no longer corresponds to the data that is actually stored on the disk. Additionally, the disk that originally had the open file does not get the directory and FAT update so the new file is lost. Ouch! The file allocation tables (FATs) on both disks have been compromised.

Although the process is incredibly tedious and requires programming skills most folks don't possess, you can restore the FATs and, maybe, save the work file that spread itself so generously around. Maybe. If you're a world-class programmer, count on three to four hours of intense labor for the process.

NOTE

If you're running DOS 4.0 or above, DOS will check to make sure that the right disk is in the drive before you can close a file.

The Installation from Hell

Most software comes with a convenient installation program. You type something like *INSTALL* and just sit calmly, following screen prompts to swap the installation disks and wait for your new program to do its work. Sometimes the program does a bit more than you bargained for.

We tend to think of a single application—any heavy-duty relational database program makes a fine example—as being just one program. It only has one name, so it's only one program, right? Not really. While you are typing away, the program itself may be, unbeknownst to you, opening and closing a large number of files and using lots of *buffers* (memory storage locations).

Because a disk must be read and written to in units called *sectors* (actually, 512 bytes per sector), DOS uses a series of memory locations called *buffers* to store a whole sector's worth of data at a time. The more buffers DOS uses, the less the disk must be accessed for data because there is a possibility that the sector is already in memory.

A buffer needs a few bytes to record information about what is stored in the buffer. Each buffer uses 524 bytes of memory in DOS versions 2 and 3 and 532 bytes in DOS 4.0. There does come a point where DOS has too many buffers. If the time it takes to search through the buffers for the data is greater than the time it would take to read the sector from the disk, fewer buffers would be more efficient. If a disk cache program such as SMARTDRV.SYS is in use, DOS needs only a few buffers because the cache already has the disk data in memory.

The number of files that a program can open at any one time depends on two DOS internal structures: the *Job File Table* (JFT) and the *System File Table* (SFT). Any program can expand the DOS default of 20 to up to 255 simultaneously open files. The number of SFT entries is more important when dealing with the number of files that can be opened at any one time. This is a 65-byte-per-open-file area that DOS uses to store all the information about the file. The number of SFT entries that DOS can handle is set at startup and cannot be changed. Even though the program can be changed to handle up to 255 open files, if the SFT is large enough for only eight entries, only eight files can be opened at one time. The FILES= line in the CONFIG.SYS file sets the number of SFT entries and thus the maximum number of files that can be opened at any one time.

When DOS is installed, there is a *default* (automatic) setting for the numbers of files and buffers that can be open at a given moment. The default settings are often insufficient for a program's needs, and in an effort to make sure the program will run once installed, the designers build in a change to the settings for files and buffers.

Settings for files and buffers are stored in the CONFIG.SYS file, which is the first file run after the bootstrap load is completed. Each setting in CONFIG.SYS is on its own line and the lines are read sequentially. Software developers assume (often incorrectly) that theirs is the only program running on a given PC. Installation programs will append their own FILES and BUFFERS requirements at the end of the CONFIG.SYS file.

It could happen—and often does—that a newly installed program requires *fewer* FILES and BUFFERS than a program already on your PC running. As DOS reads through CONFIG.SYS, it tosses out previous instructions if there are subsequent ones. You could end up with a CONFIG.SYS file that looks like this after an installation program has run:

```
DEVICE=C:\DOS\HIMEM.SYS

DEVICE=C:\DOSEMM386.EXE RAM auto 1024

buffers=30, 00

FILES=30

DOS=UMB

lastdrive=Z

FCBS=4, 0

DEVICEHIGH /L:1,12408 =C:\DOS\SETVER.EXE

DEVICE=C:\DOS\SMARTDRV.EXE /DOUBLE_BUFFER

DOS=HIGH

DEVICEHIGH /L:1,5888 =C:\DOS\RAMDRIVE.SYS     1024,512,64,/E

REM DEVICEHIGH=C:\DOS\SMARTDRV.SYS

FILES=15

BUFFERS=10

DEVICEHIGH /L:1,15792 =C:\DOS\DISPLAY.SYS

CON:=(EGA,437,1)

SHELL=C:\DOS\COMMAND.COM C:\DOS\ /E:320  /p

BREAK=ON

DEVICEHIGH /L:1,9072 =C:\DOS\ANSI.SYS

DEVICEHIGH /L:1,8208 =BRIDGE_B.DRV /PS70:1B

FILES=10

BUFFERS=30
```

As you can see from this example, you could be stranded or locked if you try to run a more needy application with the new settings.

TIP

Always read the documentation for your new program before running INSTALL. Check your CONFIG.SYS file by typing the following line and pressing Enter before you start the install process:

```
TYPE CONFIG.SYS
```

Then check to make sure that the install program won't write to CONFIG.SYS or that you have an option to say no. If changes to CONFIG.SYS are required for more buffers and files, edit CONFIG.SYS yourself by using a text editor.

Before you change CONFIG.SYS, use the DOS COPY command to copy CONFIG.SYS to a disk so that you can restore it immediately if something goes wrong.

CAUTION

Always check CONFIG.SYS after running any installation program; compare it to the check you made before installation. Otherwise, you might find yourself stranded or locked while running a program and your work will go straight down the data drain.

AUTOEXEC.BATty

Some installation programs will go so far as to rewrite (or create) their own AUTOEXEC.BAT files. This can leave you with additional instructions at the end of your existing AUTOEXEC.BAT or with the old file overwritten by the install program. A well-behaved installation program will ask whether it's allowed to perform these miracles. The naughty ones won't, and then you have the charming chore of rekeying the AUTOEXEC you want, plus adding the instructions inserted by the install procedure.

TIP

Just as you did for CONFIG.SYS, use the DOS TYPE command to find out what's in AUTOEXEC before you run an installation program. And make a disk copy of AUTOEXEC.BAT for a quick restoration if needed.

TSRs at War

Most of us use one or more *terminate-and-stay-resident* programs—called TSRs in the trade—from time to time. A complete explanation of TSRs is found in Chapter 14, but the concept is simple and important.

You can load a TSR program yourself by typing a startup command at the DOS command line, or you can set up AUTOEXEC.BAT to load the TSR automatically. Either way, the TSR takes its place in RAM and sits there, waiting, until you ask it to do something. You typically access a TSR by typing a combination of *hot keys*, like the Alt-Ctrl key combination required to access Borland's SideKick.

TIP

If all of your TSRs are loaded by AUTOEXEC.BAT, have two copies of this file (with different names) handy. For example, you might have an AUTOEXEC.BAT with no TSRs under the name AUTOEXEC.CLN and the one with all the TSRs under the name AUTOEXEC.ALL. To boot the system clean, copy AUTOEXEC.CLN to AUTOEXEC.BAT and reboot. When you want to load the TSRs, copy AUTOEXEC.ALL to AUTOEXEC.BAT and either reboot or type AUTOEXEC and press Enter.

TSRs are usually very small and a flock of them can be loaded without impairing the efficacy of your PC. If you're using a program that is RAM intensive, however, one TSR too many can bring your activity to a screeching halt, leaving you with the only choice of rebooting the machine and losing whatever data you were currently manipulating in RAM.

TIP

If you are aware of a particular program's RAM intensive needs, reboot your PC to remove active TSRs before accessing the program.

The two million members of the PRODIGY on-line service know about RAM intensive applications. PRODIGY wants—or demands—a full 640K of RAM to work its magic. A leftover TSR can bring PRODIGY to its knees and dump you back to DOS. Depending on your activity within the service, you may be able to skate through a session with a small TSR still in memory. Other times, usually after you type a six-page note, the system chokes.

TIP

If you find yourself stranded or locked in a particular program more than once, check the memory requirements in the documentation.

A proliferation of little utilities, TSRs themselves, purport to be TSR unloaders. If TSR unloaders were reliable, one would have been included on the disk in the back of this book. Handle these programs with exquisite care if you must use them.

When rebooting to clear TSRs, make sure you don't have a disk locked in drive A. This is the *only* way that the class of computer viruses known as *boot infectors* can travel.

In addition to going to war with RAM intensive applications, TSRs can also go to war with each other. No standard exists for TSR development and some TSRs are pickier than others. If you load a new TSR—either by adding it to AUTOEXEC.BAT or by calling it from the command line—and find yourself stranded or locked, it's tweak time.

TSR Tweaking

The first step in tweaking a TSR is to rename AUTOEXEC.BAT using the DOS REN command. The name AUTOEXEC.RAT works just fine.

Either jot down or print a copy of AUTOEXEC for reference. Reboot the PC. One by one, type in the names of the TSR programs at the command line until you hit the wall and everything stops. Once you've determined which program is the bad actor, reboot and rearrange your TSRs from the command line until you've got it right. What usually happens is that one program insists on being last on the list.

When the order is right, simply redo AUTOEXEC with a text editor to reflect the proper sequence, rename it back to AUTOEXEC.BAT, and reboot with the tweak in place.

Don't Do Windows?

Microsoft made a big hit with the Windows environment and its GUI. PCs packed with expanded and extended memory are in offices and homes everywhere, and users happily open two, ten, or however many windows and are completely convinced that they have multi-tasking PCs in front of them. The fact remains that the PC is still only *doing* one thing at a time; it just looks like more. And why do you need 2 Mb of memory for Windows? Because Windows *needs* a lot, that's why. And when memory requirements add up, so do possible problems.

You'll find a more technical approach in Chapter 14, but there are some Windows concerns everyone needs to understand. Put simply, some programs won't work under Windows. Or, perhaps better, some programs will work for a *while* under Windows and then stop working. You've probably seen the software products that are named *This* for Windows or *That* for Windows (enter your own product name). Common sense tells us that if Windows products include *for Windows* in their names, then the not-for-Windows products from the same developer shouldn't be run under Windows.

Microsoft's own word processing product, Microsoft Word 5.5, chokes and dies under Windows when anything more than simple typing is attempted. And every Word word goes into the byte bucket. Because other programs may be running in other windows, those programs could also lose data if Windows shuts down due to an error in one of the programs.

TIP

Make sure that any software application you want to run under Windows is Windows-compatible.

Write On/Over

DOS is practical. Each file in a directory must have a unique name. For example, if you have a file named FILENAME.EXT in a directory and you try to create another file with the same name, two things can happen, depending on the software you are using:

➤ Well-behaved software will display a pleasant query, with the following message:

```
FILENAME.EXT already exists. Replace it?  Y/N?
```

➤ Other software may offer you the option of overwriting the existing file with the new one or appending (adding) the information in the new file to the old.

In either case, at least the choice is up to you—but you still could hit the wrong key.

Less sophisticated software (for example, the early Norton text editor NE.COM was a major offender) lets you blithely overwrite an existing file without even a by-your-leave. Make sure that you know whether your software asks you to confirm the operation if you're about to overwrite an existing file or make very sure you don't type in a filename that's already in use.

SoftSell

When your favorite software company offers you an upgrade to your existing software, make sure that all data created under previous versions will translate or convert to the new version without your intervention. Read the documentation carefully to find out what, if anything, you need to do to ensure the integrity of your data. And when you put the upgrade through its paces the first few times, work from a copy of your existing data file and check the results.

More importantly, if you're changing from Product A to Product B, and Product B promises faithfully that all data created by Product A is completely convertible, test it. On a copy.

SoftWarning

Computer viruses, for the most part, travel on disks. Whenever you purchase or otherwise obtain new software, check the disk for the presence of viruses. Preformatted disks can also be carriers. When you purchase a new box of pre-formatted disks, check at least one of them for the presence of viruses.

NOTE

Pre-formatted disks carry only boot sector viruses.

Computer Viruses and Malware

The idea of computer viruses is nothing new. In 1949, John von Neumann, one of the founders of the computing community, presented a paper called *Theory and Organization of Complicated Automata*. In that paper, he put forth his theory that computer programs could multiply and included a model of what we would, today, call a computer virus. The oral tradition holds that most of von Neumann's colleagues thought he was a few bricks shy of a load, but that's understandable. The first practical electronic computers wouldn't be developed for several more years.

In an attempt to be as precise as computers, this chapter looks at the definition(s) of computer viruses and covers the expanded and more meaningful term *malware* (any software that's bent on destruction of your data). This chapter also explains the various kinds of malware and analyzes some of the solutions to the problem—and to the *solutions* that create their own particular set of problems.

The First Virus?

Bell Labs was a very busy place in the mid-Twentieth Century, producing transistors in the '40s and the first computer virus in the '50s. Three young Bell programmers—H. Douglas McIlroy, Victor Vysottsky, and Robert Morris—understood the working of transistors and computers very well, indeed. They invented a computer game called Core Wars, played on Bell Labs' monster computers, that was, arguably, the very first computer virus.

Core Wars was a one-on-one game between two programmers. Each player developed a set of reproducing programs called *organisms*. Each set of organisms attempted to destroy the other set of organisms. At the end of the game, the player with the higher number of surviving organisms won.

NOTE

It's interesting that, even then, the nomenclature indicated some sort of life force in the programs.

Today, the three would probably be encouraged to seek employment elsewhere if they were exploiting their employer's resources to develop games or computer viruses. Back then, it was probably tolerated as part of the learning experience.

NOTE

Morris' son, Robert Morris, Jr., continued in the grand tradition. He was convicted in 1991 of creating and spreading the infamous Internet Worm.

Core Wars soon spread to other high-tech sites such as the Massachusetts Institute of Technology and PARC, Xerox's research site in Palo Alto, California. The virus remained an arcane secret, known only to the initiated, until 1983 when Ken Thompson, the brilliant fellow who wrote the original version of UNIX, spilled the beans. When Thompson accepted the A. M. Turing Award, one of the computer industry's highest honors, his acceptance speech contained a recipe for viruses. Thompson told all about Core Wars and encouraged his audience to give the concept a try!

The May 1984 issue of *Scientific American* included an article describing Core Wars and offered readers the opportunity to send for a set of instructions to participate in the fun and games ($2 for postage). By this time, PCs had been on the scene for three years.

Viruses Defined

Destructive computing is not new, but the awareness of it is. Most people are aware of computer viruses, thanks to the media. Most people's understanding of the problem is flawed, thanks to the media.

> *"A virus [is] a program that can order a computer to replicate itself."*
> —Dallas Morning News

The concept of computer viruses as we know them today is more or less contained in *The Gospel According to Fred*. Dr. Fred Cohen, writing his doctoral thesis in 1983, defined the activity of a computer virus and coined the term *virus*. According to *The Gospel* and to Dr. Cohen's many disciples, computer viruses simply did not exist until Fred wrote his thesis.

It really doesn't matter. Clearly the concept, the technical ability, and the actuality existed B.C. (Before Cohen) rather than only A.D. (After Definition).

In the bleak midwinter after the first three widespread viruses— Lehigh, Jerusalem, and (c)BRAIN—captured national and international attention, the fifty "best and brightest" security and virus experts met in New York. It was an invitation-only sort of affair, and a "learned paper" was the price of admission. Two days were spent primarily arguing over the definition of the word *virus*. The key word, the one people couldn't get away from, was *replicate*. If memory serves, no conclusion was reached.

Defining a computer virus isn't that hard. A computer virus is nothing more than a set of computer instructions which will replicate them-selves, given a chance. But sometimes there is more to a computer virus than self-replicating instructions. Many computer viruses also contain instructions designed to destroy or alter data. These destructive instructions are called Trojan Horses after the famous Greek legend of the battle for Troy. A Trojan Horse can also be a stand-alone program that purports to do one thing and actually does something else. On the other hand, viruses are never stand-alone programs, but just a set of instructions appended to a program. Things get a bit dicier when worms, which also spread and may also cause damage, wriggle into the picture.

One of the best arguments and definitions currently in circulation is one propounded by A. Padgett Peterson, an internationally known virus and security expert. Peterson is a Founding Member of the Virus Security Institute (VSI) and is a member of CARO (Computer Anti-Virus Research Organization).

The answer to "What is a virus?" is becoming very confusing. Dr. Cohen would have us believe that anything that replicates or propagates is included under that heading. He would hold that, specifically, *worms* are viruses.

Cohen owns the right of first (though obscure) publication. *Scientific American* magazine's "Mathematical Games" discussion occurred at about the same time as Cohen's paper, and of course the worm concept dates back to the 1950's Core Wars and was repeated several times in fiction during the 60s. Those of us who have been working actively and publicly in the field have come to regard a virus in a more limited sense: as a parasitic organism requiring a host program to survive because it is not complete in itself.

In fact, the concept of a virus seems to be a PC phenomenon that dates back to a documented viral program in Texas in 1981, although the name *virus* did not come into popular use until 1986. The first known PC virus, the BRAIN, exhibits this characteristic because without a viable boot program to exploit, the BRAIN cannot spread. This characteristic is shared by all MBR (Master Boot Record) and BSI (Boot Sector Infectors) infectors. Without a viable partition table or parameter block that must be extracted from a functioning machine, they will not work.

NOTE

The 1981 virus was on the Apple II platform and was called Elk Cloner.

File infectors are similar in that the virus code requires a host program to function. Even overwriting viruses are nothing more than logic bombs without host programs. The group called *companion viruses* are more subtle and are stand-alone programs but still rely on the existence of a host program to ensure execution. Without a program *name*, they will not propagate.

Seven elements are found in malicious software:

1. Introduction—the means by which it is introduced into a system

2. Execution—the means by which the malicious software ensures continued operation

3. Evasion—the means by which detection is avoided

4. Propagation/Replication

5. Trigger (date, repeat count, etc.)

6. Effect (message, bomb, etc.)

7. Eradication—the removal of evidence of infection from the system

Not every characteristic need be present in each instance of malicious software. Of those listed, however, element 4 is the exclusive province of viruses and worms. Because of the different varieties of malicious software, only viruses and worms exhibit the characteristic shown in element 4.

The difference between viruses and worms is exhibited in element 2. Worms are stand-alone processes that are able to schedule their own execution, and viruses are parasitic processes requiring an external request for execution.

The important note is that this has nothing to do with propagation. Both viruses and worms can use the same means to replicate themselves—that is what makes them viruses and/or worms. (A program could be either, depending on environment.)

Understand that this definition is made in the context of *malicious software*. That is not to say that all viruses are necessarily malicious; rather, that malicious software can be classified as a virus if element 4 is met and can be separated from a worm by the means in which element 2 is accomplished.

The current discussion hinges on this last point. Dr. Cohen has provided an excellent discussion of element 4 and from that stand-point alone, a worm could be classified as a virus. My thinking is that a proper appraisal of element 2 has not been made, however, and that this reflects a fundamental difference between malicious software considered a virus and that considered a worm.

Specifically, a worm is able to create a propagating process inside a favorable computing environment without drawing on any other resources. In counterpoint, a virus requires that for propagation to occur, the environment must also contain a stored process that can be used as a host.

Early Malware

By the summer of 1985, hundreds of thousands of PCs were in use across the country. Electronic bulletin boards, accessed through a phone line and modem, were becoming all the rage. Most BBSs offered chats (although why someone would waste valuable long-distance time typing at 40 words-per-minute instead of talking at 200 words-per-minute remains a mystery) and, usually, a library of files available for *download*.

NOTE

Downloading is copying from another computer to yours; uploading is copying a file from your computer to another one.

Most of the files available on the BBSs were either utility programs or games developed by hobbyists. Often, better work was being done by hobbyists and part-timers than in the emerging PC industry itself. The first destructive program, EGABTR, promised to provide better graphics on a plain screen than those available with the then very expensive and state-of-the-art IBM Enhanced Graphics Adapter. The idea was very tempting and the price was right—free for the downloading. Only one problem. EGABTR (EGA Better) was a vicious Trojan Horse program. The first time a user ran it, it wiped out *every* file on a hard drive and closed with a message:

```
Arf, Arf!  Gotcha!
```

Other early programs bent on destruction included NUKELA, supposed to be a program that would allow you the remarkable opportunity of graphically bombing the socks off LaLaLand. Instead, it bombed the computer.

NOTE

Here at PANDA, we've been involved in the prevention of data destruction since the beginning. Andy Hopkins, who wrote many of the programs on the disk in the back of this book, was the author of the two earliest anti-destruction programs, CHK4BOMB and BOMBSQAD, both written in late 1984 when the first Trojans began to appear. In the July 1986 issue of Lotus magazine, Andy was styled as a "radio personality and talented amateur programmer." Today, his amateur status is long gone.

An important event took place on October 20, 1985. A gentleman named Tom Neff uploaded to a bulletin board system the definitive list of malware/destructive programs. Called "The Dirty Dozen," the list contained exactly twelve programs. Three years later, the Dirty Dozen had been taken over by Eric Newhouse and contained *two hundred* programs in the listing, more than half of which were warnings about pirated software, not malware. As this book goes to press, the Virus Test Center at the University of Hamburg, Germany, lists thousands of programs that fit the current definition of a virus.

What to Call Them?

From day one, viruses have been given names. Some names merely reflect the length of the virus code (1701, 1224). Other names bring notoriety to the place where the virus first appeared (Lehigh at Lehigh University) or pick up on a message displayed by the virus (BRAIN). Other virus names have been chosen because of their Trojan Horse activation date (such as Friday the 13th and Columbus Day). Sometimes the name makes no sense at all and sometimes different names are attached to the same virus. This can get even more confusing when a slight variant of an existing virus comes to light and is given yet another name, creating the impression that there are more viruses than there really are.

At this moment, no central clearinghouse exists that standardizes virus names, although the Virus Security Institute has appointed a committee on nomenclature and the members of CARO attempt to agree on what to call a newly discovered strain.

Don't be confused. The names are not as important as knowing that your computer is infected and doing something about it before you lose DATA.

Viruses Sorted Out

Viruses fall into two major categories: *boot infectors* and *program infectors*. The way that program infectors work is further broken down into *direct infectors* and *indirect infectors*.

Boot Infectors: Disk-Based

A boot infector appends virus code to the very first sector on the disk, called the *boot sector*. This sector is read into memory when the computer is first started. Usually this sector contains the instructions for loading DOS and getting the operating system up and running, but a virus adds instructions that will duplicate the infected boot sector onto other disks.

A Trojan Horse may also be imbedded within the boot sector virus code that activates under certain circumstances. Sometimes the Trojan Horse section attempts to destroy data. The Michelangelo virus activates on March 6 of any year and erases data on the hard disk. Other Trojan Horses are a little less destructive. The Stoned virus will, on a random basis, print on the screen `Your PC is Stoned. Legalize Marijuana`. Some boot sector viruses do nothing except replicate. The so-called Pakistani or (c)BRAIN virus has no Trojan Horse section.

Regardless of the existence of a Trojan Horse within the virus, boot sector viruses can be transmitted to other PCs and are thus dangerous. As a quirk, boot sector viruses are both difficult to spread and difficult to spot. There is no directory entry for the boot sector so there is no file size to check. The boot sector is always 512 bytes long whether it is infected or not.

NOTE

If the virus code is longer than 512 bytes, the virus will appropriate other sectors on the disk, corrupting the data in these sectors.

Boot sector viruses can be spread only by disk. Most PCs today boot from a hard disk, but first attempt to boot from the A: drive. If the computer is never started with a disk in drive A, it can never get a boot sector virus. But it does happen; the computer is started with a disk in the drive by mistake. Even if the disk is not a DOS disk, a boot sector virus can exist in the boot sector and the computer becomes infected.

Don't think that just because you get the `Non-system disk…` message that the virus has not spread to the hard disk. The good news is that infecting another computer involves the physical transfer of an infected disk to another computer. Even then, the second computer must be started with the infected disk in the A: drive.

Program Infectors: Execution-Based

A program infector adds virus instructions to an existing program file. These viruses can spread like a brushfire but are fairly easy to spot. When an infected program runs, the virus code usually runs first, infecting another program file, and then runs the program you requested.

The most common method virus code uses to spread itself is searching the disk for an executable file with a .COM or .EXE extension and then rewriting that file with the virus code included. The file size is increased by the length of the virus code, and sometimes the date and time stamps are changed.

The DIR command can tell you about file changes if you remember the original length of the file. Few of us remember the file length of every file on the disk and thus the virus goes undetected to the casual user. You would need another computer (or another program) to keep track of the length of every program on the disk.

Program infector viruses can spread easily and rapidly throughout the file system of an infected computer. They also can be transmitted to other computers. Any infected file transmitted to an uninfected computer can cause the spread of the virus—with one exception. If the infected file is never *run*, it cannot infect the computer. An infected program file can be stored on a disk indefinitely and until it is run will never infect the computer.

Direct and Indirect Infectors

Two methods may be used to infect other programs. Program infector viruses are further classified as *direct infectors* or *indirect infectors*.

A direct infector works only once; when it is run. When an infected program runs, the virus code seeks one or more program files to infect. After the virus finishes its task, control is passed to the host program. If an uninfected file is run, it cannot spread the infection because the virus resides on other programs. Direct infectors can rapidly infect every program file on the disk if the host program is run often.

An indirect infector operates by remaining in memory (RAM) after the infected program is run. Each time a new program is run, that program is infected and becomes a host for the virus.

NOTE

Some viruses aren't as smart as they look. Jerusalem B kept on re-infecting some files (.EXEs) until they grew too large to load.

A few very clever viruses use a combination of direct and indirect infection and can easily infect every program file on a disk.

CAUTION

Any infected program file transferred to another computer can begin to spread the virus on that computer when the program is run.

Stealth

Just like the F-117 stealth fighter that was so successful in the Gulf War, viruses tend to use techniques to hide their presence. The boot sector infectors were the first to use stealth techniques. By its very nature, the boot sector is normally hidden from view, but boot sector viruses carry this one step further. A portion (if not all) of the virus code is stored in memory and all disk operations are redirected to the virus code. If a program tries to read from or write to the boot sector, the virus redirects this attempt to the sector where the original boot sector is stored. As long as the virus is in memory, any attempt to see the virus is thwarted as well as any attempt to repair the altered boot sector.

Program infectors also go to great pains to hide their presence. Most stealth techniques involve keeping routines in memory that intercept attempts to detect any changes to the file. Every time the user tries to see the file length, the original length is returned instead of the actual length. File dates and file times are not changed. Some viruses even intercept attempts to read the file and show the real file instead of the infected file.

Stealth Techniques and Targeting

Stealth techniques have become more and more elaborate as virus programmers try to prevent anti-virus programs from discovering the virus. The proliferation of anti-virus programs has lead to a proliferation of stealth techniques. If the computing public standardizes on the Microsoft DOS anti-virus program, the virus writers will work harder at hiding their work from it.

While DOS 6 was in testing before release, at least one virus was examined that succeeded in disabling the Microsoft anti-virus. Possibly, those who rely on the DOS anti-virus program for protection will actually be more vulnerable to the targeted viruses that are successful in bypassing its protection.

Anti-Virus Solutions

Solution is a bit of a misnomer because, at least today, a computer must be already infected before an anti-virus "solution" can work. Hardly a solution—more like playing catch-up.

Even though some programs have names that indicate they're keeping viruses *off* a PC, the sad fact is that there is not currently any program that can *prevent* an attempted infection.

NOTE

Programs exist that will immediately repair a boot sector infection, restoring the original boot record after attack by a boot sector infector such as Michelangelo or Stoned.

Three methods are currently used to combat computer viruses: *scanners*, *integrity checkers*, and *behavior blockers*.

Scanners

The most widely used method is the scanner. A *scanner* is a program that reads the contents of program files and looks for a certain combination of bytes (a *signature*) that indicate the presence of a particular virus.

The major drawback of a scanner is that the programmers must know a signature for *every* virus. Not only should the signature be a combination of bytes not found in legitimate programs, but it also should be unique for every virus.

NOTE

Increasing numbers of incidents occur where a scanner picks up perfectly legitimate code and identifies it as a virus. This causes problems for the developer of the legitimate program ("You sent us a program with a virus! So-and-so's program said so!"), whose reputation can be ruined. The vendor of a scanning program that produces false positives could find itself in court.

The operative word is *every*—no one can possibly obtain a signature for every virus existing at a given moment. According to security experts, at least four new viruses appear every day that must be obtained, analyzed, added to the scanner's data list, and finally distributed to the users. Some of the major players, notably Central Point and Symantec, update only every three months. Others, like Dr. Solomon's Anti-Virus ToolKit, update monthly. Even with a monthly update, the list is likely to be six to eight weeks out of date by the time it is in users' hands and installed. Of course, often the first to get the scanners are the virus writers themselves.

Those who write viruses often change the virus just enough to alter the signature so a scanner won't recognize it. Lately, virus writers have developed mutation techniques so the virus never looks the same twice. A unique signature is much harder to find if there are an infinite number of combinations.

Integrity Checkers

The second method used by anti-virus programmers is the *integrity checker*. Integrity checking involves keeping a record of every program file and detecting any changes to the file. The changes are found by a variety of techniques, including *checksum* (the sum of the digits in the file is compared) and *CRC*, whose full name is *Cyclical Redundancy Check*. The most sophisticated integrity checkers use either a combination of checksum and CRC or their own, proprietary, methods and algorithms.

There is no need for an integrity checker to look for a specific virus as scanners do because a virus must change a program in some way to infect it. The drawback to integrity checking is that there is no way to know, for sure, whether a program is not infected in the first place, before the integrity checker is installed.

Chances are that a previously infected program will not become reinfected with the same virus. Most integrity checking anti-virus programs include a scanner to check for prior infection, just as most scanner anti-virus programs include integrity checking to guard against new viruses. The advantage of integrity checkers is that they do not have to be updated as new viruses are discovered. Updating scanners has become a major expense for large installations, not in software cost, but in direct personnel cost.

Behavior Blockers

The third type of anti-virus software is the *blocker* program. The blocker is a program that remains in memory and intercepts any activity that looks like it could be virus-related, such as writing to files with an .EXE or .COM extension. The major drawback to these programs is frequent false alarms and the requirement of a decision from the user as to whether to allow an operation to proceed. Most users have no idea whether the operation is related to a virus or to a legitimate programming function.

Point-Counterpoint

All three anti-virus techniques have advantages and drawbacks. Those who write viruses are well aware of what methods the anti-virus folks are using to combat their evil deeds. A game of sorts has evolved to see who can devise techniques to fool the other party. Unfortunately, your data is caught right in the middle. No matter how careful you are, there is a chance that a computer virus could bite you right in the ASCII.

Remember, some viruses have Trojan Horse sections that could wipe out all your data with no chance of recovery, so precaution is your best defense. Make sure that you have, stored in a safe place, a current backup of all your data files. The data files themselves will probably not be infected and can be restored to a system wiped clean by a virus.

If a virus strikes, don't restore program files from a backup because the backup itself could be infected. Returning infected programs just infects the system again. It's wiser to restore programs from the original distribution disks in the event of a virus catastrophe.

Clean-Up Caution

Most anti-virus programs say they can restore an infected program. Use this feature with caution and only as a last resort. Virus programs are usually predictable. A boot sector virus will store the original boot sector in a known sector. Program infector viruses attach a known amount of program code in a known location in the file.

To restore the boot sector to the original condition, a clean-up program needs only to copy the original back to the first sector on the disk. A program file can be repaired by restoring the program entry points to the original location in the file and adjusting the size to remove the added virus code. This works in theory. The problem is that theory sometimes takes a vacation.

One widely publicized virus was Michelangelo, a boot sector virus that erases infected hard disks on Michelangelo's birthday, March 6. This virus moves the original boot sector to the last sector of the root directory on most disks, a sector seldom used unless the root directory contained a great number of files.

One widely marketed clean-up program worked just fine on 360K, 720K, and 1.44 Mb disks. However, 5.25-inch 1.2 Mb disks are still in wide use and the clean-up program wrote the wrong sector back to the boot sector on these disks. The bark turned out worse than the byte. Disks that were supposedly fixed ended up useless. At least the infected disks were usable and, if not used to boot the computer, relatively tame.

Repair programs depend on an *absolute* identification of the virus infecting the boot sector or program file. Any variation of the virus not anticipated by the people who wrote the clean-up program could cause worse problems than the virus itself. The safest procedure is to delete infected program files and copy them back from the original distribution disks. Some experts say the space used by an infected file should be completely erased with a utility program designed for that purpose. If that makes you feel better, do it.

 Boot sectors are a bit harder to repair than programs. You can't just copy one from a distribution disk. A full discussion of how to repair an infected boot sector appears in Chapter 14.

Keep Your Fingers Crossed

With a little bit of luck, you will never come face-to-face with a computer virus or any other kind of malware. Or, if you do, hopefully you'll have the tools at hand to find the culprit before any damage is done.

Now that you have the basics of computer virology, steam ahead to the next chapter for specific examples of data destruction and recovery techniques.

CHAPTER

Disaster Recovery Plans

A few years back, a local television station broke into the regularly scheduled programming to show, live, a fire working its way up a twenty-some story office tower in downtown Philadelphia. The assembled company's comments centered, primarily, on what a good thing it was that it was a Sunday and nobody was in the building. The computer security expert in the crowd just kept mumbling, "I hope they have off-site backups."

More recently, a panicked call came through. A well-known anti-virus product had located an apparent virus on the server to a huge network. The product offered the capability to remove the virus, so the removal program was executed. The program worked a bit too well, removing all the partition data on the server drive. Off-site backups? Of course. Where? Over 2,000 miles away. The partition tables were painstakingly rebuilt "by hand" using DOS DEBUG.

On a smaller scale, a well-known writer decided to escape the gloom of a New England winter, loaded his entire manuscript on a new notebook computer, packed in a complete set of disk-based backups, chapter by chapter, and flew off to Nowhere-in-the-Sun for two weeks to complete his final work on the manuscript. His destination was ideal—no telephones, no television, no interruptions. Except the power. Rather than taking two battery packs and keeping one charging at all times, he hooked directly into the chancy wall current. Turned out, the power was too chancy, and his entire machine was fried. The international implications of getting a replacement notebook to Nowhere-in-the-Sun were almost insurmountable. His only choice was to return to the frozen tundra…with his backups.

Disasters, one and all.

Before you can prepare for the worst, you need to figure out just what the worst might be. In the world of personal computing, the worst varies from user to user, machine to machine, application to application, and maybe even day to day.

Whatever the worst is, it's going to require some time to fix, even with the best planning. The idea is to cut down to the absolute minimum both the time and expense required. This chapter looks at what can happen, what it can happen to, how to keep it from happening, and what to do if it does happen.

How Much Planning Is Enough?

This question is reminiscent of the old TV ad for a laxative. A woman queried the camera in regard to prunes. Are three enough? Are six too many? A fair assumption might be that the proper answer is "It depends."

If there were a hard and fast rule, this chapter wouldn't be necessary. Jack Bologna of Computer Protection Systems suggests a checklist approach and says:

> "Conducting computer security surveys is a time-consuming and painstaking process. The process requires an enumeration of computer resources and an assessment of the risks to which the resources may be exposed. That is, the probability of occurrence of risks and the severity of loss, damages, destruction, and theft of resources or the denial of services.

Checklists are intended to remind us of these resources and risks so that our efforts are comprehensive. But checklists, as survey tools, are not substitutes for experience, knowledge, and judgment. That means they must be *customized*. Understanding these limitations is the first step in using checklists."

Bologna, together with Tim Shabeck, developed most of the checklists included in this chapter. And, in a wry moment, Bologna commented that when the first checklist was published, "People thought I was a paranoid obsessive compulsive schizophrenic."

Management Considerations

You, in whatever setting, are the *de facto* manager of your PC. If you're in a large business setting, you have policies and procedures to follow. Often, those P&Ps are not as complete as paranoid obsessive compulsive schizophrenics might like. And, the larger your organization, the more important considering this checklist is!

Do you fully realize the value of your PCs, the software, the applications, and the data being used on your PC? Some simple math often shows that users have no idea at all what their complete systems—not just the hardware—are really worth.

Has the amount of possible financial loss from disaster, criminal act, accident, etc., been determined? This ties directly to the value of the system but with the added cost of "being out of business."

Is the selection and purchase of PCs controlled? This can be important on several levels, not the least of which is the proliferation of "gray market" sales where standard warranties may not be in place.

Has the effect of short-term and long-term downtime of PCs been determined?

Could downtime result in loss of business, customer or employee dissatisfaction, or loss of revenue?

If one PC is shut down, can another be utilized for necessary processing?

Do outsiders have access to your PCs? The ramifications of outside access range from stealing data or programs to trashing a system by inserting a computer virus—purposely or by mistake.

Has a "test" disaster been conducted? Remember fire drills?

Have emergency procedures been established that will be followed in case of disaster or criminal act?

Has a specific individual been assigned to the selection, purchase, and control of PCs?

Is there PC equipment accountability?

Has a physical inventory been conducted of all PC equipment?

Do your PC users attend classes that instruct them on proper system handling and magnetic media handling?

Are the PC users informed of their security and control responsibilities?

Have written policies and procedures been prepared and implemented that govern the security and control of micro equipment and applications?

Are stringent controls placed on any PC use that could affect the accounting records of your company?

Are there adequate controls to protect against the invasion of privacy?

Are your internal/external auditors aware of your computer systems?

Does the disaster recovery plan take into account multi-location PC operations?

Have arrangements been made to replace the micro hardware and software in case of disaster?

Has someone been assigned responsibility for disaster planning?

If you're only one person with only one PC, you will look at this checklist somewhat differently than an Information Services specialist or manager with responsibility for hundreds or thousands of machines. Looking is the important part. Most users, regardless of how or where machines are used, will find something here that rings a bell.

Vulnerability Assessment

Most of the following items are beyond your control. Consider them in terms of what needs to be done if one of them happens.

Hardware

Electro-mechanical device failure

CPU failure

Disk unit head crash

Tape drive failure

Environmental problems—dirt, dust, smoke

Circuit failure

Power problems—spikes, drops

Software

Operating system problems

Logic errors

Programming errors

Faulty design

Insufficient testing

Algorithmic errors—rounding, truncation

Poor or lost documentation

Computer viruses

Magnetic Media

Physical damage of medium

Equipment malfunction

Software problems

Operator error

Operator mishandling

Erasure

Overwrites

Computer viruses

Physical Security and Site Security

Is the perimeter security adequate?

Is the building's security adequate?
    Access control
    Proper lighting
    Alarm systems
    Environmental controls

Is internal site security adequate?
    Access control
    Hardware security devices
    Alarm systems
    Environmental controls

Are doors and docks secure?
    Keys or combinations controlled
    Combinations changed frequently
    Control log kept

If card access systems are used, are cards controlled?

Is the work area secured during nonworking hours?

Have policies and procedures been developed for access control?

Is access to electrical power controlled and secure?

Are floors and ceilings watertight?

Is there sufficient ventilation around PCs?

Is the PC placed near a window where:
    people can view the materials being processed?
    sight of the PC might tempt a thief?

Are furnishings fire resistant?

Hardware

Hardware failures tend to be dramatic and obvious. Whether you have replacement parts on hand and install them yourself or whether a trek to the local fixit place is in store, you've lost time and money. Don't lose data, too.

Of course you have a good and current backup, either on tape, floptical, or disk. If you have a warning of an impending hardware problem (funny noises coming from a disk drive, for example) *immediately* take whatever steps you can to back up anything that's not included in your backups.

It's more likely that, one fine day, your system just *isn't*. Dead. Flatlined. History. Or one of a number of handy error messages like 301 appears on your screen. (301 tells you that the CPU can't find the keyboard, even though you know it's right in front of you.)

Go back to Chapter 3 and weigh your choices about replacement or repair. And be thankful that you have your good and current backup.

Software

Software problems are the common cold or 24-hour flu of computing. Some people suffer more, some people suffer less, and some people develop complications and die.

With that cheery analogy out of the way, consider just what a software problem can mean to you and your data. With the exception of your operating system (DOS), most software is application specific. Product A develops data to be used with Product A. Product B develops data to be used with Product B. And so on. A second exception is utility software—the sort used for disk and data management—that is system-wide.

In the oldest days of personal computing, you went to the computer store, bought a computer, and were presented with the operating system disks bound in a thick manual. You took everything home and installed your system yourself, purchasing additional software at your own rate. Today, you're more likely to purchase a mail-order PC with operating system, an environment such as a DOS shell or Windows, and some applications programs already loaded. It's surprising how often these pre-loaded machines don't include the actual disks for the software in case of problems.

TIP

When purchasing a pre-installed machine, make sure, by asking specifically, that the program disks are part of your purchase. If they aren't, and that's acceptable to you, be sure to back up the programs to disk and then make a copy of the backup disk(s).

Your operating system (DOS) probably won't give you much trouble, but glitches do exist, particularly in newly released versions. Unless there's a compelling reason to upgrade DOS at the moment of release, it's wise to wait until the version has "settled" and problems, if any, have been corrected. For a number of years, DOS with a version number ending in .0 was avoided by savvy users.

Working with DOS

Most applications state clearly on the cover the system requirements of the package (640K RAM, DOS 3.3+, for example). The current standard for DOS is 3.0+ because a huge portion of the installed base is still using 3.3. Because DOS is designed to be *downward compatible*—the same functions of 3.3 are included in 6.0—the chance of a conflict between a new DOS version and your existing applications is minimal.

This is often not the case with utility programs, which are written much closer to the operating system level than applications. When you upgrade your operating system, make sure that your favorite utilities, particularly data recovery utilities, support the new DOS. If not, upgrade your utilities at the same time.

%$#@& Software

As a user, you don't have much—if any—control over how software works on your PC (as the "Stupid Software Tricks" section in Chapter 4 points out). When you *do* have control—in the setup or installation of the software—be careful. Something as simple as entering the wrong specification for a monitor can leave you puzzled, confused, frustrated, and angry. Before you answer a setup question during installation, make sure you understand the question and the answer.

TIP

If things get strange on your PC immediately after you install a new piece of software, remove the new software and restore your system to its previous state. Make particularly sure that any changes made to AUTOEXEC.BAT or CONFIG.SYS by the new software are removed. A smart idea is to copy both AUTOEXEC.BAT and CONFIG.SYS to disk or to another filename so you can easily overwrite any changes made by the installation.

WARNING

Remember that if you make any changes to AUTOEXEC.BAT or CONFIG.SYS, you must reboot the system before the changes take effect.

Making sure that your software works as advertised can be a bit more challenging. A word processing document is fairly simple. Either the document looks like it's supposed to—all the words are there and it prints properly—or it doesn't. But imagine several thousand mail-merged pieces where the name in the salutation doesn't match the name in the body of the letter. Also, remember that software written for DOS 3.3 in 1988 will not mention troubles with DOS 6.0.

Database programs, particularly those that feature relational functions, are even more of a challenge. You will need to compare carefully the results of the software's data mashing to what you know is correct.

Number crunching, the province of spreadsheet programs, is even more difficult to write and test properly. It might be OK or acceptable for a small money management program to be off a few cents here or there for a household budget of $50,000 a year. But for a $50 billion company?

RTB: Documentation

You've heard this term before. RTB is computer insider talk for Read the Book. Nothing is more annoying to technical support people than answering, over and over again, the same question—when the clear answer is on page 3 of the documentation. A universal truth seems to apply here: The more experienced the user, the less likely that the book will be read. The corollary to that universal truth is that the less the book is read, the more likely that data will be lost by an unfortunate combination of keystrokes while the user bashes around trying to make something happen.

Software developers, from lofty Microsoft to the smallest of shareware writers, include documentation with their products. Software without documentation is worse than useless—it's dangerous to your data. The usual reason a user doesn't have documentation with a product is because the product is pirated (that's a nice word for *stolen*). Wouldn't it be comforting to believe that the reason there are so many books on the shelves about how to use the most popular (and most expensive) software products is that the original vendor's documentation is obscure, abstruse, or arcane? Sometimes that's the case.

Documentation that's just plain bad is another story. Much of it is written by folks who already *know* how the software works. A lyrical description of a forest doesn't help someone who's madly searching for a specific tree. Aftermarket books can be of great help for the big commercial programs. Poor documentation for a shareware utility—or, worse, a custom program—can spell death and destruction of data because there's nowhere else to turn.

TIP

If you use shareware or any other programs where the documentation is provided on disk, print it out and put it somewhere safe. If you're in the middle of using a program and hit a wall, you may not be able to beat a hasty retreat to read the documentation on-screen without serious consequences to your data.

Lost documentation? Replace it. Period.

Media Blitz: Your Storage Media

Chapter 14 explains exactly how data is stored on disks, on tape, CD-ROM, wherever. For our purposes here, it is enough to know that data is all lumped together with the term *media*. Mistreatment of your media can result in the complete destruction of whatever data is stored there.

With the exception of CD-ROM, which is literally done with mirrors, all other storage media rely on magnetism to hold data. Exposure to magnets or magnetic fields can compromise or destroy data. Office supply manufacturers took years to figure out that the old magnetic copy holders used by secretaries were a Very Bad Idea in the computer age.

Magnetic media is also sensitive to extremes of heat and cold. Most people wouldn't put a box of disks in the trunk of a car, but what about a notebook or other portable PC? Sure. Safest place for it, right? Wrong. Unless the weather has produced the most temperate of days, a PC kept in a car's trunk for a period of time might sustain hard drive damage without any additional help. But to bring the PC, like the spy, in from the cold and immediately power up is flirting with serious danger. The same holds true for very hot days.

TIP

Make every effort to keep your PC and your media at a temperature between 65 and 85 degrees Fahrenheit. If exposed to extreme heat or cold, allow the PC or the disks to return to room temperature before using.

Disks come in those little envelopes for good reasons. And it's up to you to keep them protected. A blank disk that won't format is an annoyance. A disk full of data—especially a backup disk full of data—that won't read can be a disaster.

Disks should always be kept in some sort of protective encasement. Every office supply store sells disk banks that allow you to keep current work disks at hand but protected.

TIP

Always return 5.25-inch disks to a protective envelope before storing. 3.5-inch disks are hardier but should still be kept in closed containers.

The exposed slot on 5.25-inch disks is a particularly vulnerable area. A mote of dust, a fragment of cigarette ash, or a fingerprint can cause serious damage. Although it's arguable that the recording media is the same in top-of-the-line disks and those available from deeply discounted sources, the quality of the outer envelope is usually not. For serious work disks, don't take chances with the *el cheapos*, although they are fine for distribution disks or only occasional use.

WARNING

Even the most exquisitely controlled environments can sometimes fail. Once upon a time, in a "clean" room, a shelf pulled out of the wall, distributing microscopic hunks of drywall dust all over hundreds of disks.

If you use a tape backup system, remove the tape after backing up. A power surge to the unit could fry your tape.

Let's Get Physical: Site Security

You've already figured out what your PC and its data are worth to you. Hardware problems, software problems, and media problems are far more likely to strike than fire or outright theft.

In the case of fire or theft, however, your only hope is a backup stored somewhere safe. For fire, that means off-site...not in your home or office. For theft, off-site is best, but a carefully hidden backup might escape a computer thief's notice.

You can do some simple things to protect against theft. Never put the box that new equipment arrived in out with the trash for anyone driving by to notice. Mark your equipment obviously with your name, Social Security number, company name, and any other ID that would make a thief think twice. There are devices available (or you could construct your own) that will lash components together and allow you to cable them to a desk or other solid object.

TIP

Check your insurance policies—this is especially important for home PCs—to see what's covered in case of fire or theft. Some policies even cover replacement of equipment that has been fried by a power surge.

Remember that the cost of replacing hardware and software is a minor annoyance compared to the cost of recreating data.

BACK UP! BACK UP! BACK UP!

Stupid Human Tricks

"We have met the enemy and he is us." Pogo (Walt Kelley)

No doubt, there is someone out there mumbling, "Everything is a stupid human trick; PCs don't exist in a vacuum!" Right, but some things humans do are more stupid than others.

Most long-term PC users probably could write this chapter from painful personal experience. (By the way, any examples or additions you may have are sincerely welcomed for inclusion in subsequent editions.) The collection of *faux pas* in this chapter, taken from the collected experiences of pandas and friends, should be sufficient for flavor.

The biggest problem with stupid human tricks is that usually you don't know you've committed one until it's too late. The post-stupid human tricks phase, before you begin to try to figure out how to fix what you've broken, has its own vocabulary not found in the glossary of this book.

This chapter looks at some of the most common stupid human tricks and includes a few that you may see only once in a lifetime. Additionally, you'll look at ways to protect yourself from you.

FORMAT Me!

It's amazing. Buy a new box of disks, and you get a bonus—a neat little package of *labels*. These labels are included for a reason. You are supposed to put them on the disks and write on them. Actually, with 5.25-inch disks, whose "skins" aren't as tough as the 3.5-inch variety, you should write on the label *before* you put it on the disk or use a very soft marker-type pen if the label is already on the disk.

A disk without a label sends a single message: FORMAT ME!

TIP

Always use the DOS DIR (or similar) command to display the contents of an unlabelled disk before formatting!

Auto-Pilot

Some things we do so often with our PCs that the keystroke combination or other activity becomes as much a reflex as closing our eyes when we sneeze. After you've done something the same way a thousand times, why should the thousand-and-first be different? Stupid human tricks coming up.

For example, the Norton Editor—a basic ASCII text editor—recognizes the keystroke combination F3 E as an instruction to exit the file and save. The keystroke combination F3 Q, followed by a confirm on the Exit (Y), exits *without* saving. These two combinations are so different that you would *never* use them incorrectly, right? Wrong. Both sets become so automatic after years of use that it's remarkably easy to lose 200 lines of text by putting fingers in motion before the brain is in gear.

No standards exist in software applications for key use. That's why people tend to cling to an old reliable rather than crawling up the learning curve for a new, worlds-better package. Old dogs, new tricks. If you've been using a keystroke combination like F7 Y Y for years to exit a word processing program and save a document, you just might find yourself using that same combination in Word Blaster 96. If the designers of Word Blaster 96 were thoughtful sorts, they would make sure that "standard" combinations from other major packages wouldn't cause serious harm in their package—just in case the user is on auto-pilot. What if, in Word Blaster, F7 Y Y carried out the following commands:

1. Mark Entire Document

2. Mark for Deletion (Y/N)

3. Delete (Y/N)

Three keystrokes—keystrokes you have used thousands of times before—could delete the entire document and its associated backup files.

Thank goodness that the Y and N keys are separated by the H key, so it's not likely that you'll mistype an answer to a confirm question. But it can happen if you're talking to someone else in the room, holding something in one hand, and pecking the exit sequence without looking at the keyboard.

The magic mouse next to you holds the possibility of disaster, too. The point-and-click action becomes so automatic that a mouse skid could toss data straight to the byte bucket instead of saving it. With Microsoft Word, the distance between Save Changes and Discard Changes is about as far as the human hand travels when the human brain is startled by a sudden noise, a lap-leaping cat, or any one of a hundred other things. If your brain has already sent the click message to your finger, it may turn out to be the click of data death.

TIP

Think!

Don't Leave through the Back Door

Like many other data disasters, leaving a program in a way the programmers never intended can be averted by the RTB axiom. But everyone, it seems, loves a good shortcut. Just make sure your shortcuts don't cut you short.

DELPHI, a computer on-line service, provides E-mail capability to its members. The E-mail is stored on the corporate mainframes until you read it; then you have an option to delete the mail you have already read. If mail is left on the mainframes for storage, DELPHI imposes a storage cost.

Working your way backwards out of DELPHI's mail function is a pain. You enter a pair of ^Z commands, type EXIT from the Main Menu, and so on. It's much easier to tell the communications software "I'm outta here." Stupid human trick. Even though you carefully typed DEL after you read each message, the system won't delete them unless the proper exit procedure is followed. Many DELPHI members discover the cost of this particular shortcut when a storage fee shows up on their credit card billing.

Some programs aren't smart enough to save your data when you leave. Of course this makes no sense, but it's up to you to know how programs behave. The point-and-shoot menu bar at the top of Lotus Development Corporation's products offer the choice Save—which is a good thing. Quit doesn't save data.

After most beginners learn the Ctrl-Alt-Del method of rebooting, they will use it at least once and lose data. This usually doesn't happen a second time.

Know the Question before You Answer

Software, including DOS, sometimes has a curious nature. The program will actually ask you what you want to do. Do you really want to format that disk? Do you really want to leave the program now? Do you want to save your data? It's a good idea to know what the question means before you answer. If you're not sure, don't answer. Go directly to the manual that came with your software and *look it up*.

Some of the smartest PCs around are those in the DELL notebook series. After you turn the computer off (or think you have turned it off), the system asks you whether any data needs to be saved. If you answer no, the computer turns off.

Software Piracy

Piracy is one of the stupidest human tricks going, on several levels. First of all, piracy is illegal. Second, with pirated software, you receive no documentation, no warranty (such as software warranties are), and no technical support. (Tech support is available to you only if you are the registered licensee of the software.) And, with pirated software, the only way to get program upgrades is to steal them, too.

The Software Publisher's Association estimates that one in five copies of software in use is pirated. The proliferation of third-party books on major software packages is, possibly, attributable to the atrocious manuals published by the vendors. It's also possible to run a package quite competently with only the information found on the shelf in a bookstore.

NOTE

Shopping in a large chain bookstore one day, I was approached by a nice-looking lady and her nice-looking college-age daughter. What book would I recommend for the daughter to learn WordPerfect? Why, the beginning manual that comes with WordPerfect is a great learning tool, probably adequate for anything the daughter would need. Oops. Daughter had "copied" the software. Well, then, ladies, why don't you take three or four of these books and just stick them in your shopping bag and walk out of the store? Oh, no, that would be stealing. Indeed.

Justice does exist, however, even if it's the hit-or-miss variety. One particular PC maven, proud of his collection of bootleg software, got hold of a program that made copying (stealing) even easier. His source was an underground bulletin board system, and the SYSOP or whom-ever had uploaded the program possessed either a nasty sense of humor or a scrambled sense of ethics. The copying program contained a vicious Trojan Horse that wiped out the entire hard drive of the thief's PC.

TIP

Buy your software. Register it with the vendor. Don't give copies away.

Know Your Software

Never run a program, particularly a utility, unless you know—and know *exactly*—what it does. If you don't know, ask. Or RTB. PANDA produces a set of programs that provides secure passwords and other protection for notebook computers. Three programs are included in the suite: one to install the program, one to uninstall the program, and a third for management functions.

A prospective client, the Information Services Director for a large corporation, asked to take a look at the software. The instructions were simple: TYPE FILENAME. Before typing FILENAME, he did a DIR of the distribution disk. Aha! Look here! Other programs. Let's see what they do! First.

Of course, it would have made sense for him to test the programs on one of the brand new notebooks stacked up in the corner of his office, but his production machine was right in front of him when he opened the package. The program he chose to run was the uninstall program whose sole function is to write previously saved data from an absolute address to another, essential, absolute address. The net result was an essential part of the hard disk with *nothing on it* and a PC that no longer recognized his drive C. Short of sending the disk out for professional recovery, the data on the hard drive was gone. Backup? No.

TIP

Always back up your disk before testing new software. Always back up your disk even if you aren't testing new software.

Error (Message) Prone

Error messages are no fun to see, less fun to figure out, and dangerous to work with unless you know *exactly* what the message means and who—or what—sent it. When an error message pops up, your first job is to figure out the source. Is it the application you're running? Is it DOS? Is it, maybe, a computer virus?

What would you do if the message Fatal Error. Reboot Now! appeared on your screen? (Hint: You would *not* reboot!) First you need to figure out whether the program itself sent the message (look at the program's documentation). If you don't find the error in the list of error messages (if there's no list of error messages, the program is poorly documented), move on to your DOS manual. If the error message doesn't appear there, call the software vendor's technical support line.

Trust Me!

Never trust anyone who gives you the world's dandiest program, whether you find it on a bulletin board or are handed an actual disk. Running unknown, untested software is the number one way to catch a computer virus. Well-run BBS's and the national and international on-line services are exquisitely careful to "vet" all programs available for download. But don't take a chance. Use a scanner (there are some excellent shareware products available) to check the disk first.

Outsmarting INSTALL

Experienced users, bitten once or twice by the Installation Program from Hell, (see Chapter 4) often outsmart themselves by trying to outsmart install. The stupid human trick usually goes this way: You create a directory on your hard drive for the new software by using the DOS MD command. You then copy all the data from the installation disks to your hard drive. Then—oops—you notice too late that you didn't use the DOS CD command to move to the new subdirectory.

At least two things can happen here. First, you can write over AUTOEXEC.BAT and CONFIG.SYS, which is what you're trying to prevent in the first place. Second, with a whopping big program, you can max out the DOS limit of files in the root directory.

NOTE

The root directory is the only directory under DOS with a maximum number of files. Disks, depending upon their size, have limitations as well. For more technical information, see Chapter 13.

Ray-Ban

Most PCs provide you with the opportunity to spend even more money on special boards that install in slots inside your PC's case. The boards are easy to put in and easy to take out. Also inside your PC is an oscillator that's tossing all sorts of radio spectrum radiation. (Just in case you were wondering why there is a Federal Communications Commission label on your PC—that's why.) If you decide to remove a board from your PC and don't replace the little slot cover, you begin broadcasting from your PC.

What you're broadcasting is interference that can mess up your TV, your radio, your portable telephone...anything that receives radio waves. Your neighbors can also be affected, especially in high-density areas like apartment houses.

DELDOT

In Delaware, DELDOT often means the Delaware Department of Transportation. To PC users, DELDOT is a DOS command to be very careful with. Everyone knows that DEL *.* erases everything in the current directory. Very few people know that DEL . does the same thing.

Stupid Pet Tricks

Most people like animals; lots of people have pets. Lots of people have lots of PC problems because of pets. Ask pet-allergy sufferers and they'll tell you that there are infinitesimal particles of pet dander floating through the air. They can't see them, but they know they're there when they start sneezing. Whatever reaches the sufferers' noses can reach your PC, too. Remember how the fan draws air *across* the internal parts of your PC? A power supply fan loaded with pet glarnge will quit on you sooner than a clean one.

A strange attraction exists between pets—especially cats—and PCs. A personal favorite cat, known to one and all as Willard the Disinterested, was a moncat. (That's a cat who likes to sit on top of the monitor.) In truth, it was kind of cute to see this fluffy gray fellow lounging atop the CRT, and it was only a minor annoyance to move his tail from time to time in order to read the screen. Willard did have one interest: food. Time passed, Willard expanded, and one day, during a moncatnap, he slid off the top. Backwards. He awakened rather quickly and, in an attempt to break his fall, pulled out most of the cables plugged in to the back of the PC.

Another cat-of-the-house, Madame Pansy, the long-haired calico, likes to sleep in the well of the LaserJet printer. Pansy's a slow learner and forgets, from printer nap to printer nap, that the HP often recycles and makes *noise*! Her owner's a slow learner, too. It's impossible to count the number of times that a tidy stack of 3.5-inch disks (which *should* have been in a disk bank) has been scattered by Pansy's quick exit from her electronic nest.

Mattsa Cattsa, a quick learner, discovered at the age of six months that the most effective way to request egress from the house into the yard was to place a white-gloved paw on the keyboard. Fortunately, Mattsa has yet to learn Ctrl-Alt-Del.

All the cats have learned that they are safe from The Enforcer, a Super Soaker water gun, when they take a position anywhere near a computer.

The official PANDA Systems dog, Magabyte, the Welsh Corgi, likes to sleep under desks. In the course of dog dreams, she has been known to roll over...onto the off/on switch of the power strip. She's also been known to chase one or another of the resident felines through a snarl of cables.

Keyboard Bashing

For the most part, this stupid human trick is the province of the more experienced PC users. A new piece of software doesn't want to do what you want it to do. Well, then, try Ctrl-F3. It works with TurboSwirl! Oops. Exit without save. RTB. Or try the help key.

Real-Life Experiences

Writers are PC-intensive people. A single question, "What's the stupidest/silliest/funniest/dumbest thing you've ever done with your PC?" on the Writing Technique area of the PRODIGY Service elicited over 100 responses in less than 24 hours. The following are representative of the tales of woe that came flooding across the screen. They've been edited only to protect anonymity; the special "chat" flavor of an on-line service remains.

Stupid Human Trick #1: The Clobbered Keyboard

"Stupid Human Tricks with PCs? In my case, too numerous to mention, but there is one fresh in my memory. I spent four hours yesterday undoing what I did—whatever that was (I still don't know what happened).

"The scenario: I'm in my word processing program, working on a file. I decide to look something up in a very large book, which I had in front of me, kinda' propped up in front of the keyboard. Well, it got unpropped and fell on the keys.

"Whatever configuration of keys it struck was the one programmed to make sure that I never, ever get to work on that file again...probably an CIA/NSA code. The file is still listed in my directory, but I can't get into it, copy it, print it—nothing. Somebody or something not of this world has attached what I assume are Druid symbols to the file name.

"Honestly, I can't tell you how I finally got into it. Moral of the story: Do not place books on the keyboard while working in a file."

Stupid Human Trick #2: The Invisible Update

"I once spent two hours looking for a synopsis. Because I often update files by giving them numbers (that is, syn.001, syn.002) it is sometimes difficult to remember how many I updated. Anyway, I hunted and despaired. My last attempt before resorting to re-do (I had not printed a hard copy yet) was to go through everything on my directory...and I found it! In my sleep-induced state in the wee hours of the morning, I had filed it under Prolugue.002. Great relief."

Stupid Human Trick #3: The Backup School of Hard Knocks

"I, too, have propped books too near the keyboard, but I guess I've been lucky so far, adding only several pages of characters wherever my cursor happened to be. I did, however, lose the computer copy of my first novel. All of it. Hard disk crash, machine under warranty and all, but no back-up disk. I have a paper copy, but no desire to re-key the entire thing. Luckily, it's pretty awful so I didn't lose anything I actually want. Whew!

"I now keep two electronic copies (hard disk and a floppy) and backup big and/or important stuff every week or so. I'm considering asking a friend if he'd mind storing a couple of disks at work, just in case of fire/flood/avalanche—you know, the usual stuff."

Stupid Human Trick #4: Copy Gone Wrong

"What a relief to know I'm not alone! Although you don't have a case like this yet...

"I thought I was going to be really smart and make a backup of a completed book on a 3.5-inch disk. Following my husband's directions over the phone, I encountered an entry problem, and experimented with the closest thing I thought would work. What I was attempting was to put a copy on the hard drive, and then make another 3.5-inch disk. Instead, I creatively managed to erase several *programs* off the hard drive—to the extent that we could no longer boot up anything!"

Stupid Human Trick #5: Stewed Story Searching

"*Sure* I've done dumb things on the computer. The dumbest involve
BBSs, but that's another story. I once lost a story I was working on
because I was drinking wine while writing and miskeyed the story into
limbo. Being as stubborn as I am stupid, I drunkenly refused to sleep it
off until the morrow, so I set about trying to find the file. What had
happened was that I erased it out of the directory—but it was still
available on the disk. Not having Norton, I actually had to descend
into the damn code to find the lost file. I have *no idea* how I did this:
alcohol blocked my memory. All I know is that it worked, and I got
the story back. Felt pretty cocky about it, too."

Stupid Human Trick #6: File Hide-and-Seek

"I don't know how funny this is...it wasn't funny at all at the time. I
erased an entire manuscript from my hard drive—didn't have it on
floppy—and cried for 140 years. Due to my extensive computer
illiteracy, I didn't realize that I hadn't actually lost the file. The manuscript had just decided to fragment (like my personality, at the time).
Dear Hubby worked his computer magic on that funky lil' hard drive
and managed to coerce it back into visible reality. I still don't know
where it went. Probably on a vacation from me because I was driving it
crazy at the time...along with it driving me crazy. Fiction manuscripts
do that when they take on lives of their own, which is precisely
why mine decided to take a vacation into the land of computer
dot...dot...dash."

Stupid Human Trick #7: The Scenic Route to No Backup Canyon

"This isn't funny, and unfortunately, it's not made up.I took my 3 1/2
year-old, my 6-year-old, and my laptop on a nine month, coast-to-
coast trip in a 110,000-mile camper. Didn't know how to backup (the
files, not the camper). Lost months and miles of diary entries. *Still*
didn't learn how to backup; lost *more*. Know how to backup now.
Haven't figured out how to retrieve."

Stupid Human Trick #8: That Freebie's a Keeper

"I erased a $40 screen saver program that came with my hard drive. I could still kick myself."

Stupid Human Trick #9: DELETE Can Be Hazardous to Your Health

"I used to work with someone who erased the whole C drive! Thought she was going to stroke out."

Stupid Human Trick #10: Low Memory Laser Show

"The funniest one was when I was running WordPerfect for DOS in Windows. I minimized WP in Windows, used another gazillion-byte Windows program (I think it was Lotus 1-2-3 for Windows) and then, forgetting that WP was loaded, started it again. It loaded. While I worked in the DOS program, I forgot I was in Windows and restarted Windows—on a 386 SX with 2 Mb of RAM.

"That puppy screamed its death call. It tried really hard to juggle everything but found it had no hands to catch the programs. The screen blinked and blanked twice, and I swear smoke rose from the back of the CPU. The visual effect was like a laser light show.

"But that wasn't what was stupid. I liked the flashing effect so much that I did it again. Things were so scrambled I had to strip everything off and start over, but it was worth it. I've thought about trying it on my new 486, but..."

Stupid Human Trick #11: When It Rains, It Pours

"First, I was trying to back up my hard drive on a floppy and instead of typing C: COPY A:, I typed A: COPY C:. I heard this grating sound, sort of like Pac Man, and wondered why it was taking so long. After five minutes, I realized what had happened, threw myself on the floor, and screamed.

"Later that week, our basement flooded, and I retrieved the possessed PC and brought it to my upstairs office, to accompany my drawing board and books. It's a much more appropriate setting. Then, I spilled Pepsi all over the keyboard. The technician at the shop said that everything was fine…just a false alarm."

Stupid Human Trick #12: A Little Goes a Long Way? Not Far Enough…

"My husband is constantly bringing up the dumbest thing I ever did (or said, actually). I first began using a computer about 12 years ago and never had a problem with computer-phobia. After I left the regular workplace it was several years before we got our first PC. While shopping for a computer, we found a nice little 286 with a 20 Mb hard drive that was light years beyond anything I had used before. In discussing our purchase, I assured hubby (a computer illiterate at the time) that a 20 Mb was *huge*…we would *never* be able to fill that baby up!

"We still have that computer plus a 386 with an 80 Mb hard drive. My hubby takes great delight in teasing me about the huge 20-megger whenever I complain that I'm having trouble finding room on my little 80 Mb, and I have to keep deleting files!"

Stupid Human Trick #13: Consumer Training

"Ah…stupid human tricks. Mine involves begging, rolling over, and playing dead. One Saturday, I decided I *had* to have a computer. The logic is crystal clear. My sister gave me some software. That's kind of like having to have a pool because someone gives you giftwrapped chlorine.

"Armed with the raging desire to own a computer *today* and the ability to sign my own name, I strolled into Radio Shack. No matter that I thought RAM was a Los Angeles football player and that I assumed bytes was a typo…That's what knowledgable sales people are for, right?

"My handy dandy Tandy salesman was indeed knowledgable. He could read verbatim from the back of the box! So could I. After I determined that yes, indeed this was a computer, I bought it. The knowledgable computer salesman hurriedly printed his name on his temporary business card.

"When I called the following day with—get this—*questions*, he said he didn't know squat and told me to call the not-so-toll-free support number. Beg, roll over, play dead. Arf."

Stupid Human Trick #14: Not a Boot Disk in Sight

"The stupidest thing I have done occurred when I upgraded from DOS 3.3 to 5.0. Couldn't wait to tweak my 386 to put all my stuff up high and did so prior to making a boot disk from DOS 5.0. Guess what would not boot when I pressed Ctrl-Alt-Del?

"Lesson learned: Always have an upgraded boot disk available before you mess with AUTOEXEC.BAT and/or CONFIG.SYS!"

Stupid Human Trick #15: Eh? Can't Hear You!

"I left a box of fifty 3.5-inch disks, full of data, on top of a stereo speaker for a week. I'm still trying to recover some of that data."

Stupid Human Trick #16: Hat-in-Hand DOS Retrieval

"The night I brought home my first PC, within an hour, I reformatted my DOS system disk. The only one I had. Of course that computer didn't have a hard disk at first. I felt pretty small going back to where I bought it to get a replacement disk!"

Stupid Human Trick #17: Look before You Leap!

"I've pulled lots of stupid stunts, but the most frustrating was when I was deleting files from drive A but forgot to change to the A prompt, and deleted everything in my C directory (which naturally contained the most vital files). I've since learned to check what I've typed at the prompt before deleting anything! Undelete didn't work; what a pain!"

Stupid Human Trick #18: You Speakin' My Language?

"I was taking a class and brought home a disk with some text files on it that also had the system...3. something. Copied the disk into the root directory of the business computer that had 4.1. Got the message Bad or Missing Command Interpreter, and spent hours trying to figure out how to get the hard drive back. I learned much later that COMMAND.COM and the hidden files must match."

Stupid Human Trick #19: Curiosity Scared the Cat

"I was rearranging my drive bays and had the cover off my PC. Two floppy drives and one hard drive were unscrewed, but they were still connected by power wires and ribbon cables. My cat decided I needed help and jumped onto the motherboard, spilling the works off my desk and onto the floor. Despite sparks, screeches, and minor cardiac arrest, everything worked fine when reassembled! (I did add a few new bad sectors to my HD error map, however.) And no, we didn't have Kitty Stew for supper that night."

Stupid Human Trick #20: The Forgotten Files

"When I bought my backup tape drive I was having fun deleting files and restoring them. I decided to backup my word processor's DOC files and then delete them from the hard drive to see how much room I would save on my HD. After experimenting, I reformatted the tape but forgot to restore the files to my HD!"

Stupid Human Trick #21: AUTOEXEC.BAT by Any Other Name...

"The dumbest thing I have ever done is lose my AUTOEXEC.BAT file to the DOSSHELL Select Across Directories option. And that was after I knew about it, had watched my friends tell others about it, and preached it a little myself. And I'd kept no backup of the file. I had to recreate it from memory. Live and learn. My AUTOEXEC.BAT is stored in no less than three places now under six names."

Your Turn

Here's where you get to write down your most Stupid Human Trick. Don't forget to add what you learned from it:

_____
_____
_____
_____
_____
_____
_____
_____
_____
_____
_____
_____
_____
_____
_____
_____
_____
_____
_____
_____
_____
_____
_____
_____
_____
_____
_____
_____
_____

After you've recorded your blunders, send them to the following address:

Mike Sprague
c/o Brady Books
15 Columbus Circle, 14th Fl.
New York, NY 10023

PART

Prevention

The Backup Bible

If you don't read any other chapter in this book, read this one. You don't need to know the ins and outs of how PCs work to understand that if you *have* data, you don't want to *lose* it. You don't need to know how to use sophisticated software or learn to hand-tinker your data back to life if it's safely stored somewhere else. In short, if you read and pay attention to this chapter, the techniques you learn here will be worth every dollar you spent on this book.

Part of the human condition is our belief in our own immortality. That's the only explanation for our on-the-edge behavior. "It won't happen to me" are the watchwords of perceived immortality. "Just this once" are their corollaries.

It's also part of the human condition to undervalue our own work product. After all, it only took *time* to create it, and time we've got plenty of. A pretty sad commentary.

This chapter looks at the value of data and the ways you can keep it safe. And, in the process, you learn a bit of data management.

Silent Screams

During the Great Michelangelo Scare of 1982, TV stations spent lots of time interviewing people who were worried about their data. One interview, in particular, was memorable. A well-spoken, well-dressed gentleman of somewhat advanced years, standing in line for a "free-fix" program, told how he had spent his retirement years building a complex and complete database of his own and his wife's families' genealogy. "If Michelangelo were to strike," he said, "eight years' work would be gone."

Clearly, this gentleman did not know that his precious data could be kept and stored safely far away from his PC. And it was painful to realize that it took an over-hyped media event to bring him to the recognition of how important his work was to him. Any hour, any day, his local power company could have blasted off his files if they were open during a power surge or outage. A lap cat startled by a ringing phone could have unplugged his PC in the middle of work. Silent screams.

Our retiree was not alone. Across the country, around the world, users went bonkers with the fear of Michelangelo destroying their data. Virus and security experts' silent screams, **BACK UP! BACK UP! BACK UP!** were not heard or heeded. Strangely, the media preferred hysterical reactions to good, solid advice.

Appearing on a local PBS station during those insane days, I was asked, "What would you tell PC users?" A simple answer: "Back up your data so it's safe." That wasn't good enough for the probing young reporter. "But what if the virus is on your backup?" Silent screams. (This particular virus was a boot sector infector and did not infect files at all. In fact, most viruses infect only programs, not data files.)

Me and My Data

Whatever it is, however we created it, our data is *ours*, and it has intrinsic value. It might not be fair to compare a young teenager's lifetime accumulation of scores on SuperTetris with the Great American Novel or an elaborate spreadsheet of income tax information, but what if that kid were competing in a $1,000,000 SuperTetris tournament sponsored by Spectrum HoloByte and was a sure winner? Never underestimate the value of *any* data.

Never discount the "sweat value" of your data—the time and effort you put in gathering it. Something as simple as a Christmas card list or—horrors!—a list of wedding invitees complete with acceptances, regrets, and gifts sent can be a disaster if lost. Particularly if the *sources* of the data—old cards, old letters, notes made during phone calls to distant friends or relatives—have been discarded.

NOTE

*In 1988, I created my own millennium address list of friends and family. It was a masterpiece of what's called data modeling; with a few keystrokes, I could sort on almost any parameter, produce address labels or a printed list to work from for hand-addressing, or pop up a phone number. In fact, that list was the model for a client database I was in the process of developing. When I finished, tested my application, and found it good, I tossed out the envelopes, old address books, and varied slips of paper that had been part of my life since the mid-60s. Less than six months later, my hard drive crashed. The only—**only**—thing I needed or wanted that wasn't backed up was that list. $750 went to a data recovery company. That's a high price for being able to reach out and touch someone.*

Whether you are one of those careful folks who input each month's tax and expense data into your PC on a set date, or you are the more casual sort who digs through the shoeboxes and tidy rubber-banded stacks annually, the task of putting that data *in* is a Very Big Deal. If your data is gone, even if you've got a hard copy, you still have to go back to the keyboard.

TIP

*Think about whether some of your infrequently used data might not be better off stored on floppy disks. Or better yet—**two** identical floppy disks, with one kept at a friend's house.*

Writers, most would agree, are a strange breed in more ways than one. Most writers would agree that the first pass over material is the best. A lost paragraph, a lost chapter, a lost article, a lost anything can never be recreated. Ever.

And what about the quiet writers, those who just keep their own personal journals on their PCs? The days they've written about can never return. The loss of a long-term journal is beyond price. And we won't even think about academic papers, which require years and years of research and writing.

If writers are strange, programmers (another form of writing, it could be argued) are downright weird. In 20 years of working with computers, the only people who actually seem to *like* losing their work are programmers. Otherwise, they say, they'd never correct the stuff they figured out how to do better after they'd done it. Fortunately, programmers are prone to losing files.

In general, lost data is a disaster. How much of a disaster is simply a question of degree.

What Should You Back Up?

So now you see the value in backing up your data. But what, exactly, should you back up?

"Everything" is the easy answer. And, sometimes, it's the right answer. Just because you have a software package sitting on the shelf behind your desk doesn't mean you don't need to back it up as it sits on the disk. Some applications that you've tediously tweaked to your own exact specifications could take many hours to reinstall and fine-tune.

"Everything" is a good place to start out, regardless of the backup system you use. A good baseline backup, even though it may be months (or even years) old, can get you back up and running. Later changes, either to program installations or created data, can be added on top (as long as you have also backed up *those* changes).

How To Back Up

You *should* have a complete backup of all your data. First, run a CHKDSK of your hard disk to see how many bytes you are using on the hard disk. If you have partitioned your disk into several drives, make sure you check the number of bytes in each. If you are using 1.44M disks, plan on one disk per megabyte of file data. With 720K disks, you will need two disks per megabyte. The 5.25-inch floppies hold even less data; you will need four disks per megabyte if you use 360K floppies. This is a *very* conservative estimate, but the extra floppies will come in handy later.

To make a full backup, use the DOS BACKUP command:

```
BACKUP C:\*.* A: /s
```

This command backs up all the files in every subdirectory on the C drive to floppies in the A drive. It is much faster to have the disks already formatted, but with DOS 3.2 and later versions, you can format on the fly with the added switch /F:*xxx* (where *xxx* is the capacity of the floppy disk).

Once you have made the full backup, you are ready for the much faster *incremental* backup at regular intervals. Here is where the extra floppies are used. You can use the DOS BACKUP command to back up only the files that have changed since the last time you backed up. Use the same command line, but add the /M switch:

```
BACKUP C:\*.* A: /s /m
```

This command backs up only the files which have *changed* since the master backup. This means that only altered data files and new programs are backed up, not the entire hard disk. Backing up is much faster and easier. The /M switch turns off the archive attribute bit, so these files will not be backed up the next time. Therefore, use different disks for every incremental backup.

WARNING

A backup done before an operating system change is a recipe for further disaster. Microsoft has changed the backup file format several times and old backup files might not work with new RESTORE commands. If you upgrade your operating system, do a complete new baseline backup.

Unfortunately, "everything" is also the hard answer, requiring more time, energy, and disks than most people are willing to commit. This may be the single reason that most people don't do regular backups. But there are ways to save precious data files without all the hassle of the BACKUP program.

File Management—Naming Conventions

Good file management with all backup procedures—not just DOS—
adds immeasurably to the ability to retrieve data when it's needed.
One of the easiest ways to earmark a particular set of data files (the
chapters of this book, for instance) is with a unique *extension* (.EXT)
not used for other purposes. Another easy way to set files apart is by
always using the same *filename* and using a combination of letters and
numbers for the *extension*.

An EXTended Example

For this book, I used the extension .DRB (Data Recovery Book) for the
chapters as they were written, overriding the automatic extension of
.DOC used by Microsoft Word. I stored these files in their own
subdirectory, C:\DRB. It's fair to say that, as this book was in process,
those .DRB files were the most precious things on my hard drive. It
would have been simple enough to remember, once or twice a day, to
type the following command:

```
COPY C:\DRB\*.DRB A:
```

Using the * wildcard, this command copies to the disk in drive A all
files with the extension .DRB. (The thank-you letter to my Uncle
Steuart for the lovely Christmas fruitcake, even though I saved it to the
book's subdirectory, won't get copied.)

It was much easier to add these lines to the end of the .BAT file that
invokes Microsoft Word, WORD.BAT:

```
ECHO HEY!  Put the DRB Backup Disk in Drive A:

PAUSE

COPY C:\DRB\*.DRB A:
```

What happened with this scheme is that each time I left Word, the
ECHO message displayed and just sat there (the PAUSE command)
until I pressed Enter (presumably after I checked to make sure I had
the proper disk in drive A). Once I pressed Enter, the copy process
proceeded.

More Nomenclature

Active users of on-line services or folks who do a lot of faxing from their PCs can soon become immersed in a sea of files with relatively meaningless names. Manufacturers of fax software, in particular, seem to delight in assigning filenames that require the Rosetta Stone to dope out. Do yourself a favor and develop a meaningful naming convention for these files.

NOTE

A simple example: As a member of Board of the Virus Security Institute, I carry on voluminous correspondence over Internet with other Board members. It's important for me to save these E-letters, either to answer or for future reference. Outgoing mail **from** *me (composed off-line) is always in a file called 2VSI with an extension reflecting the date I wrote it. A message written on March 15 would be called 2VSI.315. Messages received on the same day would be called FVSI.315. (And, because someone is sure to ask, I use the numbers one through zero for the first ten months of the year, and then N and D for November and December, respectively.)*

It also makes sense not to clutter up your hard drive with files like these. Creating and saving on properly labeled floppy disks enable you to have complete, chronological records that are easy to get to when you need them.

Backup Basics: DOS

DOS itself provides two main backup methods: the program called BACKUP and another one called COPY. BACKUP is paired with RESTORE. Files backed up with COPY are identical to the original. With the addition of XCOPY in DOS 3.2 and later versions, COPY became faster and more powerful. DISKCOPY is also useful for making a second, identical, copy of a floppy.

NOTE

This book is not intended as an exhaustive treatise on the uses of DOS. Always consult your DOS manual before using DOS commands.

Many people won't need to go any further than their DOS subdirectory to make and keep a backup sufficient for their needs.

NOTE

In DOS procedures, as well as those used by commercial programs, understand the difference between the source and target (or destination) disks. The source disk is the one that has the information on it. The target/destination disk is where you want the information to go.

Most DOS commands use the structure COMMAND : SOURCE : DESTINATION. In Assembly Language programming, source and destination are reversed. This may be why so many programmers lose data.

Using BACKUP and RESTORE

If you want to back up the entire contents of a hard drive, BACKUP is the command for you. Think of all the data on your hard drive, though separated by directories and subdirectories, as one long string of symbols. Obviously, the string is too long to fit on one floppy disk, so DOS needs a way to continue to store it, uninterrupted, so that you can RESTORE it if you need to.

Once you issue the DOS BACKUP command, the operating system begins to send a data stream to a floppy drive. BACKUP is the only DOS command that can save files that are larger than the capacity of a single floppy. When you use BACKUP, you need many floppies. The very first disk you use is designated #1 by DOS. When it's full, DOS asks you to put in another disk. DOS then designates the second disk as #2. This goes on (and on, and on, depending on the size of your hard drive) until every bit of data on the hard drive has been dumped to disk.

TIP

Don't start the BACKUP procedure unless you're sure that you have enough disks to hold everything. You won't lose data if you have to stop in the middle to rush out and purchase more disks, but you may end up starting the whole procedure over again.

CAUTION

It's up to you to put labels on the disks!

WARNING

BACKUP destroys all existing data on the target disk. Be sure the disk is empty before you use it.

Unless you are using an ancient DOS version (before 3.3), you don't have to format your disks before using BACKUP. Using the /F switch with the BACKUP command formats on the fly but is slower than having preformatted floppies.

NOTE

*DOS BACKUP is not the most efficient method for most data needs. Use it when you need to be able to reproduce the contents of a hard drive **exactly** as they were saved.*

Using RESTORE is just as simple as using BACKUP. Issue the DOS command and stand by to shuffle floppies. In order. If you insert a floppy out of order, RESTORE prompts you to insert the correct floppy.

Using COPY

The COPY command is one most of us are familiar with and use often. It's the easiest way to get a file (or two or three) from one disk to another. COPY is also one of the safest ways to store a Very Important File on disk because the command requires that the entire file be stored on a single disk. With the addition of the /v switch (Verify), DOS checks the copy to see whether it can be read but does not compare it with the original.

One of the major drawbacks of the DOS COPY command is that once the floppy is full, COPY stops. If you have copied only a portion of the files you want to save, you can't easily start again with a new disk. For example, if you want to copy all the files with the extension .DRB, you enter the command:

```
COPY *.DRB A:
```

If there are more files than the disk in drive A can hold, you cannot issue the same command with another disk in A. That would only copy the same files to the new disk until it too was full. This is a situation that calls for XCOPY.

Using XCOPY

Beginning with DOS 3.2, XCOPY came on the scene to use some of the facilities of BACKUP in the copying process. It's not as fast as a speeding bullet nor as powerful as a locomotive, but it can leap small disks in a single bound. Like BACKUP, XCOPY reads huge chunks of data into memory and dumps them to disk at high speed. XCOPY reads as many files as can fit in memory before writing to the disk. COPY, on the other hand, is constantly jumping back and forth between the source disk and the target disk because it reads and writes only one file at a time.

Plus, XCOPY is smart. It can copy files in subdirectories and files that have changed since they were last copied. In other words, XCOPY can act much like BACKUP. The only thing XCOPY cannot do is copy files that are larger than the capacity of the disk.

The following sections examine some of the switches that make XCOPY a great substitute for the BACKUP command in making incremental backups.

The /A Switch

The /A switch tells XCOPY to copy only files whose archive attribute is set. The archive attribute is set every time a file is created or changed. BACKUP resets the archive attribute once the file is backed up. You can also set and reset the archive attribute by using the following command:

```
ATTRIB [+][-]a [filename].[ext]
```

Using XCOPY with the /A switch will copy only files that have changed since the last BACKUP.

The /M Switch

Like the /A switch, /M copies only files that have the archive attribute set but resets the archive attribute after the copy is made. There are two advantages to using this switch. First, you copy only the files that were changed since the last XCOPY and not every file changed since the last BACKUP. Secondly, if the destination disk is full, you can swap disks, issue the same command, and copy the rest of the files to the second disk.

The /S Switch

The /S switch tells XCOPY to copy files in any subdirectories, too. XCOPY creates matching subdirectories on the destination disk.

The /P Switch

The /P switch makes XCOPY pause and ask for confirmation before creating new files. You can use this switch to keep from overwriting files with the same name, but only if you know the file already exists on the target drive. Nice try, Microsoft!

TIP

Use the command XCOPY d:*.* /m /s as an incremental backup instead of BACKUP d:*.* /m /s.

Using DISKCOPY

You already have your Very Important File(s) on a floppy disk. You want to keep one copy close at hand, put another in a fireproof vault somewhere, and store a third with a nearby friend. The easiest way to make sure that you have three identical disks is by using the DOS DISKCOPY command, like this:

```
DISKCOPY A: B: <Enter>
```

Uh oh. You only have one floppy drive? No problem. DOS pretends that there are two floppy drives. You will have to change between the source and target disks several times, but DOS prompts you for every change.

Ok. You were smart and bought a PC with two floppies: one 3.5-inch and one 5.25-inch. DISKCOPY works only with two disks of the same capacity. Now what? No problem. Just enter DISKCOPY A: A: or DISKCOPY B: B:. DOS will prompt you to insert the source and target disks at the appropriate time. If the target disk is unformatted, DISKCOPY will format it on the fly.

CAUTION

One word of warning. DISKCOPY can work only with disks of the same storage capacity, even though the apparent size is not the same. 720K and 1.44M are the same size but different capacities. If you use the smaller 3.5-inch disks, make sure they have the same number of holes before you use DISKCOPY.

Plain Vanilla Backup (hold the jimmies)

If you just want to backup your data and don't want to bother with the expense of the fancy backup programs and devices, here's our recommendation: Use plain old vanilla DOS. With DOS, you can easily back up your vital data with a minimum amount of time and trouble. But if you are still using anything less than DOS 3.3, ask yourself why. And then consider upgrading your DOS version.

Step one.

Buy the number of disks recommended previously for a full backup of the hard disk. Buy the maximum capacity disks for your drive. This is a one-time expense in both dollars and time. And it *will* take some time.

Step two.

Format one disk as an emergency DOS bootable disk and transfer the recovery programs, by using these commands:

```
FORMAT A: /U /S

COPY RESTORE.EXE A:
  1 file(s) copied

COPY FORMAT.COM A:
  1 file(s) copied

COPY FDISK.EXE A:
  1 file(s) copied

COPY DEBUG.EXE A:
  1 file(s) copied
```

Some of these programs may have a .COM extension instead of the .EXE extension. If you get a File not found message, try the other extension or use * for the extension. Make a copy of this disk.

```
DISKCOPY A: A:
```

Give the copy to a friend, or store it in another location. One of these disks can be used as an emergency bootable disk when the hard disk crashes.

Step three.

Format all the disks you bought for backup. Even though the BACKUP program can format the disks on the fly, it's faster to do them all at once. You will also have formatted disks left over.

```
FORMAT A: /U
```

Step four.

Make a full backup of the hard disk.

```
BACKUP C:\*.* A: /s
```

This will take some time and will require you to switch disks as they become full. You can fill the time by labeling the disks. Each backup disk should be numbered in sequence. After you finish the backup, store the disks in a safe place away from the computer. With luck, you may never have to touch them again.

Step five.

Label one of the extra disks as Incremental #1, and keep it handy. You should use this disk at least once a day. If you make a change to a file that you consider vital, use the incremental disk immediately. Here's a painless way to keep files backed up.

```
XCOPY C:\*.* A: /M /S
```

Only files that have changed since the last time you typed that command are copied to the disk. If the file is already on the disk, the newer file will be copied over it, saving space.

Eventually the incremental disk will become full. When that happens, label another disk as Incremental #2 and use it after the first disk. Use the same XCOPY command and only files that were not saved to the first disk will be copied to the second. Keep adding disks until you feel it would be easier to do another full backup and begin the incremental backups from scratch.

This method takes very little time, depending on how many files were changed during the day.

If you find the incremental backup using XCOPY is copying a lot of files with a .BAK extension or some other temporary extension, you can use the ATTRIB command to prevent copying them.

```
ATTRIB -a C:\*.BAK /S
```

Use this command for any group of files you know you don't need in a backup set.

TIP

Make a BATch file called SAVE.BAT that will set the attributes of unwanted files and then copy changed files to a disk in drive A.

```
ATTRIB -a C:\*.BAK /S
ATTRIB -a C:\*,TMP /S
XCOPY C:\*.* A: /M /S
```

Other Backup Methods

 For some reason, Microsoft never included an easy to use BACKUP program with DOS until version 6. To fill the gap, many software developers market much better backup programs and one, MegaBack, is included with this book. DOS version 6 includes the backup utility from Symantec's Norton Utilities and is a great improvement over the previous versions. Most of the backup programs on the market include compression to store more information on a single disk and use high-speed direct memory access (DMA) in copying the data from one drive to another. There are options for full and incremental backups and options to include or exclude certain files from the process.

With all backup programs, the saved files are not stored in a format that DOS can use directly. Therefore the files must be restored before they can be used. Third-party backup programs usually include the restore portion as part of the same program used to backup the system. DOS uses the program RESTORE as a complement to BACKUP.

There are even hardware devices devoted exclusively to backing up a hard disk. The streaming tape drives are often referred to as "screaming" tape drives because of their speed. If you plan to make a lot of full backups from a large hard disk, this is the way to go.

We'll look at these options in the next chapter.

CHAPTER

Backup II

In the previous chapter, you were introduced to backups the hard way—using DOS. In this chapter, you explore ways to tame DOS a bit and learn about some other, easier, backup methods.

Before you begin learning about individual methods and products, remember that all your data has to be stored somewhere. Disks are the most familiar storage medium. Streaming tape backups have been around for several years, and recently *floptical* drives, which offer large storage capacities, have come on the scene.

None of these methods do any good unless they are used. That's why software manufacturers and the writers of programs for dedicated backup systems attempt to make them easy to use.

And although you hope you'll never need your backups, they are no good if you can't get to them when you need them.

What Should You Back Up?

In the previous chapter, you learned how to back up everything. And that's a good backup to have. If you went through the process, you learned how long it can take. That's enough to sour even the most security-conscious wonk.

In theory, you have a tidy shelf of boxes containing the original disks and instruction manuals for every program on your hard drive. In practice, that's not always the case. Many newer PCs come preloaded (the business term is *bundled*) with one or more programs. Sometimes the original program disks are not included.

TIP

When purchasing a computer with bundled software, insist on receiving original disks (still in the sealed envelope, if possible) with your purchase. This is especially important for DOS.

Other times, you may collect a public domain or shareware program and load it directly on your hard drive without keeping a copy on a disk. It's a good idea to keep a disk-based copy of all the programs on your hard drive.

Further, not all software lets you hit the ground—or the disk—running. Some packages, particularly the newer crop of Windows-based packages, require hours of tedious installation and tweaking. Even DOS 6.0 has its start-up headaches. That's work you don't want to lose.

TIP

If a program does require a lot of installation adjustment, read the documentation to discover which file(s) stores your personal configuration. Then make a copy of the file(s) to put in the box with the original disks.

Good data management techniques suggest that there's no reason to clutter up a hard drive with small stuff or files that may be used or worked on only once. Those files are much better off on disks. That's easy to say, but harder to practice. Many programs have a pesky way of insisting that data created or otherwise collected by that program be written to a default directory. Unless you want to haul out the manual and figure out how to designate a floppy as the default target drive, you'll have to remember to key in something like A: or C:\other\data as part of the destination path. That is easy to forget, and sometimes those extra keystrokes seem like an undue burden.

Large files that require a great deal of manipulation are usually better off on the hard drive for two reasons. First, they might not fit on a single disk, meaning you have to put them on the hard drive to work on them anyway. Second, there is an exponential increase of processing speed when the file is on the hard drive rather than on disk. Put another way, it's no chore to work on a 2,000-word feature article on a disk, but it's a drag to try to manipulate The Great American Novel.

In any case, determine which data is *essential* to you—that data without which your life or career would come to a standstill. (If there isn't any, perhaps you're undervaluing yourself or your time…) This is the stuff to concentrate most of your energies on if you're the sort who wants to put only minimum effort into the project.

When Should You Back Up?

Just as "Everything" was the answer to "What should I back up?" in the previous chapter, "Right now" is the answer to "When?" Actually, "Yesterday" is a better answer. Ideally, data should be backed up after changes are made. Many PC professionals write batch files to perform semi-automatic backups as they leave an application. Many more PC professionals know how to do this and haven't done so.

It's up to you to determine the optimum frequency of backups… perhaps daily, more likely weekly, and certainly monthly. Just be aware that the work done between backups could be lost forever.

Most smart programs will back up only the data that has been changed. This is determined by sensing the archive attribute on the file.

The best backup practice is called *grandfathering* because data is stored in generations (usually at least three). Today's backup is the son, the most recent is the father, the one before that is the grandfather. The medium you use for today's son backup is yesterday's grandfather. Most well-managed businesses use at least five iterations of backed-up data, one for each work day of the week. The disks or tapes are usually cleverly labeled with things like Monday, Tuesday… People who don't notice weekends—like writers and programmers—should use seven.

Finding the time to back up is much more difficult than designing a backup scheme or system. Although the end of a work day is a logical time to back up, it's not particularly practical. Backups are less painful to do first thing in the morning while you have your first cup of coffee and organize your thoughts and projects for the day. If you have a streaming tape backup or you back up by data transmission to a remote site (more on this later), you can automatically set your software to perform the backup at a time when the PC is not in use.

Ways to Back Up

When it comes to backing up, there are software approaches and hardware approaches. Hardware, of course, requires software to make it work, but the distinction is clear.

The method you choose for backup may also vary. A full backup is just that. A discrete backup can be a single subdirectory, a set of sub-directories, or even individual files. The most often used technique is the *incremental* backup. In an incremental backup, only those files changed since the last backup are updated; the others remain the same.

TIP

Make a full backup before using new heavy-duty utility software for the first time. Programs that de-fragment and compress your hard drives always tell you to back up first. You may wonder why, because your disk will look entirely different when you're done. Remember that these programs move other programs around and mess with the directory structure. If an error does occur, you could lose everything.

Backup Software

For backup software, there's DOS, which, with 6.0, is the Norton system. Both Norton Utilities and PC-Tools offer backup and file management utilities. Fifth Generation's Fastback Plus is the best-known standalone backup program. A fine shareware utility, Patri-Soft's MegaBack, does pretty much the same thing for a lot less money.

They all do a good job but have one common failing: you. If you don't use them, the software is no good at all.

 You'll find MegaBack on the disk in the back of this book and instructions on how to use it in Chapter 16.

Backup Hardware

For those with a few extra dollars and a strong belief in the value of their data, a streaming tape backup unit is a valuable answer to data protection. Not that long ago, tape backup units were almost as expensive as PCs and the province only of those who could rationally support the expenditure and use the tax deduction. Today, good units that store 120M of data are available for less than $400. Further good news: Technology has advanced to the point that you no longer need a special card or board inside the PC to support the system. The new units attach to your parallel port and have another parallel port attached. This means that you can daisy-chain your printer to the tape backup, running both through one parallel port.

Even better, every PC has a parallel port. The same tape backup unit can back up traveling notebooks, everyday machines, and the top-of-the-line PCs with Micro Channel Architecture. It no longer matters what's inside the PC, making tape an even more attractive option. Once you've installed the software that governs the backup unit, you're in business.

The biggest negative to tape backups is the time investment in start-up—formatting the tapes. Unless you buy tapes pre-formatted for *exactly* the unit you use, you're going to have to wait out the initialization. Plus, some of the tape backup systems are so touchy that you can't reformat a tape used by another system. Make sure, if you're buying new tapes, that they are either preformatted to your unit's specification or have been bulk erased.

Count on about a half a minute per megabyte for formatting, and add some time for the necessary information to be written to the tape by the software. Approximately seventy minutes seems to be the standard time requirement to format a 120M tape. But you only have to do it once. In theory.

One of the biggest pluses of tape drives is that the system can run unattended. You can back up on your lunch hour, overnight, or any time you want. The software includes a provision to set a time/date function. Just make sure that you have the proper tape in place and then rest easy—your data is being backed up.

CAUTION

Make it a point to remove the tape cartridge from the drive as soon as practically possible. Don't put another tape into the drive until the last possible moment. Power surges or other electrical accidents can wreak havoc with the tape and the machine.

Make sure that you have a safe place to store your stock of tapes (or any other backups). A fireproof file cabinet is a minimum standard. As an extra precaution, a master backup should be made at intervals and stored off-site. You may be tempted to keep your tapes in a tidy stack next to the backup unit for the sake of convenience. Don't. If someone decides to steal your backup unit, you can bet they will take the tapes, too! And if there is a fire...or a hurricane...or...

Off-Site Backups

An off-site backup can be as simple as routinely carrying disks back and forth from home to office in a briefcase or from lab to dorm room in a backpack. In the earliest days of the computer virus wars, one of the best-known anti-virus programmers, Ross Greenberg, always showed up at high-level conferences with a backpack. It was an unusual sight, to say the least, among all those suits, red ties, and leather attachés. What, we finally inquired, was in there? A complete backup of all his source code from both of his PCs, made before he came to the meeting. He never left his New York City apartment without taking a backup along. Never.

On a recent international trip, I noticed a small disk box in my husband's suitcase. What was it? All his current source code. Never mind that there were copies in at least three other off-site locations. You can never be too careful.

Remember to consider accessibility when choosing off-site backup locations. A friend's home is logical, but not if your friend travels a great deal and you don't have a key. A bank makes sense—just rent a safety deposit box. But what about "bankers' hours" and the sometimes interminable wait for someone to escort you to your box?

Most larger cities have commercial data storage companies that specialize in the storage and couriering of backup tapes from monster mainframes. Usually, though, they're willing to store your precious little box of disks for a modest fee. These facilities are often open 24 hours a day and have state-of-the art air-filtering systems, fire extinguishers, guard service, you name it. You may find it comforting to think that the work that enables you to pay off your credit cards is safely nestled next to the giant tapes that hold your credit card records.

If just making backups is such a drag that most people don't do it, the time investment needed to carry data to an off-site storage location almost ensures that people won't—and don't—do it. If you can't bring yourself to take those disks somewhere, at least put them somewhere at your own location well away from the computer.

CAUTION

You may be tempted to put a box of backups in the glove box or trunk of your car. Not recommended. Magnetic media is very sensitive to extremes of temperature.

Dial 1-800-BACKUPS

A 1-800 number for data backup isn't as far-fetched as it seems. Backing up data by using telecommunications isn't an everyday solution, but it's one to consider. The process is hardware intensive, requiring two PCs—one sending and one receiving—in use at the same time, two modems, two sets of communications software, and two phone lines. Backing up in this way provides you with a means of getting an off-site backup with the least amount of work on your part. It's probably easier to invite a friend over for a drink and hand her a box of backup disks than to worry about setting up a communications link and transferring files.

Remote Control

Portable computers—notebooks, handbooks, whatever—lose some of their charm if you have to carry a full set of backups with you. But what happens if—ZAPPO!—your programs or data are gone and you're 3,000 miles from home or office? Programs, of course, are as near as your nearest computer store. (Measured as the crow drives a Jeep Wagoneer, that's 62 miles in one direction from Storm Lake, Iowa, or 47 miles in the other direction.) The further from computer civilization you find yourself, the greater your need to have access to your backups. And, proven by a tried and true corollary to Murphy's law, the more likely you are to have problems.

Even if you do mount a four-wheel drive vehicle, mush through snowdrifts, and go to great expense to purchase and install new program software, what about your data? If your data is not backed up someplace you can access rapidly, your travel time's worth takes a nose dive into the negative column.

MDR (Minimum Design Requirement)

On the road, you should carry an **emergency disk** that can get you back up and running in case the worst happens. The disk should contain the essential DOS files (FORMAT, FDISK, RESTORE, and DEBUG) so that you can reformat, if necessary, and begin to reload the programs you need in order to work. Your essential program files can be on the same disk, compressed with an archiving program *and* a program to explode them back into usable form. Data files, too, can be carried along in compressed form.

WARNING

Do not keep your emergency disk(s) in the same case with your portable computer. The most likely way you could lose data is by the complete disappearance of the computer.

Homebase

If you're a multi-PC type, much of your data will be firmly ensconced on a PC either at your home or your office and, theoretically, available to you. With a telecommunications link established, you can reload from anywhere. Without special software such as Here and There, Carbon Copy, or Norton Anywhere, however, this requires a computer-comfortable person on the other end. Not easy to find in the office on weekends or at home anytime if the only ears hearing the ringing phone are Fido's or Fluffy's.

NOTE

We have yet to learn of a courier service whose employees are willing to break into a home or office to find and ship the stack of backup disks you prepared in the event of just such a problem.

So, just how *do* you access that data if you need to? First, you need a little device that will wake up an unattended PC when the phone rings. These devices cost about $150 from most mail-order sources and are cheap compared to the cost of time lost plus an airplane ticket home and then back again to wherever you were when disaster struck. In addition to the wakeup machine, you'll need either a dedicated telephone line leading to your PC (and it) or a second telephone number that rings on your main line. Most telephone companies provide this service, usually called *distinctive ringing*.

Next, you need a modem on the home/office PC (otherwise it can't hear the phone ring and you certainly can't transfer any data), a modem for the traveling PC, and software on both ends that will let you operate remotely. All told, you shouldn't have to spend more than $500 for all these goodies. This sort of setup will also give you the 1-800-BACKUPS facility from the preceding section. If you develop a great deal of new data on your travels or if you frequently need to ship data back to (or receive data from) homebase, this is a far better answer than trying to tame one of the emerging **fax packages** that depend upon OCR (Optical Character Recognition) technology to receive and store files.

The Rational Archives

You don't have to be a rocket scientist to figure out that if you just kept incrementing your backups, you'd soon have The Backup That Ate Saginaw. Some things aren't worth saving in the first place, some aren't worth saving for very long, but there are other things that Just Might Come In Handy Someday. For example, once this book is finished and in print, I'll have little need to have the files representing the individual chapters, the book as a whole, and the other associated files created along the way either on my hard drive or on a current backup. In anticipation, however, of the Second Edition, I'll make sure that everything is properly saved and stored away. The same idea works for money management and tax software that "closes out" at the end of a specified period of time. You may want to go back to it someday, but there's no reason to give it room on your hard drive or backup medium.

In short, any project that's finished should either be deleted completely—both from your PC and your backups—or archived.

Single Project Archives

Use any of the DOS commands that will place your project on one or more disks. DISKCOPY those disks to make a second, identical set. Put them in two separate, safe places—one of which is off-site.

Rolling Thunder Archives

You never know when you'll need that letter you wrote to the IRS back in '87. Or you may want to look back at the thank-you note you wrote to Uncle Steuart thanking him for last year's fruitcake so you don't say the same thing over again. It's within the scope of possibility that someone may say, "Hey, remember...?" (Writers dream of editors calling with questions like that!)

The Rolling Thunder approach requires that you have a certain amount of self-discipline by writing short-life files to a floppy—rather than the hard drive—in the first place. And unless you are incredibly verbose or under Court Order to create data 24 hours a day, seven days a week, it's hard to imagine filling up a 1.44M disk in a single month. Under the Rolling Thunder approach, all you need to do is format a new disk on the first day of each month, write to it, and store it. As long as you can remember, with any reasonable degree of accuracy, just when you wrote that letter to the IRS, you can go back to your disk archives.

Depending on the clarity of your naming conventions, you can create a perfectly usable printout of your disk's contents by using the DOS DIR command this way:

```
DIR> PRN  <Enter>
```

You can then store the printout for future reference. An entry that reads IRSLET.415 should jump right out at you.

Additionally, you can find shareware programs that create elaborate lists (complete with your own comments about the files) that print not only directories but labels, too.

Fort (Hard) Knox

Until you've had the experience of losing valuable data, the reactions to which are better described in a medical textbook, this is all academic. To continue the medical analogy, far better to get a tetanus shot in the Emergency Room than spend two months in the hospital battling septicemia.

A writer friend tells the story of hearing, in the middle of the night, her smoke alarm blasting away. Did she grab her favorite cat, her purse, her makeup? Nope. The first and only thing she grabbed was her bank of backup and work disks.

But it *will* happen. Someday. There are, it seems, two schools of thought about data loss: The San Andreas Fault Theory and the Actuarial Theory. Under the Actuarial Theory, each day you go *without* losing data makes it less likely that you *will* lose data. ("Hmm, I have used my PC 5,476 days without losing data; therefore my chances of losing data tomorrow are 1:5,476.") This is, most probably, fuzzy logic at best. Under the San Andreas Fault Theory, every day you go without losing data brings you *one day closer* to the Big One. You decide.

PART

The Data Recovery Cookbook

Troubleshooting

Sooner or later, you're going to have trouble, right here in PC City. Your stomach will sink to approximately ankle level, you'll remember that you haven't backed up since August of 1987, and you will fear the worst. That's normal. But don't panic and start madly bashing away at your PC in hopes of a miracle. This is a time for calm, patience, and precision.

My Computer Won't Start!

You flip the switch and nothing happens. Start by analyzing the obvious.

Is It Plugged in?

Yes.

Is There Power in the Wall Socket?

Plug a lamp into the socket and turn the lamp on. If it works, the answer is Yes. If it doesn't work, the answer is No (assuming the bulb is good). Check for a thrown breaker in the box, a bad wall socket, or bent pins on the plug. Don't forget to check all extension cords and surge suppressors.

Does the Computer Make Any Noise at All?

Most computers have fans that start to whirr when the power is turned on. Hard disks also make a slight noise. If the fan and the hard disk are not making noise, you may have a blown fuse in the power supply, or a connection to the power supply may have come loose. You might even have a blown power supply. This is a job for the pros. Have the unit serviced. If the power supply is bad, a new one will restore the PC and your data.

The Fan Makes Noise, but Nothing Happens

Back up a bit and examine "Nothing happens."

Do You See Any Messages on the Screen at All?

If yes, check for the message in Chapter 12 and see whether you can find your problem.

If no, is the monitor plugged in and turned on?

Does the Speaker Beep?

Yes. Just once. That's normal.

Yes. Several times in a row. This is an indication of an error in the system self-check. Usually, an error message prints on the screen following the beeps. If the problem is with the video system, you won't see the message that tells you what to do. Most AT and above class computers wait for a certain keystroke after an error in the self-test. Check your computer manual. Different brands require different actions following this type of error. If all else fails, press the F1 key to see whether processing continues.

No. Part of the startup process is beeping the speaker. If you don't hear this, you should have the system serviced by professionals. Either the power supply is not working properly or the Read-Only Memory (ROM) chips that contain the internal startup procedures are bad. The microchips inside the computer are vulnerable to heat and power surges. A fan placed inside the computer keeps the chips cool. A certain amount of power surge protection is built into the power supply, and you may even have an external surge protector at the plug. But nearby lightning can produce such a powerful spike of voltage that it could damage some chips even if the power is turned off. If you've had a recent lightning storm, and the computer won't start, that may be your problem. Have the unit serviced. Even if you need a whole new computer, you can salvage the hard disk (tell the dealer) and retain your data.

Does Drive A: Begin To Spin?

Yes. That's normal. If your computer won't start from the hard disk, place a DOS bootable disk in the A drive and try again. If you don't have a hard disk, go to the next step.

No. If you don't have a hard disk, you should see an **error message** if the A drive doesn't work. If you don't see an error message, recheck for one of the previous errors and then have the computer serviced.

Does Drive A: Stop Spinning?

Yes. That's normal. Keep reading.

No. That's not normal. Keep reading.

I Got this Far and It Still Won't Work

If you got this far and the computer still won't start normally and does not display any messages, you probably have bad program instructions in the boot sector.

...That Rhymes with "V" and Stands for Virus

It's easy to blame every problem on computer viruses. They are much in the news and do cause quite a few problems when they are encountered. Failure to boot may or may not be a virus problem. The real problem is that you can't even start the computer to see whether you have a virus.

Double-Check the Monitor

If the computer reads the disk, displays no message, and still refuses to start, double-check your monitor. Press the Print Screen key. Your video display could be burned out, the contrast could be turned all the way up, or the brightness might be turned all the way down. If the printer works when you press Print Screen, your computer has started, but you just can't see it. Twiddle the knobs on the monitor a few times. They can get dirty and make bad contact. If you still can't see, get a new monitor.

Try a New Disk

If the startup program in the boot sector of the hard disk and all your disks are bad, it could cause an endless loop. Sort of like the computer saying "You are *here*. Go to *here*." Borrow or buy a new bootable disk. Write-protect the new disk. Turn the power off and try again. If you have a bad boot sector on your disks, you should be able to start from the new disk. If the computer starts, suspect a computer virus or at least something really wrong with the boot sector. If you are a skilled computer wonk, you could try **recovery techniques** yourself; otherwise, seek professional help. Get a copy of an anti-virus program and a disk fixer program.

The New Disk Doesn't Work, Either

Another possibility exists if you have a hard disk and use a DOS version under 5.0: You could have a recursive partition table. One entry in the partition table points back to a previous entry or itself. You don't need to know what this means; the important fact is that the computer will not start if that condition exists. There is a solution. DOS 5.0 recognizes the problem and will boot where other versions of DOS will not. Your hard disk is still sick, but at least you can start up. For further information, see the section on the MBR and partition tables in Chapter 14.

I Get a Number on the Screen and It Won't Work

When the computer encounters an error in the Power-On Self-Test (POST), it either beeps the speaker or prints a number on the screen. IBM includes no documentation on what the numbers mean. Other vendors may do better. IBM PCs and IBM XTs (and compatibles) just print the number and continue. IBM PC ATs and PS/2s (and compatibles) stop and wait for a keystroke before continuing. Check the documentation for your computer. You will find out what to do in the event of a POST failure.

xxxx 201

The on-screen message xxxx 201 indicates a memory error. Run the setup program that came with the computer to check the amount of memory installed against the amount of memory the computer thinks it has. The amount of memory is indicated either by switches inside the computer or by a value in the battery-powered CMOS RAM. If this error has not happened before, one or more of the memory chips may be bad. The number preceding the 201 is the segment address (in hex) of the bad memory.

301

The error 301 is a keyboard error. Either the keyboard is not connected properly or the cord has broken. The computer starts, but will not accept input from the keyboard, which means that you can't do anything.

Try another keyboard. Borrow one from a friend. If the computer works, replace your keyboard. Most dealers will tell you that it costs more to repair a broken keyboard than it costs to buy a new one.

601

The error 601 is a disk error. The disk controller, the disk drive, or the connection between the two is bad. If the computer worked before, call the repair person.

1701

The 1701 error is the hard disk controller error. The error could be with the controller circuit itself, the hard disk, or in the connection between the two.

Most computers come with a diagnostics disk. Run that program and see whether it can fix the problem. Usually, the program just repeats the error message you see on the screen and recommends that you have the system serviced. That's a good suggestion.

The Screen Says "Parity Check 1" or "Parity Check 2"

Memory is addressed in eight-bit chunks called *bytes*. But memory chips include an additional bit for *parity*. Older chips stored one bit per address in each of nine chips. This ninth bit acts as a check on the other eight bits to make sure they contain the correct value. Anytime memory is accessed, the computer examines the parity bit. If there is an error, the Parity Check message appears and all processing stops. Parity check 1 means there is a bad chip on the motherboard. Parity check 2 indicates a bad chip on an add-in board.

Try rebooting. The problem may go away forever. If not, the rebooting process will print the address (in hex) of the bad chip. Replace the memory chip(s), or have a professional do it.

I Type a Command and the Screen Starts Scrolling...

You type a name on the command line, press Enter, and see the same lines repeated endlessly on the screen? You have the Dead C Scrolls, otherwise known as a *recursive batch file*.

One of the authors of this book (the other one) likes to name her batch file with the same name as her program file. Her WORD.BAT file contains the following commands:

```
CD \WORD
```

This means she does not have to clutter her PATH statement with the path to the WORD directory. All she needs to add to the PATH statement is her BATS directory. The CD \WORD changes to the WORD subdirectory and starts the WORD program. All is well and good unless she happens to be logged on to another drive.

If she is logged on to drive A when she types *WORD* and presses Enter, COMMAND.COM searches for the first occurrence of WORD in the PATH. That is encountered in the C:\BATS directory. COMMAND runs the WORD.BAT file. The first command in the file is to change to the \WORD subdirectory. Because the default drive is A: and it does not have a WORD subdirectory, COMMAND prints Invalid directory and goes to the next command.

The next line in the WORD.BAT file says to run Word. COMMAND searches the path for the first occurrence of Word and finds it in the C:\BATS subdirectory. Then COMMAND begins to execute WORD.BAT again. You get the picture. The batch file keeps being called by the batch file forever and ever, amen. The screen repeats:

```
A:\>CD \WORD
Invalid directory

A:\>WORD
A:\>CD \WORD
Invalid directory

A:\>WORD
A:\>CD \WORD
Invalid directory
```

TIP

Don't use program names as batch file names. Pick another name, or indicate the drive, path, and filename of your program file in the batch file. Entering C:\WORD\WORD in the example will prevent the batch file from calling itself.

Sometimes It Runs the Wrong Program

COMMAND.COM has a certain pecking order for running programs and batch files. Type the name on the command line with no extension and press Enter. COMMAND.COM adds the extension .COM, .EXE, or .BAT. Here's how it works.

First COMMAND.COM searches its internal list of commands such as DIR, COPY, DEL, and ERASE, etc. If COMMAND.COM does not find the command, it assumes you want to run a program or batch file.

Next, COMMAND.COM searches for the filename in the current directory of the current drive. If the file is not found, it checks each of the directories listed in the PATH statement in the order in which they occur. Once a match is found to the file name, COMMAND.COM adds the .COM extension. If there is not a match, it checks the .EXE extension. Finally, it checks the .BAT extension. Even if a matching filename is found, if the extension is not one of these three, COMMAND.COM continues to search directories in the PATH statement.

If no match is found in either the current directory or any directory in the PATH statement, COMMAND.COM displays Bad command or file name and waits for further input. If a match is found, COMMAND.COM runs the program or batch file.

If a file exists under four different names in the same directory—such as SAMPLE.COM, SAMPLE.EXE, SAMPLE.BAT, and SAMPLE.DAT—COMMAND.COM will always run SAMPLE.COM. If SAMPLE.COM is deleted, COMMAND.COM will run SAMPLE.EXE. If that too is deleted, the COMMAND.COM will run SAMPLE.BAT. If only SAMPLE.DAT appears in the directory, COMMAND.COM will ignore it.

If SAMPLE.COM, SAMPLE.EXE, SAMPLE.BAT, and SAMPLE.DAT all exist in different directories in the PATH statement, COMMAND.COM will run the first executable file it encounters. SAMPLE.DAT will never be run because it does not have the extension .COM, .EXE, or BAT.

TIP

To check your PATH statement, type PATH at the command line and press Enter.

I Know the File Is There, but I Can't Find It

If you use a large hard disk, you easily can forget where you stored a file. DOS has no master catalogue of where files are stored. If you have the latest version of DOS, you can use the following command to search all directories:

```
DIR [filename] /s
```

Use the WHEREIS program included with this book to locate a specific file. WHEREIS searches all directories of the hard disk, including any logical partitions. The program is a real time-saver in searching for files.

If you still can't find the file you want, you may have accidentally deleted the file. If you did, you can use a file utility to **undelete** the missing file.

I Saved the File, but When I Turned the Computer on, It Was Gone

Be careful about turning the computer off with the DOS program SMARTDRV installed, especially if you are running DOS 6.0. This disk-caching program speeds disk performance by storing file data in memory. Most cache programs are "write-through," which means that any data intended to be written to disk is written immediately. The DOS 6.0 version of SMARTDRV is *not* write-through unless specified on the command line when it is started. Data is stored in memory until idle time is detected, and then it is written to the disk. Although this speeds up performance by making fewer accesses to the disk, there is the potential of losing data when you turn the computer off.

TIP

Make sure the cache is clear before the power is turned off. Enter SMARTDRV /C to clear the cache.

Of course, if a program freezes the keyboard and you have to turn the power off to restart, you can't clear the cache. This Cache-22 situation can only be solved beforehand. Check the Help screen under SMARTDRV and see how to run SMARTDRV as a write-through cache. With a fast computer, you probably will not notice any loss of performance.

The SMARTDRV program included with DOS 6.0 is intended to help speed the performance of Windows, which uses the disk as temporary storage—virtual memory. The theory is that if the disk does not have to be accessed as often, the performance of Windows will be enhanced to make it almost as fast as the Macintosh interface. If you plan to run Windows almost exclusively, set up a partition of the hard disk to act as the Windows temporary storage drive. When you load SMARTDRV, set only this partition (drive) as a non-write through cache. Losing the data in the Windows temporary file is no big deal and Windows will recreate it when the computer is restarted.

My Disks Won't Work in another Computer

Make sure the disk is the right size and capacity. Naturally, you can't use a 5.25-inch disk in a 3.5-inch drive (and vice versa). But each size comes in two flavors: low capacity and high capacity. You can't run a 1.2M disk (high capacity) in a 360K drive (low capacity) no matter how hard you try. Nor can you use a 1.44M disk in a 720K drive. The reverse is not true. Most high-capacity drives can read low-capacity disks. But—and it's a *big* but—writing to the lower capacity disk can cause problems.

Big Disks...Big Problems

The 5.25-inch disks present a bigger problem in mismatched capacity than their smaller cousins. The lower capacity drives pack only 40 tracks in concentric rings on the surface of the disk. The opening for the head on one of these disks is about 1.25 inches, meaning that each track is about .03 inches wide (which is about half the width of the recording area on a typical audio cassette). The higher capacity 1.2M drives pack 80 tracks into the same space, reducing the track width to .015 inches wide. The read/write heads are the same width as the track, which means that the smaller heads of the high capacity drive cover only half the track of the lower capacity disk.

Reading the larger track is no problem, but writing the larger track leaves some residual data in the part of the track not covered by the read/write head. The result is that 1.2M drives can *read* 360K disks, but cannot reliably *write* to them.

Small Disks...Small Problems

Both 720K disks and 1.44M disks use 80 tracks per side, so head width is not a problem in intermixing sizes. Media capability is the problem when trying to format a 720K disk to 1.44M. It's really a physics problem, having to do with the magnetic capability of the disk media and the amount of current applied to the read/write heads for each type of drive. Both types can be used reliably in the higher capacity drive, but only 720K disks should be used in the lower capacity drive.

Different Drives...Different Problems

The head opening of the 3.5-inch disk is about one inch long. This means that each track is less than .0125 inches wide. The alignment of the heads becomes critical when dealing with so small a recording area. The drive that formats the disk will always have its heads positioned so that the track is directly under the head. After all, the track position is defined by the format process.

Another drive might have a slightly different alignment of the read/write heads in relation to the disk. If not aligned perfectly, the head may be unable to read the data as the disk spins past it. If so, a disk that appears perfectly good in one drive may not be usable in another similar drive.

Different drives may also step the head inwardly at a slightly different rate. Therefore, tracks on the outer edge of the disk read perfectly on the second drive but lose alignment as the head tries to read the inner tracks.

What To Do

If you often find that disks made on one computer fail when used in another, have a repair shop check the alignment of the heads. As a stopgap, try formatting the disk on the second computer before using it in the first. This way, at least the formatting information will be readable on the second drive. There still is no guarantee that the data written by the first computer will be readable by the second.

If you get a program distribution disk that your drive can't read, take the program back to the store and ask for a new one. The retailer will probably gladly give you a new copy of the program and take the one you returned into the back of the store, shrink-wrap it, and put it back on the shelf, waiting for someone else to buy it. If you bought the program through a mail-order house, call the company and ask about their return policy. If they say "None," don't order anything from them again, and tell all your friends. They will either change their policy or go out of business.

I Get a Message That Says...

All the DOS error messages are listed in Chapter 12. If the message comes from somewhere else—an application or Windows—check the program's manual for the error message.

If the message says something like Your PC is stoned, you have a computer virus. Screen messages that contain high weirdness or can't be found in the documentation of the program you're running (or trying to run) have to come from somewhere.

CAUTION

Here's a very good reason not to steal software and always to print out shareware or public domain documentation. If you don't have a list of legal error messages, you'll be in the dark.

S.O.L. (Stopped Or Locked Out)

No handy messages provided here. Either your PC simply stops dead in its tracks or the program that you were using dumps you, unceremoniously, back to the command line. You may end up kissing goodbye the data that you were working on (this is why you should set auto-save capabilities in software as frequently as you can tolerate); but, more importantly, you don't want it to happen again. Now is the time to invoke the most powerful problem-solving tool you possess: your own intelligence.

So What's to Lose?

The good news is that, most times, *only* the data in the file(s) currently open will fall victim to a stopped or locked out condition. If you can avoid panic, carefully consider what key or combination of keys *you might try* to revitalize your PC if you're in the middle of an application. Consider first; press the keys second.

TIP

A semi-useful test, though usually doomed to failure, is to try to activate a TSR program through use of hot keys.

Another logical progression is to try pressing Esc to see if anything happens. Next, try whatever the Help key is for the program currently running.

The CAD Method

Not to be confused with the acronym for Computer-Aided Design, this particular exercise is also known as the "Three-Finger Salute" or, more technically, a *warm boot*. It's long been suspected that the reason more PCs don't have a simple switch called Reset is that it takes *three* fingers to do this, not one. And it's unlikely that three out of ten fingers would take off on their own without proper instruction from Mission Control. Pressing Ctrl-Alt-Del at the same time sends an instruction to the PC to *reboot*, starting with AUTOEXEC.BAT.

If nothing happens after these strong measures, it's time for...

The Big Red Switch

OK, you say your computer doesn't *have* a Big Red Switch. If it were an older IBM, it would. There is no known explanation for just why IBM decided that the Off/On switch on the early PCs had to be quite so large (and inconveniently located) or *red*. But it was. In later iterations, the switch became so conveniently located that it was not difficult, if the PC was in a tower configuration (sitting on its side, under a desk) to hit the switch with a trousered or panty-hosed knee.

These days, the switches are smaller, usually the same delightful putty color as the case, and they are easier to find. Use this switch only as a last resort in an stopped or locked out condition. Turn the switch to Off, wait ten seconds for memory to clear, and turn it back on. If you're back to where you usually start when the system boots, breathe a minor sigh of relief. Now you can move on to the next step.

What's Different?

If you're stopped or locked out in the middle of a known and trusted program that you've run countless times before, *something must be different*. If you hit this state with a brand-new program, you *know* what's different.

The most likely culprit is that you have installed a new program and, whether or not you're running it at the moment you hit the invisible protective shield, look there first. Recall the Installation From Hell featured in the Software Chapter 4? Immediately check your AUTOEXEC.BAT and CONFIG.SYS files for extra, added attractions. Look *very* carefully at the last lines to see whether something has been set that supersedes previous instructions. The last ones read are the ones the computer executes.

The second most likely situation is that you've run a TSR (Terminate-and-Stay-Resident) program that you rarely use and haven't encountered its personal habits before. Sometimes these little gems gobble up so much memory (and don't release it) that big, whomping applications literally run out of room. Think back to your own activity on the PC before the stopped or locked out condition happened.

Running a distant third is the possibility of corruption of your application software (program). There are a number of ways this could happen, from a slight power surge while the program itself was running to a computer virus. Depending upon your obsession with finding out just what did happen vs. getting back in business, you can do one of two things: become Sherlock Holmes or take the easy way out.

Sherlock Holmes

Tediously compare, if possible, all the files associated with the application where the stopped or locked out condition occurred. Because today's applications are huge, are usually delivered in a compressed form on the distribution disks, and are "exploded" by the install program, this could be a major pain. But, here's how to do it.

Run the installation program all over again, but create a new subdirectory for the program. Then, file by file, use DOS FILECOMP to see whether the files are the same. No matter what you find, if you discover that one or more files are corrupted, you'll still have to...

Take the Easy Way Out (or Back In)

Reinstall the software from the installation disks.

What Did I Do Differently?

If the problem never repeats itself, you'll never know what caused it. Perhaps it was a Stupid Human Trick as simple as a fearsome flying book hitting a strange combination of keys and sending you into Never-Never Land.

It's a little-known fact that computer programmers often leave themselves a "back door" into their code through a keystroke combination. This is what's called an *undocumented feature* and can cause both data loss and lots of consternation if those keys are accidently invoked by an unsuspecting user.

Aunt PANDA's Best Advice

If you're in a stopped or locked out situation, take another shot at doing exactly what you did before. Reboot, fire up your application, and go. Take notes in case it happens again. Don't play PC Detective until you have to.

11

Disk Errors and Failures System

If you're going to receive your degree in Advanced PC Surgery, the first course you need is Anatomy. In this chapter, Dr. Panda will introduce you to how disks work. The next chapter will dissect the Disk Operating System (DOS).

Operating on Disks

The primary function of the disk operating system is to make the file system easy to understand from a human point of view. Unlike the computer, which operates in the shadowy world of binary digits, we tend to think in symbols that have meaning for us. It is easier to remember that the thank-you note to Uncle Steuart for his annual Christmas fruitcake is stored under the name C:\WORD\DOCS\ ROCKHARD.DOC than it would be to remember the drive, head, track, and sector numbers where the file is actually stored. DOS does the conversion for us. You learn how DOS handles files in the next chapter, but if for some reason any of the information DOS uses to make this conversion is lost, you need to understand the workings of the physical disk so that you can reconstruct the lost data.

Let's Get Physical

Back in 1981 when the IBM PC first entered the marketplace, things were fairly simple. There was only one kind of disk: a single-sided 5.25-inch floppy. An additional disk drive was available at a slight extra charge of close to $800. Although the single-sided floppy has joined the dinosaurs and Dodo birds as an extinct species, this relatively simple device can be used as an example of how all magnetic disks work.

A thin magnetic-coated plastic disk is encased in a square package which slides into a slot in the disk drive. When you close the door on the drive, a conical spindle drops into the round center hole and a magnetic read/record head is pinched to the bottom of the magnetic disk. The read/record head is a coil of thin wire. When the disk is set in motion, a current in the wire coil creates a magnetic field which changes the orientation of the magnetic material of the disk.

Information is stored on the disk by varying the current in the record head, which in turn varies the magnetic orientation of the magnetic material passing over it. To read this information, the magnetic material passing over the coil of wire generates a current in the coil as the magnetic orientation changes. Converting this current into a stream of binary digits is a function of the drive itself and the disk controller card.

Not All Codes Are Area

Although storing data on the magnetic media is a function of the drive and controller, it is usually accomplished by some form of encoding. The most popular form of encoding is Modified Frequency Modulation (MFM). This standard determines when changes in polarity can take place and how to interpret them into binary streams of zeros and ones. Another form of encoding that IBM has been pushing is Run Length Limited (RLL) encoding. This scheme actually uses a longer code than MFM but the bits can be interpreted more reliably. Thus a typical RLL disk can hold more data than the same-size disk using MFM encoding.

Protect Me from Myself

Most floppy disk drives contain a write-protect feature. The original single-sided floppies have a small mechanical switch along the left edge of the disk as it is inserted into the drive. When the disk is in the proper place, the switch fits into the slot on the left side of the disk and opens. When the switch is open, current can flow to the head for recording information. If you place a write-protect tab on the disk, the switch remains closed and no current can flow to the head so no information can be written to the disk. Write protection is therefore accomplished in the hardware itself and cannot be overcome by software. Later versions of the write protection mechanism use a light sensor through the slot. If light comes through, writing is enabled. No light...no write. The smaller 3.5-inch disks with the hard plastic case use a hole rather than a slot and use the light sensor method of write protection. Both systems rely on mechanical or electronic devices in the drive itself which is not dependent on software.

Head 'em Up (Move 'em Out)

The drive head itself is positioned over only a small portion of the platter at any one time. A small motor called the *stepper motor* moves the head from the outermost edge of the disk to the innermost. This motor does not move the head in one continuous fluid motion, but rather in small steps so that as the head moves, it traces concentric rings over the platter rather than a continuous spiral like the grooves in a record. These rings were called *tracks*.

The thinner the head, the more tracks it can trace on a given platter. The first disk heads traced 40 tracks on each disk. Later, thinner heads allowed 80 tracks to be placed on a 5.25-inch floppy. The smaller 3.5-inch floppies also use 40 or 80 tracks.

The thinner head and higher capacity does come with some penalties, however. The magnetic material must be of higher quality because less magnetic material appears over the head at any one time. Additionally, higher quality magnetic coatings cost more.

Fondly Fondling Floppies

When a disk comes out of the box, the magnetic material has no orientation. In order to store and retrieve information, the disk has to be formatted. The formatting process organizes and catalogues the disk so information can be stored and found.

Again using the old single-sided floppies as an example, each floppy is divided into 40 separate concentric tracks from outer edge to inner edge. The number of tracks is determined by the stepper motor and is mechanically controlled by the drive itself. The first step in making the disk usable is dividing the tracks into smaller pieces called *sectors*. Each track is divided into eight sectors, which can hold 512 bytes of data. The 512-byte-per-sector standard is a DOS convention and is not written in stone.

During the formatting process, an address mark is written to the beginning of each sector, indicating its track number and sector number. The address mark is followed by 512 bytes of data and then a checksum (the total number of flux reversals—changes in magnetic orientation—found in the sector). The address marks and checksum are for internal use only and are not available to the user.

Tracks are numbered 0 through 39 beginning at the outer edge, and sectors are numbered 1 through 8 beginning...where? If you look at one of the 5.25-inch floppies, you will notice a small hole near the hub. This is the index hole and tells the drive when the first sector of a track is in contact with the head.

During the formatting process, the address mark of the first sector of the track is written as the index passes the head and then each following sector address mark is written in sequence before the hole makes a complete revolution. The head then steps to the next track and waits for the index hole to pass again before beginning to write the address marks on that track.

IBM was quite conservative in their early estimation as to how many sectors could be placed on a track. Electrical engineers (who actually understand this stuff) soon found that there was enough room following sector number eight for another sector. Of course, DOS only accounted for eight sectors per track, so an upgrade (at a slight additional cost) allowed more data to be stored on each disk.

Once the disk is formatted, the data in any one sector can be accessed by its track and sector number. Here's how it works. All software commands are passed to the disk controller, which translates the commands into signals to the drive itself. The controller starts the drive motor, which makes the disk spin. A short delay loop waits for the disk to get up to the proper speed and then the stepper motor moves the head to the desired track. Another small delay loop waits for the head to arrive at the proper track so the disk controller can read the address marks. When the desired sector appears under the head, the controller directs the head to read or write the data. Once the data is read, the checksum is compared to the number of flux reversals. If the checksum matches, the data is considered good and the operation stops. If the disk can't find the address mark or the checksum is bad, the controller returns an error to the program requesting the disk operation.

All the instructions to the disk hardware are contained in the controller card that came with the disk drive. Different disks use different methods of storing and retrieving the data.

The double-sided disk drive added another read/write head to the top of the disk and one more factor—the head number—to the address mark. (Actually, the single-sided disk anticipated the additional head and stored the head number in the address mark.) The bottom side became side zero and the top became side one. Apparently, the crew at Boca Raton who designed the IBM PC anticipated larger capacity disks because even the original PC required a head number (always 0) to access disk data.

Because each side now had its own track numbers, the term *cylinder* was added to indicate the group of tracks passing each head. Cylinder 1 indicates track 1, side 0, and track one, side 1.

NOTE

Many users in those early days discovered that single-sided disks had magnetic coating on both sides and would work in a double-sided drive. It is easier to manufacture a disk that is coated on both sides. Disk boxes marked Single-sided and boxes marked Double-sided often contained the same disks. The only difference was the price. Double-sided disks cost more.

How Much Wood Could a Woodchuck Chuck?

If you want to calculate how much data one of the original disks can hold, remember that each sector usually holds 512 bytes of data. (This is a DOS convention and not a "written in stone" number.) Each track contains eight sectors and each disk contains 40 tracks. By simple multiplication (a calculator helps), 512 bytes per sector times eight sectors per track times 40 track per disk equals 163,840 bytes of data.

The addition of the second side will double the capacity: 512 bytes per sector times eight sectors per track times 40 tracks per side times two sides per disk equals 327,680 bytes. This means that we can make a formula to calculate the capacity of any floppy or hard disk by multiplying the number of bytes per sector by the number of sectors per track by the number of tracks per side by the number of sides:

```
Capacity in Bytes = Bytes Per Sector x Sectors Per Track x
Tracks Per Side x Number of Sides
```

Disk capacity (as well as memory) is often expressed in kilobytes. *Kilo* is a prefix taken from the Greek meaning thousand, but computer-speak adds a little kick. Internally, computers calculate using the binary number system, which is based on the power of 2 as opposed to the decimal system we use that is based on powers of 10. A kilo is 2 to the 10th power (1024) and not 10 to the third power (1000). You get an extra 24 bytes with every kilobyte! A 2.4 percent discount, blue light special. Get out the calculator again, and prove that 163,840 bytes is 160K. (Hint: 163,840 / 1024 = ?)

Because the single-sided disk and the eight sector per track disk quickly became obsolete, double-sided, nine sector per track became the standard for the 5.25-inch floppy. These disks have a capacity of 368,640 bytes, or 360K.

The high-capacity 5.25 drive introduced with the IBM PC AT features a double-sided disk with 80 tracks per side. Each track is formatted with 15 sectors and that gives these disks a capacity of 1,228,800 bytes, or 1,200K.

When disk capacity goes over the 1,000K barrier, another terminology problem arises. The prefix for million is *mega*, but is that 1000 kilobytes or 1024 kilobytes? When the IBM PC AT was introduced, the disk capacity was listed as 1.2M, meaning that a megabyte was 1000 kilobytes. The latest accepted standard is to continue the binary designation so 1M is defined as 2 to the 20th power or 1,048,576 bytes. Even though this would make the high capacity 5.25-inch disk 1.171875M, they are still referred to as 1.2M disks. Confused? Consider the 3.5-inch disks.

The latest (but probably not the last) standard for floppy disks is the 3.5-inch floppy. Smaller, but with better magnetic coatings, these disks come in two flavors. The double-density is formatted with 80 tracks of nine sectors each per side for a capacity of 737,280, or 720K. The high-density floppy is formatted with 18 sectors per track, 80 tracks per side, giving it a capacity of 1,474,560 bytes, or 1.44M using the old 1,000K per megabyte designation. Under the new designation for megabytes, these disks are rated 1.40625M.

Getting Harder

The IBM XT introduced the hard disk to the world of microcomputers. The XT hard disk had four sides (two double-sided platters), each with 306 tracks formatted with 17 sectors. This gave the disk a total capacity of 10,653,696 bytes or just a hair over 10M. At that time, the standard disk was the 360K floppy so the idea of having 10 megabytes of storage space seemed like manna from heaven. No one could conceive of a situation where these monsters would be filled. Since that introduction, hard disks have gotten smaller (physically), bigger (capacity), and much less expensive.

Physically, the hard disk operates much like the floppy. A magnetic platter rotates past a head in which a coil of wire is embedded. The coil can either create a magnetic field from a current or create a current from the magnetic field on the disk. What makes the hard disk different is that the head no longer is in contact with the platter and the magnetic coating of the platter is of much higher quality than the magnetic coating of the disk.

Inside the sealed chamber of the hard disk, not just one but a stack of platters rotate at an incredible speed, typically 3600 rpm, which means the outer edge of the platters move at over 100 miles per hour on a 5 1/4-inch diameter disk. The read/record heads are embedded at the end of long fingers which pivot much like the tone arm of a record turntable. (Records were used as a means of reproducing music before the invention of the CD.) The heads ride just above the platter surface supported by the wind that is created by the rotation of the platters. What happens if a head touches the surface of the platter at a speed of 100 mph? Consider the destruction caused by the 100 mph winds of hurricane Andrew in south Florida and you get an idea.

Because of the precision of the positioning mechanism and the thinness of the read/record head, hundreds of tracks can be recorded on the surface of each platter. The XT's 10-megabyte hard disk had two platters (four sides), which could each hold 306 tracks. Each track of the XT hard disk had 17 sectors, providing a grand total of 2,808 sectors of storage space or 10,653,696 bytes.

Larger capacity hard disks use the same principle but add more platters and pack more tracks on each platter. A 120-megabyte hard disk has 245,760 sectors. Inside the sealed box, there are a variety of ways to create this many sectors. Because the outer edge of the platter travels further on each revolution than the center, many more sectors can be packed on the outer tracks. Some hard disks even have multiple heads per side, one for the inner part of the platter and another for the outer. Regardless of the physical setup inside the box, the hard disk controller circuits make the hard disk look like a stack of platters, each with a constant number of sectors per track. Electronic deception is easy.

Just like disks, the hard disk surface must be formatted with address marks before the disk can be used. The so-called low level formatting process that places the address marks and checksum for each sector is usually done at the factory. It is inevitable that the surface of the platters contains some defects, so the manufacturer does not format these areas. In other words, no address marks appear for known defective areas of the disk. Hard disks are built to have slightly more sectors than their rating might imply so the deletion of any bad areas does not make the capacity fall below the advertised storage capacity. A 120-megabyte hard disk might actually have up to 130 megabytes of storage space. If you get a disk with few defective sectors, you get more than you pay for.

Faster Than a Speeding Bullet

The speed of the hard disk platters presents another problem to the designers. Sectors pass so quickly past the head, that the controller cannot process the data from one sector before another passes the head.

Consider a platter spinning at 3600 rpm with a track containing 32 sectors. A new sector appears under the head every .0005 seconds with 512 bytes of data. If the controller has not transferred this data to the computer before the next sector appears under the head, it must wait until the next revolution of the platter to read the next sector. To read an entire track takes 33 revolutions or approximately 1/2 second. At this rate, the hard disk can transfer only 32K per second to, or from the computer.

To speed the transfer rate, the sectors are arranged so that there are several sectors inserted between consecutive sectors. This process is called *interleaving*. A typical interleave factor is 3:1. Sectors along a track are numbered 1-4-7-2-5-8-3, etc. Now while processing the data read from sector 1, sectors 4 and 7 pass beneath the head. By the time sector 2 gets to the head, the controller has processed the data from sector 1 and is ready to process sector 2. In a 1:3 interleave, only four revolutions are necessary to read an entire track (.06 seconds), which is almost 10 times faster than with no interleave.

The interleave factor is set by either the computer manufacturer or the disk manufacturer before you get the hard disk. It's a good idea to accept the recommended interleave of the disk even though manufacturers tend to set it on the conservative side. There are programs on the market that can reset the interleave factor, but you could end up with worse performance. Best to leave the interleave to the people who designed the drive.

Needless to say, the hard disk is a precision instrument. It is very sensitive to physical abuse and mechanical failure. If any system in the computer is going to fail, it will be the hard disk. Sometimes hard disks can run for years and give reliable service, but some quit early and often and always when you have failed to back up your important data. The CMI hard disks that were part of the original IBM PC AT had a notoriously high failure rate. PC Labs reported a failure rate of 200 percent among the ATs in their office. That means each AT had two hard disk crashes. To this day, IBM denies any problem with the original AT hard disks. But they quietly switched from a second party manufacturer and began to ship ATs with their own hard disks. The failure rate dropped to almost zero, and IBM dropped a shipload of suspect drives into the sea off Boca Raton. (Note to scuba divers: Although ten years of immersion in sea water has probably not improved the performance of the CMI drives, I doubt that it hurt them either.)

Let's Get Logical

No matter what the internal structure of the hard disk may be, the computer "sees" a disk with x heads, y tracks, and z sectors per track. There is a practical limit to the capacity of the disk. The computer communicates with the controller using binary digits. The limits are as follows:

Head number: 255

Track number: 1023

Sectors per track: 62

Maximum capacity is therefore 16,173,630 sectors of 512 bytes, or 8,280,898,560 bytes (almost 7.8 gigabytes). So far, no manufacturer has risen to the challenge, but considering the speed with which technology pushes barriers, it is not out of the question that we may see one of these monsters in the future. Get out your checkbook.

The computer communicates with the physical disk through an output register assigned to one of the ports. The register is built into the disk controller card and performs all the functions of starting the motor, moving the read/write heads, and finding the correct head/track/sector combination. How DOS stores a file like C:\DATA\MYSTUFF.DAT is the subject of the next chapter.

The Operating System (OS)

The previous chapter was about the physical disk system, discussing 5.25-inch and 3.5-inch disks as well as maximum-capacity hard disks. This chapter investigates the operating system (OS). All computers—from the largest supercomputers used by NASA and the IRS to the smallest desktop model—need an operating system. This is the basic program that is always running and accepts user input and returns calculated output. Without an operating system, the computer would not...well...operate.

The History of DOS

The operating system used in the IBM and clone personal computers is called simply *Disk Operating System*, or DOS for short. Actually, DOS is geared to the Intel CPU chip within the computer and not the brand name IBM.

IBM set the standard for personal computers using the Intel 80x86 series of computer chips when it introduced the IBM PC in 1981. The IBM PC used the Intel 8088 CPU. Intel has used the 80 series numbers since introducing the 8080 chip for the Altair computer in 1978.

Before IBM, most microcomputers used eight bits to transfer data from the CPU to memory. Eight bits is commonly called a *byte* and represents numbers between 0 and 255. Intel pioneered a computer chip that used two bytes, or 16 bits, for calculation and memory transfer and called the chip the 8086. A companion chip, designated the 8088, calculated in 16-bit chunks, but transferred data in eight-bit blocks to and from memory. This is the chip IBM used when designing the IBM PC, and it quickly became the standard. The 8088 and 8086 could address memory using 20-bit addresses, which meant the new IBM computer could have up to 1M of memory. Other chips on the market at the time could use only 16-bit addresses, which limited memory to 64K. The 8088 was a bit slower than the 8086, but IBM chose this chip because most of the peripherals at that time were only eight-bit devices.

IBM had the box, but the world's leading computer manufacturer had no 16-bit operating system. The story of how young Bill Gates and his Microsoft Corporation became the supplier of the operating system to IBM could be the subject of another book, and is. Microsoft was and still is the primary producer of operating systems for the Intel-based microcomputers. IBM bought and marketed the operating system under the name PC DOS. Microsoft maintains control of the companion operating system used in non-IBM Intel-based computers and calls it MS-DOS. The only difference between MS-DOS and PC DOS is the BASIC programming language. IBM PCs come with BASIC built into the permanent memory, but clones do not. Any Intel-based computer can use either operating system. For all intents and purposes, they are the same.

Upgrade (I think I can, I think I can)

The Little Engine That Could climbed the hill on the same size tracks as every other locomotive in America. Once a standard is set, it becomes hard to adapt to new technology. When the Union Pacific railroad set the rails 4 feet 8 inches apart, it behooved the Central Pacific to follow the same standard. Think of the historic meeting at Promontory Point, Utah in 1869 if those railroads had used different standards for rail width. Where would you place the golden spike?

Computers, however, cannot rely on the technology of the 1860's or even the 1980's for a standard. So when new standards evolve, old standards must be maintained. DOS version 1.0 could be used only with single-sided disks. When the double-sided disk was introduced in 1982, DOS version 1.1 was issued to handle both sizes and both sides. DOS version 2.0 was introduced with the IBM XT and could handle both single- and double-sided disks and the new hard disk system. Users could upgrade at a slight additional cost.

Intel built the 80286 computer chip. This chip used the same instructions as the 8088, but included a new mode which allowed the chip to address 16M of memory instead of 1M. Intel, IBM, and Microsoft all produced products that maintained the old standards but introduced new methods as well. Again, users could upgrade at a slight additional cost.

Intel continued to improve the CPU with the introduction of the 80386 and 80486 chips. IBM gave up the old PC standard and began to manufacture the PS/2 line of computers, using the new Intel chips. Other manufacturers maintained the PC standard. Display technology improved from the monochrome green screen to the Color Graphics Adapter (CGA) through the Enhanced Graphics Adapter (EGA) to the Video Graphics Array (VGA). Keyboards went from 80 keys to 101 keys. Bigger and better hard disks were available. A chain reaction of technological improvements burst throughout the 80's and into the 90's with no end in sight. As always, users could upgrade at a slight additional cost.

Microsoft's DOS had to accommodate all these changes yet remain compatible with the older technologies. Upgrade fever hit the operating system market as well.

Of course...all together now...users could upgrade at a slight additional cost. Is it any wonder that Bill Gates sits near the top of the *Forbes* list?

To a programmer, each version of DOS has presented many new internal routines, but to you, the user, the changes have been less obvious. A few new utilities are found in each new version, but the screen prompt of COMMAND.COM has remained virtually unchanged. One thing that all versions of DOS have in common is the file-naming convention. Files have an eight-character name and a three-character extension. Beginning with version 2.0, you can store these files in subdirectories, but the basic naming standard has remained constant.

Don't Cry for Me...As We Peel the OS Onion

Like an onion, the operating system is composed of many layers. In the previous chapter, you saw the inner core of the disk system: the physical disk connected to a controller card. Just on top of that core is the *Basic Input Output System* (BIOS), which acts as a bridge between DOS and the physical system.

Basic Input Output System

BIOS is part of the computer itself or the plug-in peripheral boards and is contained in Read Only Memory (ROM) chips. Most devices communicate through *Input/Output Address Ports*. These address ports connect to data registers, which are usually located on the device controller card. In the case of the disk system, the controller card contains five registers for disk functions (I/O address 3F2 through 3F7) and eight registers for hard disk functions (I/O address 1F0 through 1F7). The BIOS contains routines to issue the commands to these registers, which make the disk function.

Basic Input Output

The next layer is not fixed like BIOS, but is stored in a system file on a bootable disk. This file is the *Basic Input Output* (BIO) file and is the first file on a bootable disk. The name of the BIO file used to be standardized as IBMBIO.COM, but that name is only used on the IBM version of recent DOS releases. Microsoft DOS (MS-DOS) now calls this file IO.SYS. The BIO program contains routines that determine the configuration of the system on start-up by reading the hard disk partition table and the disk BIOS parameter block (explained later). BIO also loads the DOS file, called IBMDOS.COM in the IBM version PC DOS or MSDOS.SYS in MS-DOS.

Disk Operating System

The program contained in the IBMDOS file sets up the *logical* file system which the BIO converts into the *physical* file system. Despite the name, DOS is more than just a *disk operating system*. The DOS program contains hundreds of routines that application programs can use when dealing with attached devices such as disks, the screen, keyboard, printer, modem, and even networks. All of these routines are backwardly compatible with the 43 functions that were introduced in version 1.0 of DOS. All programs can use DOS services without knowledge of the actual physical parameters of any attached device. DOS presents input from a file, the keyboard, or a modem in exactly the same way to any program. Likewise, programs can direct output to any device through DOS functions and let DOS filter the data down through the BIO and BIOS to the device.

The Outer Shell

DOS itself is not the top layer of the operating system onion. On start-up, DOS loads a shell program called COMMAND.COM. This is the only part of the operating system that is not either built-in or a hidden file. In the very first DOS release, IBM stated that other shells could be substituted for COMMAND.COM and although a few have appeared on the market, COMMAND.COM has generally won favor as the user interface of choice.

COMMAND.COM prints a prompt on the screen, usually the current drive letter followed by a greater-than symbol (C:>) and waits for you to type something on the keys. After you type something and press the Enter key, COMMAND.COM tries to interpret what you want to do. COMMAND.COM either runs an internal routine or searches for a program file, loads it in memory, and starts the program. When the program is finished, COMMAND.COM resumes and waits for the next input.

COMMAND.COM is the outer skin of the operating system onion. Sometimes you use another layer on top of COMMAND.COM to make the computer easier and more intuitive to use. DOSSHELL and Windows both have a *graphical user interface* (GUI) and perform many of the same (and sometimes more) functions as COMMAND. But

COMMAND.COM always sits in memory in case you exit one of the GUI shells.

Is That Device Logical?

The whole idea behind DOS is to convert human symbols to computer symbols. To make the computer easier for us to understand, DOS sets up a logical device system that becomes independent of the actual physical devices connected to the computer. A *device* is anything that can accept output or can input data and does not have to be some physical device attached to the system. Each device is given an easy-to-understand name. The names used for the disk system begin with A: and progress through the alphabet. The names are two characters long and the colon indicates that A: is a device and not a one-character filename. Other device names include PRN and LPTx: for the printers and NUL for a null device connected to nothing. Because data recovery is usually confined to the disk devices, this discussion omits the other DOS devices.

WARNING

DOS device names, like filenames, can be eight characters long. Device drivers, programs loaded by the DEVICE=... line in CONFIG.SYS, can assign names to a device. Device names cannot be used for filenames.

Drives A: and B: are reserved for the first two disk drives. If only one drive is connected, DOS sets up a logical B: drive using the same physical drive as drive A:, but keeps the data separate just as though there were two physical drives. In this case, DOS can prompt you to change disks when switching from drive A: to drive B:.

Drive C: is reserved for the first hard disk if it is attached to the system. If no hard disk is attached, DOS can use the C: drive for additional disks. If a hard disk is attached, the first DOS partition on the hard disk becomes drive C:. Assigning drive designations above drive C: depends on the DOS version and how many hard disks are connected to the computer.

Prior to DOS version 3.3, a hard disk could contain up to four logical partitions, and each partition could be a logical drive (C:, D:, E: and F:). Version 3.3 and up changed the partition setup so there could be an almost unlimited number of partitions, and each partition could be a separate logical drive.

A hard disk has two types of DOS partitions: a *primary* DOS partition and an *extended* DOS partition. Extended DOS partitions can be divided into a primary DOS partition and another extended DOS partition or could be just a primary DOS partition. Just how the hard disk is divided into partitions is up to you or whomever set up the hard disk in the first place with the FDISK program.

If only one hard disk is used, DOS assigns C: as the first primary DOS partition of the hard disk. Each extended DOS partition that contains a primary DOS partition is assigned the next letter in sequence until all primary DOS partitions are assigned drive letters.

If two hard disks are used, DOS still assigns C: to the primary DOS partition of the first hard disk. If the second hard disk contains a primary DOS partition, it gets the D: designation; otherwise the extended DOS partitions of the first hard disk get the next letters followed by the extended DOS partitions of the second hard disk. This may seem complicated, but you need to know which DOS drive corresponds to which physical drive in order to recover lost data.

Although DOS uses letters and a colon to designate logical drives, the BIOS uses numbers to indicate the physical drives. The disks are assigned drive numbers beginning with 0 for physical drive A:, 1 for physical drive B:, etc. There is no number for a logical drive B: if a second physical disk drive does not exist. Hard disks are assigned numbers 128 (80hex) and 129 (81hex).

Logical drive letters can exist beyond the number of physical drives attached to the system. Just as physical drive 0 can double as drives A: and B:, the DOS SUBST command can assign drive letters to the entire drive\subdirectory combination. For example, the command SUBST F: C:\DOS makes the DOS subdirectory on drive C: accessible by using just the drive designation F:. DIR F: shows a directory of the C:\DOS subdirectory.

Logical Sectors

The DOS logical disk is a visible part of the file system. COMMAND.COM and most GUIs maintain the DOS drive-naming scheme. Not as visible is the DOS logical sector structure. As described in the previous chapter, the disk is divided into head, track, and sectors where information is stored. DOS sets up a logical sector-numbering scheme starting at sector 0 and numbering sectors sequentially through the total number of sectors on the disk. On disks, this logical sector-numbering scheme begins with track 0, head 0, sector 1. On hard disks, the partition table indicates which track, head, and sector number begins each logical drive.

The 32-Megabyte Barrier

Early versions of DOS (before 4.0) counted logical sectors in 16-bit (two-byte) units. The maximum number of sectors that can be counted under this system is 65,536. Because each sector contains 512 bytes of data, disks using this scheme can be no larger than 33,554,432, or 32M. Beginning with DOS 4.0, sector numbers are stored as 32-bit (four-byte) numbers. Now DOS can count up to 4,294,967,296 sectors or 2048 gigabytes worth of data. The previous chapter showed how the BIOS can handle a disk of up to 7.8 gigabytes, so the DOS number seems adequate.

How DOS Does It

You probably think of a file as an eight-character filename and a three character extension separated by a dot or period. You also know the drive where you stored the file (or the disk) and the directory name. It may be easier to think in terms of office filing cabinets. The drive is the particular filing cabinet, the directory is the drawer in that cabinet, and the filename itself the particular folder within the drawer. The file data can be thought of as the contents of the folder. In fact, many office filing systems work this way. To retrieve a particular contract, you first go to the correct file cabinet, open the proper drawer, remove the folder, and find the document you need inside. Some graphical computer interfaces even try to simulate the office filing environment with cute little icons of file folders, trash cans, and assorted other cartoons.

It's fine to think in terms of a filing cabinet—especially if you use a GUI that encourages that analogy. But DOS manages files in a much different way—more like a lending library than a filing cabinet. You tell a librarian what you want and the librarian disappears into the stacks and returns with your book. What happens back in the stacks is of no particular concern to you. All you need to know is that you give the librarian the title of a book and the librarian finds it for you. But what happens if the librarian returns to the desk and says, "The book is missing"? Can you go into the stacks and find it yourself? Not if you don't know how the library arranges the books back in the stacks.

DOS is the computer librarian. You tell DOS the title of the information, and DOS either gets it for you or stores it. Unlike a library, there is some information you need to know about where the file is stored. In a library, if you know the title and author, the librarian can find your book no matter where it is in the stacks. In the world of computers, you sometimes have to help the librarian by supplying the drive and directory where the file is located. You can use the PATH statement to help you search for a program file. The PATH merely helps the librarian by suggesting which drives and directories to search for the file.

The Inside Story

Behind the librarian's desk are the stacks where the books are stored. Picture a disk drive as several racks of shelves each neatly divided into little cubbyholes. The cubbyhole is a sector, capable of holding 512 bytes of information. Each shelf of the rack is a track holding many cubbyholes and each rack represents a head on the disk drive. Some "books" (files) are larger than others and need more than just one cubbyhole, so the librarian has devised a scheme to catalogue just where the various parts of the file are stored.

There are enough systems for storing data on a file system to keep computer science majors busy for several semesters. Theory is one thing, practicality another. Here is how the designers of DOS chose to utilize the disk.

DOS converts drive name, directory name, filename, and extension into physical disk, track, head, and sector numbers. If there is one thing a computer can do well, it is...er...compute. So all DOS needs to know is how the physical disk is arranged and off it goes computing.

The BIOS Parameter Block

At the very beginning of the disk (logical sector 0), DOS keeps a set of statistics about the disk. This area, called the *BIOS Parameter Block* (BPB) contains the following information:

```
Number of bytes per sector
Number of sectors per allocation unit
Number of sectors in reserved area
Number of FAT copies
Number of root directory entries
Total number of sectors
DOS media descriptor
Number of sectors per FAT
Number of sectors per track
Number of heads
Number of hidden sectors
```

Converting from logical sectors to physical sectors is easy. The hard part is figuring out how to allocate all those sectors and keeping track of which file occupies which sectors. DOS uses two special areas on the disk for this cataloging.

Keeping the FAT Slim

The next sector on the disk (logical sector 1) is the beginning of what is known as the *File Allocation Table* (FAT) and its size (number of sectors) is indicated in the BPB. The designers of DOS thought that the FAT was such a critical area that in all versions of DOS up to 6.0, two copies of it are stored on the disk. That number could change because the number of FAT copies is one of the statistics kept in the BPB. Even though DOS writes the second copy of the FAT, it never reads it unless there is an error reading one of those sectors.

The FAT is the master catalogue of what sectors are occupied by which file and which sectors are unoccupied and can be used when new space is needed. It would have been easy for the designers of DOS to have one entry in the FAT for each sector on the disk. The original single-sided disk had 320 sectors. To represent the number 320 in byte-sized units takes two bytes because one byte can represent only up to 255. 320 two-byte entries take 640 bytes, meaning two sectors would be devoted to each copy of the FAT, robbing the disk of precious data space.

To conserve space, the original FAT was made up of 1 1/2 byte entries, or 12 bits. Each sector is represented by one 12-bit FAT entry and takes only 480 bytes, which fit neatly into one sector of the disk. When upgrade fever hit the disk drive industry and double-sided disks were introduced, DOS had a problem. The FAT had to grow to twice the size and would no longer fit in one sector. Out of necessity (the mother of all invention) came the *File Allocation Unit* which was originally referred to as a *cluster*.

A cluster merely designates a group of two or more consecutive logical sectors. By calling two consecutive sectors a cluster and storing the cluster number in the FAT, the disk capacity could double, but the FAT size stayed the same. All DOS has to do is add another calculation to convert from cluster number to sector number, and we know that computers are good at computing.

As disk capacity grew and upgrade fever hit hard at the checkbook, so did the cluster size and the FAT size. The FAT is no longer confined to one sector and entry size has increased to 16 bits (two bytes) on all FATs except disks and small hard disks. Cluster sizes vary from disk to disk and all the information needed to make cluster-to-sector calculations is stored in the BPB.

OK. So the FAT has an entry for every allocation unit on the disk. How is it used? The FAT is also one of the hardest structures to visualize but is critical in determining just what section of the disk is in use and by what file.

If every file was small enough to fit in one cluster, life would be easy. Allocate one cluster to the file, mark the cluster as used in the FAT, and be done. But in real life, a file can occupy many clusters and may need more as time goes by and the data is expanded.

The method Microsoft chose was to have every cluster entry be a number, indicating the next cluster used by a file. If the FAT entry is the last cluster used by the file, then a special *End Of File* <EOF> marker is used for that FAT entry. All bits on (FFF hex or FFFF hex) were chosen as the <EOF>. If the FAT entry is a 0, then the cluster is free and can be allocated the next time space is needed on the disk. One other special entry in the FAT marks the cluster as not occupied but not available. This is the Bad Sector mark, which prevents DOS from trying to store data in areas that were found during the formatting process to be physically damaged.

Here's an example of part of the FAT for a file occupying four clusters, beginning with cluster 2. (DOS never allocates clusters 0 and 1):

```
FAT ENTRY    0    1    2    3    4    5    6    7 …
            xxx  xxx  003  004  005  FFF  000  FF7 …
```

FAT entry 2 points to 3, which points to 4, which points to 5, which indicates <EOF>. DOS knows that this file occupies clusters 2, 3, 4, and 5 in that order. Cluster 6 is available for another file or expansion of this file. Cluster 7 is bad and should not be used.

Direct(ory) Me to the Proper Cluster

After the FAT, the next most important DOS structure on the disk is the *directory*. Every file stored on the disk has a directory entry, either in the root directory or a subdirectory. This is the card catalogue of the disk library. Only the root directory is located at a fixed place on the disk. The subdirectories can be anywhere, but the subdirectory branch eventually leads back to an entry in the root directory.

The sectors that are used for the root directory are immediately following the second copy of the FAT. Each directory entry is 32-bytes long and the maximum number of allowable entries is another variable stored in the BPB. The size and location of the root directory is fixed and the directory cannot be expanded. Directory entries have the following form:

```
8 bytes      filename
3 bytes      extension
1 byte       attribute
10 bytes     reserved
2 bytes      time
2 bytes      date
2 bytes      first allocation unit
4 bytes      file size
```

The DIR /a command displays all the data in the directory with the exception of the attribute and the first allocation unit. ATTRIB *.* displays the attribute of every file in the directory. The first allocation unit field is the only part of the entry that cannot be displayed with normal DOS commands.

OFFSET 00h: FILENAME (Eight Bytes) EXTENSION (Three Bytes)

The filename and extension are stored as ASCII characters in upper-case. The filename always occupies eight bytes. If the name of the file is not that long, DOS stores the ASCII space character (32) in the remaining bytes. Likewise, the extension is always three bytes long and is padded with spaces. It's interesting to note that *any* character can be used for filenames and extensions—even imbedded spaces. Unfortunately, COMMAND.COM interprets a space entered on the command line as the end of a string of characters and not as part of a filename, so you can't access a file containing embedded spaces from the command line. Programs that call DOS file services directly easily can include a space within a filename or extension.

DOS does not store the dot that separates the filename and the extension. Before creating or reading a directory entry, DOS parses the filename, converts it to uppercase, and pads it to the proper length. The filename "file.x", for example, is converted to "FILE   X ".

The first character of the filename (which is the first byte of the directory entry) has a special meaning. If this byte is 0, the directory entry is empty and no more entries follow. If the byte is E8 hex, the entry has been deleted and may be reused. Any other value is the first character of a valid filename.

OFFSET 0Bh: Attribute (One Byte)

The attribute byte is bit coded and can be one or more of the following:

```
1       read only
2       hidden
4       system
8       volume label
16      sub-directory
32      archive
64      unused
128     unused
```

Volume Label is the only attribute that cannot be used in combination with other attribute bits.

The only two attribute bits that are special are the volume label and subdirectory bits. Only one volume label entry per disk can be used. (There can be more, but DOS ignores any after the first.) The volume label is not a file; it is just an entry in the directory. The volume label entry is a holdover from prior versions of DOS. The volume label is now stored in the first sector of the disk along with the BPB.

The subdirectory attribute bit indicates that the entry is another directory and not a normal file. Even though subdirectories take up space on the disk and are allocated clusters just like data files, the size field in the directory is always zero.

Notice that there is no distinction in the directory between a data file and a program file. The designers of DOS could have chosen to use one of the attribute bits to designate an executable program, but did not. Instead, the file extension is used for this purpose. COM and EXE are the extensions used by the DOS command processor (COMMAND.COM) to locate and load program files. Although COM files and EXE files have different internal formats, COMMAND.COM does not distinguish between the two formats based on extension, but rather on the first two bytes of the file. A program file that begins with the ASCII coded letters MZ is an EXE file; otherwise it is a binary memory image file (COM).

OFFSET 0Ch: Reserved (0A Bytes)

This 10-byte area is not used in any version of DOS up to 6.0 and is normally set to 0.

OFFSET 16h: File Time (Two Bytes)

The file time reflects the system time when the file was created or last changed. The time is stored in a bit-coded format. The top five bits represent the hour (0 to 31), the next six bits are the minute (0 to 64) and the lower five bits represent the seconds divided by two (0 to 31). Because the seconds bits can only represent 32 digits, the time is only accurate to the nearest two seconds.

OFFSET 18h: File Date (Two Bytes)

Like the time field, this field represents the date when the file was created or changed. The date is also stored in a bit-coded format. The upper six bits are the year minus 1980 (0 to 63). The next four bits are the month (0 to 15) and the final six bits the day of the month (0 to 31). Apparently, Microsoft feels confident that we will all switch to OS/2 by the year 2043 when it runs out of years in the date field. WOW! That's the year Willard Scott wishes me a happy birthday on the "Today" show.

OFFSET 1Ah: Starting Cluster Number (Two Bytes)

This field indicates which cluster holds the first part of the file. It is also an indication of the maximum number of clusters a disk can have because a two-byte number's maximum value is 65,535. DOS uses 65,535 as the <EOF> in the FAT and reserves all cluster numbers greater than 65,520 (FFF0h), less the first two unused clusters, for a maximum of 65,518 usable clusters. Keep that in mind when you buy that 1024-gigabyte monster drive. Each cluster will be 65,554 sectors long. It would take 32M of disk space just to store a 10-byte batch file.

OFFSET 1Ch: File Size (Four Bytes)

This field indicates the total number of bytes in the file. The four-byte number can range from 0 to 4,294,967,295. That should be large enough for most practical work.

Data Area

The data area begins on the sector following the root directory. This is where the file data is stored. The first sector of the data area corresponds to the second data cluster. Data clusters 0 and 1 are not used for storing data and those entries in the FAT are used to store the *media descriptor byte* of the disk. The media descriptor byte is also part of the BPB, so its inclusion in the FAT is redundant and a holdover from the first version of DOS.

The size of the data area can be calculated by subtracting the number of boot sectors, FAT sectors, and directory sectors from the total sectors on the disk. All these values are stored in the BPB.

Storing and Retrieving Files

In the beginning, the disk was void. DOS saw the void and created files to fill the void. Creating a file is the first of many sequential steps to storing and retrieving data. Files must be *opened* before being used and *closed* after use. There is no COMMAND.COM command to open or close a file. This is all handled internally by the programs you use, even COMMAND.COM. But things go wrong. If you understand how programs use files, you can understand what went wrong and discover how to get the data back.

Creating Files

When DOS creates a file, it needs the full filespec, not just the filename and extension. If you don't supply the full drive, path, and filename, DOS will fill in the blanks using default values. When DOS starts, the default drive is the drive used to boot the computer and the root directory is the default directory. Typing another drive letter followed by a colon changes the default drive and the command CD, followed by a directory path, changes the default path.

WARNING

Any program can change the default drive and the default directory on any drive. The defaults might be different when a program ends and returns you to the COMMAND prompt.

TIP

To see the full path for any filename, use the undocumented command TRUENAME followed by a filename and extension. This also works on any substituted or joined drive.

The first step DOS performs is to create a directory entry for the file in the appropriate directory. The new directory entry has an initial length of 0 and the first allocation unit field is set to zero. At this point, none of the data space is used by the file. Once the file is created, it is automatically *opened* for reading and writing, even if the read-only attribute is set.

Opening Files

Before DOS can do anything to a file, it must set up some internal structures to keep track of the file operations. This is called *opening a file*. If a file already exists in a directory, DOS can open the file for reading and/or writing unless the read-only attribute bit in the file's directory entry is set. If this bit is set, the file can only be read; it cannot be written to or deleted.

Any application program that uses DOS to access a file must open the file before it can be used. One of the internal DOS structures is assigned to keep track of operations on that file. A number called a *file handle* is used to refer to this structure in all file operations. There is a limit to the number of files that can be open at any one time. That limit is set in the CONFIG.SYS file with the statement FILES=nnn. If there is no CONFIG.SYS file or there is no FILES= statement, the default is eight files.

Four files are automatically available to every program: the NUL file (or bit bucket), which has no input or output device; the CON file, which is the keyboard for input and the screen for output; the PRN file, which is the standard printer; and the AUX file, which can be assigned to the COM port. With the default setting, this leaves only four files available for disk operations.

Some applications never have more than one file open at a time, but other file-intensive programs like a relational database may require more open files than the default setting allows. If there is no space for a file to be opened in the DOS internal structure, DOS returns an error to the application. COMMAND.COM displays the message No more file handles, although any application is free to use another error message.

Writing to Files

A newly created file contains no data and uses no disk space. As data is added to the file, the application uses DOS services to write the data from memory to the disk. The application tells DOS the file handle, the address where the data is located in memory, and the number of bytes to write to the disk. DOS then does all the work involved with actually writing the data to one or more free clusters on the disk and updating the FAT and directory entry. But it does not all happen instantly. DOS follows a specific set of steps in actually writing the data to the disk.

First, DOS reads the directory into memory and checks the initial allocation unit field in the file's directory entry. If this field is zero, then space must be assigned for the data. DOS reads the FAT sectors into memory from the first copy of the FAT and checks the FAT for the first free allocation unit on the disk. Then DOS begins to build a chain in the FAT with each entry indicating the next available free allocation unit until enough allocation units are assigned to hold the number of bytes that will be written to the disk. The last FAT entry in the chain is set with the <EOF> marker. The FAT sectors are then written back to the disk with the new chain in place. DOS writes both copies of the FAT, even though it only read the first copy.

If the file is an existing file, DOS will not allocate new allocation units unless the number of bytes to be written exceeds the length of the existing chain. If the file is to be written at the beginning, DOS frees all previously assigned allocation units and proceeds just as though the file were new. There is no guarantee that the new allocations units will be the same as those just freed. If the data is not to be written to the beginning of the file, DOS frees any allocation units past the point where the data is to be written and allocates new units. The FAT sectors are then written back to the disk as before.

After the FAT is safely written to the disk, DOS updates the directory entry with the new initial allocation unit, the new length of the file, and the current time and date. This information is stored in memory and is not written to the disk at this time.

The file data is transferred to one or more of the DOS disk buffers. If enough buffer space is available, all the data remains in these areas of memory and is not written to the disk. Each DOS buffer holds one sector's worth of data (512 bytes) and the number of buffers is set in the CONFIG.SYS file with the BUFFERS=nn statement. Because memory is faster than accessing the disk, the more buffers, the faster the DOS file operations.

DOS writes the new data to the disk only when it runs out of buffer space or receives a "flush buffers" signal from the application program. Before the buffers are flushed, your data is vulnerable. It has not been written to the disk and will be lost if the power is cut off at this point. CHKDSK will report the allocated clusters as lost, but they do not contain the data from the file. The data that was in the buffers is gone.

Reading from Files

Reading from files is the reverse of the writing operation except that DOS does not have to update the FAT or the directory entry. The application tells DOS the handle number of the open file, the number of bytes to read from the disk, and the memory location where DOS should store the file data. DOS then reads the FAT chain for the file and reads the appropriate sectors into the DOS buffers. DOS will read as much of the file as there is space in the buffers, even if fewer bytes are requested by the application. The data is then transferred from the buffer to the memory location indicated in the read request.

If another read request is received, DOS does not have to go to the disk to get the data because it is already in the buffers. The data can just be transferred from the buffer to the application's memory area.

Closing Files

The file remains open for reading and/or writing until DOS receives a *close file* request. If the file was open for reading only, DOS merely frees the internal structure that was assigned to the file and makes no more disk access. However, if the file was opened for writing and a write operation was performed, DOS flushes the buffers associated with the file by writing the data to the disk and finally writes the updated directory information to the disk. The longer a file remains open, the higher the risk of corrupting the FAT by a power loss or reboot. The FAT is updated immediately, but the data and directory information remain in memory until DOS gets the "flush buffers" and close signal.

Erasing Files

When DOS erases a file, only the first byte of the directory entry is changed to indicate that the entry has been released. All other directory information remains intact. DOS frees all allocation units used by the file in the FAT and writes the new directory and FAT sectors to the disk.

Un-erasing Files

It's no secret that DOS does not erase the data in a file when a file is deleted. There are many utilities that can recover a file from an accidental deletion. Here's what happens: DOS marks the first character of the directory entry with a special character that indicates that the entry has been deleted and the space is available for another file. The file's entries in the FAT are marked as available, but the initial allocation unit entry in the directory is not changed. All the directory information remains, with the exception of the first character of the filename. This is why you need to supply that letter when you use undelete programs.

How well do undelete programs work? The answer is "It depends." It depends on whether any other file was created since the file that needs undeleting was deleted. When DOS creates a file, it searches for the first available directory entry. If that entry is the file that was accidently deleted, recovery is almost impossible because the directory entry gets reused.

Recovering the FAT chain is the hard part of file undeleting. All the FAT entries used by the original file are marked as unused so the trail of the chain is completely obliterated. However, there is a system that DOS uses in allocating sectors for a file. As a file grows, DOS assigns the next available allocation unit in the FAT to the file unless the end of the disk is reached. Only under that condition will DOS go to the beginning of the disk to search for free allocation units. Because few disks get totally full, the chance is good that each allocation unit that was assigned to the file is further into the disk than the previous one. Because the file directory contains the initial allocation unit, an undelete program can begin to reconstruct the allocation chain by looking for free FAT entries which follow the initial allocation unit. Only if all free units toward the end of the disk are exhausted will the undelete program begin to look from the beginning of the disk. If the undelete program can find enough free allocation units in sequential order to account for the file size, the chances of full recovery are good.

Problems in recovery can arise if more than one file was deleted. It is possible that the allocation of the two files was intermixed; that is, the files were not written in sequential allocation units. For example, FILE.1 may have been allocated units 2 and 3, and FILE.2, units 4 and 5. Then, if FILE.1 added two more clusters, it would get units 6 and 7. This means that FILE.1 occupies clusters 2, 3, 6, and 7, and FILE.2 occupies clusters 4 and 5. If both files are deleted, allocation units 2 through 8 are all marked as free and there is no way to tell which allocation unit belonged to which file. Most recovery programs would assume that if you wanted to recover FILE.1, it would have been stored in allocation units 2, 3, 4, and 5. Only by examining FILE.2 would the recovery program know that allocation unit number 4 was the initial allocation unit for FILE.2 and not part of FILE.1's chain.

It's also impossible to know for certain that FILE.2 was not deleted before FILE.1 was created and therefore allocation unit 4 was available to FILE.1. Some undelete programs allow you to examine the sectors that could have been part of the original file. This will work if the file was text but is of little help for binary files and program files. Deciphering the data and making a decision as to whether a particular allocation unit was part of the original file can be frustrating at best.

The probability of successful recovery increases if the recovery is attempted immediately after deletion and if only one file was deleted. But many times, a wanted file is deleted with the command DEL *.*. In this case, many files are deleted at once and the fact that a file was accidently erased is not discovered until later. Many times the needed file is overwritten before the mistake is realized. This is a case where an ounce of prevention is worth more than the proverbial pound of cure.

The UNDELETE command available with DOS 5.0 and later versions and with PC-Tools (the DOS version is licensed from Central Point Software, the makers of PC-Tools) can use a tracking file so that no file is truly deleted until the disk is full. The DOS 5.0 and DOS 6.0 versions work differently and you are advised to check the documentation of whichever version you are using. If you are using a version of DOS prior to 5.0, you should probably upgrade to version 6.0 or get the PC-Tools or Norton Utilities undelete programs.

In version 5.0 of DOS, the MIRROR utility sets the deletion tracking by using the /dt switch. DOS 6.0 sets the deletion tracking by using the UNDELETE program itself. The appropriate tracking program should be part of the AUTOEXEC.BAT file so that tracking is started at the beginning of each session.

Deletion tracking in DOS version 6.0 comes in two flavors: DELETE TRACKING and DELETE SENTRY. DELETE TRACKING creates a file with the deleted file's name and the clusters it occupied. When the file is undeleted, the tracking file is checked for the clusters that the file occupied and those clusters are checked to make sure they are still free. If those conditions are met, the file is unerased.

DELETE SENTRY is a better method to assure the file data is intact. DELETE SENTRY does free the allocation units when a file is deleted. The directory entry is "moved" to a hidden subdirectory called SENTRY. Only when the disk approaches capacity are the files actually deleted. The oldest files are deleted first. Deletion tracking is well worth the bytes used by the memory-resident portion of the program and worth the cost of upgrading to the latest version of DOS.

Other Problems

When a program uses a data file, it must open the file before it can read or write data to it. Once data is written to the file, it must be properly closed before the updated directory is written back to the disk. Some programs will open the file, write the data, and then close the file in succession. Other programs leave the data vulnerable by opening the file at the beginning of the session and leaving it open until the program ends. The method used is strictly up to the people who wrote the application program and each method has advantages and disadvantages.

Files that are opened and closed frequently produce a lot of disk activity, which is not only inherently slow, but also can cause wear on the mechanical parts of the disk drive. Leaving the file open increases the speed, because disk activity is less, but if the session is interrupted, the data written to the file can be lost.

Programmers are encouraged not to leave a file open and DOS now includes a FASTOPEN utility which speeds up the process of opening frequently used files. Windows programs should never leave a file open according to Windows programming strictures, but sometimes programmers play a little fast and loose with the rules.

Sometimes a little utility like FASTOPEN can leap up and bite you. During the production of this book, one of the hard disks became close to full. It was time to drain the swamp. We copied several megabytes of files to disk and deleted them from the hard disk. To improve performance, we ran a defragging program to force all the remaining files into consecutive clusters. After the defragging process finished, we started Word to resume the creative process of producing a book. What we got was a recursive batch file that called Word endlessly.

After breaking out of the batch file, we ran CHKDSK and found hundreds of lost clusters in dozens of files and several invalid directories. We were up to our necks in alligators! Or were we?

continues

When the initial shock wore off and we concluded that we were the experts in recovering data, we set about the task of finding what went wrong. (If you know what went wrong, it's easier to make it right.) The first thing we did was to check the AUTOEXEC.BAT file to see what TSR programs were in memory. There was a line that read C:\DOS\FASTOPEN C:. Problem solved. Data recovered. All it took was a three-finger-salute to reboot the computer.

Here's what happened: FASTOPEN stores directory information in memory. When the defragging program relocated the subdirectories on the hard disk, FASTOPEN was not updated with the new information. It only appeared that the data was lost. Once the computer was restarted, the updated clusters were reported correctly.

Moral: When the defragmenting program says reboot, do it!

Abnormal Termination of Programs

A good rule to follow is to run CHKDSK anytime a program has an abnormal termination. If you lose power or have to reboot in the middle of a program, check to see whether the program has left lost allocation units on the disk.

You might also want to check to see whether the data files used by that program are there. Sometimes a program will rename a data file and use that file as a temporary file while writing the data to the original file. In this case, the data file could be missing entirely if the program does not run to completion. Usually, but not always, the data will be in the temporary file and can be recovered. The name of the temporary file will vary from program to program, so there is no hard-and-fast rule as to how to recover the data.

13

DOS Error Messages

Just as you would flip through your omnibus cookbook looking for a recipe for Hollandaise sauce or chocolate mousse, this is the chapter to turn to when you need a solution to a problem. Here are quick explanations of what's probably gone wrong and instructions on what to do about it. This chapter is your basic *The Joy of Cooking*; later chapters are the data recovery *Larousse Gastronomique* that deal with problems in more intricate detail.

Disk Problems

Everyone encounters a disk problem from time to time. It may be as simple as failing to close the door of a floppy drive or as fatal as a hard drive that's gone so far south it reached Rio de Janerio before you noticed it was gone. Because error messages appear rarely, you need to know—or at least have a good guess—about what happened.

Your Computer Won't Boot from the Hard Disk

You turn the computer on, expecting to boot from the hard disk but all you see is the cursor in the upper-left corner of the screen. You get no error message and nothing happens.

Several things could be wrong:

➤ Partition table bad

➤ DOS system files corrupt

➤ Corrupt program in CONFIG.SYS

➤ Corrupt program in AUTOEXEC.BAT

➤ Bad CMOS in AT-class computer

First, try to boot the computer with a system disk in the A: drive. This, at least, tells you that the PC is working. If you're not using the original DOS disk that came with your PC, make sure the bootable disk contains the same DOS version used to set up the hard disk (FDISK and FORMAT).

 Many computers are now shipped with the hard disk already format-ted, and you may not be sure which version of DOS has been used to set up your hard disk. For that reason, a utility program called BOOTINFO is included with this book which will tell you what version of DOS was used to set up the hard disk.

If you see a disk controller error message (1701 Error), it is possible that the hard disk motor is not working, the head positioning sole-noids are stuck, or the CMOS drive information has been corrupted. The CMOS battery also could be dead, and CMOS data can't be read as part of the bootstrapping process. If the battery is not dead, you can correct CMOS problems with the setup program included with most systems.

When you have an A:> prompt on the screen, try to access the C drive. If you get the message Invalid Drive Specification, chances are that the partition table has been corrupted. Norton Disk Doctor or PC-Tools can be used to try to correct the partition table information.

NOTE

PC-Tools Disk Fix can repair the partition table only if the file PARTNSAV.FIL is available on a disk. You must build the PC-Tools emergency disk while the hard disk is still good. Norton Disk Doctor can sometimes rebuild the partition information even if it was not previously saved.

If you can access drive C, try to get a listing of the files in the root directory by typing DIR C: and pressing Enter. If you are using DOS 5.0 or above, type DIR C: /a to get a listing of the hidden system files IBMBIO.COM and IBMDOS.COM (IO.SYS and MSDOS.SYS in MS-DOS).

Rename the CONFIG.SYS and AUTOEXEC.BAT files to CONFIG.TMP and AUTOEXEC.TMP. Remove the disk from drive A and press Ctrl-Alt-Del to reboot from drive C. If the computer still does not boot after the CONFIG.SYS and AUTOEXEC.BAT files are removed, there may be an error in the hidden system files. Start the computer with a DOS disk in drive A and type SYS C: to recopy the system files to the hard disk.

If the computer boots, but hangs, chances are that there's a problem in either the CONFIG.SYS or the AUTOEXEC.BAT file. Try CONFIG.SYS first. Rename CONFIG.TMP to CONFIG.SYS and reboot. If the computer hangs, boot from drive A as before and edit CONFIG.SYS by typing REM before each DEVICE=xxx line. Boot from drive C and remove the REM from each line, one line at a time, until the computer hangs. This is the offending line. Replace the program from the original and try again.

If CONFIG.SYS doesn't hang the system, try AUTOEXEC.BAT. Rename AUTOEXEC.TMP to AUTOEXEC.BAT and try to boot from C. If the computer hangs now, start from a disk in drive A and edit each line of the AUTOEXEC.BAT file, placing a REM before each command. Reboot and remove the REM statement from each line one at a time. You do not have to reboot each time you change the AUTOEXEC.BAT file; just type AUTOEXEC and press Enter. If the computer hangs, the last line contains the corrupt program. Replace the bad program file with a good one or remove it from the AUTOEXEC.BAT file.

NOTE

For the most part, unless you have the Taj Mahal of AUTOEXECs, you can enter the contents of AUTOEXEC.BAT from the command line, one line at a time, and press Enter. When the system hangs, you've got the culprit.

Your Computer Won't Start from the Hard Disk ("Starting MS-DOS" Message)

The Starting MS-DOS message appears only with DOS version 6 and indicates that the boot process has begun and that DOS is about to process the CONFIG.SYS and AUTOEXEC.BAT files. You can step through the CONFIG.SYS file by pressing F8. This should allow you to see which program in CONFIG.SYS is causing the problem. Replace the program from the original disk or remove it from the CONFIG.SYS file.

If CONFIG.SYS operates properly but the system hangs during the processing of AUTOEXEC.BAT, reboot and skip AUTOEXEC.BAT by pressing F10 at the Starting MS-DOS message. Edit AUTOEXEC.BAT by placing a REM statement before each line and then one by one eliminate the REM and type AUTOEXEC at the DOS prompt. If the system hangs, the last removed REM statement contains the offending program. Replace the program from the original disk or remove the line from the AUTOEXEC.BAT file.

Deleted File

Deleted files aren't really deleted. DOS simply puts the non-ASCII character σ 229 or E5 hex in place of the first letter of the filename so that it won't be picked up by a DIR listing. This character tells DOS that the directory entry has been deleted and can be used again if another file is created. The contents of the file remain right where they were until they are overwritten by another file or moved by a de-fragging program. The sooner you realize you've deleted a file—like immediately—the better your chances of recovery.

Fix: Run UNDELETE from DOS version 5.0 or later, UNDELETE from PC-Tools, or UNERASE from the Norton Utilities. If you have not written any files since the file was deleted, recovery chances are good. Each of the above utilities has a companion program that will set delete tracking so the recovery chances are enhanced. This works only if you ran the tracking program before deleting a file. A delete tracking program keeps a record of the deleted files' space on the disk so it can be recovered more easily. A full technical explanation of how DOS allocates and releases disk space is covered in Chapter 14.

Removed Subdirectory

It's not too easy to remove a subdirectory. You can't do it without deleting all files in the subdirectory (or subdirectories of the subdirectory!). If you have gone to all the trouble to remove a subdirectory and suddenly realize that you've deleted an essential file, *do not* attempt to recreate the subdirectory using the MD command because that, alone, might overwrite the file you want back.

CAUTION

With DOS 6, you can blast off an entire subdirectory and any directories within it by using the DELTREE command. Handle this command with the same care you use with the DEL *.* command.

Fix for DOS and PC-Tools users: UNDELETE (DOS or PC-Tools) cannot automatically recover entire missing subdirectories. Unlike a file listing in the directory, DOS does not store the length of the subdirectory, so UNDELETE recovers only the first allocation unit associated with the subdirectory. Then you must use a manual recovery option to bring back the rest, which is tedious work. After the removed subdirectory is restored, recover the deleted file.

NOTE

The UNDELETE function is exactly the same in DOS and PC-Tools.

Fix for Norton users: Norton UNERASE doesn't need to jump through all these hoops. Norton looks though unused clusters on the disk for lost filenames, finds the file, and restores it.

Bad File Allocation Table (FAT)

A mucked-up File Allocation Table means one thing: You can't get to your files. DOS stores two copies of the FAT, so there is a small chance that only the first copy is bad. Because DOS writes to both copies of the FAT every time there is a change to the FAT, however, it's more likely that both copies are bad.

Fix: PC-Tools and Norton Utilities have programs that attempt to repair a damaged FAT. If you have previously run PC-Tools (or DOS) MIRROR or Norton IMAGE, you can restore the previously saved FAT with UNFORMAT. This does not guarantee a perfect FAT because there may have been changes made since the FAT was saved—but it's better than nothing.

Accidental Floppy Disk Format

Remember the FORMAT ME! Stupid Human Trick? If you don't do a DIR of a floppy before formatting, you can end up losing lots of valuable data.

Early DOS versions (before 5.0) destroy the entire contents of a floppy disk when it is formatted. There is no recovery. Starting with DOS version 5.0, unless the /u (Unconditional) switch was used with the FORMAT command, the disk can be restored with UNFORMAT.

Fix: The PC-Tools FORMAT and UNFORMAT programs are the same as the equivalent programs in DOS version 5.0 and up. The Norton flavor is SAFE FORMAT and UNFORMAT.

TIP

If you're using DOS 5.0 or above, use the /u switch with care.

Accidental Hard Disk Format

FORMAT C: isn't as scary (or as easy) as it used to be. Worse to FOR-MAT A: or B:. Unlike formatting a floppy, formatting a hard disk does not erase any of the sectors in the DATA area of the disk, but the FAT and root directory information are deleted. The data is still there, but without the FAT and root directory, DOS can't find it. All you have to do is restore those areas to undo the format effectively. Of course, you can't restore this information unless you saved it before formatting the drive.

TIP

Disable or tinker with your FORMAT command so that FORMAT C: is no longer a choice to any user.

Fix: If you have saved the hard drive information with MIRROR (DOS and PC-Tools) or IMAGE (Norton), the disk can be unformatted with UNFORMAT.

TIP

DOS version 5.0 and later automatically saves the previous FAT and directory unless you format with the /u option.

Lost or Damaged Subdirectories

This particular fix has caused great consternation in the PANDA halls. Nobody can quite figure out how you can "lose" a subdirectory and the guesses about how one might be damaged are more suitable for science fiction treatises than a technical book on data recovery. DOS is very careful about manipulating the directory entries, but sector editors can sometimes cause the best precautions to go haywire. Who know how it happens. (See "Stupid Human Tricks" in Chapter 7.)

A subdirectory can be lost by changing the first character of the directory listing to 0 or E5 hex. The subdirectory is considered damaged if the first filename in the directory is something other than "." or the second is something other than "..". Nevertheless, if there *is* a fix, the problem must have happened to someone, sometime. If it happens to you, here's what to do.

Fix for DOS users: CHKDSK provides a minimal repair option for damaged subdirectories, but it could lose all the information they contain. If the first entry is not "." and the second is not "..", CHKDSK can only convert the subdirectory to a file, which loses all the other entries (files) in the subdirectory. Not recommended.

Fix for PC-Tools and Norton users: Norton Disk Doctor or PC-Tools Disk Fix should be used for repair according to both packages' documentation.

Missing File(s)

Sometimes a **missing file** is really there, as you learned from the Stupid Human Tricks. Other times, the file has been deleted.

The wildest possibility, but one that is real, is that the directory could have been damaged so that a previous entry is marked as unused (binary 0 as the first character). If that happens to any directory entry, any file whose entry is listed after the damaged entry will be "missing" because DOS stops searching the directory when it gets to an unused entry. The tough part is knowing that this is indeed what has happened to the directory, because neither DOS nor CHKDSK will be able to tell you. You will have to use a sector editor to look at the directory in order to find this problem.

Fix for DOS users: DOS stops searching a directory when the first character of the filename is binary 0. To allow a search to continue past that point, use a sector editor and change the 0 to hex E5, which indicates that this entry is available, but there is more to follow.

Fix for PC-Tools and Norton users: Use Norton Disk Doctor or Disk Editor to repair the bad directory entry. PC-Tools Disk Fix will also allow you to make the necessary repairs.

Fix for users who want to do it the hard way: if you do not have Norton or PC-Tools, you can still repair the subdirectory by creating enough dummy files to fill the space in the directory between the beginning and the valid file. DOS will create new directory entries in the first available space in the directory. If you create enough files to fill the entries between the bad entry and the lost entry, DOS will be able to find it again. To create a dummy file, type the following line at the DOS prompt and press Enter:

```
ECHO ON>TEMP01.DAT
```

This creates a 0 length file in the current directory. Keep making entries until the missing file shows up. You can then DEL all the temporary files.

Overwritten Files

This one is a "stupid human trick" that we have all done at one time or another. If you save a file with the same name as an existing file, the new file will overwrite the data of the old file. It's entirely possible that you might like to have the contents of *both* files. Despite what you might like, the only way to save the old, overwritten data is to plan ahead.

Fix: If you use the Norton ERASE PROTECT program, the old file can be recovered. If you use the DOS (or PC-Tools) UNDELETE with the SENTRY enabled, you can also recover overwritten files. You will be given the option of specifying a new name for the recovered file because the new file uses the old filename.

NOTE

Overwritten files can be recovered only if one of the delete tracking programs was previously installed.

Bad Root Directory

Here's an error that has us perplexed. No matter how hard we try to mess up the entries in the root directory, we can't get this error. But it's there in COMMAND.COM, and root directory problems can be fixed.

Fix for DOS users: Use DEBUG as a sector editor to repair the **root directory**.

Fix for PC-Tools and Norton users: A bad root directory can be fixed by Norton Disk Doctor or PC-Tools Disk Fix.

DOS Error Messages (COMMAND.COM)

COMMAND.COM contains an extensive list of error messages that can appear when you are operating from the command line. That's easy. On the dicey side, many of these errors can also pop up when a program uses a DOS function. It works this way: DOS informs the program of the error, but what the program does about the error varies from program to program. Whenever you get an error message from inside a program, consult the documentation to figure out whether the error message was generated by the program or by DOS.

Abort, Retry, Ignore, Fail?

When one of the attached hardware devices, such as the disk drive or the printer encounters an error condition, DOS generates what is known as "Critical Error." Because these problems can sometimes be fixed, DOS prints a message that details the problem and then gives you a choice on how to continue.

The `Abort, Retry, Ignore, Fail?` message follows the device error message and means that you're not getting anywhere until you make a decision about what to do next. When this message appears, DOS is waiting for your input on what to do about the problem. The problem is reported on the line above this message, so see the section on that error before answering. (See the section on Critical Errors for a full explanation of possible causes.) Choose the option by pressing the first letter (A, R, I or F). But it's wise to know just what you're choosing, for example:

```
Drive not ready, reading Drive A: Abort, Retry, Fail?
```

Abort ends the current program and returns control to COMMAND.COM.

Retry tries again. If you solved the problem (like closing the drive door), this option repeats whatever operation sensed the error.

Ignore tells whatever program developed the problem that there is no problem and to continue as though the operation was successful.

WARNING

Use Ignore carefully—it could cause loss of your data.

Fail continues the current operation, but DOS tells the program that the requested service was not successful.

Access denied

The Access denied message is displayed if you try to delete or write to a file that is read-only or try to open a subdirectory as a file. You cannot open a subdirectory as a file, but you can change a read-only attribute. To remove the read-only designation from a file, use the following command line:

```
ATTRIB -r filename.ext
```

Bad command or filename

The Bad command or filename error is an easy error message to solve. You typed something that is not a valid DOS internal command or there's no file in the current directory or path with that name and either a COM, EXE, or BAT extension.

Check your spelling and the PATH= statement to make sure the file's directory can be accessed. If you do not need to access the program from all directories, change to the directory where the file is located and try again.

 If you cannot remember where the file is located, use WHEREIS (included with this book) to find the file. If the file is missing, check the section on deleted files.

Maybe it wasn't so easy. If the program is not there, it may have been erased or the subdirectory may have been damaged. See the section on recovering erased files for more information.

WARNING

Computer viruses can cause the mysterious disappearance of programs. If you didn't erase the program, maybe a virus did.

Bad or missing command interpreter

In this case, the command interpreter is usually COMMAND.COM, but could be another program if you are not using a normal DOS setup.

If COMMAND.COM is not the same DOS version as the hidden system files, you get the Bad or missing command interpreter message. That doesn't mean COMMAND.COM is bad; rather, the file is just the wrong version. Of course, if you are booting the system from a hard disk and get this message, the computer will not start and you won't be able to make any corrections.

Fix: Boot from a DOS disk in drive A. Copy the correct version of COMMAND.COM to the root directory of C and start the computer again.

DOS also needs to locate COMMAND.COM in order to go to work. If Bad or missing command interpreter appears, DOS couldn't find COMMAND.COM. If COMMAND.COM is not in the root directory of the boot disk. You will have to edit CONFIG.SYS and AUTOEXEC.BAT to let DOS locate it.

Fix: Edit the CONFIG.SYS file to include the following line:

```
"SHELL=[d]:[\path\][filename].[ext]".
```

If you use a command interpreter other than COMMAND.COM, indicate its name on this line. If COMMAND.COM is not located in the root directory, AUTOEXEC.BAT must contain the following line:

```
"SET COMSPEC=[d:][\path\][filename][.ext]".
```

Make sure that COMMAND.COM exists in the root directory or the path indicated in the CONFIG.SYS and AUTOEXEC.BAT files. In DOS 6.0, COMMAND.COM can be in the root directory or the C:\DOS directory.

WARNING

Some computer viruses will attack COMMAND.COM only if it is in the root directory. For that reason, you might want to keep COMMAND.COM in a subdirectory where you store all your other DOS programs.

Cannot find system files

The Cannot find system files error message means that the two system files (called IBMBIO.COM and IBMDOS.COM in IBM's PC-DOS, and IO.SYS and MSDOS.SYS in Microsoft's MS-DOS) are not located in the root directory of the disk. These files are marked "hidden" and "system" and will not appear in a normal DIR search. To see the names of the hidden system files on your system, you can include the switch /a after the DIR.

Fix: Boot from a DOS disk in drive A. Use the SYS command to transfer these files to the disk. Make sure that you boot from a disk that is the same version of DOS that you have on the hard disk.

NOTE

The most common mistake is having the PC-DOS version and the MS-DOS version mixed up. The boot sector contains the name of the system files. If the disk was formatted for PC-DOS, the boot sector contains the names IBMBIO.COM and IBMDOS.COM. If you change to MS-DOS, the names of the files are IO.SYS and MSDOS.SYS, and the boot program cannot locate them.

Cannot load COMMAND, system halted

When you are finished running a program, DOS occasionally needs to reload a portion of COMMAND.COM. If the file cannot be loaded, the operating system stops. This can happen if the program you just ran did not free memory properly and DOS cannot safely load COMMAND.COM. You will probably also see the Memory allocation error message. Check with the program's manufacturer if the problem persists.

Fix: Reboot.

Data error reading/writing drive x

The error message Data error reading/writing drive x is usually caused by a hardware error from the drive. This may mean that the sector is defective and the data does not match the CRC for that sector. The message could be a one-time error or an indication that something is (seriously) physically wrong with the disk.

CAUTION

With hard disks, Data error reading/writing drive x *can be a warning of impending catastrophic failure. Backup immediately and have the hard disk serviced or replaced.*

Fix: PC-Tools Disk Fix and Norton Disk Tools can be used with floppy disks to revive the disk. Disk Fix and Norton Calibrate can be used with hard disks to attempt repair to the sector.

WARNING

Norton Disk Doctor and PC-Tools Disk Fix have options that attempt to repair any damaged sectors, but the options should be used only as stopgaps until the disk can be replaced or repaired.

Disk boot failure

Ouch. One or both of the DOS system files is damaged.

Fix: Boot from a DOS system disk and run SYS.

WARNING

There is no logical reason for the DOS system files to be damaged in the course of everyday computing. Suspect a computer virus if you see this message.

Divide overflow

The Divide overflow error is caused by a program that attempted to divide by zero. Even though most of us learned this in third grade arithmetic, programmers sometimes forget.

Fix: Reboot the computer to clear the error. If the error persists, contact the program's manufacturer.

Drive not ready error reading/writing drive x

The error message Drive not ready error reading/writing drive x is almost always caused by a disk not properly seated in the drive or by an open drive door.

Fix: Close the disk drive latch and choose the Retry option.

WARNING

If this error appears when you try to access a hard disk, it is a sign of impending doom. Turn the computer off and let it cool for several hours. Once you restart the computer, try to back up the hard disk if you have not recently done so. After you have a back up, have the drive serviced or replaced.

Error in EXE file

The message Error in EXE file means that an executable file is corrupted.

Fix: Replace the file with a new copy.

WARNING

Unless this is the first time you ran the program, this message could mean a computer virus has altered the file.

Error loading operating system

The message Error loading operating system means that an error occurred while loading the hidden DOS system files.

Fix: Reboot the computer from a DOS disk and run SYS to replace the system files.

Error writing fixed disk

The error message Error writing fixed disk usually implies physical damage to an area of the hard disk.

Fix: Back up what you can and have the disk serviced or replaced.

NOTE

Norton Disk Doctor and PC-Tools Disk Fix have options to attempt repair to any damaged sectors, but they should be used only as stopgaps until the disk can be replaced or repaired.

Error writing directory

The error message `Error writing directory` indicates possible physical damage to the disk in the area where the root directory is stored.

Fix: Copy the file off the disk and try to reformat the defective one using the UNCONDITIONAL /u switch or throw it away. Disks are cheap.

CAUTION

If the error appears on a hard disk, there may be physical damage to the sector. Back up the disk and have it replaced or repaired.

NOTE

Norton Disk Doctor and PC-Tools Disk Fix have options to attempt repair to any damaged sectors, but they should be used only as stopgaps until the disk can be replaced or repaired.

Error writing FAT

The `Error writing FAT` message and the remedies are the same as for `Error writing directory` except that the damaged sector is located in the FAT and not the root directory.

Error writing partition table

The partition table is stored on the first sector of the disk. The partition table holds data that describes how the hard disk is allocated. If you try to redefine the partitions using FDISK, you see the message Error writing partition table if there is an error writing to this sector.

Fix: Check to make sure that you have not installed any software that prevents changing the partition table. Some anti-virus programs will not allow this sector to be changed. If you do not have any such protection, the drive has a defective sector. Have the drive serviced or replaced.

File allocation table bad, drive x

When you see the message File allocation table bad, drive x, a sector of the FAT has developed a physical problem and cannot be read or written. If the problem is with a disk, you may not be able to copy the files to another disk using the DOS COPY command—but you *will* want to try.

Fix: Try using the DOS DISKCOPY command to make a mirror image of the damaged disk. Choose Ignore to any read errors during the copying. If you have trouble reading only the first copy of the FAT on the bad disk, you can copy the second FAT to the first by using a sector editor or DEBUG.

If this problem occurs on a hard disk, you should try to make a backup and have the drive serviced or replaced.

Fix: Norton Disk Doctor and PC-Tools Disk Fix have options to attempt repair to any damaged sectors, but they should be used only as stopgaps until the disk can be replaced or repaired.

File creation error

Several things can keep a file from being created. The directory is full, the disk is full, or you are trying to overwrite an existing file that has a read-only attribute.

Fix: If the root directory is full, create the file in a subdirectory. If the disk is full, delete unwanted files. If you really want to overwrite a file with the read-only attribute, remove the read-only attribute with the following command:

```
ATTRIB -r filename.ext
```

CAUTION

The File creation error *will not cause loss of data at the DOS command prompt, but if you are running a program that has stored data in memory and needs to save it to a file, do not exit the program. Try to save the file to a subdirectory or a disk before exiting. If you exit to DOS before saving the information, you could lose all your work from that session.*

File not found

When you see the File not found message, the specified file does not exist in the directory. You probably misspelled the name or included the wrong drive and directory information.

Fix: Use WHEREIS to locate the file. If the file is not found, it may have been deleted. Refer to the section on undeleting files.

General failure reading/writing drive x

The error message General failure reading/writing drive x is a non-specific error that occurs when DOS attempts to read from or write to an unformatted floppy disk. Using a high-density disk in a low-density drive (1.2M in a 360K drive) can also cause this error.

Fix: Replace the disk with one that's properly formatted.

If a hard disk has a general error, it usually indicates some physical problem with the drive mechanism or missing low-level formatting information.

Fix: The hard disk should be serviced or replaced. If the problem is in the drive mechanism, you really *must* recover the data. (See the section "When All Else Fails" and have your checkbook handy.)

If the problem is with the format information on the disk, Norton Disk Doctor and PC-Tools Disk Fix have options to attempt repair to any damaged sectors, but they should be used only as stopgaps until the disk can be replaced or repaired.

Incorrect DOS version

The DOS hidden system files and COMMAND.COM must be from the same version of DOS. Many DOS utility programs also require a particular DOS version be used.

Fix: Delete any portions of a previous DOS version after you upgrade to a newer version.

TIP

Before you upgrade to a new version of DOS, move all the DOS files to a new subdirectory. Don't forget to remove from the root directory the old COMMAND.COM.

Insert disk with \COMMAND.COM in drive x

DOS loads a portion of COMMAND.COM in the upper part of memory but allows other programs to use this memory area. When a program ends, DOS may need to reload this transient portion of COMMAND.COM. DOS looks for the file COMMAND.COM on the disk used to start the computer and complains if you have changed the disk.

Fix: Replace the disk in drive A with any disk containing COMMAND.COM. If you frequently work from disks, copy COMMAND.COM to your program disks to prevent this error in the future.

If you started the computer from the hard disk and get this message when exiting a program, you do not have COMMAND.COM in the root directory where DOS expects it to be. Check your CONFIG.SYS file for the line SHELL=.... This line describes the location of COMMAND.COM for the boot process. If COMMAND.COM is not in the root directory, you have to edit your AUTOEXEC.BAT file to include the line SET COMSPEC=... so DOS knows in which directory to search for COMMAND.COM.

Fix: Reboot and edit AUTOEXEC.BAT to add the line

```
SET COMSPEC= [d:][\path\]COMMAND.COM
```

Alternatively, you can copy COMMAND.COM to the root directory.

NOTE

DOS version 6 also will search the directory \DOS for COMMAND.COM.

Insufficient disk space

When you see the message Insufficient disk space, there are not enough free allocation units remaining on the disk to accommodate the file being written. An *allocation unit* is the least amount of space DOS uses for a file. The number of bytes per allocation unit varies, depending on the size of the disk. CHKDSK will tell you how many bytes are in each allocation unit and how many allocations units are on the disk.

Fix: Run CHKDSK to check for the possibility of lost allocation units. You may be able to find some extra space on the disk.

Another fix: Remove some files.

Yet another fix: If you are in the middle of an application and need to save your work, use a floppy to save your file until you can clear some space on your hard disk.

Invalid drive specification

If you see the Invalid drive specification message, the drive you have specified does not exist. Okay, you can see it—but for some reason, DOS can't. The drive may be disconnected, or a hard drive may have an invalid partition table. This error can also be caused by booting from a DOS 2.X floppy and trying to access a head disk formatted with DOS version 3.0 or later.

NOTE

Make sure you booted with a DOS version equal to or greater than the version that initialized the hard disk. The program BOOTINFO (included with this book) tells you which version of DOS formatted the disk.

If the hard disk partition data has been corrupted, you can attempt to repair it with Norton Disk Doctor or PC-Tools Emergency Disk. If you do not have access to these programs, you can attempt to rebuild the partition information with the tools supplied on the disk enclosed with this book. See Chapter 15 for details.

Invalid partition table

The `Invalid partition table` error, which occurs only when you boot the hard disk, means that the partition table contains incorrect information. If you boot from a floppy, you will most likely get the `Invalid drive specification` message when you try to access the hard disk.

Fix: Norton Disk Doctor and PC-Tools Emergency Disk can attempt to repair the damaged partition table.

NOTE

PC-TOOLS Disk Fix can repair the partition table only if you have previously saved the information to an emergency disk. Norton Disk Doctor can sometimes calculate the disk partition information.

Use the program, PARTINFO, supplied with this book. See Chapter 15 for details.

Invalid path, not directory, dir not empty

Wow! Three errors in one message. All appear after an RD (Remove Directory) command.

`Invalid path` means that what you typed does not match any path on the disk. Maybe you forgot to start with a backslash (\) to indicate the root directory. Maybe you misspelled the name of a subdirectory.

`Not directory` means that the final name in your path is a file and not a directory. You can't RD a file; you must DEL it.

`Dir not empty` means that there are still files or subdirectories in the directory you are trying to remove. You cannot remove a directory that still contains files or subdirectories unless you use the DELTREE command in DOS 6. Check for hidden files in the directory by using the DIR /a command in DOS version 5.0 or later. You can't remove a directory if it contains hidden or read-only files.

Fix: Use the ATTRIB command to change hidden and read-only attributes so the files can be deleted before you attempt to remove a subdirectory. To remove the Read-Only attribute, enter the following command:

```
ATTRIB -r *.*
```

To remove the Hidden attribute, enter this line:

```
ATTRIB -h *.*
```

To prevent carpal tunnel syndrome from too much typing and remove both the Read-Only and Hidden attributes at the same time, enter the following:

```
ATTRIB -h -r *.*
```

If a file is marked with the System attribute, use the following line:

```
ATTRIB -s *.*
```

CAUTION

Beware of files that contain illegal DOS characters. For example, you cannot enter a space from the command line, but a file can be created with a space in the name. FILE 1.DAT (with a space between E and 1) is a legal filename, but an illegal name on the DOS command line. To delete it, you will have to type DEL FILE?1.DAT.

Memory allocation error

The Memory allocation error message tells you that a program has overwritten the DOS **memory control block information**.

Fix: Your only recourse is to reboot the system. Contact the manufacturer of the offending program.

Missing operating system

The display of the Missing operating system error message means that the DOS **Boot Record** of the hard disk is missing or is corrupted.

Fix: Boot with a DOS disk, and run SYS to restore the Boot Record to the hard disk.

WARNING

There is no good reason for the Boot Record to become corrupted. Check for a computer virus.

Non-DOS disk error reading/writing drive x

The message Non-DOS disk error reading/writing drive x means the DOS media descriptor byte in the FAT is invalid. The first byte of the FAT indicates the type of disk. If this byte is corrupt, it could mean that the entire FAT is corrupt also.

Fix: Norton Disk Doctor and PC-Tools Disk Fix can correct this byte.

Another fix—the hard way: DEBUG can correct the problem. Run DEBUG, and at the dash (-) prompt, type

```
L100 (x) 1 1
```

In this line, (x) is the drive number (A=0, B=1, C=2, etc). Then edit the media descriptor byte by entering the following:

```
e 100
```

The current byte is at location 100. Just enter the correct byte from the following table:

160K disk	FE
320K disk	FF
180K disk	FC
360K disk	FD
1.2M disk	F9
720K disk	F9
1.44M disk	F0
Fixed Disk	F8

Once the media descriptor byte is changed in memory, write the sector back to the disk by entering the following line:

```
W 100 (x) 1 1
```

Here, (x) is the same as used in the L command. Now you can quit DEBUG by entering Q.

Non-system disk or disk error

The Non-system disk or disk error message tells you that either the DOS system files are missing or there was an error in reading the system files from the boot disk.

Fix: With a floppy error, replace the disk and try again. If the error occurred while trying to boot from a hard disk, boot from a DOS floppy and copy the hidden system file to the hard disk by using the SYS command.

Not ready error reading/writing drive x

See the section "Drive not ready error reading/writing drive x".

No room for system on destination disk

To make a bootable disk, DOS must place the system files in the first two entries in the root directory. In addition, in versions of DOS prior to DOS 5.0, there must be enough allocation units for all of IBMBIO.COM (IO.SYS) and the first allocation unit of IBMDOS.COM

(MSDOS.SYS) at the very beginning of the data area. If these two conditions are not met, DOS cannot place the system files on the disk. In DOS version 5.0 and later, you will see this message only if there is not enough space on the disk for the system files.

Fix: To make room for these files, copy all files off the disk and delete them. Run SYS and then copy the needed files back to the disk.

NOTE

Some versions of DOS require that the first two root directory entries be clear and not just available. In this case, it is best to copy all files off the disk and FORMAT using the /s switch to transfer the system files following the format. The files can then be copied back to the disk.

Path not found

You see the Path not found error most likely when you entered a spelling error or forgot to specify the backslash (\) root directory in the path specification. If the subdirectory is truly missing, see "Undeleting Subdirectories."

Read fault error reading drive x

When the Read fault error reading drive x message appears, for some reason DOS is unable to read from the disk. This could indicate mechanical failure of the head-positioning mechanism or missing format information.

Fix for floppy problems: If this error occurs with a floppy disk, try another disk and see whether the error persists.

TIP

A good way to test the disk is to use an almost full disk and enter COPY *.* NUL. This forces DOS to read all the files on the disk. If the error persists on many disks, some sort or mechanical failure is indicated. If other disks do not incur the error, it may mean that format information is lost from the disk. Copy all the files you can to another disk and either discard or reformat the damaged disk.

Fix for hard disk problems: If this error occurs with a hard disk, it may mean mechanical or media failure. Either way, back up all the data you can and have the drive serviced or replaced.

NOTE

Norton Disk Doctor and PC-Tools Disk Fix have options that attempt to repair any damaged sectors, but they should be used only as stopgaps until the disk can be replaced or repaired.

Sector not found error reading/writing drive x

See "Read fault error" earlier in this chapter.

Seek error reading/writing drive x

See "Read fault error" earlier in this chapter.

Top level process aborted, cannot continue

This error will not occur if you use COMMAND.COM as your DOS shell. However if you run another program such as DEBUG in the DOS shell and exit that program, you get this message:

```
Fix: reboot.
```

Write protect error writing drive x

The Write protect error writing drive x means that the disk you are using is write protected.

Fix: Remove the write-protect tab or slide the write-protect switch; then reinsert the disk and choose Retry.

WARNING

Do not insert another disk into the drive and choose Retry. If DOS does not recognize the disk change, the FAT and directory information in memory will be written to the wrong disk. Newer versions of DOS check for this possibility, but it's better to be safe than sorry.

Some software disk or virus protection schemes programs can write protect all or a portion of the hard disk. Otherwise, you should always be able to write to a hard disk.

Fix: Disable the hard disk write protection software.

Let's Get Technical

For the wonks in the crowd, this is what you've been waiting for. For wonks-to-be, this is what you *really* need to attain full wonk status. Here, at last, you will learn how to tinker with the inner soul of your PC. Some of the information in this chapter was covered briefly in the beginning chapters which you may have skipped as being too elementary. Here it is repeated and expanded upon.

WARNING LABEL

It seems that all products now come with warning labels. It's easy to see why a rotary lawn mower has to warn the user that the blades spinning at high speed designed to break off the tough cellulose fibers of lawn grasses and eject them at high velocity into a catch bag might do the same with toes. Although one suspects that the user who has to be told this fact may not have sufficient brain capacity to read or heed the warning label.

Now there's even a warning on the back of football helmets used by the NFL. Unfortunately the resolution of most television sets is not fine enough to read the actual warning message, the word

"WARNING" is clearly visible when the TV cameraman zooms in for a dramatic shot of the back of someone's head. What could that warning possibly be? "Carrying an inflated leather spheroid while wearing this piece of plastic can attract a crowd of eleven 250 pound behemoths who are paid to do you bodily harm. The manufacturer accepts no responsibility for torn or broken limbs. Warranty void if point spread not covered."

OK. Here's what it actually says:

WARNING
Do not strike an opponent with any part of this helmet or face mask. This is a violation of football rules and may cause you to suffer brain or neck injury, including paralysis or death. Severe brain or neck injury may also occur accidently while playing football.
NO HELMET CAN PREVENT ALL SUCH INJURY.
USE THIS HELMET AT YOUR OWN RISK.

It's almost enough to scare a linebacker.

With this trend toward all inclusive warning labels, here is the warning label for the data recovery routines discussed in this section.

WARNING
Improper use of the recovery techniques discussed in this book could cause the permanent loss of all data. Data loss could also occur accidently while operating a personal computer.
NO RECOVERY TECHNIQUE CAN PREVENT ALL SUCH LOSS.
USE THESE ROUTINES AT YOUR OWN RISK.

Pocket Protectors Optional

This is the "WHEN ALL ELSE FAILS" section for "do-it-yourselfers." If you have a passing knowledge of programming and want to try the recovery techniques yourself, this section will guide you through the intricacies of DOS. First, ways to use DOS CHKDSK to diagnose and repair problems. Next, a familiarization with the program DEBUG and an explanation of the hexadecimal number system which is used with DEBUG.

Diagnosis and Repair with CHKDSK

Since the beginning, Microsoft has included the utility Check Disk with every release of the operating system. Check Disk is called CHKDSK.COM in DOS versions through 5, although the DOS 5.0 CHKDSK.COM is actually in EXE format. DOS 6 uses the CHKDSK.EXE filename. This program is designed to find and, if possible, correct any errors in the directory structure and *File Allocation Table* (FAT). Normal DOS operations rarely cause problems with the FAT, but not all programs follow normal DOS operations. Of course there is always the possibility of "stupid human tricks" mucking up the directory and FAT.

Here is the normal CHKDSK screen of the distribution diskette of DOS version 3.3 in drive A.

```
A:>chkdsk

 724480 bytes total disk space
  52736 bytes in 3 hidden files
 543232 bytes in 50 user files
 128512 bytes available on disk

 654336 bytes total memory
 599504 bytes free
```

DOS version 6.0 CHKDSK of the same diskette shows a slightly different message.

```
C:>chkdsk a:

 724480 bytes total disk space
  52736 bytes in 3 hidden files
 543232 bytes in 50 user files
 128512 bytes available on disk

    512 bytes in each allocation unit
   1415 total allocation units on disk
    215 available allocation units on disk

 655360 total bytes memory
 562480 bytes free
```

The allocation unit report was added to DOS version 5, although DOS has always allocated disk space in terms of allocation units, also called clusters. A cluster is just a series of consecutive sectors on the disk. The number of sectors per cluster is always a power of 2 and can be 1, 2, 4 or 8 sectors long. 1.44 MB diskettes allocate 1 sector per cluster, while 720 kb diskettes have 2 sectors per cluster. This is not a hard and fast rule. Notice that the DOS 3.3 distribution diskette illustrated above bends the rule and allocates space in terms of 1 sector per cluster (512 bytes). The typical hard disk of today has 4 sectors per cluster although many old XT models use 8 sectors per cluster.

The *File Allocation Table* (FAT) is a section of the disk beginning with a known sector (usually sector 1) that DOS uses to keep track of which files use which clusters on the disk. Ever since DOS version 1, two copies of the FAT are stored for each disk although DOS never uses the second copy. No matter how many sectors comprise a cluster, there is one entry in the FAT for each of the clusters on the disk. In order to keep track of which clusters a file uses, the file's directory entry points to the FAT entry of the first cluster occupied by that file. Each FAT entry contains the FAT entry of the next cluster used by the file with the last cluster marked by a -1 (end of file marker). This forms a chain of FAT entries from directory to end of file, each entry indicating the next. For example the file README.TXT has a directory entry which contains the file name, extension, attribute (read only, hidden, etc), date, time, size and first cluster number. That cluster number is an index into the FAT. If the first cluster is 2, then FAT entry number 2 contains the number of the next cluster occupied by the file or the end of file marker. Each file should have a valid chain of unique FAT entries from the first cluster to the end of file marker.

Unused clusters are marked in the FAT with a zero to indicate that this cluster can be allocated when a new file is created or an existing file needs more space. Bad sectors on the disk are also marked in the FAT with a special number so that DOS will not allocate that portion of the disk to a file.

Normally the FAT chain is intact. Each directory entry points to a unique FAT entry and each FAT entry follows a logical chain to the end of file marker. No FAT entry should be part of more than one chain, and every FAT entry not marked as available or bad should be part of a valid chain. Occasionally errors do appear in the FAT chains. Two directory entries may point to the same FAT chain, a FAT chain may loop back on itself so that the end of file marker is never reached, or a chain of entries may exist in the FAT with no directory entry pointing to it.

Another important aspect of the FAT chain is that the size of the file as indicated in the directory must match the number of clusters allocated in the FAT. CHKDSK detects all of these errors and corrects some of them by changing the directory entry to match the FAT. CHKDSK does not correct the FAT, even if there are errors, nor does it compare the two copies of the FAT. All problems are reported on the basis of the information in the first copy of the FAT.

Using CHKDSK to Correct Errors

Keep in mind that CHKDSK is designed to find and correct errors in the File Allocation Table and directory. It is not intended to be a data recovery tool.

CAUTION

In fact, CHKDSK can sometimes make your data disappear.

For this reason, CHKDSK only reports the condition of the disk and does not repair the directory unless you include the /F (Fix) switch on the command line. To save data that might be lost by fixing the directory entries, always run CHKDSK without the /F switch first and then understand the problem before fixing it.

Lost Clusters (Allocation Units)

Sometimes there is a chain of clusters in the FAT but no directory entry that points to this chain. This error can be caused by turning off the power or rebooting between the time when DOS updates the FAT and the time it updates the directory. There is probably a 0 byte file in a directory.

```
Volume Serial Number is 3219-10D9
Errors found, F parameter not specified
Corrections will not be written to disk

   31 lost allocation units found in 1 chains.
     15872 bytes disk space would be freed

1457664 bytes total disk space
 130560 bytes in 3 hidden files
  62464 bytes in 3 user files
1248768 bytes available on disk

    512 bytes in each allocation unit
   2847 total allocation units on disk
   2439 available allocation units

655360 total bytes memory
562480 bytes free
```

In this example, CHKDSK reports that one file chain exists without a valid directory entry. CHKDSK only reports the error and does not correct it because the /F switch was not used.

To correct the problem, run CHKDSK again with the /F parameter on the command line. You get a choice to either create a directory entry for the lost file chain, or free the space in the FAT, in effect, delete the file. If you choose to create a directory entry, CHKDSK makes a file named FILE0000.CHK in the root directory of the disk. If more than one lost chain is found, CHKDSK makes multiple entries in the root directory using the names FILE0001.CHK, FILE0002.CHK etc.

```
C:\>chkdsk a: /f
Volume Serial Number is 3219-10D9

   31 lost allocation units found in 1 chain.
Convert lost chains to files (Y/N)?
```

Choose "Y" and the directory shows the new file.

```
C:\>dir a:

 Volume in drive A has no label
 Volume Serial Number is 3219-10D9
```

```
Directory of A:\

COMMAND    COM          52841 01-28-93     6:00a
ND         DAT           1536 02-26-93     5:09p
BF         EXE           7208 02-16-93     8:19p
FILE0000 CHK            15872 02-27-93    10:06a
        4 file(s)             77457 bytes
                            1248768 bytes free
```

Was the file chain worth saving? What was it supposed to be? View the contents of the file with the "TYPE" command piped through "MORE".

```
C:\>type a:file0000.chk¦more

È¸¶Qè µ"Â.ä.HYuⵎÁ=P-P+¿ÄÿÇ&q X£. - P-+¿Äÿ ÷qÇ-
XtÇÃÇDDœ÷-Çt°XÎœ÷¬Î÷¬ÎΩ'Ô=P-P+¿ÄÿÇ&q X£. -TP-+¿Äÿ÷qÇ-
XtÇÃDDœ÷-t°XÎœÇ¸u¥ÇœSPRªŒ/.èÇ¸t¥Õ¶$0u¥)Î<0u¥ÉÎ¥ZÎ¥Õ¶Z÷-Ç¥Ét¥
[è\ɵ╨╨╨╨╨╨╨╨╨╨╨╨╨╨╨╨╨WW╔┒Å&~∅à tⅣÉ3Ä'&áP'&áR'&áⓊ8á'Ùⅇ─π
¸≤ñ  ·&«∅î»-&ú2√Äÿ∫P ¶¥%Õ!X∫IP ¥%Õ!X.∆'∫‹4RË∅.∆─∆ É[XZ^_
√     É@ The IBM Personal Computer Mode command Version 3.30
(C)Copyright IBM Corp 1987 Licensed Material - Program Prop-
erty of IBM Authors - Kerry Sayers, Ed Kiser, Ron Heiney and
Mel
HäⅡⅇⅉⅽⅆⅇⅆⅉⅉ╨┰┰┰┰┰╨╨        d╓╢╖╖╜╓╚╚╙╟╟╟╟╟╚╙╚╙╙┌╓╓╟╟┌┰┰╓╚╚╚╚╚┌/
STAT₊₊₊₊─ More ─
```

If you can figure out what file it is, you can rename FILE0000.CHK or copy it to the correct subdirectory. If you don't know what it is, delete it.

Lost chains are the most common problem reported by CHKDSK and are usually caused by "stupid human tricks." If you are curious, you can check the section which describes the file creation process in Chapter 2. Sometimes a poorly written program can cause lost chains. The first edition of the IBM Pascal Compiler wrote several temporary files to the disk when compiling a program, but if it encountered a syntax error in the source code, it would stop and return to the DOS prompt without freeing the FAT space used by the temporary files. Many Pascal programmers found themselves with a full disk but no files listed in the directory! The only cure was to run CHKDSK every time the Pascal Compiler was used. Very few programs have this particular bug, but orphaned clusters still occur. Turning the power off while DOS is writing a file to the disk, or rebooting to exit a program which has open files is a good way to end up with lost clusters on the disk.

Cross-Linked Files (Directory Entry)

Sometimes two directory entries point to the same first allocation unit. This is known as cross-linked files. CHKDSK cannot correct cross-linked files. In the example shown below, the directory entry of file ND.DAT was intentionally altered to point to the allocation chain used by the file BF.EXE. DOS does not allow this to happen in normal operation, but you could UNDELETE a file whose original space has been overwritten by another file.

```
C:\>chkdsk a:

Volume Serial Number is 3219-10D9
Errors found, F parameter not specified
Corrections will not be written to disk

A:\ND.DAT
    Allocation error, size adjusted
    3 lost allocation units found in 1 chains.
        1536 bytes disk space would be freed

A:\ND.DAT
    Is cross-linked on allocation unit 395
A:\BF.EXE
    Is cross-linked on allocation unit 395

    1457664 bytes total disk space
     130560 bytes in 3 hidden files
      61440 bytes in 4 user files
    1264128 bytes available on disk

        512 bytes in each allocation unit
       2847 total allocation units on disk
       2469 available allocation units on disk
```

```
655360 total bytes memory
562480 bytes free
```

CHKDSK did not make any corrections since the /F parameter was not entered on the command line. Here is what CHKDSK found. The file ND.DAT size is reported as 1536 bytes yet it is allocated 15 allocation units of 512 bytes for a total of 7680 bytes. Three clusters are lost in one chain for a total of 1536 bytes. (These are the clusters that were allocated to ND.DAT.) CHKDSK reports the cross-linking of two files because the directory entry for ND.DAT and BF.EXE both point to the same cluster.

To make corrections to the directory entry for ND.DAT run CHKDSK with the /F parameter. CHKDSK adjusts the size of ND.DAT to make it agree with the number of clusters in its allocation chain. In this case CHKDSK changes the file size to 7680 bytes since the file uses 15 clusters. You also have the option to save the lost clusters to FILE0000.CHK. CHKDSK does not repair the crossed-linking of the files ND.DAT and BF.EXE. Be careful. You can lose data trying to repair cross-linked files.

If you have another copy of the two cross-linked files, repair is simple. Delete both files and then copy the backups to the disk. If you do not have a backup, you may still be able to restore the missing pieces, but you must be careful.

When two files are cross-linked, only one of them is correct. The other file contains all or part of another file. Sometimes you can tell instantly which file is correct and which is corrupt. In the example, ND.DAT is obviously corrupt since the size needed adjusting. But both files share the same FAT entries. If you attempt to delete either of the files, DOS marks the FAT entries as available. The directory entry of the deleted file is eliminated, but the other directory entry points to a cluster that is marked available. This produces another CHKDSK error, "Invalid initial cluster", and CHKDSK changes the file size to 0. Now the data from both files is lost! Thank you, CHKDSK.

Here's how to save at least the good file. Before deleting either of the cross-linked files, COPY both files to other names. This creates two new chains in the FAT which are not cross-linked although the data in both chains is the same. Now delete both original files.

```
C:\>COPY a:nd.dat a:temp1.dat
     1 file(s) copied

C:\>COPY a:bf.exe a:temp2.exe
     1 files(s) copied

C:\>DEL a:nd.dat

C:\>DEL a:bf.exe
```

CHKDSK reports no errors. You are left with the choice of what to do with the two temporary files and the CHKDSK file FILE0000.CHK. In the example, FILE0000.CHK contains the data from the original ND.DAT and TEMP2.EXE is the original BF.EXE. This is not quite so obvious in the field where there are hundreds of files on a disk. Trying to decide which file is valid may be difficult. In some cases it could be dangerous. Consider the reverse case of the example where the directory entry for BF.EXE points to the file ND.DAT. The EXE extension indicates to DOS that the file contains executable program instructions. Files with a .DAT extension are not program code. If the files were cross-linked, and you typed "BF" on the command line, the data contained in the file ND.DAT would be read into memory and executed as if it were program instructions. In the best possible case the computer just freezes and you reboot. The worst case is damage to the file system.

WARNING

Never give a file an extension of EXE or COM unless your are certain that it is a legitimate program file.

Cross-Linked Files (FAT Entry)

A very rare error is the cross-linking of files within the File Allocation Table. If the computer loses power and only a portion of the FAT sector is written, you might get a cross-link. The more likely cause of this error is the "stupid human trick" of intentionally changing the FAT with a sector editor. In the next example, two files were intentionally cross-linked by making the last FAT entry of README.TXT point to the last cluster of MOVE.EXE.

```
A:\>DIR

 Volume in drive A has no label
 Volume Serial Number is 3468-13E4
 Directory of A:\
MOVE      EXE      50197 12-23-92   6:00a
README    TXT      76052 12-23-92   6:00a
         2 file(s)       126249 bytes
                        1330176 bytes free

A:\>CHKDSK

Volume Serial Number is 3468-13E4
A:\MOVE.EXE
   Is cross-linked on allocation unit 100
A:\README.TXT
   Is cross-linked on allocation unit 100

   1457664 bytes total disk space
    126976 bytes in 2 user files
   1330688 bytes available on disk

       512 bytes in each allocation unit
      2847 total allocation units on disk
      2599 available allocation units on disk

    655360 total bytes memory
    562480 bytes free
```

This time there are no lost clusters, because there is no size discrepancy. Both files have the correct number of clusters in the FAT chain. CHKDSK does not repair the FAT chain to remove the cross-linking. One of the files contains one or more wrong clusters, but which one? Although not a foolproof method, you could run CHKDSK again with the *.* parameter to get a report on fragmentation. CHKDSK reports the name of any files which do not occupy a continuous block of clusters.

```
A:\>CHKDSK *.*

Volume Serial Number is 3468-13E4
A:\MOVE.EXE
    Is cross-linked on allocation unit 100
A:\README.TXT
    Is cross-linked on allocation unit 100

    1457664 bytes total disk space
     126976 bytes in 2 user files
    1330688 bytes available on disk

        512 bytes in each allocation unit
       2847 total allocation units on disk
       2599 available allocation units on disk

     655360 total bytes memory
     562480 bytes free


A:\README.TXT Contains 2 non-contiguous blocks
```

Since MOVE.EXE is contiguous and README.TXT is not, chances are that README.TXT is the file which contains the allocation error. To repair the damage, copy both files to other filenames.

```
A:\>COPY move.exe move.tmp
    1 file(s) copied

A:\>COPY readme.txt readme.tmp
    1 file(s) copied
```

Now delete both README.TXT and MOVE.EXE and rename the temporary files back to the original names. Be sure to copy both files before deleting either one since the common FAT entries will be marked as available as soon as one file is deleted. Since the fouled up file is a text file (hence the TXT extension), you can use a text editor to clean out any extraneous material developed during the cross-link. If the cross-link had been the other way, that is MOVE.EXE pointed to clusters occupied by README.TXT, you should DELETE the executable file since it probably contains corrupt data.

Allocation error (size adjusted)

A discrepancy between the file size as stored in the directory entry and the number of clusters allocated in the file allocation chain causes CHKDSK to report an allocation error. This error is the inverse of the lost clusters error. DOS was interrupted between updating the FAT and updating the directory, but this time the file was shortened. In the next example, the FAT was deliberately altered to make the file README.TXT one cluster shorter than the file size indicates.

```
A:\>DIR

Volume in drive A has no label
Volume Serial Number is 3468-13E4
Directory of A:\
MOVE     EXE     50197 12-23-92   6:00a
README   TXT     76052 12-23-92   6:00a
        2 file(s)      126249 bytes
                      1331200 bytes free
```

README.TXT should occupy 149 clusters, but the FAT chain is only 148 clusters long. CHKDSK reports:

```
A:\>CHKDSK

Volume Serial Number is 3468-13E4
Errors found, F parameter not specified
Corrections will not be written to disk


A:\README.TXT
   Allocation error, size adjusted

   1457664 bytes total disk space
    126464 bytes in 2 user files
   1330688 bytes available on disk

       512 bytes in each allocation unit
      2847 total allocation units on disk
      2600 available allocation units on disk

    655360 total bytes memory
    562480 bytes free
```

In the example, running CHKDSK with the /F parameter truncates the directory length to match the allocation length, 75776 bytes (148 clusters * 512 bytes per cluster).

Allocation size errors are rarely caused by DOS with executable files (EXE and COM) since these files are usually never written, only read. Data files can become corrupt by rebooting between the time DOS writes the FAT to the disk and the time the directory is written to disk. Since the FAT sectors and directory sectors are written sequentially there is a small window of opportunity for the "stupid human trick" of interrupting this process by rebooting or turning the power off. But the odds of hitting just the right moment are less than winning the Irish Sweepstakes. More than likely the cause of allocation problems is someone deliberately manipulating the directory entry or the FAT with a sector editor, or a computer virus.

Computer viruses are increasingly becoming the culprit in size allocation errors where EXE and COM files are concerned. Many viruses attempt to hide from the user by adjusting the size reported when you type DIR to subtract the length of the virus addition to the file. Here's what can happen: the virus adds 1024 bytes (2 clusters on a diskette) to the length of the file then hides in memory and intercepts any attempt to read the length of the file by DOS. When the virus sees a request for the file length, it subtracts 1024 bytes and returns that value. CHKDSK then checks this value against the number of clusters allocated to the file and finds a mismatch of 2 clusters. If the /F parameter is specified, CHKDSK adds 1024 bytes to the file size recorded in the directory entry. In effect, CHKDSK adds *another* 1024 bytes to the file size further corrupting the directory entry.

WARNING

Allocation size errors in EXE and COM files may be an indication that a computer virus is lurking in the system.

Invalid subdirectory entry

What is an invalid subdirectory? Glad you asked. Subdirectories are stored just like data and program files with a directory entry and a FAT chain. The difference is indicated by the attribute byte in the directory entry itself. If the directory entry attribute of a file such as README.TXT is changed to indicate that it is a subdirectory, DOS treats it as such. You can even Change Directory (CD) to a bogus subdirectory and type "DIR." What you see on the screen depends on the contents of README.TXT, but it sure won't look like a normal directory listing to you. Nor will it to CHKDSK.

```
A:\>CHKDSK

Volume Serial Number is 3468-13E4
Errors found, F parameter not specified
Corrections will not be written to disk

A:\README.TXT
    Invalid subdirectory entry

    1457664 bytes total disk space
      76288 bytes in 1 directories
    1381376 bytes available on disk
        512 bytes in each allocation unit
       2847 total allocation units on disk
       2698 available allocation units on disk


     655360 total bytes memory
     562480 bytes free
```

Including the /F parameter and CHKDSK gives you the option to convert the invalid subdirectory to a file.

```
A:\>CHKDSK

Volume Serial Number is 3468-13E4

A:\README.TXT
    Invalid subdirectory entry
Convert directory to file (Y/N)?y

    1457664 bytes total disk space
      76288 bytes in 1 directories
    1381376 bytes available on disk
        512 bytes in each allocation unit
```

```
2847 total allocation units on disk
2698 available allocation units on disk

655360 total bytes memory
562480 bytes free
```

CHKDSK converts README.TXT to a file by changing the attribute byte in the directory entry. The next time CHKDSK is run, the report will reflect the change.

How does it know? Another good question. Glad you asked. Valid subdirectories have two special entries. The first entry is the subdirectory itself with the filename '.' (Dot). The second entry is the parent directory and uses the file name '..' (Double Dot). You see these special names everytime you "DIR" anything except the root directory. If these entries are not valid, the CHKDSK gives you the option of converting the subdirectory to a file, or fixing these two entries. How it handles the error depends on the type of error. If either of these two special entries contains an invalid starting cluster number or the file name begins with the "deleted" mark (E5 hex), CHKDSK corrects the entries. A file name in either of these two entries that does not begin with Dot triggers the option to convert the subdirectory to a file.

If the Dot or Double Dot entries are corrupted but the rest of the subdirectory is valid, you have a problem. After the initial entries are deemed to be invalid, CHKDSK considers the other entries in that sub-directory to be lost allocation units. Your only option with CHKDSK is to convert the subdirectory to a file and save the lost allocation chains to FILE0000.CHK etc. Here's an example where the Dot entry was changed to "FAKEDIR". This is the "DIR":

```
A:>dir \TESTDIR

 Volume in drive A has no label
 Volume Serial Number is 0C3E-12ED
 Directory of A:\TESTDIR

FAKEDIR      <DIR>       02-28-93  11:36a
..           <DIR>       02-28-93  11:36a
README   TXT    76052 12-23-92   6:00a
        3 file(s)         76052 bytes
                        1380864 bytes free
```

Here is how CHKDSK reports on the disk:

```
A:\>CHKDSK

Volume Serial Number is 0C3E-12ED
Errors found, F parameter not specified
Corrections will not be written to disk

A:\TESTDIR
   Invalid subdirectory entry

   149 lost allocation units found in 1 chains.
    76288 bytes disk space would be freed

 1457664 bytes total disk space
     512 bytes in 1 directories
 1380864 bytes available on disk

     512 bytes in each allocation unit
    2847 total allocation units on disk
    2697 available allocation units on disk

  655360 total bytes memory
  562480 bytes free
```

This looks simple enough. Convert the subdirectory to a file, save the lost chain and rename FILE0000.CHK to README.TXT. But in the real world the subdirectory may contain many files. The WINDOWS subdirectory and all its subdirectories may contain over 300 files. Think of renaming that many files! Fortunately there is a better way.

You can copy the files from the corrupt subdirectory to another directory, and then delete them from the corrupted subdirectory. Run CHKDSK, convert the subdirectory to a file, and delete it. With DOS 6, use the "MOVE" command to move the files to another directory saving the space used by copying all the files.

Another solution to this particular problem is to use a sector editor like Norton Utilities DISK EDIT or PC-Tools DE to change the first entry back to the correct file name. This instantly restores the subdirectory and eliminates the need for CHKDSK repairs.

Using DEBUG.COM (DEBUG.EXE)

When computers were still in their infancy following the end of the Second World War, they were built with vacuum tube and relays instead of the "chips" we now associate with all types of electronic gadgets. The computer at Harvard University suddenly ceased operations and the boys in the white lab coats began to search for the cause of the mishap. After an exhaustive test of the circuitry, they found a moth wedged between the contacts of a relay. Upon removing this pesky insect, the computer once again resumed normal operations. One of the "boys", Grace Hopper (the inventor of COBOL), dubbed this problem a "BUG", and removed the moth to the Naval Computing Center in Virginia where it rests in peace, if not pieces, to this day. Got a problem with your computer? Suspect a bug.

Many of the recovery techniques in this section rely on the DOS program DEBUG.COM. This utility comes with all versions of DOS so it is readily available to every user. If you do not have a diskette version of DEBUG.COM, take a few seconds to copy it to a diskette. In case something goes wrong with the hard disk, you will need to have this program available. DOS version 6 calls this program DEBUG.EXE.

The documentation that comes with DOS 5 gives a full explanation of all the DEBUG commands. Before DOS 5, the documentation is, to say the least, somewhat sketchy. This section gives you an idea as to what DEBUG can do with the emphasis on the techniques needed to perform the recoveries outlined in this book. For a full explanation, refer to the DEBUG section in the DOS manual.

You begin DEBUG.COM just like any other program by typing its name (without the file extension) on the command line and pressing <Enter>. Unlike most programs, DEBUG has no opening message, only the DEBUG prompt which is the hyphen character "-".

To display the commands accepted by DEBUG enter a question mark at the prompt.

```
-?
assemble        A [address]
compare         C range address
dump (display)  D [range]
```

```
enter (edit)    E address [list]
fill            F range list
go              G [=address] [addresses]
hex             H value1 value2
input           I port
load            L [address] [drive] [firstsector] [number]
move            M range address
name            N [pathname] [arglist]
output          O port byte
proceed         P [=address] [number]
quit            Q
register        R [register]
search          S range list
trace           T [=address] [value]
unassemble      U [range]
write           W [address] [drive] [firstsector][number]
allocate expanded memory       XA [#pages]
deallocate expanded memory     XD [handle]
map expanded memory pages      XM [Lpage] [Ppage] [handle]
display expanded memory status XS
```

Most DEBUG commands are only one letter (upper and lower case are accepted) and need one or more parameters. If the parameter is shown in square brackets, it is optional. If the optional parameter is not entered, DEBUG uses a default which depends on the command.

Parameters:

➤ address: This can be either SEGMENT:OFFSET or just OFFSET. If only the offset is given, the segment value of the appropriate segment register is used.

➤ range: A range of memory needs two values and can be expressed in two ways. The beginning address can be expressed as either SEGMENT:OFFSET or just OFFSET. If just the offset is given the segment value is taken from one of the segment registers. The second value in RANGE is the ending address or length. As an ending address, just the OFFSET is needed since the SEGMENT is the same as with the starting address. If length is desired, use "L" (upper or lower case) before the number of bytes desired. For example:

```
"1234:0 L200" is 200 hex bytes from address 1234:0.
"1234:0 200" is Segment 1234 from offset 0 to offset 200.
```

➤ list: A list of byte values in hex or ASCII code delineated by single quotes. Byte values are 2 two hex digits ("3f 4c 01 00") and are separated by a space.

➤ drive: The logical drive number not letter. 0=drive A:, 1=drive B: etc.

➤ register: CPU register name. DEBUG does not support 32 bit register names of the 386 or 486 but does support 16 bit register names.

8 or 16 bit general purpose registers

AX (AH/AL)	Accumulator
BX (BH/BL)	Base
CX (CH/CL)	Count
DX (DH/DL)	Data

16 bit Index Registers

DI	Destination Index
SI	Source Index
BP	Base Pointer
SP	Stack Pointer
IP	Instruction Pointer

16 bit Segment Registers

ES	Extra Segment
DS	Data Segment
CS	Code Segment
SS	Stack Segment

All numbers in DEBUG are expressed in hexadecimal notation. If you enter a decimal number, the hexidecimal equivalent is assumed. For instance if you enter 10, it is assumed to be 10 (hex) or 16 decimal. If you mean to enter 10 decimal, you will have to use the hex equivalent which is 0A. Read the next section on hexadecimal numbering if you have any doubts.

STUPID MATH TRICKS (Hex on you)

Douglas Adams suggested in one of the five books of the "Hitchhikers Guide to the Galaxy" trilogy that it was really the porpoises who ruled the earth and not man. After all, they just swim around in a tank, jump up in the air like Micheal Jordan and get fed a lot of fish. Humans, on the other hand toil from dawn 'till dusk (at least during a Republican administration) and get pictures of dead Presidents for their troubles. Unless, of course, we can jump in the air like Michael Jordan. In which case we get a lot of dead Presidents' pictures for 48 minutes a night, 80 nights a year.

The porpoises have never had a President. For that matter the porpoises have never even had an election which means there is little work for porpoise pollsters or porpoise tax collectors. For this reason, porpoises have never had to deal with much arithmetic. They kept it rather simple; only two numbers, 1 and 0. Add 1 to 0 and get 1. Add 1 to 1 and get 10. No need to bother with any other numbers when you don't have fingers.

Humans not only have Presidents (alive and dead) but also elections, taxes, pollsters and ten fingers. We get to deal with 10 numbers from 0 to 9 so we can figure out our taxes and how the Electoral College works. At first humans had no zero, only I, V, X, L, C, D, and M. Imagine math class in Ms. Mammeata's Latin school (Latin was easy then). Little Caesar could not subtract X from X. No wonder he started making two Pizzas for the price of one instead of conquering the known world. It was probably during the Spanish Inquisition that the zero was added to the number system. Prisoners were told to divide by zero or be burned at the stake. Oh what a day for an *auto de fe*! What form of torture would come next? Trigonomic functions? Calculus? (Calculus was devised by a Frenchman...that says it all.) And who invented the circle? Some demented monk who spent too much time in the vineyard? If you're going to have a number system, at least come up with one where the ratio of the circumference to the diameter is a rational number and not a Greek letter.

Fortunately the number system computers use is the one invented by the real masters of the earth, the porpoises. The computer "knows" only 2 numbers, 1 and 0. Each succeeding digit is the next power of two as the chart below shows.

1	2^0	=	1
10	2^1	=	2
100	2^2	=	4
1000	2^3	=	8
10000	2^4	=	16
100000	2^5	=	32
1000000	2^6	=	64
10000000	2^7	=	128

Math turns out to be really simple, which is why schools of porpoises always seem to be at recess playing.

Addition:

```
1+0=01      One plus zero equals one.
1+1=10      One plus one equals zero carry the one.
```

Subtraction:

```
1-0=1       One take away zero is one.
1-1=0       One take away one is zero.
```

Multiplication:

```
1x0=0       One times zero equals zero.
1x1=1       One times one equals one.
```

Division:

```
1/1=1       One divided by one equals one.
0/1=0       Zero divided by one equals zero.
```

At this point the porpoises got bored with math and gave up before defining what 1/0 would be.

When IBM saw the simplicity of the number system devised by the porpoises they adapted it for use in the computer. Unfortunatly there were now humans involved and they tried to make it more complicated.

IBM saw a group of 8 binary digits (bits) and called it a byte. Using the human numbering system this byte could represent binary digits between 0 and (2^8)-1 or 255. This seemed to be a little too complicated even for a company whose ledger sheet looks like the GNP of most countries. The byte was divided in half to four bits and called a nibble. Someone got a plaque on the wall for that name.

Four bits can represent numbers from 0 to 15 or (2^4)-1. Now all that had to be devised was what to call each of these digits. 0 through 9 was easy since they had already been invented, but 10 through 15 created a problem since they represented carries to the next place in the decimal system. Another plaque was presented to the scientist who suggested that A through F be used to represent the 6 extra digits.

Now one digit could represent each of the 16 combinations represented by a group of four binary digits. Each place in this new number system would represent a power of 16. IBM saw that it was much more complicated than even the decimal system, pronounced it good and called it hexadecimal.

Binary	Decimal	Hexadecimal
0000	0	0
0001	1	1
0010	2	2
0011	3	3
0100	4	4
0101	5	5
0110	6	6
0111	7	7
1000	8	8
1001	9	9
1010	10	A
1011	11	B
1100	12	C
1101	13	D
1110	14	E
1111	15	F
===
10000	16	10
.		
.		
.		

Maybe it is a bit easier to represent the contents of computer memory, but math is complicated even further. For humans, it seems to be easier to convert the hex digits into decimal, run them through a calculator and then convert back to hex. Those who need to do this a lot spend a couple of dead President's portraits and obtain a calculator that does hex math.

Just as in our decimal system where each digit represents one tenth part of a power of ten, each hex digit represents one sixteenth part of a power of 16. For example the decimal number 1234 could be represented as follows:

```
1 * 10³ = 1 * 1000  = 1000
2 * 10² = 2 *  100  =  200
3 * 10¹ = 3 *   10  =   30
4 * 10⁰ = 4 *    1  =    4
                      ====
                      1234
```

The hex number 1234 could be written as follows:

```
1 * 16³ = 1 * 4096 = 4096
2 * 16² = 2 * 256  =  512
3 * 16¹ = 3 * 16   =   48
4 * 16⁰ = 4 * 1    =    4
                     =====
                     4660
```

Converting from decimal to hex is only a little more difficult. Let's use the decimal number 1234 and convert to hex. The basic principle is to divide by a power of 16 the remainder of the previous division.

```
1234 / 16³ = 1234 / 4096 = 0     r 1234
1234 / 16² = 1234 /  256 = 4     r  210
 210 / 16¹ =  210 /   16 = D     r    2
   2 / 16⁰ =    2 /    1 = 2     r    0
```

The 13 becomes D in the hex numbering system so the hex equivalent of 1234 decimal is 04D2 hex.

There are some standard numbers used in computers which are best thought of in hex terms.

```
Standard Disk Sector = 512 bytes or 200 hex bytes
One kilobyte (2¹⁰)   = 1024 decimal or 400 hex
One megabyte (2²⁰)   = 1048576 decimal or 100000 hex
```

Repairing the DOS BOOT SECTOR

Let's start at the very beginning.

A very nice place to start.

When you read, you begin with "A B C."

power of 16. For example the decimal number 1234 could be represented as follows:

```
1 * 10^3 = 1 * 1000  = 1000
2 * 10^2 = 2 *  100  =  200
3 * 10^1 = 3 *   10  =   30
4 * 10^0 = 4 *    1  =    4
                       ====
                       1234
```

When you sing you begin with "Do Re Mi."

Oscar Hammerstein II, *Do Re Me*

When you compute, you begin with the *BOOT SECTOR*. There are two kinds of Boot Sectors, depending on the type of disk. The *DOS Boot Sector* is the first sector on a diskette. On hard disks the first sector is the *Master Boot Record* (MBR). The MBR contains instructions for loading the DOS boot sector from the hard disk. Each logical drive of the hard disk begins with a DOS Boot Sector.

When the computer is started, it is the DOS boot sector which loads the operating system from the disk. The operating system on IBM PCs and clones is called DOS, an acronym for Disk Operating System. The operating system consists of two disk files named IBMBIO.COM and IBMDOS.COM. These files are the first two files on the disk and their directory entry is marked "Hidden" and "System" so their names do not appear on ordinary directory searches. This prevents accidental erasure of these vital files. Without them, the operating system cannot be loaded and the computer will not operate.

Here's what happens when you flip the "Big Red Switch" which, strangely, isn't very often red these days. Once power is applied, the CPU (the Intel microprocessor chip which is the brains of the computer) begins to execute instructions stored in memory. The first set of instructions is stored in the system ROM (Read-Only Memory) and is a series of routines that check everything in the computer. This routine is called the Power On System Test (POST). Once the POST is complete, the built-in instructions call for the loading of disk A sector 1 into memory at location 0:7C00. If this load fails (there is no diskette in drive A) the POST tries to load the hard disk's first sector into memory. If this too fails, IBM computers start the BASIC program stored in ROM and clones prompt for a diskette in A.

After the first sector of the diskette or hard disk is loaded into memory, the instructions contained in that sector are run. With hard disks, the instructions are the Master Boot Record instructions (covered elsewhere) and they load the DOS boot sector. Diskettes have no MBR and load the DOS boot sector directly.

The DOS boot sector contains computer instructions and data. The data area includes the disk's BIOS Parameter Block (BPB), a 23 byte structure that can be used by DOS to calculate the logical structure of the disk. The BPB was first used with DOS version 2 and allows DOS to deal with any type of diskette or hard disk. DOS version 1 supported only the 8 sector per track, 40 track per side diskette. Since the introduction of the BPB, DOS can deal with any type of disk as long as the first sector is the DOS boot sector containing the BPB 0B (hex) bytes from the beginning of the sector.

BIOS PARAMETER BLOCK

Offset	Length	Data
0B	2 bytes	Bytes per Sector
0D	1 byte	Sectors Per Cluster
0E	2 bytes	Reserved Sectors
10	1 byte	Copies of FAT
11	2 bytes	Root Directory Entries
13	2 bytes	Total Number of Sectors
15	1 byte	DOS Media Descriptor
16	2 bytes	Sectors per FAT
18	2 bytes	Sectors per Track
1A	2 bytes	Number of Sides
1C	2 bytes	Hidden Sectors
20	4 bytes	Total Sectors (if offset 13 is 0)

Booting Up

The DOS boot sector is loaded into memory at absolute location 0:7C00 and begins the process of loading DOS. Each version of DOS has a slightly different start up code. All versions begin the process by setting up the segment registers and the stack pointer.

DOS version 5 then loads the Disk Base Table into the area occupied by the first several bytes of the instructions since they will not be used again. The Disk Base Table contains information used by the BIOS disk services, including how long to wait for the motor to start, when to turn the motor off and how long it takes for the heads to move. The start up instructions set a very conservative head move time and the number of sectors per track into the Disk Base Table.

Following this housekeeping chore, the instructions calculate the logical sector numbers for the start of the directory and the start of the data area. The directory is read into memory at location 0:500 and the first two entries are searched for "IBMBIO COM" and "IBMDOS COM". Some versions of MS-DOS look for "IO SYS" and "MSDOS SYS", others look for different names. The file names in the directory must match the names in the boot sector or DOS will not be loaded.

Once the filename matches are made, the starting cluster number of the BIO file is extracted from the directory entry and the logical sector number of that cluster is calculated. A subroutine calculates the head, track and sector number of the file and the first 3 sectors are read into memory at location 70:0. (Early versions of the boot code skip the calculation of the cluster and assume IBMBIO.COM begins in the first cluster.)

If there are no errors encountered, a far jump instruction to 70:0 ends the DOS boot sector process. If for any reason IBMBIO.COM cannot be loaded, the following message is displayed:

```
Non-system disk or disk error.
Replace and press any key when ready.
```

Once you press a key, control passes back the ROM BIOS through an interrupt and the boot process begins again with the new disk. The ROM BIOS does not clear memory or reset the disk BIOS interrupt (INT 13), but merely loads the new diskette's boot sector and transfers control back to that sector's instructions. This is an important point to remember in dealing with computer viruses.

Virus in the Boot Sector

Not all diskettes have the DOS system files, but all must have a boot sector with at least a BPB. Since the instructions contained in this sector are the first to be executed when the computer is started, the boot sector has become a target for computer viruses. Some boot sector viruses move the original boot sector to some other place on the disk, others replace the boot sector completely. No matter which method is used, the computer becomes infected with the virus whether or not disk contains the DOS system files. Any subsequent diskette used in the drive will also become infected unless the computer is powered off and then restarted with an uninfected diskette.

The good news about boot sector viruses is that the instructions contained in the boot sector are only run at start up. An infected diskette can be used for years without harm if it is never inserted in the A drive at boot up. The bad news is that hardly anyone inspects the code contained within the boot sector to see if it is legitimate. A boot sector virus can sit undetected for a long time waiting to be activated.

Most anti-virus software can identify the known boot sector viruses and replace the infected boot sector with the good one, but sometimes the cure can be worse than the disease. One widely used virus clean up program published by McAfee Associates would identify the "Michelangelo" virus as the "Stoned" virus and write a directory sector to the boot sector of the 1.2 meg diskettes. In this case, DOS would fail to find the BPB and the user would be unable to use the diskette at all.

Viruses and anti-virus programs are not the only things that can cause the DOS boot sector to become damaged. While most programs do not use the boot sector, some disk utility programs have the ability to read and write this sector. There is also the possibility of physical damage to this sector.

REPLACING THE BOOT SECTOR (Diskettes)

You can easily repair damage to the boot sector of diskettes with DEBUG if there is no physical damage to the media. This will cure corruption by viruses and inattentive use of disk utility programs.

WARNING

If you are replacing the boot sector of a virus infected diskette, turn the computer off and restart from a bootable diskette that you know is not infected.

Get a new diskette and FORMAT it so its the same size as the damaged diskette. If you start from a cold boot and format another diskette, the new disk's boot sector will be written as DOS intended.

Start the DEBUG program and insert the damaged diskette in the A drive. At the DEBUG prompt (-) enter "L 100 0 0 1". This reads the damaged diskette's boot sector into memory at location 100. If you get the DOS message "Error reading drive A:. Abort, Retry, Fail", or something to that effect, the boot sector has physical damage and cannot be recovered.

If the DEBUG read the boot sector successfully, recovery is possible. Replace the damaged disk with the new disk and enter the same command: "L 100 0 0 1" or just press F3 and enter. This reads the good boot sector of the new diskette into location 100.

Replace the good diskette with the damaged diskette. Write the good data in memory to the bad diskette with the command "W 100 0 0 1".

Enter "Q" to quit DEBUG and you are done. If the diskettes were the same capacity, all should be well.

REPLACING THE BOOT SECTOR (Hard disks)

Don't!

Here is a case where the old saying "an ounce of prevention is worth a pound of cure" is certainly true. In the case of a diskette, it's a simple matter to format a duplicate diskette and then transfer the DOS boot sector from one to the other. Unless you have a duplicate hard disk sitting on the shelf, this cure won't work. The problem is that once you lose the BIOS Parameter Block of the hard disk, it is difficult to reconstruct. Although the MBR gives you the total number of sectors in the partition, it gives you no clue as to how it is divided into sides, tracks, and sectors. You have also lost the number of FATs, FAT sectors, and directory entries.

TIP

Use MIRROR before trouble strikes.

The *ounce of prevention* in this case is to make a copy of the DOS boot sector before the sector is lost or corrupted. The MIRROR program included with DOS version 5+ saves the DOS boot sector along with other vital areas. If you use MIRROR with the "/partn" switch, it saves the MBR and DOS boot sectors to a diskette. To restore these areas, run the UNFORMAT program with the "/partn" parameter. If the hard disk is divided into several partitions, MIRROR saves the information for every partition on the disk. It is well worth the 10 seconds it takes to run MIRROR.

Virus Removal with Anti-Virus Programs

If a computer virus overwrote the DOS boot sector, you will probably be able to recover. Very few computer viruses replace the DOS boot sector of the hard disk. Most will replace the Master Boot Record (partition table) located on the first sector of the disk. (The Master Boot Record is discussed elsewhere in this book.) It is likely that the virus merely moved the DOS boot sector to another sector on the disk. Anti-virus programs repair the DOS boot sector by knowing where the virus has stored the original sector.

WARNING

Before running anti-virus software to fix an infected DOS boot sector, use "MIRROR /partn" to make a copy of the infected disk.

The anti-virus program might not identify the virus correctly. It could make a bad assumption about where the original DOS boot sector is stored. As in the case of the McAfee Associates CLEAN program with the 1.2 meg diskette, you might get a directory sector written to the DOS boot sector of the hard disk. The cure is worse than the disease. If the anti-virus program writes the wrong sector to the boot sector, you can use the "UNFORMAT /partn" to undo the damage and then proceed to remove the virus the hard way.

Virus Removal the Hard Way

You can still replace the DOS boot sector if a computer virus has moved it. In order for the hard disk to operate, the BIOS parameter block must still be in place, at least according to DOS. Some viruses contain code which redirects any attempt to read the DOS boot sector to the sector that contains the original boot sector. If the virus does not redirect a read attempt, then the corrupted Boot sector must contain a proper BPB.

Begin the replacement procedure by starting the computer from the infected hard disk. With the virus in memory, DEBUG can read the BIOS Parameter Block. Start the DEBUG program and then load the DOS boot sector into memory by entering "L 100 2 0 1". (Drive 2 is drive C to DEBUG since numbering begins with A=0.)

After the DOS boot sector is loaded into memory by DEBUG, use the "D" (Display) command to print the first section of the DOS boot sector. Enter "D" or "D 100". If you have a printer attached, press <Ctrl><PrintScreen> and the output from DEBUG is echoed to the printer. If you don't have a printer, write down all of the numbers on the first three lines of the display.

After you have saved the numbers in the BPB, turn the computer off at the switch. Turning off the power clears memory and removes any virus instructions. Restart the computer with a write-protected bootable diskette in drive A. Once the computer has rebooted, start DEBUG again and load the DOS boot sector of the diskette into memory with the command "L 100 0 0 1". First, use the "U" (Unassemble command) to see where the data section ends and the code section begins. You will notice that the first instruction is "JMP xxx" where xxx is the location of the next instruction. If, for example, the instruction is "JMP 13E", place a mark on your paper at location 13E.

Edit the bytes starting at memory location 103 to match the bytes written down from the hard disk's DOS boot sector. Begin by entering "E 103" and then just type the numbers as they appear on your paper separating each by a space. If you hit <Enter> by mistake, just enter "E" again and you can begin where you left off. Copy all the numbers up to the mark on your paper.

After all the proper numbers have been entered, write the sector back to the hard disk. But first, make a diskette copy of what you have done just in case something goes wrong. Enter "N A:BOOT.SEC" to name the file. Change the CX register to 200 by entering "RCX" and then "200". This tells DEBUG how big the file is. To write the file "A:BOOT.SEC" enter "W 100". Now that a copy has been saved on diskette, write the sector to the hard disk boot location. Enter "W 100 2 0 1". If you get an "Invalid drive specification" error message you have to go to alternate plan B. If not, you have restored the DOS boot sector and removed the virus. Reboot and see if the computer starts from drive C.

Alternate Plan B

It makes sense to always have an "Alternate Plan B". Something did not go right on the first attempt at a repair to the boot sector. If you are dealing with a computer virus on the hard disk and could not write the new DOS boot sector, the virus is also affecting the Master Boot Record (MBR). Deal with that problem first, and then retrace your steps to replace DOS boot sector.

Repairing the MASTER BOOT RECORD

The Master Boot Record (MBR) is the single most important sector on a hard disk. Do not attempt to alter this sector unless you know what you are doing. Before doing *anything* to the MBR make sure you have a DOS diskette with DEBUG.COM (or DEBUG.EXE) on it.

The Master Boot Record Explained

The Master Boot Record is the first sector of a hard disk, side 0, cylinder 0, sector 1. This sector contains both instructions for starting the computer disk system and data about the partitions on the hard disk. You cannot read the MBR using the DEBUG L (load) command because it resides outside the DOS logical disk structure. In fact, it defines the logical disk structure.

To read the Master Boot Record using DEBUG, write a small assembly language program in DEBUG. Enter the DEBUG command "A" (Assembly) and get to the following prompt:

```
XXXX:100 _
```

The segment address "XXXX" will vary from system to system. Enter the following instructions (you can omit the comments following the ";"):

```
MOV     AX,201          ;Read 1 sector
MOV     BX,200          ;into ES:200
MOV     CX,1            ;Sector 1, Track 0
MOV     DX,80           ;Head 0, Drive 80 First hard disk
INT     13              ;BIOS disk call
MOV     AH,4C           ;DOS Terminate Function
INT     21              ;DOS Function Call
NOP                     ;No Operation
```

This code sets up the registers for BIOS disk interrupt call (INT 13) which reads the first sector of the hard disk into the memory at location ES:200. You can run this small program either entering "G" at the DEBUG prompt or pressing "P" until after the call to INT 13.

Once the MBR has been read into memory at location 200, you can enter the DEBUG "U200" (Unassemble) command to see the start up code.

The computer loads the MBR into the boot location, absolute memory address 0000:7C00. Here is what this short piece of code does. Interrupts are disabled the Data Segment (DS), Extra Segment (ES), and Stack Segment (SS) are all set to 0. The Stack Pointer (SP) is set to 7C00. The entire 200 bytes of code and data is moved from 0000:7C00 to 0000:600 using a REP MOVSW instruction. Then a far jump continues execution of the code at location 0000:600 plus the offset of the next instruction.

The code is moved to clear the boot location (0000:7C00) for the DOS boot sector. The MBR startup code begins checking the *Partition Table* located 1B8 bytes from the start of the Master Boot Record. At this point in the boot process, the Partition Table is located at 0000:7BE.

There is room in the Partition Table for four separate logical partitions of the hard disk. The data for each partition occupies 10 hex bytes and its structure is defined as follows:

```
Offset        Size      Function
_ _ _ _ _ _ _ _ _ _ _ _ _ _ _ _ _ _ _ _ _ _ _ _ _ _ _
00            1         Boot indicator (80=bootable)
01            1         Beginning head number
02            2         Beginning track (10 bits)
                        Beginning sector (6 bits)
04            1         Type (1=primary DOS 12 bit FAT)
                            (2=XENIX)
                            (4=primary DOS 16 bit FAT)
                            (5=extended DOS)
                            (6= >32MB primary DOS)
                            (8=non-DOS)
05            1         Ending head
06            2         Ending track/sector
08            4         Starting sector
0C            4         Number of sectors
```

Primary DOS partitions (types 1, 4, and 6) all have a DOS Boot Sector at the beginning of the logical disk. The location of the DOS boot sector is indicated by the beginning head, track and sector numbers. Generally, the first DOS partition of the hard disk begins at head 1, track 0, sector 1. Some older versions of DOS place the beginning of the DOS partition at the second sector of the first head and track.

The MBR start up code searches for the boot indicator (80 hex) in one of the 4 possible partitions. This value is loaded into the DL register and becomes the disk number for an INT 13 call. The beginning head number is loaded into the DH register and the beginning track/sector number at offset 2 is loaded into the CX register. The BX register is set to 7C00 (the boot address) and AX is set to 201 to read one sector. The MBR code then reads the DOS boot sector and jumps to 0000:7C00 to begin the DOS boot code. (The DOS boot code was explained above.)

There are three errors that can occur while the MBR code loads the DOS boot sector. There could be no bootable partition defined. There could be a read error in reading the DOS Boot Sector. Or the DOS Boot Sector could be missing. In each case one of the following error messages will appear:

```
Invalid partition table.
Error loading operating system.
Missing operating system.
```

The action taken upon one of these errors depends on the brand of computer. An IBM with built in BASIC is booted to the CASETTE BASIC program. Other brands will prompt for a bootable diskette in drive A. No matter which action your computer takes, the hard disk (drive C) will not exist for normal DOS operations. Only diagnostic programs can access the hard disk at this point.

If the partition is an extended DOS partition, the bytes at offset 1 and 2 are the head, cylinder and track values for the partition table of the extended partition. That extended partition could have a primary and another extended partition and so on. There can an unlimited number of extended partitions of the hard disk each with a DOS primary partition and another extended partition. Every primary partition in the chain becomes a different logical drive under DOS. DOS ignores any non-DOS partition.

WARNING

Recursive Extended Partitions will prevent the computer from starting with DOS version 4 and in some cases DOS version 3, even when booted from a diskette. DOS versions below 3 do not recognize extended partitions and DOS version 5+ will issue a warning on bootup that logical drives past Z: exist.

If the partition table is invalid, you can't start the computer from the hard disk. You must boot from a diskette. Even when booting from a diskette, DOS reads the Partition Table part of the MBR to set up the logical drive. If the Partition Table does not contain valid information, DOS ignores the hard disk.

The message "Invalid drive specification" means that DOS does not recognize the drive. Either the Master Boot Record could not be read or DOS has determined that the Partition Table information for the hard disk is not valid.

Replacing the MBR start up code.

If the Partition Table information is valid, but the startup code at the beginning of the MBR is corrupt, you can replace the startup code by using an undocumented feature of the FDISK program or you can do it the hard way with DEBUG.

The Easy Way (FDISK)

Normally FDISK should be used only once, when the hard disk is originally set up and partitioned. Once the disk is up and running there is probably no good reason for using FDISK. Changing the partitions will destroy all the data on the hard disk. Therefore it's a good idea to keep FDISK on a diskette for emergency use and remove it from the hard disk.

There is one undocumented feature of FDISK that comes in handy in a data recovery sense. When FDISK is used with the "/MBR" switch, it replaces the startup code at the beginning of the MBR but leaves the partition information intact. As a matter of fact, when FDISK is run with that parameter, it does not even go the to the normal screen which give 4 options on how to partition the disk. It merely replaces the startup code and returns to the DOS prompt.

The Hard Way (DEBUG)

Start the DEBUG program from the diskette in A. Since DOS is useless in reading and writing the MBR, you need to write a program to read the MBR sector into memory. DEBUG sets the instruction pointer (IP) to 100 and all segment registers (DS, ES, SS, and CS) to the same value. The segment values vary from system to system. All memory references are offsets to whatever segment is occupied by DEBUG. Remember that all numbers are in hexadecimal (base 16) and not decimal (base 10).

To begin assembly, type "A" at the DEBUG prompt "-". Press <Enter> after each command.

```
-A

XXXX:0100          MOV   AX,201
XXXX:0103          MOV   BX,200
XXXX:0105          MOV   CX,1
XXXX:0109          MOV   DX,80
XXXX:010C          INT   13
```

```
XXXX:010E          NOP
XXXX:010F          <ENTER>
```

This sets up the correct registers for a call to the disk BIOS interrupt (INT 13) to read the first sector of the disk into memory offset 200. The AX register says read 1 sector. BX is the address where the sector data is read. CX is track 0, sector 1. DX is set to head 0, disk 80 (1st hard disk). INT 13 is the call to the Disk BIOS routine.

To run this short program, enter "G 10E" at the DEBUG prompt, or enter "P" 6 times. DEBUG displays the register set and the next instruction. Check the flags register for "NC", no carry. If the flags include "CY" then the call to INT 13 failed and the MBR is unreadable. Here is the complete startup code as it would be written in DEBUG assembler mode. Remember that you are writing this code to offset 200 even though it executes from offset 7C00. To begin assembly enter "A 200".

```
xxxx:0200    CLI
xxxx:0201    XOR    AX,AX
xxxx:0203    MOV    SS,AX
xxxx:0205    MOV    SP,7C00
xxxx:0208    MOV    SI,SP
xxxx:020A    PUSH   AX
xxxx:020B    POP    ES
xxxx:020C    PUSH   AX
xxxx:020D    POP    DS
xxxx:020E    STI
xxxx:020F    CLD
xxxx:0210    MOV    DI,0600
xxxx:0213    MOV    CX,0100
xxxx:0216    REPNZ
xxxx:0217    MOVSW
xxxx:0218    JMP    0000:061D
xxxx:021D    MOV    SI,07BE
xxxx:0220    MOV    BL,04
xxxx:0222    CMP    Byte Ptr [SI],80
xxxx:0225    JZ     0235
xxxx:0227    CMP    Byte Ptr [SI],00
xxxx:022A    JNZ    0248
xxxx:022C    ADD    SI,+10
xxxx:022F    DEC    BL
```

```
xxxx:0231    JNZ      0222
xxxx:0233    INT      18
xxxx:0235    MOV      DX,[SI]
xxxx:0237    MOV      CX,[SI+02]
xxxx:023A    MOV      BP,SI
xxxx:023C    ADD      SI,+10
xxxx:023F    DEC      BL
xxxx:0241    JZ       025D
xxxx:0243    CMP      Byte Ptr [SI],00
xxxx:0246    JZ       023C
xxxx:0248    MOV      SI,068B
xxxx:024B    LODSB
xxxx:024C    CMP      AL,00
xxxx:024E    JZ       025B
xxxx:0250    PUSH     SI
xxxx:0251    MOV      BX,0007
xxxx:0254    MOV      AH,0E
xxxx:0256    INT      10
xxxx:0258    POP      SI
xxxx:0259    JMP      024B
xxxx:025B    JMP      025B
xxxx:025D    MOV      DI,0005
xxxx:0260    MOV      BX,7C00
xxxx:0263    MOV      AX,0201
xxxx:0266    PUSH     DI
xxxx:0267    INT      13
xxxx:0269    POP      DI
xxxx:026A    JNB      0278
xxxx:026C    XOR      AX,AX
xxxx:026E    INT      13
xxxx:0270    DEC      DI
xxxx:0271    JNZ      0260
xxxx:0273    MOV      SI,06A3
xxxx:0276    JMP      024B
xxxx:0278    MOV      SI,06C2
xxxx:027B    MOV      DI,7DFE
xxxx:027E    CMP      Word Ptr [DI],AA55
xxxx:0282    JNZ      024B
xxxx:0284    MOV      SI,BP
xxxx:0286    JMP      0000:7C00
xxxx:028B    DB       'Invalid Partition table',0
xxxx:02A3    DB       'Error loading operating system',0
```

```
xxxx:02C2    DB      'Missing operating system,0
xxxx:02DB <Enter>
```

Reset the Instruction Pointer to offset 100. Enter "RIP" and then enter "100". To write the new code to the MBR sector, you only need to change the first instruction of the code that you used to read the sector.

```
-A 100
xxxx:100 MOV   AX,301
xxxx:103    <Enter>
```

Make sure the Instruction Pointer (IP) register is 100. Enter "G 10E".

Boot Sector Virus (MBR)

Other than inadvertant repartitioning by FDISK, the most likely cause of a corrupt MBR is a computer virus. Computer viruses that attack the DOS Boot Sector of diskettes will often attack the MBR of a hard disk since this is the first sector on the disk. There are many boot sector viruses and they all work in slightly different ways. The primary defense against these rogue programs is never boot the machine with a diskette in drive A. This is the only way a boot sector virus can be transmitted from PC to PC. Just a little care can go a long way toward preventing this kind of damage as seen in the following example.

The secretary to the General Manager of a major market radio station wrote many documents on her word processor (the boss was a memo freak). She would put a diskette in the A drive, and write all of her word processing documents to the diskette instead of the hard disk. At the end of each day she would turn the computer off and go home or to a nearby watering hole if the boss had been in one of his moods. The next morning, she would arrive at work bright and early and turn on the computer. Some mornings she would forget to remove the diskette from A and would see the message "non-system disk. Replace and press any key."

One morning she removed the disk from the diskette, pressed a key, and was greeted by the message "Your PC is stoned!" *Had she been a little more careful about the diskette in A, she could have written files to the infected diskette for years without infecting her hard disk with the "Stoned" virus. Her hard disk had been infected for some time and consequently all her diskettes were now carriers of this computer virus. Fortunately, she was the only one who ever used these diskettes so the virus had not spread to other computers within the office.*

The easy way to prevent this type of corruption of the MBR would be diligence on the part of the operator. But once the damage has been done, it must be undone.

Fortunately, "Stoned" is a well known boot sector infector and repair methods are easy and reliable. Almost any anti-virus software can repair the MBR of a "Stoned" infected disk. Not all boot infectors are so easy to remove.

There are several kinds of boot infecting viruses. One kind overwrites the MBR with the virus code. That is, it replaces the original MBR start-up code with the virus itself. The partition information is still intact, and repair is made by replacing the virus code at the end of the beginning sector with the correct startup code using "FDISK /MBR" from DOS version 5 and up. If the partition data is missing, reconstructing the MBR is a little more tedious, but it can be done.

Another type of boot sector virus moves the MBR intact to another sector of the disk. When the infected computer is started, the disk BIOS interrupt (INT 13) points to the virus in memory and references to the first disk sector are redirected to the sector that contains the original MBR. This has the effect of hiding the virus contained in the first sector on the disk. Any diagnostic program attempting to read the MBR sector reads the sector with the original MBR and not the infected sector. To repair the damage done by this kind of virus, you have to copy the original MBR sector back to the first sector of the hard disk.

Most anti-virus repair programs rely on the fact that a known virus stores the original MBR in a specific location on the disk. The anti-virus software copies the original MBR back to where it should be. But if the anti-virus software misidentifies the virus or the virus has been altered so the original MBR is not in the expected location, the anti-virus repair can make matters worse by writing a non-MBR sector to the MBR making the disk unuseable. At least with the virus, you could still access your data.

Some boot sector viruses like "Stoned" mentioned above, do nothing except replicate the virus code onto any diskette used by the computer. Others, like the "Michelangelo" virus and the "Data Crime" virus have trigger dates for a destructive phase. These viruses destroy hard disk data on a specific date. "Michelangelo" destroys the MBR, boot sector, FAT table and root directory on March 6. "Data Crime" formats the hard disk on any day after October 12. These viruses can cause enough damage to make you drop back 10 and punt. The damage to data might be so severe that the only recourse is to repartition and reformat the hard disk.

Reconstructing the Partition Table (the Hard Way)

There is no easy way. If the Partition Table is destroyed by a virus, an anti-virus program, or stupid human trick, the hard disk will not be accessible through DOS. You cannot start the computer from C. You get the message "Invalid drive specification" when you try to access drive C.

Unfortunately running "FDISK /MBR" is not enough to repair the damage to the Partition Table. Even though FDISK replaces the code at the beginning of the MBR, it will not replace the partition data. If the Partition Table is invalid, you can repartition the hard disk using FDISK program with no switches.

WARNING

Repartitioning the hard disk could cause the loss of all data.

If you have a current backup, you can repartition, reformat and restore. If you don't have a backup, you can't make one since the hard disk is inaccessible.

Unfortunately, FDISK destroys the DOS Boot Sector when you repartition the hard disk. FDISK does nothing to the root directory and FAT, but to restore the DOS Boot Sector, you need to run FORMAT which initializes the root directory and the FAT.

If you save the existing DOS Boot Sector before running FDISK to replace the partition information, it's possible to restore the existing data on the disk.

To begin the restoration process, save the existing DOS Boot Sector using DEBUG. Start DEBUG and write a small program to read the DOS Boot Sector into memory.

```
-A
xxxx:0100      MOV    AX,201
xxxx:0103      MOV    BX,200
xxxx:0106      MOV    CX,1
xxxx:0109      MOV    DX,180
xxxx:010C      INT    13
xxxx:010E      NOP
xxxx:010F  <Enter>
-G 10E
```

Check the sector just read to verify the DOS Boot Sector. Enter "D 200 LB" to display the first 11 bytes of the sector.

```
-D 200 LA
xxxx:0200   EB 3C 90 4D 53 44 4F 53 35 2E 30   .<.MSDOS5.0
```

Display the BPB and write down the numbers that appear in the next 25 bytes.

```
-D 20B L19
```

The 2 bytes at offset 213 are the total number of sectors in the partition. If these bytes are 0, then the 4 bytes at offset 220 contain the total number of sectors. You need this number to calculate how large the partition was. These are hexadecimal numbers and are stored backwards in memory. For example, if the two bytes at offset 213 are 0 and the 4 bytes at offset 220 are 78 DB 01 00, then the total number of sectors for this partition is 1DB78 hex. Using a hex calculator multiply the number of sectors by the number of bytes per sector (2 bytes at offset 20B) which is almost always 200. Divide the result by 10000 hex to get the number of Megabytes. If bytes per sector number is 200, you get the same result dividing the number of sectors by 800 hex. Convert the number to decimal and write down the answer.

Save the DOS Boot Sector to the diskette using the following sequence:

```
-N A:BOOT.DAT
-R BX
BX 0200
:0
```

```
-R CX
CX 0001
:200
-W 200
Writing 00200 bytes
-Q
```

Run FDISK to check for any existing partitions.

FDISK presents four options in the opening screen.

```
1) Create DOS partition or Logical DOS Drive.
2) Set active partition.
3) Delete partition or Logical DOS Drive.
4) View partition information.


Press Esc to exit FDISK
```

Only option 4 (View partition data) is safe to use. Options 1 and 3 both have the potential of losing all the data on the hard disk. View the partition information and verify that there are no defined partitions. If there are non-DOS defined partitions, they must be removed before you can proceed. FDISK will not remove a non-DOS partition, so you will have to use DEBUG.

Start DEBUG from a diskette. Enter "A", and write a program to read the MBR sector. Press <Enter> after each command.

```
-A

XXXX:0100          MOV   AX,201
XXXX:0103          MOV   BX,200
XXXX:0105          MOV   CX,1
XXXX:0109          MOV   DX,80
XXXX:010C          INT   13
XXXX:010E          NOP
XXXX:010F   <ENTER>
-G 10E
```

Check the Flags Register for "NC". If you see "CY", the sector could not be read. The number in the AH register (first two digits of AX) contains the error code.

Zero all the bytes in the Partition Table section of the MBR. Enter "F 3BE L40 0" for "Fill offset 3BE for a length of 40 bytes with 0".

```
-F 3BE L40 0
-
```

Change the Instruction Pointer (IP) register back to the beginning of your program. Enter "RIP" (cute) and then enter "100".

```
-R IP
RIP 010E
:100
-
```

Change the first instruction to "write sector" instread of "read sector". Enter "A 100".

```
-A 100
xxxx:0100      MOV  AX,301
xxxx:0103   <Enter>
-
```

Write the change back to the MBR sector. Enter "G 10E". Quit debug, enter "Q".

```
-G 10E
-Q
A:>
```

Run FDISK again and verify that there are no partitions defined for the hard disk. Once this is done, choose option 1, "Create DOS partition or Logical DOS drive." Set the partition size as the number of megabytes derived from the DOS Boot Sector. The Partition Table and the DOS Boot Sector should both indicate the same disk size.

Exiting the FDISK program forces a reboot, but **DO NOT FORMAT!** You will have to reboot from the diskette again.

FDISK resets the Partition Table but fills the DOS Boot Sector with the byte F6. Before DOS can recognize the disk, you need to restore the DOS Boot Sector which you saved to diskette. **DO NOT FORMAT** because FORMAT initializes not only the DOS Boot Sector but also the root directory and the FAT.

Start the DEBUG program and load the saved DOS Boot Sector into offset 200.

```
A:>DEBUG
-N A:BOOT.DAT
-L 200
-
```

Write a small program to save this data back to the DOS Boot Sector.

```
-A
xxxx:0100     MOV  AX,301
xxxx:0103     MOV  BX,200
xxxx:0106     MOV  CX,1
xxxx:0109     MOV  DX,180
xxxx:010C     INT  13
xxxx:010E     NOP
xxxx:010F     <Enter>
-G 10E
-Q
A:>
```

Reboot again to force DOS to read the changes to the DOS Boot Sector, otherwise you will get the message "Invalid Media Type."

RECONSTRUCTING PARTITION DATA (The Harder Way)

If the partition data is missing, replacing it without using FDISK requires some guess work and some hexadecimal math. If you do not have a calculator that does hexadecimal math, then you need to check that section in this book.

Using the method described above, record the BPB information from the DOS Boot Sector. You will need all of this information in order to proceed.

The first partition is defined in the 10 (hex) bytes beginning at offset 01BE in the MBR. By now you should know the DEBUG sequence to read this sector into memory at offset 200. Because you are constructing that sector beginning at offset 200, add 200 to 1BE and begin construction at offset 03BE. Edit each field of the Partition Table as described below.

(offset 00) BOOT INDICATOR

First, assume that the first partition is a bootable partition so enter "80" for the byte at 03BE.

```
-E 3BE
xxxx:03BE  00.80
-
```

(Offset 01) STARTING HEAD

The next two fields are the head (1 byte) and sector/track (2 bytes) of the starting sector of the disk. This is the sector where the DOS boot record is located. You need to find this sector and look at it before proceeding. Different versions of FDISK place the start of the partition at different places. The early versions of FDISK begin the partition immediately following the MBR, that is sector 2 of track 0, side 0. Later versions of FDISK begin the partition in sector 1 of track 0, head 1.

Most likely, you partitioned (or the manufacturer did it for you) the disk with a version of FDISK later than DOS 2. In this case the DOS boot sector is at sector 1, track 0, head 1. If you have not done so before, read this sector into memory above the MBR sector that you are reconstructing by using the following assembly instructions:

```
NEW FDISK              OLD FDISK

MOV   AX,201           MOV   AX,201
MOV   BX,400           MOV   BX,400
MOV   CX,1             MOV   CX,2
MOV   DX,180           MOV   DX,80
INT   13              INT   13
NOP                    NOP
```

To run these instructions use the DEBUG "G xxxx" command where xxxx is the offset value of the NOP instruction. If you use the "G" command, be sure you specify where to stop or DEBUG will continue to execute instructions beyond the end of your program! It's safer to use the "P" command and step through the instructions one at a time. You can then double check the registers at the INT 13 instruction just to make sure they are set correctly before the disk BIOS call is executed.

Verify that you have read the DOS boot sector into memory at offset 400. Use the "D" (Dump Memory) command by entering "D 400" at the DEBUG prompt.

The first byte should be "EB" which is a JUMP instruction. The 8 bytes at 403 should be readable ASCII (on right of display) and indicate the DOS version used to FORMAT the disk. On later versions of DOS, the bytes at 42E are the volume label or "NO NAME" and the bytes at 436 indicate the FAT size ("FAT12" or "FAT16"). Finally the last 2 bytes in the sector should be the DOS boot signature bytes "55 AA". Display 5FE for a length of 2 bytes to check the signature: "D 5FE L2".

If you are satisfied that this sector is indeed the DOS boot sector, you are ready to proceed in reconstructing the partition data. If not, repeat the process by looking at the sector immediately following the MBR.

The field of the partition data at byte 1BF is the head number of the start of the disk. Since data is being reconstructed starting at offset 200, add that offset to 1BF to get 3BF. Edit byte 3BF to either 1 or 0 depending on which method you used to find the DOS boot sector: 1 for the newer FDISK and 0 for the old FDISK.

(Offset 02) Starting Track/Sector

The WORD (2 bytes) at offset 3C0 (1C0+200) is the sector/track where the DOS boot sector is located. Remember that computers store numbers "back words" in memory. That means that the hex number 1234 would be stored in memory as "34 12". The DOUBLE WORD (4 bytes) 12345678 would be stored in memory as "78 56 34 12". If the DOS boot sector was found at sector 1, track 0, head 1 then the value at 3C0 would be "01 00". If the DOS boot sector was located immediately following the MBR then the value would be "02 00". To edit two bytes in DEBUG, enter "E 3C0" and then "01 <space bar> 00" followed by <Enter>.

```
-E 3C0
xxxx:3C0 00.01 00.00
```

(Offset 04) PARTITION TYPE

Assuming that you are reconstruction the primary DOS partition, this value can be either 1, 4 or 6 depending on the FAT size and the disk size. If the total number of sectors exceeds 10000 hex, then the type is 6, BIGDOS. If the total number of sectors is less than 1000 hex, then the type is 1, FAT12. Otherwise the partition is type 4, FAT16. Enter the appropriate type into offset 3C2:

```
-E 3C2
xxxx:3C2  00.6
-
```

(Offset 05) ENDING HEAD

At this point you need to gather some data from the BPB in the DOS Boot Sector. You should have the BPB either in memory beginning at offset 400 or written down from when you saved it to disk. In the second case, the DOS Boot Sector began at offset 200. Get a piece of paper and a crayon (pen or pencil will do) and write down the following values using either a 2 or 4 for the first part of the address:

```
Sectors per Track  WORD (2 bytes) at offset x18
Number of Heads    WORD (2 bytes) at offset x1A
Total Sectors      WORD (2 bytes) at offset x13
Total Sectors      DWORD (4 bytes) at offset x20
```

If the WORD at x13 is "00 00" then write down the total number of sectors as the DOUBLE WORD (4 bytes) at x20.

If you wrote down these values in the order they appear in memory, then you need to reverse the pairs. For example, an IBM 120 megabyte hard disk with a 32 megabyte primary DOS partition shows the following in memory order:

```
Sectors per Track  20 00
Number of Heads    40 00
Total Sectors      E0 F7
```

Reversing these pairs and dropping the leading zeros shows:

```
20   (hex) 32 (decimal)    Sectors per Track
40   (hex) 64 (decimal)    Heads
F7E0 (hex) 63456 (decimal) Total Sectors
```

To find the ending head number apply these numbers to the following formula:

EndHead = (TotalSectors / SectorsPerTrack) MOD NumOfHeads.

(In case you are not familiar with the term MOD in a mathematical formula it is simply the remainder of a division.)

TotalSector/SectorsPerTrack   63456/32=1983

Since most calculators do not do modulus here's how to do it the hard way.

```
1983/64=30.984375    Do the division
30*64=1920           Multiply the integer part
1983-1920=63         Subtract integers to get remainder
```

You could do long division on the paper and not use a calculator to get the remainder if you remember how.

So this partition ends on head 63 (decimal) or 3F (hex). This is the value that goes in offset 3C3. The value you would get will be different.

```
-E 3C3
xxxx:3C3  00.3F
-
```

(Offset 06) ENDING SECTOR/TRACK

This WORD contains the sector and track of the end of the partition. The two values are combined in a funny way so that the sector value occupies 6 bits and the track number occupies 10 bits. If you looked at the two bytes you would see the bits dedicated this way in memory:

```
ttssssss tttttttt
```

The two bits of track value in the first byte are the HIGH bits of the sector number.

To figure out the sector number use the formula:

```
Sector=(TotalSector-1) MOD SectorsPerTrack
```

Again using the values for the example partition and doing the MODULUS the hard way:

```
63455/32=1982.96875
1982*32=63424
63456-63424=32
Sector=32 (decimal)   20 (hex)
```

That was a piece of cake!

Get the ending track using the formula:

```
Track=TotalSectors/(SectorsPerTrack * NumberOfHeads)
```

Good no MODULUS!

```
Track=63456/(32*64)
Track=63456/2048
(ignore remainder)
Track=30 (decimal)   1E (hex)
```

Now pack the two values together in the form ttssssss tttttttt. In this example the two bytes are "20 1E".

Since the track value is less than 8 bits you don't have to worry about packing the upper two bits into the upper two bits of the first byte. This is a procedure that is easy for a computer, but very difficult to accomplish by hand. If you need to do it, consider writing the two values as BINARY digits and moving bits 8 and 9 of the track number to bits 15 and 14 of the sector number. As an example assume Sector 20 (hex) and ending track number 3A0 (hex). The binary equivalent would be:

```
6  bit SECTOR   20           00 0010
10 bit TRACK    3A0       11 1010 0000
```

Move two upper track bits to two upper sector bits:

```
8 bit SECTOR   C2        1100 0010
8 bit TRACK    A0        1010 0000
```

Enter the sector byte and the track byte into the partition table.

```
-E 3C4
xxxx:03C4  00.C2  00.A0
-
```

(Offset 08) STARTING SECTOR FROM BEGINNING

This is an easy one. The starting sector number is a DOUBLE WORD value (4 bytes) and indicates the total number of sectors from the start of the disk (MBR) to the DOS boot sector. Since you have already found the DOS Boot Sector and know its head, track and sector numbers you can apply the following formula:

StartSector=(Sector - 1) + (Head * SectorsPerTrack) + (Track * SectorsPerTrack * NumberOfHeads)

Using the same hard disk as an example, you would get the following values:

```
                  hex   decimal
Sector:           01    1
Track:            00    0
Head:             01    1
SectorsPerTrack:  20    32
NumberOfHeads:    40    64
```

Plugging in the numbers:

```
StartSector=(1-1)+(1*32)+(0*32*64)
StartSector=0+32+0
StartSector=32 (decimal)   20 (hex)
```

Since you need a DOUBLE WORD the hex equivalent is 00 00 00 20. But remember to store the value "back words" in memory, so enter "20 00 00 00".

```
-E 3C8
xxxx:3C8  00.20  00.00  00.00  00.00

-
```

(Offset 0C) TOTAL NUMBER OF SECTORS

This one has been calculated for you and is stored in the DOS boot sector. Remember you wrote down the Total Sectors value? Convert this number to a 4 byte value and add the Start Sector number from the preceeding field. The DOS partition size is always a bit less than the physical partition because of the sectors reserved by the Partition Table.

```
Total DOS sectors    F7E0
+Boot Sectors        0020
Total Sectors        F800

-E 3CA
xxxx:3CA  00.00  00.00  00.F8  00.00
  -
```

COMPLETING THE MBR

You need to check one more detail. The MBR must have the DOS boot signature in the last two bytes of the sector. Check for "55 AA" at offset 3FE. If it is not there, add it.

```
E 3FE
xxxx:03FE  00.55  00.AA
  -
```

The MBR is now complete in memory beginning at offset 200 for 200 bytes. Write yet another small assembly program to store this sector back in the disk. It is actually only one byte different from the instructions used to read the sector from the disk. Using the DEBUG "A" command enter the following code, being careful that you are not overwriting the data stored beginning at offset 200:

```
MOV    AX,301
MOV    BX,200
MOV    CX,1
MOV    DX,80
INT    13
NOP
```

Use the DEBUG "G xxxx" command where xxxx is the address of the NOP instruction, or use the "P" command to step through the instructions. If the "CY" flag does not appear after the INT 13 instruction, the new sector has been safely written to the first sector of the disk. Your reconstructed MBR is in place.

Conclusions

These procedures only reconstruct the primary partition of the hard disk. That should be enough to get you up and running. If there are extended DOS partitions, you will need to construct another Partition Table entry following the first which describes the extended partition.

The extended partition should begin on the first sector on the next head following the Primary DOS partition. With luck, the extended partition's Partition Table is intact and the reconstruction process will be finished.

Repairing The FAT

Repairing the FAT is best left to programs that are designed specifically for that purpose. The NORTON UTILITIES contain an excellent sector editor that can help you repair the FAT. Most FAT problems are concerned with deleted and cross-linked files and with lost allocation units. For cross-linked files and lost allocation units, refer to the section on CHKDSK earlier in this chapter. To recover deleted files, refer to that section.

There is one FAT problem that can be cured using DEBUG, the Media Descriptor Byte, which is stored as the very first byte of the FAT. This byte is checked by DOS to verify the integrity of the FAT. If it is not the expected value, DOS displays an "Unknown media" message and ignores the disk.

How does this byte get changed? DOS does it. Some versions of DOS use the first two bytes of the FAT to store an unknown value which is sometimes written to the disk, and then almost immediately changed. This action was discovered when we wrote an anti-virus program to verify that the Media Descriptor was correct before the FAT sector could be written. A power loss at occurring before DOS writes the correct Media Descriptor leaves the FAT corrupt.

The following table lists the Media Descriptor Byte for most of the current DOS disk formats:

160 KB	FE
320 KB	FF
180 KB	FC
360 KB	FD
1.2 MB	F9
720 KB	F9
1.4 MB	F0
HARD DISK	F8

The Media Descriptor can also be found in the BPB of the Boot Sector. To edit this byte in the FAT, run DEBUG and load the first sector of the FAT into memory. The DEBUG command sequence is "Load to 100 drive x sector 1 for 1 sector."

```
A:\>DEBUG
_L 100 3 1 1
-
```

The DEBUG Load command works with logical drives so the drive number begins with A=0, B=1, C=2 etc.

Edit the first byte in the FAT.

```
-E 100
xxxx:0100    00.F8
-
```

Write the sector back to the disk using the same parameters as the Load command and Quit DEBUG.

```
-W 100 3 1 1
-Q
A:\>
```

Repairing the Root Directory

Most directory problems can be repaired with CHKDSK or a sector editor such as DISK EDIT included with the NORTON UTILITIES. DEBUG can be used, but you need to calculate the sector where the root directory begins.

Load the Dos Boot Sector and locate the BPB. You can load the DOS Boot Sector using the DEBUG Load command where x is the drive number.

```
-L 100 x 0 1
```

Locate the BPB (see the section on the DOS Boot Sector) and write down the "sectors per FAT" and "FAT copies" numbers. Multiply the two numbers. Add the number of DOS Boot Sectors, usually 1. This is the first sector of the Root Directory. Get the "Root Directory Entries" number and divide by 16. This is the number of sectors occupied by the Root Directory. Use the DEBUG Load command using x for the drive, d for the first sector and n for the number of sectors calculated above.

```
-L 100 x d n
```

Each sector of the Root Directory will occupy 200 hex bytes from offset 100. To make it easier to calculate, adjust the DS register so the directory begins at offset 0. Add 10 hex to the value in the DS register.

```
-R DS
DS 24AF
:24BF
-
```

Now the Root Directory begins at offset 0 from the DS register which is the default segment for Display and Edit commands.

After any changes, write the sectors back to the disk using the same parameters you used to load the sectors.

```
-W 100 x d n
```

You still use offset 100 since the Load and Write commands are offsets to the CS register which you did not change.

What to Look for

You should have a good reason for editing the Root Directory. You may want to remove imbedded spaces from file names or change the "System" attribute of a non-system file so it can be deleted. These are things that you cannot do from the DOS command line.

You can find missing files. Scan down the entries searching for a 0 in the first byte of a file name. This is the point where DOS stops searching for files. If there are entries following the one with a 0, they are lost until the entry marked with a 0 is used. To allow DOS to find the missing file, replace the 0 in the bad entry with E5, the deleted mark.

Unless you are having trouble, don't try to change any of the values in the directory. You could cause more trouble than you bargained for.

Repairing Subdirectories

The same techniques involved in editing the Root Directory apply to editing subdirectories. The problem is in finding them. The NORTON DISK EDIT program provides an easy way to edit subdirectories and is recommended for that work. To use DEBUG, find the subdirectory entry in the Root Directory and note the starting cluster number. Calculate the sector number for that cluster using the following formula with values taken from the BPB in the Boot Sector:

```
Sector=(Cluster - 2) x SectorsPerCluster) +
(SectorsPerFat x NumberOfFATs) +
(RootEntries / 16) + BootSector
```

Load the first cluster of the subdirectory by using the DEBUG Load command. Use d=drive number, s=sector of directory, and n=sectors per cluster.

```
-L 100 d s n

_
```

If the directory uses more than one cluster, it is doubtful that the next cluster follows the first. When subdirectories are created, only one cluster is assigned to it. As files are added, and the subdirectory needs to grow, more clusters are added. By this time the cluster immediately following the subdirectory has probably been used by one of the files.

To find the next part of the subdirectory, you have to check the FAT entry and find the next cluster in the chain. This is not easy with a 16 bit FAT and very difficult with a 12 bit FAT.

Deciphering the FAT

If the FAT has 16 bit entries, load the entire FAT into memory and change the DS register so that the beginning offset of the FAT is 0. Mulitply the cluster number by 2 and check the two bytes at that offset into the FAT. This is the cluster number of the next cluster in the chain.

NOTE

Suppose you were looking for the next cluster number for FAT entry number 2. Load the FAT into memory and adjust the DS register. Multiplying 2 times 2 gives an offset of 4.

```
-L 100 2 1 7c
-RDS
DS 1234
:1244
-D 4 L2
xxxx:0000            03 00
```

FAT entry 2 points to FAT entry 3. (Numbers are stored in reverse order in memory.) To see the entry for cluster 3, display the two bytes at offset 6 (3x2).

```
_D 6 L2
xxxx:0000                    FF FF
```

This marks the end of the FAT chain for that file <EOF>.

If the FAT has 12 bit entries, again begin by loading the FAT into memory and changing the DS register. To find the offset of the cluster into the FAT, multiply the cluster by 3 and divided the result by two. The two bytes at that offset contain one and a half FAT entries. Reverse the bytes to get a 4 digit hex number. If the cluster number is even, discard the first digit and use the last three as the 12 bit entry number. If the cluster number is odd, discard the last hex digit and use the first three hex digits as the 12 bit entry.

NOTE

Assume you want to see the FAT entry for cluster 10 hex. Load the FAT and adjust the DS register. Multiply 10 times 3 and divide by 2. Check the three bytes at offset 18.

```
-L 100 0 1 4
-RDS
DS 1234
:1244
-D 18 L2
xxxx:0000         11 20
```

Reverse the two bytes (20 11) and discard the first digit. The result is 011.

To find the entry for cluster 11, multiply 11x3=33 and divide by 2: 19 (ignore remainder). Display the two bytes at offset 19.

```
-D 19 L3
xxxx:0000                20 01
```

Reverse the two bytes (01 20) and discard the last hex digit. The result is 012 hex. This is the next entry in the FAT chain. You can proceed until the result is FFF which is the <EOF> marker.

WARNING

Making any changes to the FAT could really foul up the file system beyond all recognition. FUBAR!

<EOF>

The information contained in this chaper is not for the fainthearted or the novice. It's obviously a last resort and, just maybe, you'd be better off shipping your hard drive to a professional data recovery operation.

15

Tips, Tricks, and Traps

This chapter is the computer-book equivalent of Fibber McGee's famous closet (remember that?). Here you'll find all the bits, bytes, and other stray pieces that didn't fit logically elsewhere but are too important not to include.

We have a drawer named after McGee in our kitchen and, always, among the rubber bands, retired toothbrushes, and pet-savaged orthodontic retainers, small bits of treasure can be found.

In this chapter, you'll find reiteration of technical concepts too important not to mention again, and, sometimes, an expansion of something briefly mentioned before. You'll also find a few common-sense treasures based on years of experience. There's no particular order in this chapter, but we start off slow. Just read on.

There's Safety in Shrinkwrap

A certain imputed margin of safety exists in anything we buy that is neatly enclosed in shrinkwrap, especially computer software. Think again. Most computer stores have their very own shrinkwrap machine in the back room.

Shrinkwrap does *not* ensure that you're receiving straight-from-the-factory merchandise.

TIP

Look closely at the shrinkwrap surrounding the package. If the seams don't look straight, compare it to another package on the shelf. If it still doesn't look right, ask for another package.

Problems with "new" merchandise aren't just limited to software.

A client firm needed a new, high-speed modem. A runner was dispatched to a well-known cost-cutting computer outlet, and the modem was acquired and brought to the office. After several frustrating hours, they decided the modem was bad. Back went the runner; the store refused to accept the return. A manager, properly attired in suit and tie, grabbed the package and stomped back to demand an exchange. Finally, the clerk agreed and, as the manager watched, put the damaged modem back on the shelf for the next unsuspecting purchaser.

Take particular care with demo packages that you can take home from the store to try out. You don't know who took the last look and what extras might inadvertently have become attached. Ask the store clerk to run a good anti-virus scanner on the disks before you accept them and run a check yourself before installing them.

Beyond Repair(shops)

Sad but true, the people we want to trust the most may be the most dangerous to our PCs' health. Consider the repair technician who may service ten or twenty PCs a day with the same set of utility disks. She can't go chasing back to the shop after each call to make sure she didn't pick up a computer virus along the way. And it's not likely she's going to take the time to install an A-V product on your PC, check her disk, and uninstall her A-V product before rushing off to her next appointment. This doesn't preclude *asking* that your system be checked when she's done. And you should ask.

As an example, most diagnostics disks *require* that the system be booted with the diagnostic disk in drive A. If a machine is already infected with Michelangelo, the virus will most likely infect the diagnostics disk. The next time the technician boots a machine (maybe yours) with that disk, Michelangelo will begin to paint the equivalent of the Sistine Chapel ceiling on your computer.

In-shop technicians are often a harried bunch. Everyone wants his or her PC back *yesterday*. Even the best procedures can sometimes be ignored under the pressure of time.

TIP

Have your own Anti-virus scanning program on a disk. After every repair, run it from the disk.

Beware the Jabberwock

Always remember that the people who work in computer stores are there to sell products. In some of the largest outlets, the only computer the salespeople know anything about is the cash register. Beware.

While doing research for a magazine article on Windows-based fax software, we took an excursion into a local computer store just to see what a prospective purchaser might encounter. Ah, there was one of the packages. The young man whose tag said Manager gave this answer when asked how the program worked: "Works great." When pressed for specifics, he didn't know any. But he was more than willing to sell it!

Another time, when we were attempting to purchase a printer, the salesperson flatly stated, "We don't support that printer." Now, what could that mean? Did it mean that the printer wouldn't *work* with the computer I had already purchased? Did it mean they didn't sell a printer stand for it? Did it mean they didn't have the right cables? No—what the salesperson meant was that the profit margin on that printer wasn't high enough and the store didn't *sell* it.

Knowledge is power. Gird yourself for combat before you sally forth into enemy territory.

TIP

This is a nasty one. If you think you're being snowed by a salesperson, ask a meaningless question to see what sort of an answer you get. "Oh, yes, I understand all that, but what's really important to me is whether or not this system will address the W-7 standard for memory caching." (Hint: There is no W-7 standard for memory caching.)

Before you make a purchase, know what you need or want to buy. Do you *really* need a math co-processor if your number one use is word processing? Do you need the 7,481 features of package A when all you are going to use are the 13 features that package B does just fine? There's all kinds of snobbery in the world of PCs—don't fall victim to it at the expense of your wallet and your patience.

Beware the Jabberwock II

Everybody knows one of these Jabberwocks. You buy your new PC, a great new piece of software, a MIDI interface, *anything*—and the Jabberwock will tell you (a) how he could have gotten it for you cheaper or (b) why you bought the wrong thing. These people are best ignored unless they do, in fact, have a great deal of technical knowledge. In that case, give them food and drink, agree with them, and tell them they're right (you never know when you'll need help).

And here's where it gets dicey. Beware the Jabberwock who wants to "help" you with a problem. There is an ever-widening class of PC users who know just enough to be dangerous...to *your* data. The stories are legion.

> *"Never in the history of the world has so little been known by so many."* - Kane

Unless you are *absolutely certain* of your personal Jabberwock's capabilities and technical knowledge, decline his kind offer.

Beware the Jabberwock III

There's a class of Jabberwock known as "The Reviewer." You find their work in any one of a hundred computer magazines. They're always writers, often free-lancers, and, sometimes, are seriously *under-knowledged* about their subject.

In all fairness, we can't expect these folks who make their living writing about word processing one day, telecommunications the next, and anti-virus programs the following week to be experts in every field. And, in truth, they don't often fail us in our expectations.

Some syndicated columnists seem to work directly from a vendor's press kit, right down to the list of features included in the article—often in exactly the same order as the features are listed on the back of the box.

Are comparative reviews skewed? Possibly. It's never a surprise when a product with a huge advertising budget takes first place in the review sweepstakes. Serious money changed hands after a recent product review in a major magazine—not a bribe, a bet. The wager went that the two best-advertised (and lame performing) products would win. They did. Take reviews with a grain of salt.

In another remarkable instance, one program, marketed under two different names, received different scores. Curiouser and curiouser.

And we at PANDA are still scratching our ears with bamboo shoots over a reviewer that categorically stated our product didn't include a scanning utility. Elsewhere in the same article, the scanner received the highest available rating. Maybe you should take reviews with a *box* of salt.

The Bleeding Edge of Technology

If you're a regular—or occasional—reader of computer publications, you will have noticed the emphasis on the latest and greatest technology. With the advent of the Intel Pentium chip (go ahead, call it a 586), it would appear to the uninitiated that we might as well toss out our 486s, 386s, 286s, and 8088s. We should also immediately upgrade to DOS 6.0, which is little more than DOS 5.0 with a few bells and whistles licensed from other companies. And while we're at it, let's trade those 2400bps modems for snappy new 9600s or 14400s. No, thanks. At least, not yet.

The day may come when your 286 gives up the ghost and it's cheaper to buy a new 486 than replace the ("...out of stock, and it's a two week wait, sir...") motherboard of the 286. And that's the best news about the rapid advance of technology: the rapidly falling prices on "outdated" stuff.

It's easy to forget, when reading these mags and trade newspapers, that, until the exact moment of release of the new technology, *everybody* was using the old technology. Unless you have an absolute, quantifiable need to purchase the very newest whatever (and if you know that you need it, you won't be reading this...) the best advice is to wait. Not only will you end up paying less than on the day of release, but you'll also have the benefit of other folks being the guinea pigs.

Vaporware

The vaporware concept is particularly prevalent in the software side of things. Every week, the trade press is flooded with announcements of new products. Many of them don't exist except in a raw development state. A few are imaginary. Some of the more responsible companies hold off their new product announcements until the new release is at least half-way through the beta testing process. Getting products out the door on time is such an unusual happening that Lotus Development Corporation once threw a huge party, complete with a decorated semi-trailer truck, for the on-time ship date of a 1-2-3 release.

TIP

Don't hold up the purchase of needed software for a new release which just might be vaporware. Better to purchase the current version, probably well-tested and debugged, and pay a few dollars more for an upgrade when the new release has had some field time.

Also, beware upgrade offers from software companies. Often the upgrade ("Save $20! Order now!") form appears in your mail at about the same moment that programming work is begun on the upgrade.

Weirdware

Across the country, around the world, there are computer wonks thinking "Wouldn't it be nice if..." They usually have perceived a tiny niche that's not filled by either software or hardware and set out to invent it. This is a Good Thing. If fewer people had spent time in garages messing with PCs in the early 80s, we'd still be back in the '80s, technologically speaking. Check the back pages of any computer publication and you'll see tiny ad after tiny ad for either software or hardware that does something only about 1,000 people in the free world would need. If you're one of those 1,000 people, you may have stumbled onto something wonderful that far outpaces what's available from the big commercial developers. Small companies can keep abreast of technology far better than the giants.

TIP

When you purchase Weirdware or any other software from a small shop, you will usually hit the jackpot with technical support...the person answering the phone, more often than not, will be the wonk who developed it!

Be *very careful* with Weirdware, especially if it involves electricity. And, if at all possible, pay with a credit card so you have some recourse if it doesn't work as advertised.

NOTE

Weirdware does not include shareware.

Adopt-A-Wonk

Most newly-purchased computers come with warranty schemes serviced by large national organizations. A warranty is comforting. The service may not be. Additional years' service contracts are expensive, too. Consider the "benefits" carefully.

Remember the *gurus* from Chapter 1? Many of them are happily ensconced in small workshops doing what they like to do best...fix computers. Unfortunately for them, PCs are becoming more and more reliable all the time so there are fewer and fewer repair shops these days. Nevertheless, the best time to find a computer repair person is before you need one. And knowing that you can call Bolivar on the phone and show up 20 minutes later with your ailing PC is a comfort beyond price when many service companies *guarantee* an appearance by a technician within 24 hours. Maybe.

With more and more of the big companies going to centralized service points and parts depots, chances are that a local person can provide speedier service and will have the same—if not better—access to needed parts. It's also quite probable that Bolivar will have *years* more experience than the fresh-faced youngster who's not too sure which end of a screwdriver to use.

The PANDA people have adopted a wonk named Dave. We haven't needed or used Dave's services in about three years, but he's always on the other end of the phone as we proceed to work through problems we haven't seen before. In return, he calls us with virus questions that we answer if we can. Every now and then one of us stops by his shop to drop off a case of JOLT! Cola or National Bohemian beer (a local treat) and pass the time of day. And we always refer clients and friends with problems to Dave.

TIP

Find a wonk. Adopt him. Or her.

(Black) Mail Order

Some of the best deals on hardware and software today are offered through mail-order houses. It makes sense. No expensive overhead, just a bunch of phones, some ads in computer magazines, a billing system, and a warehouse full of goodies. Just remember...if the price is too good to be true, it probably is.

The best mail-order houses (PC Connection of Marlowe, New Hampshire, comes immediately to mind) also have strong, competent tech support staff. And their warehouses are well-stocked at all times. A three- or four-day wait for shipment from a mail-order house (unless the item is really hot) usually means that there's no stock at all and the warehouse is non-existent. The supplier takes your order, charges your credit card, and then orders what you want from another source.

TIP

Before placing an order with an unknown mail-order house, ask to speak to a tech support person, and then ask a simple question about the product you intend to order. If there's no tech support person "available," beware. Ask for a callback before you place your order.

You won't find much variation in prices from one mail-order outlet to another. One will be higher on one item, lower on another.

Flee Markets

Often held on weekends in huge auditoriums, most computer flea markets charge an admission fee, the auditorium management sells soft drinks and hot dogs at a price best described as rapacious, and hundreds of vendors try to sell you *something*. The prices are often terrific, but the bargains may not be.

Be suspicious of anything that seems too good to be true, particularly items that are normally expensive. This isn't to suggest that the software or printer offered at 1/4 retail just fell off the back of a truck and might be too hot to touch, though that can be the case. Attempt, if you're purchasing hardware, to open the box, set the thing up, and watch it run. If nothing else, *insist* on paying by credit card so you have some recourse. Never pay more in cash than you're prepared to lose. Also understand that technical support from these vendors may be non-existent. Sometimes the vendors, themselves, are non-existent the following week.

You will encounter software vendors with, literally, thousands of disks. Some software sorts are exceedingly careful that they can, in fact, "sell" you a program. Some are also exceedingly careful to make sure that the disks they're selling are virus-free. Then there are the other ones. Be warned.

The Dangers of Defrag

As you delete and create files on your hard disk, DOS uses the space that it finds available to write the new information. It's possible that a single file could find itself spread all over the hard dive—here a cluster, there a cluster—and the time it takes to read in the file is increased by the seek time to locate all the bits and pieces.

In order to speed up operations, use a disk compression, or "de-frag" (for *fragment*), utility. These utilities are usually fun to watch with small symbols dancing across the screen, indicating that work is indeed progressing. When the process is complete, you'll be amazed at how much more quickly your PC responds. Usually.

Defraggers work by hauling huge amounts of data into memory, mashing it around, then writing it back where it ought to be—in tidy, contiguous blocks. But remember, in order for the data to be written in location A, whatever was already *in* A has to be removed, awaiting shipment to its new locations. Too much can go wrong in the process not to take special care. *Never* begin a defrag process without a current backup. Ever.

 And make sure that you have no TSR programs in memory. Most compression utilities remind you before they run to (a) back up and (b) remove all TSRs. If you're not sure whether you have any TSRs, the program Dr. Hook, included on the disk in the back of the book, will tell you.

TIP

Here's the easy way to make sure no TSRs are loaded: Boot your PC from a DOS disk in drive A, change to the hard drive and the subdirectory where your defrag utility is located, and start the program. This ensures that no TSRs can be loaded.

BATs in the Belfry: BATch Files

Those little BAT files can sure come in handy. You probably have many of them scattered about your hard disk. You may not be aware of the incredible amount of disk access it takes to run just one little batch file.

Every time you run a BAT file, COMMAND.COM searches through the PATH for the file, opens it, reads the file into memory, closes it, and executes the command in the first line. Then COMMAND.COM searches through the PATH again for the file, opens it, reads the file into memory, closes it, and executes the command in the second line. This search, open, read, close, and execute process continues for every line in the file. Depending on the cache and buffer status of the drive, you are subjecting the mechanical parts of the drive to an incredible amount of wear just to run a batch file.

Here's a tip. Set up a RAM drive in memory. DOS includes one called RAMDRIVE. You create the RAM drive by placing RAMDRIVE in either the CONFIG.SYS file or the AUTOEXEC.BAT file, depending on your DOS version. This will create a pseudo disk in memory. RAMDRIVE displays the drive designator when it creates the drive. If you have a hard disk with one partition, the RAM drive will be drive D:. If you have more than one partition on the hard disk, the RAM drive will be one letter above the last logical hard disk drive.

Edit your AUTOEXEC.BAT file to include the RAM drive's root directory as the first directory in the PATH statement, as follows:

```
PATH=D:\;C:\DOS;C:\LOTUS…
```

After the PATH statement, copy all the batch files to the RAM drive. If you store all of your BAT files in a subdirectory called BATS, you can copy the entire subdirectory, like this:

```
COPY C:\BATS D: >NUL
```

NOTE

Redirecting the output of COPY to NUL suppresses the n file(s) copied *message.*

If your batch files are scattered around the disk, use XCOPY with the /S switch:

```
XCOPY C:\*.BAT D: /s >NUL
```

Now when you run a BAT file, COMMAND.COM will find it in the RAM drive. Not only will your batch files run faster, but you will also save wear and tear on your hard disk.

Can You EXE(cute) a COM(mand)?

Since day one of MS-DOS, there have been two kinds of program files: those with an EXE extension and those with a COM extension. You may wonder what the difference is.

COM (short for *COMMAND*) files are binary memory images. The file is an exact copy of what the program looks like when it is stored in memory. The COM extension is fast becoming extinct. In its place, you will begin seeing BIN (for *BINARY*).

EXE (short for *EXECUTABLE*) files are program files that need some help to become a program in memory. Every EXE file contains a section called a *header*, which contains information DOS needs to load the program into memory. A special section within DOS reads the header and uses this information when loading the program into memory.

What's in a Name? An EXE by Any Other Name Would Load as Sweet

You would think that COM and EXE are the Montagues and Capulets of computing because they require different methods of loading. But only COMMAND.COM cares about the extension. EXE and COM are merely extensions that COMMAND.COM looks for when you type a filename on the command line. You can freely switch extensions between EXE and COM, and the program will work just fine no matter which kind of file it is. You can even patch COMMAND.COM so that it searches for different extensions such as PRG and BIN.

When DOS loads a program, it first checks the two initial bytes of the file. If those bytes are ASCII "MZ", the file is loaded like an EXE file. If not, the file is loaded as a binary memory image. Not surprisingly, *Mark Zbikowski* was the principal architect of DOS. (Strange, we never see WG or BG.)

The COM before the Workhorse

EXE files are the workhorses of computer programming. They can be as large as memory allows. COM files must fit into a single memory segment (64K or 65,535 bytes). The original design for DOS included internal commands, which where built into COMMAND.COM (such as DIR and COPY), and external commands, which, although part of COMMAND.COM, were stored as files to be used when needed (such as DISKCOPY and CHKDSK). Programs were to be EXE files. Therefore COMMAND.COM always looks for a command first.

When you type something on the command line and press Enter, COMMAND.COM is the program that interprets your input. First, COMMAND.COM checks a list of internal commands. Next, it checks for an external command (COM file); and finally, it checks for a program file (EXE). As a last resort, COMMAND.COM checks for a batch file containing further commands.

Be careful about where you place executable files. Remember the order in which COMMAND.COM searches. A filename with an EXE extension in the same directory as the same filename with a COM extension will never be run. There are exceptions. Some programs use a COM extension as an initialization program that runs an EXE file by the same name. In this case, COMMAND.COM runs the COM program, which in turn runs the EXE program.

WARNING

Be alert to a special type of virus called a Companion Virus. This virus does not change the EXE file, but it makes a hidden COM file with the same filename containing the virus code. COMMAND.COM always runs the companion instead of the EXE file.

Go To...

One of the most important memory areas of the computer is the first 1K, the Interrupt Vector Table. This area stores 255 four-byte addresses that literally tell the computer where to go. An interrupt can be generated by the hardware or software and is identified by an interrupt number. When the microprocessor (CPU) receives an interrupt signal, it stops what it is doing, looks up an address of the Interrupt Service Routine (ISR) for the interrupt number in the Interrupt Vector Table, and starts processing at that address. The ISR contains an Interrupt Return (IRET) instruction which returns the CPU to what it was doing before the interrupt occurred.

The Interrupt Vector Table can be accessed just like any other area of memory. It is not uncommon for programs to change the vector addresses (see the next section on TSRs). If an interrupt vector is changed so that no ISR appears at that address, the system could crash. Most likely, you will have to reboot to reset the interrupt vectors. You might possibly need to turn the computer off because the Three Fingered Salute (Ctrl-Alt-Del) causes an interrupt that performs the warm restart.

TSRs: A Hitchhiker's Guide to the Memory

TSR is the computer acronym for Terminate-and-Stay-Resident. It's a DOS gift that keeps on giving and can be somewhat akin to its biological counterpart if not used properly. TSRs can be the little utilities that pop windows onto the screen when you press a certain key combination or DOS's own PRINT program that (sort of) allows you to continue computing while a file is being printed. Several TSR programs are included with DOS and thousands more are available in the software market.

Rules? We Don't Need No Stinking Rules!

Yes, there are rules that all TSRs should follow. But for years the rules were kept secret within the confines of Microsoft and only bits and pieces received public notice. As a result, hundreds of programmers wrote TSR utilities that do not follow the rules. A TSR may work properly for years without following the letter of the law and then suddenly—ZAP!—you're out of luck.

 How do you know a TSR is following the rules? You don't. That's the sad part. How do you know what TSRs are in memory? That's easy. Run the Dr. Hook program that comes with this book or enter the MEM command at the DOS prompt. You see all the programs that are still sitting in memory and how much space they are using.

DOS Memory Allocation

DOS keeps track of memory by dividing it into blocks. Each DOS memory block begins with a 16-byte header that indicates which program owns the block and how big it is:

```
DOS MEMORY BLOCK HEADER

Signature      1 byte
                          'M'=Memory Block
                          'Z'=Last Memory Block
Owner          2 bytes
Length         2 bytes (number of 16 byte paragraphs)
unused         3 bytes
Owner's Name   8 bytes (DOS 4.0+)
```

If the Owner is 0, the memory block is free. To find the next memory block, add the length times 16 to the address of the header. There will not be another header if the signature byte is Z instead of M. (Mark Zbikowski's initials appear yet again.)

When DOS runs a program, it normally gets two memory blocks. One block is for a copy of the "environment," and the other is for the program. You can see what's in the environment by entering SET on the command line. DOS usually allocates all remaining memory to the program. Programs can use DOS functions to resize memory blocks, allocate memory blocks, and free memory blocks. Once the program terminates (ends), all memory that was allocated to that program is once again freed, unless the program uses a DOS function to terminate and stay resident. In that case, DOS resizes the program's memory block and keeps it as part of the memory chain. All subsequent programs are loaded after the TSR's memory block.

Rule: Save only as much memory as the TSR needs, not too much (Hog) and not too little (Crash).

Getting Control of the Situation

Just because it remains in memory does not mean that the TSR program can *do* anything. There must be some way for the TSR to gain control. Therefore, most TSRs hook one or more of the INTERRUPT vectors.

Rule: Pass control to the previous interrupt handler or else (Crash).

We Don't Do DOS (Again)

It may seem that those TSR programs allow you to do two things at once, but that is an illusion. DOS is a single-tasking operating system. Only one process runs at a time. A TSR cannot use a DOS function if another DOS function is in progress.

Rule: Do not call a DOS function in the middle of a DOS function or else (Crash).

Let Me Outta' Here

Some TSRs can be removed from memory by pressing a certain key or running the program again with a special switch on the command line. The TSR releases the DOS memory block and returns any hooked interrupt vectors to their previous values. However, if another TSR was loaded subsequently, it's possible that it passes control along to the one being released. Resetting the interrupt vector could effectively bypass the other TSR.

Rule: Don't reset interrupt vectors that don't point to the TSR about to be released or else (Crash).

Rule: Don't reset memory if another TSR has hooked the interrupt or else (Crash).

Devices and Files...What's in a Name Revisited

DOS uses eight-character names for both files and devices, and you can't use the same name twice.

Workin' on the Chain Gang

As DOS initializes, it builds a chain of device headers that can be used to access any peripherals. Each device is given a name which can be up to eight characters long (just like filenames). DOS automatically assigns the names NUL, CON, AUX, PRN, CLOCK$, COM1 through COM4, and LPT1 through LPT4.

Devices loaded by the command DEVICE= in the CONFIG.SYS file are inserted into the device header chain following NUL in the order in which they appear. Two types of device drivers can be loaded: block devices, like disk drivers, and character devices. Block devices are assigned drive letters, and character devices have eight-character device names.

 To see the device chain on your computer, run the program Dr. Hook supplied with this book and press F2. The name of every character device is listed. Block devices indicate how many units (drives) are associated with the device driver.

A Device Is Not a File

DOS will always search the device chain for a name before searching for a file. This means you can't name a file CON or PRN. If you use one of the device names on the command line, DOS will not even look for a file by the same name:

```
C:\>COPY MYFILE.DAT PRN.DAT
```

This sends the file MYFILE.DAT to the PRINTER and not to a file named PRN.DAT on the current drive.

The following command will create the file PRN.DAT on device A:.

```
C:\>COPY MYFILE.DAT A:PRN.DAT
```

Now it begins to make sense. DOS first searches for a device—in this case, A:—and then for the file PRN.DAT. Only if there is no device match, as in MYFILE, will DOS assume the current drive as the device.

WARNING

If you save a file and use a device name as the filename, the data goes to the device instead of to a file.

Supporting Cast

Computing can be a lonely activity. There's usually only room for one at the keyboard and activity can be intense. Tales of computer widows (and widowers) float across the land. And, strangest of all, even the most highly placed computer professionals speak of "playing" with a new system or a new program.

Unless you're working (or playing) in an environment with its own support group, consider joining a PC users' group. On-line services like CompuServe, GEnie, PRODIGY, and DELPHI also offer areas to ask questions and get answers about PCs and almost anything else you can imagine. Reach out.

At Last It Can Be Told

The following exchange of inter-office messages actually took place in mid-1985 and have been carefully saved for just such a moment. If nothing else, they provide a commentary on how bargains can get out of hand. In absolute fact, it's why Kane decided that marrying Hopkins was cheaper than supporting his bargain-hunting activities on company time.

Date: 4/17/85

To: Pam Kane

From: Andy Hopkins

Re: Bargain hard disk

I was able to purchase a Tandon 40 megabyte hard disk to upgrade the old PC-1 at a computer flea market in King of Prussia, PA. This was a new, still in the original packaging, hard disk valued at $849 retail. Cost of the hard disk at the flea market was $250.

For accounting purposes, please add 50 miles of automobile expense at $.20 per mile, $5.00 admission to the flea market, and $4.57 for lunch.

Hard disk 250.00

Automobile Expense...................10.00

Admission 5.00

Lunch...4.57

                              ======

Total   269.57

Date: 4/19/85

To: Pam Kane

From: Andy Hopkins

Re: Additional items for hard disk

In order to install the new hard disk I have had to order a few pieces of additional equipment.

The 75-watt power supply of the PC will not support the requirements of a hard disk. I have ordered a new 150-watt power supply from PC Connections for $149.95.

Also, the PC's ROM chips need to be upgraded to support the addition of a hard disk. I have picked up the required replacement chip from the IBM store in King of Prussia for $53.00.

For accounting purposes, add 54 miles of automobile expense (to IBM in King of Prussia to pick up the new ROM chip).

Power supply 149.94

Automobile expense 10.80

======

Total   160.74

Date: 4/20/85

To: Pam Kane

From: Andy Hopkins

Re: A few more things

I have discovered that the Tandon hard disk does not include the controller board. I have ordered a Western Digital hard disk controller from B&S Supply for $99.95. These are not in stock at the moment, but they expect a shipment at any time. I'll advise you when it arrives.

Western Digital Hard
Disk Controller 99.95

Data cable 15.95

Control cable 12.95

                                     ======

Total   128.85

Date: 6/15/85

To: Pam Kane

From: Andy Hopkins

Re: Hard disk progress

The backordered controller card arrived today from B&S Supply along with the cables. Unfortunately, I could not install the hard disk because all 5 slots on the PC are in use in the following manner:

1. Color video controller

2. Disk controller

3. Additional memory

4. RS-232C

5. Printer controller

I have ordered a multi-function board from PC Connections to replace the RS-232C and Printer Controller with one card. This will not only free a slot for the hard disk controller, but will allow me to upgrade the memory from 512K to 640K. I have ordered the additional memory chips also.

Multi-function board 149.95

18 64K memory chips
(128K) 102.90

            =======

Total   252.85

Date: 7/6/85

To: Pam Kane

From: Andy Hopkins

Re: Hard disk update

Before installing the Tandon hard disk, I noticed that one
of the disk drives would have to be removed. Because the
hard disk is a half-height hard disk, this will create a hole
in the front of the PC. Prices on disk drives are dropping
rapidly and I have ordered a half-height disk drive to fill
the hole for only $249.95. This will allow us to continue
disk copy operations on this machine.

Half-height disk 249.95

Date: 7/15/85

To: Pam Kane

From: Andy Hopkins

Re: Problems

All the pieces for the upgrade of the PC are in place. Unfortunately the PC does not have a mounting bracket for half-height drives. I was able to fashion a bracket from pieces obtained at the hardware store so the hard disk and half-height disk can be mounted in the drive bay.

Hardware 6.38

Automobile expense
(2 trips) 1.50

=====

Total   7.88

Date: 7/16/85

To: Pam Kane

From: Andy Hopkins

Re: Hard disk installed!

The hard disk, half-height disk, multi-function card, new power supply, and ROM chips have all been installed in the PC. Upon starting the system the screen displayed 1701 and when drive C: was accessed, I got the message Invalid drive specification. I called IBM and was told that 1701 is the message indicating that the hard disk controller has returned an error to the ROM on bootup. They opined that the hard disk had no low level format.

I called Tandon and was told that disks are shipped unformatted and the low level format program was contained on ROM on the controller card.

I called Western Digital and they walked me through a low level format of the hard disk, but the PC would still not recognize the disk. They suggested I call Tandon to see whether the controller matched the disk.

I called Tandon again and was told that Western Digital controller WD1049A was the proper controller for that particular disk.

I called Western Digital again and they told me how to figure out which controller I had. Turns out that the controller B&S advised me to get was the wrong one.

I called B&S about the controller problem and they apologized and agreed to replace the controller with the WD1049A. That particular controller was backordered but they expected a shipment at any time.

Long distance phone calls 53.12

Controller price difference 12.00

=====

Total   65.12

Date: 8/20/85

To: Pam Kane

From: Andy Hopkins

Re: Hard disk WORKS!!!!!!

The Tandon 40M hard disk has been successfully installed in the PC and all programs and data have been transferred to the hard disk from disks. I would suggest that the external hard disks on the other PCs be upgraded to larger internal hard disks as soon as we can find another flea market in the area.

Date: 9/12/85

To: Pam Kane

From: Andy Hopkins

Re: Dead disk drive

The hard disk died last night. When the PC was turned on this morning, the hard disk apparently froze. There is no indication that the disk is turning. I called Tandon and they advised me that this particular model was discontinued over a year ago because of problems with the motor bearings. They had sold their remaining stock as surplus.

They know of no way to recover the data because the bearings are sealed in the motor housing and cannot be replaced. In retrospect, I probably should have made a backup of the data. I think I can reconstruct all source code before the end of October.

One additional note. Even though the warranty has expired they offered to trade the defective disk for a new one for $750.

Advise.

Long distance phone call 6.50

Date: 9/21/85

To: Andy Hopkins

From: Pam Kane

Re: What a bargain!

Please review the spreadsheet from accounting on the hard disk upgrade for your PC.

Hard disk	250.00
Automobile expense	10.00
Admission	5.00
Lunch	4.57
Power supply	149.94
Automobile expense	10.80
Western Digital hard disk controller	99.95
Data cable	15.95
Control cable	12.95
Multi-function board	149.95
18 64K memory chips (128K)	102.90
Half-height disk	249.95
Hardware	6.38
Automobile expense (2 trips)	1.50
Long distance phone calls	53.12
Controller price difference	12.00
Long distance phone call	6.50
	======
Total	1141.46

Because I can no longer afford your bargains, I have ordered a new IBM PC AT for you with a 40M CMI hard disk. This state-of-the-art technology should last well into the next century.

EOF Marker

As mentioned much earlier, the fate of that PC AT with its monster 40M CMI hard drive cannot be recalled. Andy Hopkins now works with a minimum of one 386 and two 486 PCs in his office (that's on a slow day). He eagerly awaits a bargain on a Pentium (586). Pam Kane awaits an inter-office memo requesting one.

IV

The Disk In Back

16

The Disk Bank

There are 18 utility programs on the disk bound into the back of this book. Ten of them were developed by PANDA Systems, eight of them are new especially for this book. Three are from a fine shareware vendor, Patri-Soft, the remainder are in the public domain. Here's the list:

PANDA UTILITIES

NODEL   A small TSR that prevents the DEL(ete) and ERASE commands from being used from the command line. Allows additional programs, such as FORMAT to be disabled.

DRHOOK   Part of the DR. PANDA Utilities, it displays TSR programs currently in memory and which interrupts are hooked by those programs. Also displays all installed devices.

DISKINFO   Shows the informaton in the DOS Drive Parameter Block.

MONITOR	A TSR program which prevents Data destruction through the disk access interrupt. Can also trap disk, read, and write calls in a laboratory setting.
BOOTINFO	Shows the information in the Boot Sector BIOS Parameter Block.
PARTINFO	Shows the partitioning information of the hard drive(s).
FINDPART	Shows existing partitions and boot sectors. Displays a warning if the information seems incorrect. Can find lost partitions and boot sectors.
WHEREIS	The PANDA version of an old favorite. Finds "missing" files.
DELALL	Deletes files in any subdirectory after confirmation.
BROWSE	A full screen version of the TYPE command which allows you to scroll back and forth through the file.

PATRI-SOFT UTILITIES

You can spend lots of money and take up lots of disk space with a huge commercial package and not have the ease of use and functionality of these three programs:

MEGABACK	Lets you back up to any medium, compresses files, keeps a list of backups on the hard drive.
STOWAWAY	Archives files to any medium, deletes files from the hard drive, maintains a list on the hard drive for easy retrieval.
PCOPY	Faster and better than DOS XCOPY.

The Patri-Soft Utilities are *shareware* and are included in this book for your evaluation. If you like and use them, please register them. Technical support for these utilties comes directly from Patri-Soft.

FROM THE PUBLIC DOMAIN

These are programs whose authors have "donated" them to the greater good of computer users everywhere. No warranty is made, either by the authors or publisher of this book, as to whether or not these programs will work for you. They worked for us, or we would not have included them.

HOWBAD	The "Shame on You" utility.
LHARC	Fast data compression program.
CHKDIR	Works like CHKDSK, but on specified directories.
CMOS	Backs up CMOS information.
DELBUT	Lets you exclude files from a DEL *.* command.

The Disk

All the files on the disk are archived using the LHARC program. The LHARC program itself (LHA.EXE) is not archived and can be used to un-archive the files. There is an INSTALL.BAT file which will copy the files to your hard disk in the PANDA directory. The files on the disk are:

INSTALL.BAT	Installation batch file.
HOWBAD.EXE	The HOWBAD program.
LHA.EXE	The LHA program.
LHARC93.LZH	Archived documentation and associated files for LHARC.
MBACK93.LZH	Archived MBACK program, install and associated files.
PCOPY93.LZH	Archived PCOPY program and documentation.
PANDA93.LZH	Archived PANDA utilities.

PUBDOM93.LZH	Archived public domain utilities and documentation.
STOW93.LZH	The STOW program, installation program and associated files.

The INSTALL Batch File

The INSTALL.BAT file can be used to copy the files on the disk to your hard disk, and un-archive the files. Both the MBACK and the STOW programs need to be installed with their own INSTALL programs. The batch file will run these programs automatically, but if you do not install them at this time, you will have to run the install programs separately later. MBACK installs with the MINSTALL.EXE program, and STOW installs with the SINSTALL.EXE program.

To use the INSTALL batch file, you will need to supply the destination drive letter, followed by a colon. The colon is important. If you don't include it, the batch file will unarchive the programs onto the diskette.

To install the programs in a directory called PANDA on the C: drive, place the diskette in the A: drive, log on to that drive and enter:

```
A:\>INSTALL C:
```

Once you have run the install program, you may want to edit your AUTOEXEC.BAT file to include the \PANDA directory in the PATH= statement. Then you can run the utilities from any directory or drive.

If you do not want to use the INSTALL batch file, you can un-archive any of the files with the LHA.EXE program. The syntax is:

```
LHA x [filename]
```

The "x" means extract the files. The filename is the name of the archive without the LZH extension. To see a complete list of LHA syntax, enter "LHA /?".

The PANDA Programs

The PANDA Systems programs on the disk in the back of the book are to be treated as shareware. By purchasing this book, you have purchased a shareware license in the PANDA shareware. You have *not* purchased a license in the other shareware included from Patri-Soft. The rest of the programs are in the public domain. This means that you can share them freely with others and are under no obligation to register them with the author.

PANDA Programs

The following PANDA Systems programs are included on the disk:

```
INFORMATIONAL:

BOOTINFO.EXE
BROWSE.COM
DISKINFO.EXE
DRHOOK.EXE
PARTINFO.EXE
WHEREIS.EXE


TSR:

MONITOR.EXE
NODEL.EXE


FUNCTIONAL:

DELALL.EXE
FINDPART.EXE
```

These programs are © Copyright PANDA Systems, Wilmington, DE. All rights reserved. You may make copies for your personal use, but you may not give copies or sell the programs to others.

BOOTINFO.EXE

BOOTINFO displays the information in the BIOS Parameter Block (BPB) located in the boot sector of the selected drive.

SYNTAX:

BOOTINFO [*drive:*]

PARAMETER:

[*drive:*] The drive you want to see. Defaults to A:.

KEYS:
None:

EXIT:
Automatic.

```
15:38:35  Sat 03-27-1993   Directory  C:\WORD\DOCS
C>bootinfo c:
System ID:            MSDOS5.0
Bytes Per Sector:     200
Sectors Per Cluster:  4
Reserved Sectors:     1
Copies of FAT:        2
Root Dir Entries:     200
Total Sectors:        f7e0
Format ID:            f8
Sectors per FAT:      3e
Sectors per Track:    20
Sides:                40
Special Reserved:     20

C>
```

Figure 16.1. Output from BOOTINFO.

BROWSE.COM

BROWSE is a full screen version of the DOS TYPE command. Instead of the text scrolling up the screen, BROWSE allows you to use the arrow keys to move the text up, down, left and right. You can go to the end of the file by pressing the <End> key, or the beginning of the file by pressing the <Home> key. To exit BROWSE, press <Esc>.

SYNTAX:
BROWSE [*drive:*][path]filename

PARAMETERS:
[*drive:*][*path*]filename

Specifies the location and name of the file you want to view.

KEYS:	DOWN ARROW:	Moves text up one line.
	UP ARROW:	Moves text down one line.
	RIGHT ARROW:	Moves text left ten characters.
	LEFT ARROW:	Moves text back to first column.
	PAGE DOWN:	Moves text up one screen.
	PAGE UP:	Moves text down one screen.
	END:	Moves to end of file.
	HOME:	Moves to beginning of file.
	<Esc>:	Returns to DOS.

NOTE

Written out the keys seem backwards, but using them is really intuitive.

EXIT: Press <Esc>. The screen returns to the same display as before BROWSE was invoked.

DISKINFO.EXE

DISKINFO displays the information in the DOS Drive Parameter Block (DPB) for the selected drive. The information is displayed in both Hex and Decimal.

SYNTAX:
DISKINFO [*drive:*]

PARAMETERS:
[*drive:*] The drive you want to see. Defaults to A:.

KEYS:
None:

EXIT:
Automatic.

```
15:38:54  Sat 03-27-1993  Directory: C:\WORD\DOCS
C>diskinfo c:
2          C           Drive
2          2           Unit Within Driver
200        512         Bytes per Sector
3          3           Sectors Per Cluster -1
2          2           Cluster to Sector Shift
1          1           Number Reserved Sectors
2          2           Number of FAT Copies
200        512         Number of Root Directory Entries
9d         157         Sector of First Data Cluster
3dd1       15825       Number of Clusters
3e         62          Sectors per FAT
7d         125         Sector of Root Directory
0A2F:20C4              Address of Device Header
f8         f8          Media Descriptor Byte
0          0           0 if accessed
0129:13CB             Next DOS Disk Block
3bb2       15282       Read/Write Head Location (Cluster Number)
ffff       -1          Number of Free Clusters (-1 is Unknown)

C>
```

Figure 16.2. Output from DISKINFO.

DRHOOK.EXE

DRHOOK displays memory used by Terminate and Stay Resident (TSR) programs and the interrupt vectors associated with each. An option lets you display the memory used by the device driver chain. To exit press <Esc> or <F10>.

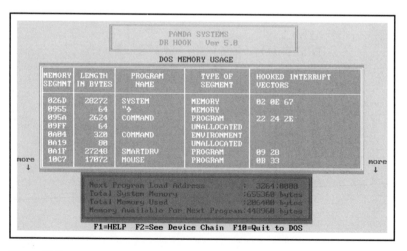

Figure 16.3. DRHOOK's DOS Memory Usage screen.

SYNTAX:
DRHOOK

PARAMETERS:
None.

KEYS: UP ARROW: Move screen down one line.
       DOWN ARROW: Move screen up one line.
       RIGHT ARROW: Move screen left one character.
       LEFT ARROW: Move screen right one character.
       <F2>:   Display Device Driver information.
       <F3>:   Display TSR information.
       <F10>:   Return to DOS.
       <ESC>:   Return to DOS.

EXIT: Press <Esc> or <F10>. The DRHOOK display remains on the
screen and the cursor is placed on the bottom line.

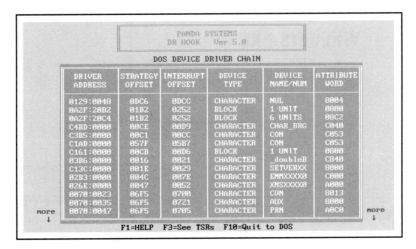

Figure 16.4. DRHOOK's Device Driver screen.

PARTINFO.EXE

PARTINFO displays information about the partitions of your hard
drives. This program is menu driven. The menu can be accessed by
clicking the left mouse button on the desired choice or pressing the

<Alt> key and moving the highlight to the desired selection. Pressing <Enter> or a highlighted Hot Key selects the menu choice.

SYNTAX:
PARTINFO

MOUSE:
Click the left mouse button on the menu choice.

KEYS:

<Alt>:	Opens menu.
ARROW:	Moves highlighted menu selection.
<Enter>:	Selects menu option.
HotKey:	Selects menu option by highlighted letter.
<Esc>:	Closes menu.

EXIT:
Select "Exit" choice in "Quit" menu.

WHEREIS.EXE

WHEREIS allows you to do a DIR search for a file or group of files through all subdirectories.

SYNTAX:
WHEREIS [*drive:*]*filename.ext* [*drive:*]*filename.ext* ...

PARAMETERS:
[*drive:*] Limit search to one drive. Default, all drives from C: to last drive.
filename.ext The name of the file you want to find. DOS wild cards * and ? may be used. You can search for several files by entering more than one filename.

KEYS:
None.

EXIT:
Automatic.

```
15:52:13  Sat 03-27-1993  Directory: C:\WORD\DOCS
C>whereis find*.bak
Copyright (c) Panda Systems 1992.  All rights reserved.
F:\SOURCE\RECOVER\FINDMENU.BAK          2915 bytes   03/25/93   07:26:14
F:\SOURCE\RECOVER\FINDDISP.BAK          8590 bytes   03/26/93   08:51:38
F:\SOURCE\RECOVER\FINDBOOT.BAK          6838 bytes   03/26/93   08:52:28

            3 File(s)              18343 bytes

C>
```

Figure 16.5. The WHEREIS utility.

MONITOR.EXE

MONITOR is a TSR program that can be used as both an informational tool and as a malware protector. In the default configuration, MONITOR examines writes to the critical disk areas, the Master Boot Record, the DOS Boot Sector and the FAT through the BIOS disk interrupt (13 hex). No writes are allowed to the MBR or DOS Boot Sector. Only data that "appears" to be FAT chain data can be written to the FAT sectors. The blocks on misbehaved activity are absolute and cannot be overridden by the user. MONITOR also prevents any attempt to FORMAT a disk.

Additional options include a display of head, track and sector (HTS) for every read and/or write call. A "Professional" mode allows you to proceed or cancel any disk operation.

SYNTAX:
MONITOR [/p][/r][/w][/v][/f][/x]

SWITCHES:

/p	Professional mode. Allows proceed/bypass of any disk call.
/r	Displays HTS information of "Read" calls.

/w	Displays HTS information of "Write" calls.
/v	Displays HTS information of "Verify" calls.
/f	Displays HT information of "Format" calls.
/x	Disables MONITOR and (if possible) removes TSR.

KEYS:

(In Professional Mode)

\<Enter\> Proceed with call.

\<Esc\>   Cancel call with error.

(In default Mode)

Any key.

EXIT:

Automatic. Remains in memory.

INTERRUPTS HOOKED:

INT   13

INT   2F

NOTE: If the /r, /w, /f, or /v switch is used, MONITOR displays the status of every disk call to that function. There can be a LOT of disk calls in any application program.

To change the switch settings, run MONITOR again with the new switches. Old settings are discarded.

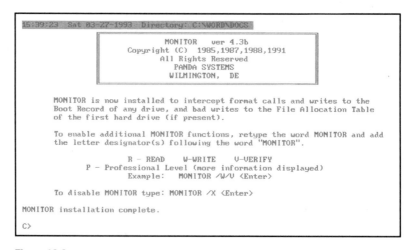

Figure 16.6. The MONITOR installation screen.

NODEL.EXE

NODEL is a memory resident (TSR) program that overrides the COMMAND.COM DEL and ERASE commands. With NODEL installed, you or anyone else who wanders by will be unable to delete a file from the command line. If you want to disable other commands (or programs) you can enter them as parameters on the command line.

SYNTAX:
NODEL [*command*] [*command*]... **/d**

PARAMETERS:
[*command*] DOS internal command or program file that is to be disabled. You can enter more than one command.

SWITCH:
/d Disable NODEL and (if possible) remove TSR from memory.

KEYS:
None.

EXIT:
Automatic. Program remains in memory.

INTERRUPTS HOOKED:
INT   2F

NOTE

NODEL always disables DEL and ERASE. If you want to change any parameters, just run NODEL again and the new parameters go into effect.

EXAMPLES:

```
C:\>NODEL
```

The DEL and ERASE commands will not work.

```
C:\WORD\DOCS>DIR *.BAK

Volume in drive C is PANDA C
Volume Serial Number is 2A27-1DD1
Directory of C:\WORD\DOCS
```

```
COOKBOOK BAK      45568 03-09-93   7:50a
PHYSICAL BAK      20992 03-17-93   4:19p
LOGICAL  BAK      47616 03-17-93  11:16p
TECH     BAK      75776 03-23-93   7:20a
EIGHT    BAK      23552 03-16-93  11:50a
TROUBLE  BAK      14848 03-24-93   8:14a
PROGRAMS BAK       5120 03-27-93  10:00a
        7 file(s)      233472 bytes
                      2717696 bytes free


C:\WORD\DOCS>ERASE *.BAK


C:\WORD\DOCS>DIR *.BAK

 Volume in drive C is PANDA C
 Volume Serial Number is 2A27-1DD1
 Directory of C:\WORD\DOCS

COOKBOOK BAK      45568 03-09-93   7:50a
PHYSICAL BAK      20992 03-17-93   4:19p
LOGICAL  BAK      47616 03-17-93  11:16p
TECH     BAK      75776 03-23-93   7:20a
EIGHT    BAK      23552 03-16-93  11:50a
TROUBLE  BAK      14848 03-24-93   8:14a
PROGRAMS BAK       5120 03-27-93  10:00a
        7 file(s)      233472 bytes
                      2717696 bytes free



C:\>NODEL FORMAT
```

The DEL, ERASE and FORMAT commands are disabled.
COMMAND.COM will not even look for a file named FORMAT.COM,
FORMAT.EXE or FORMAT.BAT.

```
C:\>FORMAT C:


C:\>
```

DELALL.EXE

DELALL allows you to delete a file or group of files in any sub-directory. You must confirm each deletion.

SYNTAX:
DELALL [*drive:*]*filename.exe* [*drive:*]*filename.ext*

PARAMETERS:
[*drive:*] Limits subdirectory search to one drive.
filename.exe The file(s) you want to delete.

KEYS:
<Y>   Delete file.
<N>   Do not delete file.

EXIT:
Automatic.

FINDPART.EXE

FINDPART is an informational program to detect trouble within the Partition Table and Boot Sector of a hard disk. You see a warning window if the partition information does not match the boot sector information. You also see a warning window if the partition information does not match the disk information stored in the BIOS. If there is a mismatch, you can scan the disk for additional partition sectors and boot sectors. The HTS of these "lost" sectors help you repair the partition information.

SYNTAX:
FINDPART

MOUSE:
Click the left mouse button on the menu choice.

KEYS:
<Alt>:   Opens menu.
ARROW: Moves highlighted menu selection.

<Enter>:   Selects menu option.
HotKey: Selects menu option by highlighted letter.
<Esc>:   Closes menu.

EXIT:
Select "Exit" choice in "Quit" menu.

MegaBack

MegaBack is a personal backup system for your computer.
MegaBack software automates and organizes backup processing
for your system. It also provides comprehensive abilities to restore
backup files when needed.

MegaBack is designed to be easy for all PC users. Its menus are simple
and understandable. MegaBack makes backup simple by surrounding
all complex backup terms and requirements with a menu driven
system.

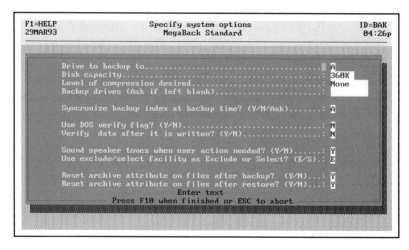

Figure 16.7. MegaBack System options.

MegaBack Features

Lets you control, backup, and type by selecting full volume, or incremental backup of updated files.

Saves you time by letting you optionally view files to be backed up before backup begins.

Simplifies restore by locating backup files quickly using backup indexes maintained by MegaBack.

Reduces backup time and diskettes required through a comprehensive exclusion facility that lets you mark directories and files to exclude from the backup process.

Saves time and effort by formatting new diskettes automatically.

Saves backup space by appending daily backup of updated files to the last backup disk used.

Saves backup space through very high compression and smart disk storage techniques. Lets you store the maximum amount of data on a minimum number of diskettes.

Provides flexibility by optionally restoring files to any specified location.

Uses multiple storage media. Backup to diskette, removable hard disks, or optical disks.

Provides transportability of backup data to other systems using portable backup volumes.

Provides peace of mind through extensive capabilities to recover from backup errors and disk losses.

Enhances backup data integrity by letting you create multiple backup disk sets to keep spare backup copies of your data.

Adapts to your operation preference of menu or command line operation.

Simplifies learning and operation through instant access to context sensitive help at any time (F1 key).

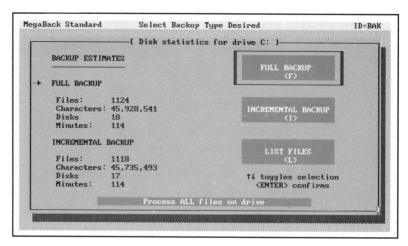

Figure 16.8. MegaBack backup options.

Backing up with MegaBack

MegaBack keeps compressed and compacted copies of files on off-line diskette volumes and maintains records for every file in a backup index on your hard disk. The backup index lets you immediately examine all information about your backup files without having to scan through backup diskettes.

MegaBack compresses each file as it is backed up to make maximum use of diskette storage. Compression usually results in storing files in 1/2 the space they would normally require on diskettes.

MegaBack also compacts data on backup disks to improve performance and further reduce disk space required for backup. All files backed up to a single diskette are compacted into a single backup file. Writing this single file is much faster and more efficient than writing multiple files on a backup diskette. In addition to performance, compaction saves disk space used by unoccupied cluster space at the end of each DOS file.

Unlike some other backup systems, MegaBack uses standard DOS disk I/O routines when reading and writing backup data. This makes MegaBack much more reliable as it does not depend on unsupported, nonstandard, I/O techniques that may fail on some computers.

MegaBack organizes your backup volumes (diskettes) in simple numerical order so it is easy to file and locate backup volumes. All volumes are numbered sequentially starting at 1. Newly backed up files are stored in the next available space on the last used backup volume.

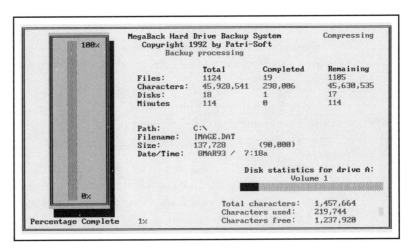

Figure 16.9. MegaBack backup processing.

Volumes are completely used before new volumes are started. Mega-Back tracks volumes by number and records information about the exact location of every stored file in its hard disk index.

MegaBack's backup index provides a backup directory containing valuable information about every file backed up. The backup index lets you determine if you have a backup of any file from any directory, and tells you the date and time the backup was made.

The following information is maintained about every backup file:

File name

Drive where file was backed up from

Directory where it was backed up from

File Size

Date the file was created or last changed

Time the file was created or last changed

File attributes

Date the file was backed up

Time the file was backed up

The number of the backup disk(s) holding the file

The compressed size of the backup file

When you need to restore files or an entire volume, you specify the drive, directory, and file information for all files to be restored.

These specifications may be for an exact file or may specify wildcard names for qualifying multiple files. \MegaBack can immediately restore all matching files, or it will provide a scrollable selection list for you to select one or more files to be restored.

Once you have selected files to be restored, MegaBack determines where the backup files are stored and requests volumes by number. This organization lets you keep many volumes of backup data while still maintaining easy access to any file.

Stowaway

Stowaway is a personal archival system for your computer. Stowaway releases space on your hard disk by archiving inactive files to off-line storage media such as diskette.

The files and software on our PC systems are changing at a rapid pace. We are constantly creating new data, trying new software, and updating old systems. Our hard disks become vessels holding massive amounts of information we want to keep at our fingertips.

In our fast paced world, much of what we use today is old tomorrow! Old data and software clutter our hard disks files and do little more than take up space. These files get in our way when we search for the files we need.

Deleting old files is not a solution, as we may have use for them in the future, so we end up purchasing more hard disk space to increase our storage capacity.

Although we do have need for larger hard disks to accommodate today's larger software and more complex systems, we can also use what space we have more efficiently. Hard disks are expensive storage locations for inactive data. Based on disk storage prices in 1992, it costs about $5.00 to store 1,000,000 characters of data on a hard disk. You can store the same amount of data in archive format on diskette for less than $0.50. This example shows a substantial savings to be gained archiving data. Inactive data should be stored on inexpensive media and in a place where we no longer have to deal with it each day.

Stowaway is a solution to the storage and maintenance of your inactive files. It manages the process of storing and tracking inactive data on less expensive storage media such as diskettes. Stowaway automates the task of moving files to off-line storage and cataloging them so they may be quickly located and restored when you need them. Stowaway is a data and software archival system for your personal computer.

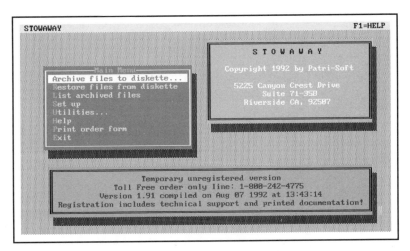

Figure 16.10. Stowaway Main menu.

Stowaway Features

➤ Age and select files for archival automatically based on your specification criteria.

➤ Select files to be archived from optional scrollable selection lists.

➤ Locate archived files quickly using hard disk archive indexes maintained by Stowaway.

➤ Format new diskettes automatically.

➤ Compressed data over 50%.

➤ Recover files to their original or new location.

➤ Archive to diskette, removable hard disks, or optical disks.

➤ Transport archives to other systems.

➤ Create multiple archive sets to keep archives for different users on the same system.

➤ Categorize archive files into groups.

➤ Add descriptive text to archive files.

➤ Archive and restore directories or trees.

➤ View WordPerfect and text files.

➤ Assign expiration dates to archived files.

➤ Run with command line parameters or menus.

➤ Examine context sensitive help at any time.

➤ Copy archive volumes easily to off-site storage.

➤ Archive files in a network environment.

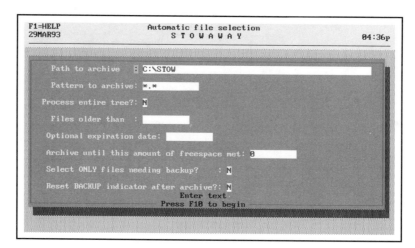

Figure 16.11. Automatic File Selection screen.

Archiving with Stowaway

Stowaway moves files to off-line disk volumes and keeps indexes of them on your hard drive. You retain the same access to inactive files that you had when they were on your hard disk. The index is instantly accessible to let you locate files. When you need a file again, Stowaway will bring it back from storage for you.

Stowaway organizes your archive volumes in simple numerical order so it is easy to file and locate archive volumes. All archive volumes are numbered sequentially starting at 1. Newly archived files are stored in the next available space on archive volumes.

Volumes are completely used before new volumes are started.

Stowaway tracks volumes by number and records information about the exact location of every stored file in its hard disk index.

Archive volumes are stored in numeric order. During restore processing, Stowaway determines where the archived file is stored, and requests archive volumes by number.

This organization lets you keep hundreds of volumes of archive data while still maintaining easy access to any file.

Use Stowaway to save all your old and seldom used files.

Archive:

> Old versions of software
>
> Old documentation
>
> Old data files
>
> Old system configuration information
>
> Picture and graphic files
>
> Faxes

PCOPY and PMOVE

PCOPY is an advanced replacement for the DOS COPY command, one of the most used of the DOS commands. Unfortunately, the DOS COPY abilities are very limited and are not sufficient for many disk maintenance chores. PCOPY is similar to the DOS COPY command in that it copies file data between disks and hard disk directories. In addition, PCOPY provides intelligent file selection and processing options.

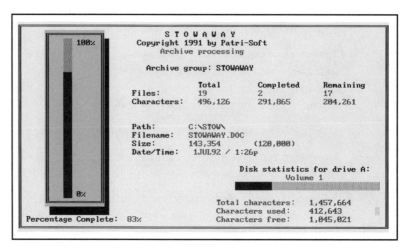

Figure 16.12. Stowaway archiving screen.

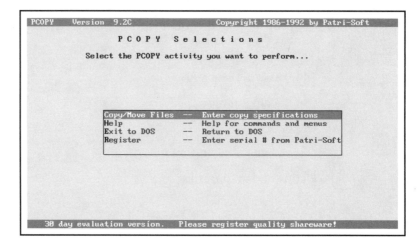

Figure 16.13. PCOPY Main menu.

PCOPY options allow you to use a single PCOPY command to perform a function that would require many complex DOS COPY commands.

PCOPY also provides a safer way to copy files than that provided by the DOS COPY command. It allows you to copy only newer files or update a directory with the contents of another. PCOPY will never allow you to overlay a file unknowingly.

PCOPY allows you to specify standard DOS wildcard file names in the source file specifications, and standard pathnames for the target directory specification.

PCOPY attempts to anticipate your needs and then help you accomplish your intent. For instance, if PCOPY determines that the target directory name does not exist, it will ask you if it is to be created. If you respond <YES>, PCOPY will create the directory. With the /SAVE option, if you are about to overlay a file with another file with the same name, you will be asked if the older duplicate file is to be renamed with a version number.

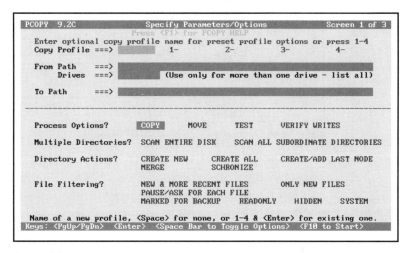

Figure 16.14. PCOPY options screen.

The PMOVE Option of PCOPY

PMOVE is an option of the PCOPY command you can use to move files between disks and directories on disks. PMOVE combines the functions of DOS COPY and DELETE commands to simplify the moving of files. In addition to just moving files, PMOVE also allows you to specify selection criteria to better qualify the files to be moved.

PMOVE automatically determines the environment in which the move is requested and determines if the data must be physically moved or if it can be moved by simply renaming it. The file will be moved by renaming it if the move is to another directory on the same disk device. This is much faster than physically moving the file. In addition, it reduces free space fragmentation, and allows you to move very large files between directories when they could not otherwise be moved with DOS COPY because of insufficient space.

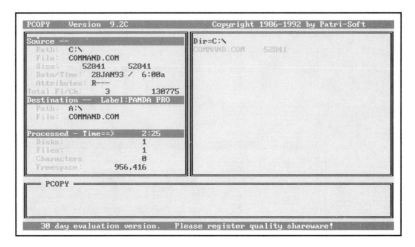

Figure 16.15. PCOPY transferring files.

The only difference between PCOPY and PMOVE is that PMOVE removes the file from the source location after it has been successfully copied to the target location.

PMOVE is implemented as a .BAT file that invokes PCOPY with the /X parameter.

PCOPY Features

Copies files to and from any disk or directory.

Allows you to save older versions of files with new names before replacing them.

Moves files by copying them or renaming them to the new location.

Deletes the original file if /X is specified.

Creates target directories if needed.

Makes sure the DOS archive flag is set correctly for each file as it is moved.

Preserves the DOS date and time for each file moved.

Allows you to pause processing at any time by pressing any keyboard key. Once stopped, the program can be terminated by pressing <ESC>.

Provides file selection and processing control options to tailor the move process to your own needs.

Allows commands to be tested so you may be sure that commands are specified as you desire.

Copies updated files to a special disk or directory.

If there is not sufficient space on the current target disk, PCOPY allows you to place another disk in the drive and continue processing. This lets you copy groups of files larger than disk size to other computers.

Starts with a specific file in a directory.

Ends with a specific file in a directory.

Processes files based on the date stored in the directory entry.

Warns you before overlaying a file unless specific parameters indicating otherwise are specified.

Checks target disk for available space before starting to copy files. This saves time when the copy will not be able to complete.

Gives you constant status of the progress of the command.

Runs with windows or using standard DOS screen output.

Formats new floppy disks as they are needed by pressing <F3> at any prompt.

Processes one directory, a single directory subtree or all directories on a disk (/S).

Allows you to indicate that multiple input disks are to be used and prompts for the next one after each disk is processed.

Creates a series of output disks filled efficiently with files from the source location.

DOS ERRORLEVEL set to indicate error conditions. PCOPY may be used in .BAT files to copy files and you may confirm results are good.

Special wildcard matching allows you to select all files with specific text in filename.

LHARC

A file compression utility can be a major space-saver for data that you don't need all the time but want to have available when you do need it. It's also a money saver if you need to tranfer files via modem to another computer directly or through an on-line service. Compressed files are about half the size of their "normal" version. There's a small security factor, too. Files that have been compressed can't be viewed by anyone who doesn't have the software to "explode" it back to "normal."

If you're unfamiliar with the technology (usually called "arcing" for archiving) you might have wondered just how so many programs got crammed onto the disk in the back of this book. That's easy: LHARC.

You might also wonder just how such a thing can be done. Remember the magazine ads for a shorthand method called Speedwriting? "Gt a gd jb w mo pa." It's the same idea, but a little more scientific. The proper name for the scheme used is the "Dynamic Hoffman Algorithm" and it's the programmer's job to figure out which common words can be represented symbolically in the arced program and how to replace the symbol with the word(s) in the exploded (back-to-normal) version.

As you will see on the on-disk documentation, there is an almost staggering number of ways to "tweak" LHARC. The documentation is lengthy and complete but somewhat difficult to assimilate on the first couple of passes. This could be due to the fact that it was originally written in Japanese and translated. Once you've got the flavor of the program's basics, though, the document begins to make more sense.

The two basic functions are making (or adding to) an archive file and un-archiving (exploding) it. All you need to do is decide on a filename for the archive file. How about SAVEIT? Now, let's assume that you have five new faxes on your hard drive, all with the extension .FAX and you want to archive them. This is the command you'd use:

```
LHA A SAVEIT *.FAX <ENTER>
```

In that command sequence, LHA started the program, the letter A said "Add" the specified files to the archive file SAVEIT. The *.FAX told the program to archive *any* file with the extension .FAX.

To restore the files to their original glory, use the command

```
LHA X SAVEIT <ENTER>
```

Quick thinkers will already have discerned that the "X" means eXtract.

LHARC also lets you view the contents of an arced file by typing

```
LHA V SAVEIT <ENTER>
```

V for View. Check Figure X.X to see a view.

CAUTION

Don't send files compressed with LHARC to anyone who doesn't have LHARC on the receiving end.

CMOS.EXE

This utility was written by Vertical Solutions of Los Angeles, California. It lets you save and restore the setup information of AT Class PCs. You could do this manually, but could you remember where you'd put the information if you needed it? This is much easier.

```
SYNTAX:  CMOS -SAVE/-RESTORE FILENAME -CLOCK
```

Choose the -SAVE or -RESTORE switch based on what you want to do. The logical first thing to do is -SAVE.

When you choose -SAVE FILENAME.EXT, CMOS.EXE writes the contents of the CMOS RAM into the file specified (FILENAME.EXT). The new file will hold all the setup information about your display adaptor, the initial display mode, the number of disk drives and their capacities, the number of hard drives installed and their drive types, the amount of RAM installed (both conventional and extended), the current date and time and any other information that your machine stores in CMOS RAM.

When you -RESTORE FILENAME.EXT, CMOS.EXE reads the file (FILENAME.EXT) and writes the information into your PC's CMOS RAM. Note that the disk file will contain the date and time you used the -SAVE switch. Check the on-disk documentation for instructions on using the -CLOCK switch to set a new date and time.

DELBUT.COM

DELBUT is a handy little extension of the DOS DEL or ERASE command. It allows you to DELete all BUT what you want to save. A prime example is a large file full of chapters of a book like this one. There are the "real" files, all with the extension .DAT (for DATA) and there are the backup files created by Microsoft Word. They have the extension .BAK. In addition there are draft files lurking around with various extensions like .NEW or .BAH. In order to clean up the subdirectory once there's no longer a need for the backup files, a DELBUT.DAT would delete everything BUT the .DAT files.

DOS wildcards are allowed. For example:

```
DELBUT *.COM

DELBUT DEL*.COM

DELBUT D*.*
```

CHKDIR

This is a scaled-down version of the DOS CHKDSK command. It checks against an individual subdirectory (or subdirectories) rather than an entire drive.

```
SYNTAX:  CHKDIR [-s/-a/-c/-d] DRIVE PATH
```

Thus, to check a subdirectory of Microsoft Word called DATA, this would be the command line syntax:

```
CHKDIR C:\WORD\DATA
```

The switches are put in the command before the drive and path.

-s - Search subdirectories

-a - Add subdirectory files to report

-c - Report only on files not backed up

-b - Report only on files backed up

HOWBAD

If you followed the instructions in the Introduction, you've already made friends with Ed Ross's HOWBAD. And, possibly, had your socks shocked off.

The syntax is simple, just type HOWBAD and <ENTER> for the latest update on the state of your backups.

For the more curious, you can add two switches, /D and /N ... /D will give you the date of the oldest file not backed up, /N the filenames that go with the date information.

The world of software utility developers is a small one. When I located HOWBAD on ZiffNet, it was called something else and the document didn't quite match the program. Fortunately, Ed had included his CompuServe ID. I sent him mail, he sent me mail. A genuinely nice fellow, he re-wrote HOWBAD the way I wanted it and even changed the name to HOWBAD. (Later, he told me that was the original name of the program!)

When I received the new version, I ran it and it told me that I had a file that hadn't been backed up since 1985! I knew that was impossible, since I had recently backed up my entire system and had been backing up current work twice a day. PLUS, the PC I was working on was less than a year old.

Ed had included his phone number in an E-mail message, so I decided it was time to give him a jolt. "Try the /N switch," Ed suggested. (I hadn't paid attention to the little file called README.PAM which would have told me to do just that. RTB.)

Ed may never be the same. One moment he was speaking to a professional writer and software developer — a reasonably composed human being — the next moment a woman was hysterically laughing on the other end of the line. The file not backed up? The 1985 version of Ed's program.

PANDA Programs Not On This Disk

Beginning in 1987, PANDA has been a leader in the development of leading-edge anti-virus and security utilities. The PANDA approach and philosophy is a simple one: Make it easy and make it WORK.

The DR. PANDA UTILITIES include an up-front scanning utility to ensure a clean hard drive before installation and the premiere suite of integrity-checking and diagnostic programs.

A new release of the DR. PANDA UTILITIES was prepared especially for readers of this book and includes the latest version of PHYSICAL which prevents infection by boot-sector viruses such as Michelangelo and Stoned. Further, it catches polymorphic viruses, companion viruses and stealth viruses.

This new version of the DR. PANDA UTILITIES (DOS 2.1 - 6.0) is available, with documentation on-disk in ASCII, Word Perfect, and Microsoft WORD formats for $39.95 *only* with the coupon in the back of this book.

Technical Support

For technical support for the PANDA products on the disk, please write to Brady Books. Patri-Soft provides technical support to its registered users, so be sure to register MEGABACK, STOWAWAY, and PCOPY with Patri-Soft.

A

A P P E N D I X

Virus Facts and Fun

A lot of people have a little knowledge about computer viruses. Most know enough to fear them, perhaps unreasonably or illogically. Misunderstandings abound—from the woman who really believed that her husband could catch something perfectly dreadful from his PC and taped over the drive slots, to the folks who believe turning off your PC on a virus' target date is a safe practice.

The following information, prepared by Rob Rosenberger with the assistance of one of the world's best-known virus-busters, Ross Greenberg, explains viruses in detail. This is the 9th Edition of this work because Rosenberger is very careful to stay up-to-date. We've added our notes to Rob and Ross' comments here and there. (When you see PANDA:, that's us.)

Virus Myths Explained

A number of myths have surfaced about the threat of computer viruses—myths about how widespread they are, how dangerous they are, and even myths about what a computer virus really is. We want you to know the facts.

The first thing you need to learn is that a computer virus falls in the realm of malicious programming techniques known as Trojan horses. All viruses are Trojan horses, but relatively few Trojan horses can be called viruses.

That having been said, it's time to go over the terminology we use when we talk about viruses:

BBS. Bulletin Board System. If you have a modem, you can call a BBS and leave messages, transfer computer files back and forth, and learn a lot about computers.

Bug. An accidental flaw in the logic of a program which makes it do things it shouldn't really be doing. Programmers don't mean to put bugs in their programs, but they always creep in. Programmers often spend more time debugging programs than they do writing them in the first place. Inadvertent bugs have caused more data loss than all viruses combined.

Hacker. Someone who really loves computers and who wants to push them to the limit. Hackers have a healthy sense of curiosity: they try doorknobs just to see whether they're locked, for example. They also love to tinker with a piece of equipment until it's "just right." The computer revolution itself is largely a result of hackers. PANDA: Unfortunately, the term *hacker* has become a pejorative for people bent on destruction.

Shareware. A distribution method for quality software available on a try-before-you-buy basis. You must pay for it if you continue using it after the trial period. Shareware authors let you download their programs from BBSs and encourage you to give evaluation copies to friends. Many shareware applications rival their retail-shelf counterparts at a fraction of the price. (You must pay for the shareware you continue to use—otherwise you're stealing software.) PANDA: The three programs on the disk in the back of the book, all from Patri-Soft, are *shareware*.

Trojan Horse. A generic term describing a set of computer instructions purposely hidden inside a program. Trojan horses tell programs to do things you don't expect them to do. The term comes from the legendary battle in which the ancient city of Troy received a large wooden horse to commemorate a fierce battle. The "gift" secretly held soldiers in its belly and, when the Trojans rolled it into their fortified city...(you know the rest).

Virus. A term for a very specialized Trojan horse that spreads to other computers by secretly "infecting" programs with a copy of itself. A virus is the only type of Trojan horse that is contagious, much like the common cold. If a Trojan horse doesn't meet this definition, then it isn't a virus.

Worm. A term similar to a Trojan horse, but there is no "gift" involved. If the Trojans had left that wooden horse outside the city, they wouldn't have been attacked. Worms, on the other hand, can bypass your defenses without having to deceive you into dropping your guard. An example would be a program designed to spread itself by exploiting bugs in a network software package. Worms usually come from someone who has legitimate access to the computer or network.

Wormers. What we call people who unleash destructive Trojan horses. Let's face it, these people aren't angels. What they do hurts us. They deserve our disrespect.

Viruses, like all Trojan horses, purposely make a program do things you don't expect it to do. Some viruses will just annoy you, perhaps only displaying a "Peace on earth" greeting. The viruses we worry about will try to erase your data (the most valuable asset of your computer!) and waste your valuable time in recovering from an attack.

Now you know the differences between a bug and a Trojan horse and a virus. Let's get into some of the myths:

All purposely destructive code spreads like a virus.

Wrong. Remember, *Trojan horse* describes purposely destructive code in general. Very few Trojan horses actually qualify as viruses. Newspaper and magazine reporters tend to call almost anything a virus because most of them have no real understanding of computer crime.

PANDA: Or programming.

Viruses and Trojan horses are a recent phenomenon.

Trojan horses have existed since the first days of the computer; hackers toyed with viruses in the early 1960s as a form of amusement. Many different Trojan horse techniques have emerged over the decades to embezzle money, destroy data, fool investors, etc. The general public really didn't know of this problem until the IBM PC revolution brought it into the spotlight. Banks still hush up computerized embezzlements to this day because they believe customers will lose faith in them if word gets out.

Viruses are written by teenage hackers.

Yes, hackers have unleashed viruses—but so has a computer magazine publisher. And according to one trusted military publication, the U.S. Defense Department creates viruses for use as weapons. Trojan horses for many decades sprang from the minds of middle-aged men; computer prices have only recently dropped to a level where teenagers could get into the act. We call people *wormers* when they abuse their knowledge of computers.

You shouldn't fear hackers just because some of them know how to write viruses. This whole thing boils down to an ethics issue, not a technology issue. Hackers know a lot about computers; wormers abuse their knowledge. Hackers as a whole got a bum rap when the mass media corrupted the term.

Viruses infect 25 percent of all IBM PCs every month.

If 25 percent suffer an infection every month, then 100 percent would have a virus every four months—in other words, every IBM PC would suffer an infection three times per year. This mythical estimate surfaced in the media after researcher Peter Tippett wrote a complex thesis on how viruses might spread in the future.

Computer viruses exist all over the planet, yes—but they won't take over the world. Only about 500 different viruses exist at this time; many of them have never existed "in the wild" and some have since been completely eliminated from the wild. You can easily reduce your exposure to viruses with a few simple precautions. Yes, it's still safe to turn on your computer!

Only 500 different viruses? But most experts talk about them in the thousands.

The virus experts who claim much larger numbers usually work for antivirus companies. They count even the most insignificant variations for advertising purposes. When the Marijuana virus first appeared, for example, it displayed the word *legalise*, but a miscreant later modified it to read *legalize*. Any program which can detect the original virus can detect the version with one letter changed—but antivirus companies count them as two viruses. These obscure differentiations quickly add up.

And take note: The majority of "new" computer viruses discovered these days are only minor variations on well-known viruses.

A virus could destroy all the files on my disks.

Yes, and a spilled cup of coffee could do the same thing. You can recover from any virus or coffee problem if you have adequate backups of your data. Backups mean the difference between a nuisance and a disaster. You can safely presume there has been more accidental loss of data than loss by all viruses and Trojan horses.

Viruses have been documented on over 300,000 computers {1988}.

Viruses have been documented on over 400,000 computers {1989}.

The Michelangelo virus alone was estimated to be on over 5,000,000 computers {1992}.

These numbers originated from John McAfee, a self-styled virus fighter. If we assume it took him a mere five minutes to adequately document each viral infection, it would have taken four years of effort to document a problem only two years old by 1989. We further assume McAfee's statements included every floppy disk ever infected up to that time by a virus, as well as every computer involved with the Christmas and InterNet worm attacks. (Worms cannot be included in virus infection statistics.)

McAfee prefers to "estimate" his totals these days and was widely quoted during the Michelangelo virus hysteria in early 1992. Let's do some estimating ourselves by assuming that there are about 80 million IBM PC-compatible computers around the world. McAfee's estimate means one out of every 16 computers on the planet supposedly had the virus. Many other experts considered it an astronomical estimate based on the empirical evidence.

Viruses can hide inside a data file.

Data files can't wreak havoc on your computer—only an executable program file can do that (including the one that runs every time you turn on or reboot a computer). If a virus infected a data file, it would be a wasted effort. But let's be realistic: what you think is data may actually be an executable program file. For example, a batch file on an IBM PC contains only text, yet DOS treats it just like an executable program.

Some viruses can completely hide themselves from all antivirus software, making them truly undetectable.

This myth ironically surfaced when certain antivirus companies publicized how they could detect so-called Mutation Engine viruses. The myth gained national exposure in early 1993 when the Associated Press printed excerpts from a new book about viruses. Most viruses have a character-based signature that identifies it both to the virus (so it doesn't infect a program too many times) and to antivirus software (which uses the signature to detect the virus). A Mutation Engine virus employs an algorithm signature rather than a character-based signature—but it still has a unique, readily identifiable signature.

The technique of using algorithm signatures really doesn't make it any harder to detect a virus. You just have to do some calculations to know the correct signature—no big deal for an antivirus program.

BBSs and shareware programs spread viruses.

Here's another scary myth, this one spouted as gospel by many "experts" who claim to know how viruses spread. "The truth," says *PC Magazine* publisher Bill Machrone, "is that all major viruses to-date were transmitted by [retail] packages and private mail systems, often in universities." [*PC Magazine*, October 11, 1988.] What Machrone said back then still applies today. Over 50 retail companies have admitted spreading infected master disks to tens of thousands of customers since 1988—compared to only nine shareware authors who have spread viruses on master disks to less than 300 customers since 1990.

Machrone goes on to say "bulletin boards and shareware authors work extraordinarily hard at policing themselves to keep viruses out." Reputable sysops check every file for Trojan horses; nationwide sysop networks help spread the word about dangerous files. Yes, you should beware of the software you get from BBSs and shareware authors, but you should also beware of retail software found on store shelves. (By the way, many stores now routinely re-shrinkwrap returned software and put it on the shelf again. Do you know for sure only you ever touched those master disks?) My computer could be infected if I call an infected BBS.

BBSs can't write information on your disks—the communications software you use performs this task. You can only transfer a dangerous file to your computer if you let your software do it.

And there is no "300bps subcarrier" by which a virus can slip through a modem. A joker who called himself Mike RoChenle ("micro channel," get it?) started this myth after leaving a techy-joke message on a public network. Unfortunately, some highly respected journalists got taken in by the joke.

So-called boot-sector viruses travel primarily in software downloaded from BBSs.

This common myth—touted as gospel even by experts—expounds on the supposed role bulletin boards play in spreading infections. Boot-sector viruses spread only if you directly copy an infected floppy disk, or if you try to boot a computer from an infected disk, or if you use a floppy in an infected computer.

BBSs deal exclusively with program files and don't pass along copies of boot sectors. Bulletin board users thus have a natural immunity to boot-sector viruses in downloaded software. (And because the clear majority of infections stem from boot-sector viruses, this fact alone exonerates the BBS community as the so-called "primary" source for the spread of viruses.)

We should make a special note about "dropper" programs developed by virus researchers as an easy way to transfer boot-sector viruses among themselves. Because they don't replicate, dropper programs don't qualify as viruses. These programs have never appeared on BBSs to-date and have no real use other than to transfer infected boot sectors.

My files are damaged, so it must have been a virus attack.

It also could have happened because of a power flux, or static electricity, or a fingerprint on a floppy disk, or a bug in your software, or perhaps a simple error on your part. Power failures, spilled cups of coffee, and user errors have destroyed more data than all viruses combined.

Donald Burleson was convicted of releasing a virus.

Newspapers all over the country hailed a 1989 Texas computer crime trial as a "virus" trial. The defendant, Donald Burleson, had released a destructive Trojan horse on his employer's mainframe computer. The software in question couldn't spread to other computers, and prosecuting attorney Davis McCown claimed he "never brought up the word *virus*" during Burleson's trial. So why did the media call it one?

1. David Kinney, an expert witness testifying for the defense, claimed Burleson unleashed a virus. The prosecuting attorney didn't argue the point and we don't blame him—Kinney's claim may have actually swayed the jury to convict Burleson.

2. McCown gave reporters the facts behind the case and let them come up with their own definitions. The Associated Press and *USA Today*, among others, used such vague definitions that any program would have qualified as a virus. If we applied their definitions to the medical world, we could safely label penicillin as a biological virus (which is, of course, absurd).

Robert Morris Jr. released a benign virus on a defense network.

It supposedly may have been benign, but it wasn't a virus. Morris, the son of a chief computer scientist at the National Security Agency, decided one day to take advantage of bugs in the software which controls InterNet, a network the Defense Department often uses. These tiny bugs let Morris send a worm throughout the network. Among other things, the "InterNet worm" sent copies of itself to other computers—and clogged the entire network in a matter of hours due to bugs in the worm module itself. The press called it a virus, like it called the 1987 "Christmas worm" a virus, because it spread to other computers. Yet Morris's work didn't infect any computers. A few notes:

1. Reporters finally started calling it a worm a year after the fact, but only because lawyers on both sides of the case constantly referred to it as a worm.

2. The worm operated only on Sun-3 and Vax computers which employ the UNIX operating system and were specifically linked into the InterNet network at the time of the attack.

3. The 6,200 affected computers cannot be counted in virus infection statistics (they weren't infected).

4. It cost way less than $98 million to clean up the attack. An official Cornell University report claims John McAfee, the man

behind this wild estimate, "was probably serving [him]self" in an effort to drum up business. People familiar with the case estimated the final figure at slightly under $1 million.

5. Yes, Morris could easily have added some infection code to make it both a worm and a virus if he'd had the urge.

6. InterNet gurus have since fixed the bug Morris exploited in the attack.

7. Morris went on trial for launching the worm and received a federal conviction. The Supreme Court refused to hear his case, so the conviction stands.

The U.S. government planted a virus in Iraqi military computers during the Gulf War.

U.S. News & World Report in early 1992 claimed the National Security Agency had replaced a computer chip in a printer bound for Iraq just before the Gulf War with a secret computer chip containing a virus. The magazine cited "two unidentified senior U.S. officials" as their source, saying "once the virus was in the [Iraqi computer] system,…each time an Iraqi technician opened a 'window' on his computer screen to access information, the contents of the screen simply vanished."

Yet the USN&WR story shows amazing similarities to a 1991 April Fool's joke published by *InfoWorld* magazine. Most computer experts dismiss the USN&WR story as a hoax—an "urban legend" innocently created by the *InfoWorld* joke. Some notes:

1. USN&WR continues to stand by its story, but did publish a "clarification" stating "it could not be confirmed that the [virus] was ultimately successful." The editors broke with tradition by declining to print any letters readers had submitted about it.

2. Ted Koppel, a well-known American news anchor, opened one of his *Nightline* broadcasts with a report on the alleged virus. Koppel's staff politely refers people to talk with USN&WR about the story's validity.

3. *InfoWorld* didn't label their story as fiction, but the last paragraph identified it as an April Fool's joke.

Viruses can spread to all sorts of computers.

The design of all Trojan horses limits them to a family of computers, something especially true for viruses. A virus written for IBM PCs cannot infect an IBM 4300 series mainframe, nor can it infect a Commodore C64, nor can it infect an Apple Macintosh.

My backups will be worthless if I back up a virus.

No they won't. Let's suppose a virus does get backed up with your files. You can restore important documents and databases and spreadsheets—your valuable data—without restoring an infected program. You just reinstall the programs from master disks. It's tedious work, but not as hard as some people claim.

Antivirus software will protect me from viruses.

There is no such thing as a foolproof antivirus program. Viruses and other Trojan horses can be (and have been) designed to bypass them. Antivirus products also can be tricky to use at times and they occasionally have bugs. Always use a good set of backups as your first line of defense; rely on antivirus software only as a second line of defense.

PANDA: This is especially true of the product included with DOS 6.0. Months before its announced release date, a number of programs to disable it appeared around the world.

Read-only files are safe from virus infections.

This common myth among IBM PC users has appeared even in some computer magazines. Supposedly, you can protect yourself by using the DOS ATTRIB command to set the read-only attribute on program files. Yet ATTRIB is software—what it can do, a virus can undo. The ATTRIB command cannot halt the spread of most viruses.

Viruses can infect files on write-protected floppy disks.

Another common IBM PC myth. If viruses can modify read-only files, people assume they can also modify files on write-protected disks. However, the disk drive itself knows when a floppy has a write-protect tab and refuses to write to the disk. You can't override an IBM PC drive's write-protect sensor with a software command.

We hope this dispels the many computer virus myths. Viruses *do* exist, they *are* out there, they *want* to spread to other computers, and they *can* cause you problems. But you can defend yourself with a cool head and a good set of backups.

Virus Prevention Guidelines

The following guidelines can shield you from viruses and other Trojan horses. They will lower your chances of getting infected and raise your chances of recovering from an attack.

1. Implement a procedure to back up your files regularly and follow it religiously. We can't emphasize this enough! Consider purchasing a user-friendly program or a tape backup device to take the drudgery out of this task. You'll find plenty of inexpensive programs and tape backup hardware to choose from.

2. Rotate between at least two sets of backups for better security (use set 1, then set 2, then set 1…). The more sets you use, the better protection you have. Many people take a master backup of their entire hard disk, and then take a number of incremental backups of files which have changed since the last time they backed up. Incremental backups might require only five minutes of your time each day.

3. Download files only from reputable BBSs where the sysop checks every program for Trojan horses. If you're still afraid, consider getting programs from a BBS or "disk vendor" company which gets files direct from the authors.

4. Let newly uploaded files "mature" on a BBS for one or two weeks before you download them (others will put it through its paces).

5. Consider using a program that searches (scans) for known viruses. Almost all infections involve viruses known to antivirus companies. A recent version (no more than four months old) of any scanning program will in all probability identify a virus before it can infect your computer. But remember: There is no perfect antivirus defense.

6. Consider using a program that creates a unique signature of all the programs on your computer. Run this software once in a while to see whether any of your program files have been modified—either by a virus or perhaps just by a stray gamma ray.

7. *Don't panic* if your computer starts acting weird. You might have a virus, but then again you might not. Immediately turn off all power to your computer and disconnect it from any local area networks. Reboot from a write-protected copy of your master DOS disk. Do *not* run any programs on a regular disk—you might activate a Trojan horse. If you don't have adequate backups, try to bring them up-to-date. (Yes, you might back up a virus as well, but it can't hurt you if you don't use your normal programs.) Set your backups off to the side. Only then can you safely hunt for problems.

8. If you can't figure out the problem and you don't know what to do next, just turn off your computer and call for help. Consider calling a local computer group before you call for an expert. If you need a professional, consider a regular computer consultant first. (Some "virus removal experts" charge prices far beyond their actual value.)

Virus Fun

It could be argued that there's nothing funny about viruses, but the following list proves that even virus-busters have a sense of humor. There are rumors about the origin of this well-circulated list, but none can be confirmed:

Paul Revere Virus: This revolutionary virus does not horse around. It warns you of impending hard disk attack—once if by LAN and twice if by C.

Politically Correct Virus: Never calls itself a "virus," but instead refers to itself as an "electronic micro-organism."

Right-to-Life Virus: Won't allow you to delete a file, regardless of how old it is. If you attempt to erase a file, it requires you first to see a counselor about alternatives.

Ross Perot Virus: Activates every component in your system, just before the whole thing quits.

Mario Cuomo Virus: It would be a great virus, but it refuses to run.

Oprah Winfrey Virus: Your 200M hard drive suddenly shrinks to 80M and then slowly expands to 250M again.

AT&T Virus: Every three minutes it tells you what great service you are getting.

MCI Virus: Every three minutes it reminds you that you are paying too much for the AT&T virus.

Ted Turner Virus: Colorizes your monochrome monitor.

Arnold Schwartzenegger Virus: Terminates and stays resident. It'll be back.

Dan Quayle Virus I: Prevents your system from spawning any child processes without joining into a binary network.

Dan Quayle Virus II: There is sumthing rong with yur computer, ewe just can't figyour out watt.

Government Economist Virus: Nothing works, but all of your diagnostic software says everything is fine.

New World Order Virus: Probably harmless, but it makes a lot of people really mad just thinking about it.

Federal Bureaucrat Virus: Divides your hard disk into hundreds of little units, each of which does practically nothing, but all of which claim to be the most important part of the computer.

Gallup Virus: Sixty percent of the PCs infected will lose 38 percent of their data 14 percent of the time (plus or minus 3.5 percent margin of error).

Terry Randle Virus: Prints "Oh no you don't" whenever you choose Abort from the `Abort, Retry, Fail` message.

Texas Virus: Makes sure that it is bigger than any other file.

Adam and Eve Virus: Takes a couple of bytes out of your Apple.

Michael Jackson Virus: Hard to identify because it is constantly altering its appearance. This virus won't harm your PC, but it *will* trash your car.

Congressional Virus: The computer locks up, the screen splits erratically with a message appearing on each half blaming the other side for the problem.

Airline Virus: You're in Dallas, but your data is in Singapore.

Freudian Virus: Your computer becomes obsessed with marrying its own motherboard.

PBS Virus: Your PC stops every few minutes to ask for money.

Elvis Virus: Your computer gets fat, slow, and lazy and then self-destructs, only to resurface at shopping malls and service stations across the country.

Ollie North Virus: Turns your printer into a document shredder.

NIKE Virus: Just does it.

Sears Virus: Your data won't appear unless you buy new cables, power supply, and a set of shocks.

Jimmy Hoffa Virus: Nobody can find it.

Congressional Virus II: Runs every program on the hard drive simultaneously, but it doesn't allow the user to accomplish anything.

Kevorkian Virus: Helps your computer shut down whenever it wants to.

Imelda Marcos Virus: Sings you a song (slightly off-key) on boot up, then subtracts money from your Quicken account, and spends it all on expensive shoes it buys through Prodigy.

Star Trek Virus: Invades your system in places no virus has gone before.

Health Care Virus: Tests your system for a day, finds nothing wrong, and sends you a bill for $4,500.

George Bush Virus: It starts by boldly stating "Read my test...no new files!" on the screen, proceeds to fill up all of the free space on your hard drive with new files, and then blames it on the Congressional virus.

Cleveland Indian Virus: Makes your 486/50 machine perform like a 286/AT.

LAPD Virus: Claims it feels threatened by the other files on your PC and erases them in "self-defense."

Chicago Cubs Virus: Your PC makes frequent mistakes and comes in last in the reviews, but you still love it.

Moving Right Along...

Now that you've had a chuckle, see Appendix B for a current list of viruses on the prowl.

The Virus List

The following list of almost 2,500 computer viruses was as up-to-date as possible on the day this book went to press. The list was compiled by S&S International of the United Kingdom, whose founder, Dr. Alan Solomon, is one of the world's leading anti-virus researchers.

Stoned	a new boot	Abs 3	Aircop
AircopNG	Aircot	Alive	Angelina
Anthrax-b	Anticad 1 boot	Anticad 4 boot	Archub
Azusa	BE boot	Boot-437	Brain
Brasil	Cannabis	Catman-b	Changshaboot
Chinese Fish	Clock	Crazy Eddie-b	Comptrojan
Comptrojan-2	Denzuk 1	Denzuk 2	Denzuk 3
Denzuk 4	Dinamo	Disk Killer	EDV
EkoTerror boot	Empire	Exebug	Face
Falling boot	Filler-b	Filler-p	Flip
Form	GrandYork boot	Gullion	Horse-boot
Horse boot C	Hybryd boot	Installation Check	Joshi
Joshi-b	JKTK	June 4th	Telefonica boot
Keydrop	Keytrick	Kiev 2049 boot	Kilroy
Kitty	Laodoung	Leszoptad	Leszoptad-2
Liberty boot	Lovechild-B3	Lucifer	Malaga boot
Mardi	Mardi-2	Michelangelo	Microbe
Micro Cops	Military	Mothering	MPHTI

Mugshot	Music Bug	Neardark	Nichols
NJH-LBC	NJH-LBC-2	Noint	Nov-7
Nu-way boot	Horseboot b	Parity boot	Pentagon
Ping-Pong	Ping-Pong.Big	Print screen boot	QQ-1513 boot
Quox	Saigon	Shifter boot	Smiley boot
Spook	Starship boot	Stealth boot	Stoned-2
Stoned-8	Stoned-16	Stonehenge	SVC 6.0 partition
Swedish disaster	Tequila partition	Thanksgiving boot	Tony boot a
Tony boot b	Twelve tricks part	V-Sign	Vienpart
Whirl	W-boot	Windmill	X-boot
Yale	CR	10past3	1759x
5lo	99%	99%-o	Ada
Adolf	Advent	Advent-demo	Advent-nw
Aids 2	Aids Information 1	Aids Information 2	Aircop dropper 1
Aircop dropper 2	Aircop dropper	Aircot dropper	Akuku
Alabama dropper	Alabama	Albania-429	Albania-506
Albania-575	Albania-606	Albanian	Alex 368
Alex 818	Alex-1951	Alphabet	Ambulance
Amoeba	Amoeba-0	Anarkia	Andryushka
Angarsk	Anna	Ansi bomb	Ansi bomb-c
Anthrax dropper	Anthrax	Anthrax-c	Anticad 1
Anticad 2	Anticad 3	Anticad 4	Anticad 5
Antichrist	Antimit	Anti Pascal 400	Anti Pascal 440
Anti Pascal 480	Anti Pascal 529	Anti Pascal 605	Antimon
Antix	Arab	ARCV	Argentina
Armagedon	Arriba	Ash	Astra
Astra-976	Astra-1010	AT II	AT-132
AT	AT-149	Atas-384	Atas-400
Athens	Attention	Backfont	Backfont-765
Backtime	Bad-389	Bad Boy	Bad Boy 2
Bad Brains	Bad Guy	Bad Taste dropper	Bad Taste
Banana	Bandit dropper	Bandit	Baobab
Batch	Batch-1	BE File	Beast-NB
Bebe	Beech-439	Best Wishes-1	Best Wishes-2
Beta Boys	Better world	Beware	Big Joke
Bios	Birdie hop	Bit Addict	Black Monday
Black Wizard.a	Black Wizard.b	Black Wizard dropper	Black Jec
Black Peter	Blaze	Blood	Blood lust
Bobas	Bomber		

Bonk	Boojum	Boot dropper	Border
Boys-500	Brain 2	Brain dropper.b	Brain dropper
Brain dropper.a	Brainy	Breeder	Breeder son
Brothers	Bryansk-673	Budo	Bugs
Bugs resident	Bupt,Burger.382	Burger.405	Burger.560
Burger-1310	Burghofer	Bushishiro	Capital
Cara	Carioca	C-J dropper	C-J dropper-2
Cascade.1701	Cascade.1701-S	Cascade.1621	Cascade.1661
Cascade.1704	Cascade.1706	Casino	Casper
Catman	CAZ	CC	Cemetery dropper
Cemetery	Cerberus	Chad	Chameleon.
Chameleon-0	Chameleon	Chameleon.de	Changsha
Chaos.4	Chaos	CHCC	Checksum
Cheeba	Cheef	Christmas-exec	Cinderella
Cinderella II	Civil War	Clonewar	Close
CLS-853	Cod	Codezero	Coffeeshop
Coldir	Com2Con	Comasp-472	Commfix
Commy	Como	Comp-16850	Compiler-2
Compiler	Cookie	Cookie-2232	Copmpletly
Copyright	Cossiga	CPW	Crazy Daisy dropper
Crazy Daisy	Crazy Eddie-f	Crazy Eddie-0	Crazy Imp
Creeper	Creeper-252	Crew 1	Crew 2
Criminal	Crooked	CSL dropper	CSL
Cvir	Cvirus	Dada	Damien
Danish Tiny 126	Danish Tiny	Dark Avenger 1	DA-MIR dropper
DA-MIR	DA-1801	DA-Quest	Dark Avenger 1800
DA 2000 dropper	Dark Avenger 2000	DA2100 dropper	Dark Avenger 2100
Dark Avenger-1530	Dark Avenger-Milena	Dark Av-Slowdown	Dark end
Dark Lord	Darth 1	Darth 2 dropper	Darth 2
Darth 2.b	Darth 3-a	Darth 3-b	Darth4 dropper
Darth 4	Dash-em	Datacrime dropper	Datacrime-1a
Datacrime-1b	Datacrime-2	Datacrime-2-0	Datacrime-2b
Datalock	Dazzler	Dbase	DBT
December 24	Deicide-1	Deicide	Delyrium dropper
Delyrium	Demolition	Demon	Denzuk dropper
Destructor	Devil's dance	Dewdz	Diabolik
Diamond	Diamond-b	Diamond dropper	Diamond-b dropper
Diamond-Damage drp	Diamond-Damage	Diamond-Damage-b drp	Diamond-Damage-b
Diamond-David drp	Diamond-David	Diamond-Greemlin drp	Diamond-Greemlin

Diamond-Lucifer drp	Diamond-Lucifer	Digger	Digital FX
Dima	Dir-II	Dir-II dropper	DIR III
Dir	Disk plus 1	Disk spoiler	Dismember
DM-92	DM-400-c	DM-400	DM-330
DM-310	Doom II-752	Doom II-1240	Doomsday
Doshunter	Dossound	Dot Eater	Dr Q
Dr Q II	Dr W	Drop	Dutch Tiny
Dyslexia	Dyslexia dropper	Ear	Eddie 2
Eddie dropper	Eddie.F dropper	Eight tunes	Eko Terror file
Eliza	Eloi	EMF 404	EMF 625
Emmie	End-of	Enigma	Enola
ENUN	Erasmus	Error	ETC
Europe-1992	Even Beeper	Evil Genius	Exebug file
Exev	Explode	Exterminator	F-you
F1-337	Falling dropper	Farenheit 121	Father
FaX Free	FCB	Feist	FGT
Fichv fexe 1.0	Fichv 2.0	Fichv 2.1	Filedate
Filehider	Filename-512	Finger joke	Finger dropper
Finger	Finnish-357	Finnish-709	Fire
Fish dropper	Fish 6	Flash	Flash-dr
Flip	Flip 2153	Flower	FMCIK
Forger	Freddy	Freew-692	Freew.718
Friday 13th	Friends	Frodo	F-soft-458
F-soft-563	Froggie	Frogs	Fu Manchu.3
Fu Manchu	Fumble	Fune-921	FVHS
Geek	Gergana-182	Gergana-222	Gergana-300
Gergana-450	Gergana-512	Ghost-A	Ghostballs
Girafe	Girl-2273	Gliss	GMB
Goblin dropper	Goblin	Gosia	Got You
Gotcha-A	Gotcha-B	Gotcha-C dropper	Gotcha-C
Gotcha-D	Gotcha-E dropper	Gotcha-F Nonvirus	Gotcha-E
Grab	Grand York file	Grapje	Green Caterpillar
Grower-268	Grune	Grunt	Guppy dropper
Guppy	Guru	Gyorgyi	Gyro
Ha	Haddock	Hafenstrasse	Haifa
Mozkin	Halloechen	Halloween	Happy
Happy New Year 1614	Happy New Year 1560	Happy New Year 1600	Harakiri
Haryanto	Hate	Headcrash	Hell first
Helloween	Hellraiser	Hey YOU	HI-460
Hide and seek	Highlander	Hitchcock	HIV-1 dropper

HIV-1	Horror	Horse-1 dropper	Horse-1
Horse-2 dropper	Horse-2	Horse-3	Horse-4
Horse-5	Horse-6	Horse-7	Horse-8-0
Horse-8	Horseboot dropper	House	Hungarian-473
Hungarian-482	Hybryd	Hydra	Hymn
Hymn demo	Hymn-2144	Ice-9	Ice-Friends
Icelandic.Saratoga	Icelandic-1	Icelandic	Ieronim-I
Ieronim-II	ILL	Impotence	Incom
Indos 552	Indos 2618	Infector	Infinity
Installation Check	Int13	Int78	Int80
Int86	IntF0-732	Interceptor	Internal
Intruder	Involuntary	Involuntary-B	Involuntary-B DD
Ionkin	Iper	Iron Maiden	Itavir
Itti	Jabberwocky	Japanese Xmas	JD
Jeff	J-Inject	Jerusalem	Jerusalem-UCNDER
Jerusalem-1663	Jerusalem-1767	Jerusalem-count	Jeru-2187
Jeru-Antiscan	Jerusalem-Barcelona	Jerusalem-Captrip	Jerusalem-Carf
Jeru-Clipper	Jeru-Czech	Jeru-Discom	Jerusalem-Einstein
Jerusalem.Mendoza	Jeru-Nemesis	GP1 dropper	Jeru-GP1
Jeru-Groen	Jeru-IRA	Jeru-Kylie	Jeru-Spanish
Jeru-Sunday	Jeru-Sunday2	Jeru-Swiss	Jeru-Timor
Jerusalem-Yellow	Jihuu	Joanna	Jojo
Joker	Joker-01	Jonekey	Joshi dropper.a
Joshi dropper.b	June 16	July 13.a	July 13.b
Junior	Justice	K-Lame	Kalah
Kalah-499	Kamasya	Kamikaze	Kamikaze-trashed
Kampana-3784 dropper	Kampana-3445	Kampana	Karin
Kemerovo	Keybug-1596	Keybug-1596-0	Keybug-1720-0
Keybug-1720	Keydrop dropper	Keypress	Keypress.b
Keypress.chaos	Kiev 2049	Kiev 2049 dd	Kiev-483
Kinnison	Kiss	Kit	KLF-356
KO-408	Kode	Kremikov	Kthulhu
Kukac-Nagytud	Kukac-Turbo	kuku-448	Kuzmitch
Lancspwei	Lancspwei-cmp	Larry	Lazy
Leapfrog	Leech 1	Leech 2	Leech 2b
Legalize	Lehigh	Leningrad	Leprosy-I
Leprosy-II	Leprosy	Liberty	Liberty dropper
Liberty-SSSSS	Lippi 286	Lisbon	Little Brother 1
Little Brother 2	Little Girl	Little Pieces	Lock dropper

Lock	Loki-354	Loki	Lokinator
Lovechild-B3 dropper	Lovechild	Lovechild trojan	Lowercase
LV 1.2	Lycee	Lycee-1975	Macedonia
Made	Maffy	Magnitogorsk	Magnitogorsk-3000
Malaga	Maltese Amoeba	Mannequin	Manuel
Many Fingers	Marauder.560	Marauder	Matura
Mayak-2339	Mayak-2339 dd	Mayak-2370	Mayak-2370 dd
Mega-F	Metka	MG1	MG2
MG3	MG4	MG5	Mgtu dropper
Mgtu	MH-757	Micro-128	Migram
Miky	Mini-207	Minsk-1075	Minsk Ghost
Mirror	Mithrandir	Mix 1	Mix 1b
Mix 2	Moctezuma	Mono	Month 4-6
Monxla	Mosquito	MPS OPC	MPS OPC 4.01
Mr-Virus	MS-748	Mshark	Mshark-889
MSJ	MSK	MSTU-532	MSTU-554
MtE	MtE.c	MtE.f	MtE.g
MtE.h	MtE-O	MtE	MtE.d
MtE.e	MtE-Pogue.a	MtE-Pogue.b	MtE-Pogue.c
Mubark	Mule	Multi	Multiface
Mummy 1.0	Mummy 1.2	Mummy 2.1	Munich
Murphy-1	Murphy-2	Murphy-3	Murphy-4
Murphy-5	Murphy-a dropper	Murphy-Amilia	Mushroom
Mutant 1680	Mutant 1744	MVF 1	MVF
My Adidas	Nazgul	Ncu-li	Necropolis-A
Necropolis	Necros	Necrosoft	New BadGuy
New Generation	Nice day	Nin	Nina-256
Nines complement	Ninja	No Bock	No Frills
Noint dropper	Nomenklatura	Noon beep	November 17
November 30	Null-256	Number 1	NOTB Dropper
NOTB w	No. of the beast	No. of the beast.b	No. of the beast.t
No. of the beast.u	No. of the beast.c	No. of the beast.d	No. of the beast.e
No. of the beast.i	NTKC	Nu-way	Nygus
Ogre dropper	Old Yankee-1	Old Yankee-2	Omega
On 64 dropper	On 64	Ondra	Ontario
Ontario 730	Orion	Oropax	Oscar
Otto	Outland-drp	Outland	Overwriting 4870
Padded	Parasite	Paris	Parity
Pas-5220	Pascal-3072	Pascal-7808	Pathhunt

PC Byte Bandit	PCBB-3072	PC-FLU	PC-FLU II
PcVrsDs	Peach	Penza	Perfume-Slash
Perfume	Perfume-731	Perry	Perry-2
Perv	Pest dropper	Pest dropper-2	Pest
Phalcon dropper	Phalcon	Phantom	Phoenix-927
Phoenix 800	Phoenix 1226	Phoenix 1226 dropper	P E drp
Phoenix Evil	Phoenix Phoenix	Phoenix Proud	Phoenix-2000
Phoenix-2000 trojan	Phoenix-2000 dropper	Pif-paf	Ping dropper
Pipi	Pirate	Pisello	Piter
Pixel-847	Pixel	Pixel.740	Pixel.892
Pixel.877	Pixel.345	Pixel.299	Pixel.277
Pixel-2xx	Pixel-9xx	Pixel-457	Pixel-550
Pixie 1.0	Plague	Plaice	Player
Plovdiv 1.1	Plovdiv 1.3	Plutto	Polimer
Polish tiny	Portugese	Possessed-1.03	Possessed-1.08
Possessed-1.07	Possessed-2438	Power pump	Prague
Prague-Joker	Pregnant	Press	Prime Evil
Pro	Problem	Proto-T	PrtSc1024
Prtsc dropper	Prudents	McWhale-dropper	PS-MPC
PS-MPC.c	PS-MPC.a	PS-MPC.b	PS-MPC.d
PSQR	Ps!ko dropper	Ps!ko	PSQR
Psycho	QQ-1513	Quake	Quake-O
Quiet	Quit-1992	Radyum	Rage
Rape 1.0	Rape 1.1	Rape 2.2-0	Rape 2.2
Raubkopie	Ray	RBBS	Reaper man
Reboot-715	Reboot-patcher	Red Diavolyata	RedX-Boom
Reklamowy	Releave	Relzfu	REQ
Requires	Revenge	Rjabber	RNA.1
RNA2	Rob	Rock Steady	Rock Steady II
Rosen	Rostov dropper	Rush Hour	Russian Mirror
Russ Mutant	Russian Tiny	Rust	Ryazan
S-Cadet	Sad	SADAM	Sadist
Samsoft	Satan	Sathanyk	Saturday 14
SBC	Schizo	Schizo-S	Scotts Valley
Scorpio	Screaming Fist	Screaming Fist II	Screaming Fist IIb-d
Screen+1	Screen-1014	Scroll	SD-123
Seacat	Secret Service	Sector-Zero	Semtex-0
Semtex	Seneca	Sentinel dropper	Sentinel-b dropper.a
Sentinel-b dropper.b	Sentinel misc	Sentinel 5402	Sentinel 4636

Sentinel 5173	Sentinel-4	Sentinel 4625	Sentinel 4571
Seventh Son	Seventh Son.284	Stoned.sr drp	Shadowbyte
Shake	Shake a-d	Shake-2	Shhs
Shifter	Shirley	SI-492	Sicilian mob 1a
Signs	Silence	Silent night	Silly-178
Silly-189	SillY-302	Silly Willy	Silver Dollar
Simulate	Siskin-Hero-506	Siskin-Hero-394	Siskin.Resurrect
Siskin.839	Siskin.948	Siskin.1017	Sistor.1
Sistor	SK	Skism	Slovakia 1b
Slovakia 2.00	Slovakia 2.02a	Slovakia 2.02b	Slovakia 3.b
Slovakia 4	Slow Format	Slowload	SMA-108
Smack dropper	Smack	Small-115	Smiley
Snow	Socha	Something 1.1	Spanish Fool
Spanz	Sparse	Squawk	Squeaker
Squisher	Squisher dropper	Stack	Staf
Stahlplatte	Stanco	Stardot-600	Stardot-789
Stardot-801	Starship	Stinkfoot-1	Stinkfoot-2
Stone 90	Stoned dropper 1	Stoned dropper 2	Stoned dropper 3
Stoned dropper 4	Storm	Stranger	Striker
STSV	Stupid	Subliminal	Suicide
SUM-1569	Suomi	Superhacker	Suriv-1
Suriv-2	Suriv-3	Surrender	SVC 3.1
SVC 4.0-a	SVC 4.0-b	SVC 5.0	SVC5B
SVC 6.0	SVC 6 DD	Sverdlov	Svir dropper
Svir	Swami	Swedish boys	Swedish boys-SH
SD dropper	Swiss-143	Sylvia	SYP
Syslock	Tabulero	Tack	Taiwan-708
Taiwan-743	Taiwan-Doom I	Taiwan-Doom Ib	Tenbytes drp-A
Tenbytes drp-B	Tenbytes	Tequila dropper	Tequila.
Tequila	Terminator a	Terminator b	Terminator-1501
Term-2294	Terminator-526	Terror	Testvirus B V1.4
Tet	Thanksgiving	The Rat	Thimble
Thirteen minutes	Thursday-12	Tic	Timemark
Timeslice	Timid	Tiny.198	Tiny.167
Tiny.15x	Tiny.13x	Tiny.133	Tiny-DI
Tiny-GM	Tired	Todor	Tokyo
Tony dropper	Tony	Torm-205	Tormentor
TP Worm	Traceback-0	Traceback	Traceback-2930
Trash	Traveller Jack	Trivial-25	Trivial-26

Trivial-30	Trivial-30.c	Trivial-42	Trivial-II
Trivial	Trivial-46	Trivial	Troi
Troi two	Trojan-17	Tula-419	Tula-1480
TUQ	Tumen	Tumen.1092	Twelve tricks
Twer-1000	Twin	Typeme	Typeme dropper
Ufa-1201	Ungame	Updown	Urfydus
Uruguay	Uruguay 5	Use killer	USSR-1049
USSR-707	V1244	V2P6	V377
Vac	Vacsina	Vacsina Convert	Vbasic-0
Vbasic.a	Vbasic.b	Vbasic.c	VCL a
VCL b	VCL c	VCL d	VCL e
VCL f	VCL g	Vcomm.a	Vcomm.b
VCS	VCS-created	VDV-853	Vengence-A
Vengence-B	Vengence-CD	Vengence-E	Vengence-F
VFSI	Victor	Video mode	Vienna-648
Vienna m1	Vienna m2	Vienna.m3	Vienna-test
Vienna-7xx	Vienna-774	Vienna-774 trojan	Vienna-Iraqui
Vienna-733	Vienna.644a	Vienna-reboot damage	Vienna-547
Vienna-5xx	Vienna-528	Vienna-510	Vienna-435
Vienna-m4	Vienna-367	Vienna-361	Vienna 348/353
Vienna-TS	Vienna-W13	Vienpart dropper	Vindicator
Violator	Violetta	Virdem Irus	Virdem
Virdem-2	Virus-101	Virus 3	Virus-90
Vivaldi	VMS-Xmas	Void Poem	Voronezh-370
Voronezh-600	Voronezh-1600	Vorpal	Vote
Vote-II	VP	Vriest	VVF 3.4
Wake	Walker	Warpcom	Warrior
Weak	We're here	Westwood	Wisconsin
Whale	Whale 1	Whale 2	Whale 3
Whale 4	Whale 5	Whale 6	Whale 7
Whale 8	Whale 9	Whale 10	Whale 11
Whale 12	Whale 13	Whale 14	Whale 15
Whale 16	Whale 17	Whale 18	Whale 19
Whale 20	Whale 21	Whale 22	Whale 23
Whale 24	Whale 25	Whale 26	Whale 27
Whale 28	Whale 29	Whale 30	Whale 31
Whale 32	Whale 33	Wilbur.a	Wilbur.b
Winvir 1.4	Witch	Witcode	Wizard3
Wolfcheat	Wolfman	Wonder dropper	Wonder

Wordswap-1069	Wordswap-1085	Wordswap-1503	Wordswap-1387/1391
Worthless	WW-217	WW.c	WWT
X-1	X-2	Xabaras	XA1
X-Fungus	XPEH.3600	XPEH.3840	XPEH.4016
XPEH.4048	XPEH4	XPEH5	Xuxa
Yafo	Yale dropper	Yankee-1150	Yankee-1202
Yankee Doodle	YD-2505	Yankee Doodle	Yankee Doodle.44
Yankee Doodle	YD-44.83	YD-44.Login	Yap
Yaunch	YD	YD Wobble	Year1992
Yeke	Youth	Yukon	Zero bug
Zero hunt 1	Zero hunt 2	Zerotime	Zero-to-O
Zherkov	ZK900	ZZ	Ice
PKLite	LZexe	Kvetch	CPAV com
CPAV exe	TAV	TAV-2	TAV
F-XLOCK			

MegaBack

MegaBack
Comprehensive Backup for PC Systems
March, 1992
User's Guide

IMPORTANT WARRANTY INFORMATION

TRIAL USE (SHAREWARE EVALUATION VERSION) WARRANTY:

The Shareware evaluation (trial use) version is provided AS IS. Patri-Soft MAKES NO WARRANTY OF ANY KIND, EXPRESSED OR IMPLIED, INCLUDING WITHOUT LIMITATION, ANY WARRANTIES OF MERCHANTABILITY AND/OR FITNESS FOR A PARTICULAR PURPOSE.

REGISTERED VERSION ONLY WARRANTY:

Patri-Soft warrants the physical diskette(s) and physical documentation provided with registered versions to be free of defects in materials and workmanship for a period of ninety days from the date of registration. If Patri-Soft receives notification within the warranty period of defects in materials or workmanship, and such notification is determined by Patri-Soft to be correct, Patri-Soft will replace the defective diskette(s) or documentation.

The entire and exclusive liability and remedy for breach of this Limited Warranty shall be limited to replacement of defective diskette(s) or documentation and shall not include or extend to any claim for or right to recover any other damages, including but not limited to, loss of profit, data, or use of the software, or special, incidental, or consequential damages or other similar claims, even if Patri-Soft has been specifically advised of the possibility of such damages. In no event will Patri-Soft's liability for any damages to you or any other person ever exceed the lower of suggested list price or actual price paid for the license to use the software, regardless of any form of the claim.

Patri-Soft SPECIFICALLY DISCLAIMS ALL OTHER WARRANTIES, EXPRESSED OR IMPLIED, INCLUDING BUT NOT LIMITED TO, ANY IMPLIED WARRANTY OF MERCHANTABILITY AND/OR FITNESS FOR A PARTICULAR PURPOSE.

About MegaBack

MegaBack is a personal backup system for your computer. MegaBack software automates and organizes backup processing for your system. It also provides comprehensive abilities to restore backup files when needed.

MegaBack is designed to be easy for all PC users. Its menus are simple and understandable. MegaBack makes backup simple by surrounding all complex backup terms and requirements with a menu-driven system.

MegaBack Features

➤ Lets you control backup type by selecting full volume, or incremental backup of updated files.

➤ Saves time by letting you optionally view files to be backed up before backup begins.

➤ Simplifies restore by locating backup files quickly using backup indexes maintained by MegaBack.

➤ Reduces backup time and diskettes required through a comprehensive exclusion facility that lets you mark directories and files to exclude files from the backup process.

➤ Saves time and effort by Formatting new diskettes automatically.

➤ Saves backup space by appending daily backup of updated files to the last backup disk used.

➤ Saves backup space through very high compression and a smart disk storage techniques. Lets you store the maximum amount of data on a minimum number of diskettes.

➤ Provides flexibility by optionally restoring files to any specified location.

➤ Uses multiple storage media. Backup to diskette, removable hard disks, or optical disks.

➤ Provides transportability of backup data to other systems using portable backup volumes.

➤ Provides peace of mind through extensive capabilities to recover from backup errors and disk losses.

➤ Enhances backup data integrity by letting you create multiple backup disk sets to keep spare backup copies for your data.

➤ Adapts to your operation preference of menu or command line operation.

➤ Simplifies learning and operation through instant access to context-sensitive help at any time (F1 key).

Backing up with MegaBack

MegaBack keeps compressed and compacted copies of files on offline diskettes volumes and maintains records for every file in a backup index on your hard disk. The backup index lets you immediately examine all information about your backup files without having to scan through backup diskettes.

MegaBack compresses each file as it is backed up to make maximum use of diskette storage. Compression usually results in storing files in half the space they would normally require on diskettes.

MegaBack also compacts data on backup disks to improve performance and further reduce disk space required for backup. All files backed up to a single diskette are compacted into a single backup file. Writing this single file is much faster and more efficient than writing multiple files on a backup diskette. In addition to performance, compaction saves disk space used by unoccupied cluster space at the end of each DOS file.

Unlike some other backup systems, MegaBack uses standard DOS disk I/O routines when reading and writing backup data. This makes MegaBack much more reliable as it does not depend on unsupported, nonstandard, I/O techniques that may fail on some computers.

MegaBack organizes your backup volumes (diskettes) in simple numerical order so it is easy to file and locate backup volumes. All volumes are numbered sequentially starting at 1. Newly backed up files are stored in the next available space on the last used backup volume. Volumes are completely used before new volumes are started. MegaBack tracks volumes by number and records information about the exact location of every stored file in its hard disk index.

MegaBack's backup index provides a backup directory containing valuable information about every file backed up. The backup index lets you determine if you have a backup of any file from any directory, and tells you the date and time the backup was made. The following information is maintained about every backup file:

- ➤ File name
- ➤ Drive from where file was backed up
- ➤ Directory from where it was backed up
- ➤ File Size
- ➤ Date the file was created or last changed
- ➤ Time the file was created or last changed
- ➤ File attributes

➤ Date the file was backed up

➤ Time the file was backed up

➤ The number of the backup disk(s) holding the file

The compressed size of the backup file

When you need to restore files or an entire volume, you specify the drive, directory, and file information for all files to be restored. These specifications may be for an exact file or may specify wildcard names for qualifying multiple files. MegaBack can immediately restore all matching files, or it will provide a scrollable selection list for you to select one or more files to be restored. Once you have selected files to be restored, MegaBack determines where the backup files are stored, and requests volumes by number.

This organization lets you keep many volumes of backup data while still maintaining easy access to any file.

Full/Incremental Backup

It is not reasonable to expect you to take the time to backup your entire hard disk volume every time you want to backup. MegaBack provides two backup types.

Full backup backs up all the files on your hard disk. Use Full backup the first time you use MegaBack, and then periodically to refresh your backups. Full backup is only needed when you have used all your backup disk volumes and want to condense multiple backup copies of the same file down to a single copy. It is also useful after you have deleted many files from your hard disk and want to free up backup disk space used to hold the files. Unbelievably, most users only need to perform a full backup about once every three months. They use incremental backup on a daily basis.

Incremental Backup is the term given to the process of backing up only files that have been modified since they were last backed up. DOS always keeps track of modified files for you by marking their directory entries with an archive (changed) attribute.

The DOS attribute command (ATTRIB in DOS 5.0) can be used to inspect or change the archive attribute. Whenever a file is created, copied to a new location, or changed by an application, DOS marks the directory entry with the archive attribute. If you have never run backup, the archive attribute will be set for each file on your system. Backup programs remove the archive attribute from files after they have been backed up. MegaBack's Full and Incremental Backups reset the archive (changed) indicator. For testing or special situations, you can disable resetting this attribute through MegaBack options.

Incremental Backup can quickly identify all changed files on your system and append them to your backup set. Since many people only update a few documents or files each day, incremental backup often only takes a minute or two a day. Since Incremental Backup only backs up a small amount of information, you may use incremental backup each day for months before needing a full backup.

Incremental Backup has the effect of storing multiple copies of the same file in the backup set if the file is changed between backups. This would occur when you were editing a word processing document over a period of days. Each day, the current status of the document will be saved to the backup set. Although you may at first think this is a waste of backup disk space, it is really a very beneficial feature. Incremental backups of the same file provide a history of changes to the file. In the event you need to restore an earlier version of the file, you can always find it in MegaBack's backup set.

MegaBack's Incremental Backup lets you backup often. In fact, you may want to backup more than once a day when working on critical information you cannot afford to lose. Since Incremental Backup only takes a minute, you won't hesitate to use it.

Multiple Hard Disks

MegaBack keeps track of all files by drive letter, and pathname so you may backup multiple hard disk volumes using the same set of backup disks and index. When restoring data, simply specify the originating drive to restore data from.

Complements Tape Backup

Those of you with tape backup systems know how time consuming tape backup can be. Tape backup is great for full volume backup, or for regularly backing up very large systems, but it is often not efficient for regular daily or even hourly backup. Tape processing takes too long!

MegaBack does not currently backup to tape devices, but is still a great complement to tape backup systems. Consider using your tape system to do full volume backups of your hard disk drive. Then use MegaBack for Incremental Backup of changed data. Your incremental backups will only take a couple of minutes a day. You will be much more likely to take the time to do daily backup and your hard disk files will be better protected from loss.

To restore a system from a combined tape/MegaBack backup, restore the entire backup from tape and then restore from MegaBack. MegaBack will update the changed files with its copy.

Select/Exclude

Not all files need backing up! This may sound a little reckless, but there are often many files kept on hard disks that are easily replaced and do not justify using backup time and space. Software developers don't need to backup intermediate compiler .OBJ files and test .EXE files. Word processing systems often create .BAK or .BK! files that are redundant copies of their original files.

MegaBack provides a Select/Exclude capability to let you select only the files to be backed up, or to exclude files or directories from backup processing. Use this facility to reduce your backup time and the amount of backup disk space needed. MegaBack options indicate if you want to select files for backup, or back up an entire drive except specified files. You select how its processing is to operate.

Reliability

The most important question to ask of any backup system is how reliable it is? MegaBack has been designed to safely backup your files and double check the backups to make sure they are accurate and correct. In addition, file and index recovery utilities are provided to make sure files can be restored even when hard disk indexes are lost, or when sections of backup disks are lost or destroyed. MegaBack goes to great lengths to recover as much data as possible from your backup set in the event errors are found. Following are MegaBack's data integrity features:

➤ MegaBack uses standard, reliable, DOS I/O routines to read and write backup data. You do not have to worry about it being compatible with your system.

➤ You may activate optional DOS VERIFY checking to confirm data is properly written to disk. This causes DOS to verify each record is correctly written to diskette before writing the next record.

➤ A second MegaBack backup verification feature rereads all data on a backup volume before continuing to the next volume. Backup data is verified before backup is considered complete.

➤ MegaBack keeps a CRC check value on each backup file to confirm files are restored exactly as they were when they were originally backed up.

➤ A backup volume verify feature lets you compare backup data with actual hard disk files at any time. You may use it to verify that a backup is accurate.

➤ MegaBack detects recovered, and unrecoverable disk I/O errors during backup, and asks you if it can take another backup of all files on the disk to a new volume. MegaBack knows if one file on the diskette has a problem, the diskette cannot be trusted and should be replaced.

➤ Restore processing recovers from disk I/O errors and restores all possible files from the bad disk volume.

➤ The backup indexes stored on the hard disk are also backed up to the last backup volume, and may be restored from the backup set if they are lost.

➤ If the backup indexes stored on the last backup volume are not recoverable, a MegaBack utility is available to scan individual backup disks and recreate the hard disk index.

➤ You may think all these precautions are excessive, but users have different and sometimes very stringent requirements for the integrity of their data. MegaBack strives to provide the best data recovery and integrity found in a backup system. You may optionally deactivate the verify features to improve your backup performance if you like.

System Setup/Installation

To install MegaBack take the following steps:

Place distribution diskette in any diskette drive.

Enter the following INSTALL command. (If you are not using drive A, substitute the appropriate drive letter as the first letter in the command.)

`A:INSTALL`

Once the installation is complete, you will find the following files installed in the selected directory on your hard disk:

`MB.EXE`

The MegaBack program file, MegaBack.HLP, contains the context-sensitive help.

The first time MegaBack is started it builds files it needs for its general operation. They are:

`BAKOPT.DAT`	The options file. These options are set using the Setup option from the MegaBack menu.
`BAKVOLIX.DAT`	MegaBack's index containing information about each backup volume it maintains.
`BAKFILIX.DAT`	MegaBack's index containing information about each file maintained in backup sets.

NOTE

Each of the installed file names begins with the letters "BAK." MegaBack allows multiple backup disk sets to be created. Each set is assigned a three-letter identification. MegaBack's index and option file names will be prefixed with the three-letter identifier on secondary backup sets so backup set data is maintained independently. Alternate backup sets will be discussed further in subsequent sections of this manual.

Setting system options

MegaBack is installed with default system options. Verify these options before using MegaBack. Enter the MB command from the DOS command line:

```
C> MB<Enter>
```

From MegaBack's Main Menu, select the SetUp function by pressing 'S' or by using the menu selection bar.

MegaBack's options will be displayed. Examine and modify the options as they are appropriate for you. The following descriptions will help you decide what options to choose. Help is always available by pressing <F1> at any time.

Drive to backup to/from?

Enter the letter of the DOS device you will use to write backup data. This may be the drive letter of any valid DOS mountable disk device. You may use 5 1/4 or 3 1/2 diskette formats or large capacity demountable hard disk type devices.

Level of compression desired?

Use the Right and Left cursor positioning keys to select the level of compression desired for data written to backup volumes.

➤ **NONE:** Do not compress backup data. Will provide the fastest possible backup, but you will use additional backup disks.

➤ **MINIMUM:** Provides about 40% compression of data, but is not as slow as higher compression levels. This is the recommended level of compression.

➤ **STANDARD:** Provides about 45% compression on data, but is not as slow as MAXIMUM compression.

➤ **MAXIMUM:** Provides 50-60% compression, but is slower than other compression.

Disk capacity?

Specify the size of disk you will be using for backup. Each backup disk should be the same size. This size is used when MegaBack formats new diskettes for the backup set.

If you incorrectly specify a size of a high-density disk and place a low-density disk in the drive, MegaBack will format the disk as a high-density disk and format errors will be encountered.

Backup drives

Enter the drives you wish MegaBack to backup. If left blank, MegaBack will request a drive letter. Otherwise, MegaBack will automatically scan each specified disk.

Verify data after it is written? (Y/N)

For data integrity, MegaBack can verify backup volume contents after writing all data to a backup volume.

The verify process is performed just before you are asked to remove a backup volume from the drive. Verification rereads the entire disk to make sure the data is accessible.

Synchronize backup index?

MegaBack can check the hard disk to see if the files in the backup index are still on the hard disk. If they are not, then MegaBack will mark that record as deleted and will not attempt to restore that file.

Use DOS Verify flag? (Y/N)

DOS provides a Verify feature to check that data is properly written during disk write processing. This feature adds additional time to verify disk data during processing, but provides an additional level of assurance that backup data is properly written to disk and can later be accessed. This verification may also be activated through the DOS VERIFY command. Documentation about VERIFY may be found in DOS reference manuals.

Enter 'Y' to have MegaBack activate the DOS VERIFY feature during its operation. We recommend you use this feature.

Sound speaker tones when action needed? (Y/N)

If you dislike the speaker sounds MegaBack makes during processing, specify <N> to have MegaBack disable all sounds during its operation.

When <Y> is specified, you will hear a quiet tic as each file is backed up. This gives you audible signal that backup is currently working. You will also be beeped whenever MegaBack is waiting for you to take an action, such as placing another volume in the drive.

Use exclude/select facility as exclude or select? (E/S)?

You may set up MegaBack to backup selected files and directories on your hard drive, or to process all files except those specifically excluded. Enter <E> to make MegaBack's file selection facility an exclusion facility. Enter <S> to have the file selection facility specify all files and directories to backup. The file select/exclude facility is found in MegaBack's utilities menu and may be found by pressing <U> from the main menu.

Reset archive attribute on files after backup? (Y/N)

Backup processing normally resets DOS's archive attribute (indicating files have changed since backup) after backing up each file. This lets Incremental Backup locate only newly changed files during its processing. Enter <N> if you do not want the DOS attribute reset.

You may want to specify <N> when testing MegaBack, or to run a special backup to a secondary backup diskette set.

Reset archive attribute on files after restore?

This option indicates how the DOS archive attribute will be set after MegaBack restores files. If set to N, MegaBack will mark the file as "Not backed up" and will back up the file at next backup time. Recommended setting is Y.

Test to verify installation

After MegaBack is successfully installed you will want to take a few minutes to learn how it works and develop come confidence in it. You may test MegaBack without resetting the DOS archive (file changed) flag by setting the "Reset archive attribute" Setup option to <N>.

Explore MegaBack's features by backing up and restoring files and directories. When restoring files, always specify an alternate restore target pathname so you will not replace the files on your hard disk during your evaluation.

Since MegaBack allows multiple backup sets to be created, you can create a special backup set to test or demonstrate MegaBack. If you would like to use this feature specify /ID:TMP on the MegaBack command line or set a DOS environment variable with the backup set id desired.

```
SET MegaBack=/ID:TMP
```

You may delete the test backup set by using the Clean option from MegaBack's utility menu.

Backup volumes used for the test backup set may be reused for any other backup set. You do not need to delete the files on the disk before reusing them as MegaBack will do this for you.

Quick Start Guide

If you dislike reading manuals and want to get right to the action, this section will get you started using MegaBack. Remember the <F1> key provides direct access to information about your current action in MegaBack. The context-sensitive help system provides complete information for using the system.

Starting MegaBack

Use the MB command to start MegaBack. MegaBack may be started from any directory or disk. MegaBack uses indexes and options from the directory \MegaBack.

You may place the MegaBack directory in your PATH environment variable (see your DOS manual), or you may specify the pathname where the MB command exists as the command prefix. Following are some command examples:

```
MB

\MegaBack\MB

C:\MegaBack\MB
```

MegaBack can be run from the DOS command line using command line parameters. Command line parameters are documented later in this manual. This section assumes you are using menus to direct MegaBack's operation.

We assume you have already used the Setup of the Main Menu to specify system options. If you have not done this yet, do it now.

Backing up files

1. Starting from the menu.

   Select the Backup function from MegaBack's main menu. MegaBack will scan the selected hard drive to determine how many files exist on your volume to be backed up, and it will also count all files that are marked with the DOS archive attribute as changed since their last backup.

   You will be presented with a selection screen that shows totals for full and incremental backup. These totals indicate how many files will be backed up in each type of backup, how many backup disk volumes are to be used, and approximately how long backup will take. The estimated backup time may be off considerably during your first run of MegaBack since it has no history of your computer's performance. After the first backup, MegaBack uses the previous backup's performance statistics to estimate required time for backup.

2. Backup processing.

MegaBack will present a backup status display. You will immediately be asked to place a backup volume in the output drive. Place any formatted or unformatted disk in the drive. IF THE DISK CONTAINS DATA, IT WILL BE ERASED! Press <Enter> to indicate the volume is ready.

Backup processing will progress while continually updating the status on the display. You will be asked for additional disk volumes as they are needed. Label each backup volume with the number indicated by MegaBack. It is usually sufficient to place a label with a large number on it on each diskette.

3. Backup termination.

When backup processing ends, MegaBack saves its own indexes and options at the end of the backup data on the volume. This may be used if you need to recover the indexes on another machine.

Three actions are possible from this screen. Use the cursor arrow keys to select an option and then press enter, or press the letter associated with the selection you desire.

➤ **Full Backup:** MegaBack will back up all files on your hard disk. If you have selected or excluded files for backup, only those files designated for processing will be backed up.

Full backup begins by asking if you want to start a new backup set or continue adding to an already existing one. Once this decision is made backup processing will begin.

➤ **Incremental Backup:** Process only files marked with the DOS archive (file changed since backup) attribute. These will be added to an already existing backup set. If no full backup has been completed, MegaBack will warn you before starting Backup.

➤ **List Files:** You may obtain a scrollable list of all files to be backed up with Full or Incremental backup. After selecting this option, you will be asked if ALL files are to be listed, or if CHANGED files to be included in Incremental backup are to be shown.

The list files feature lets you verify what data is to be processed before starting backup. It is especially useful to verify Incremental Backup in processing only those files you desire to be backed up. You may want to review this list and make changes before backup.

Active Keys

Several keys are active in the listing.

X	Exclude all files in the directory of the current files.
<SPACE>, *<RIGHT ARROW>*	Exclude the specific file under the highlight bar. <SPACE> toggles.
D	Delete the file under the highlight bar.
ALT-D	Delete file without confirmation.
O	Show Other information about the listed files.
F10	Save the changes made to exclude file.
Exit back *to main menu*	Press the <Escape> key to return back to MegaBack's main menu.

Restoring files

1. Restoring files.

   From the MegaBack Main Menu, select restore to begin processing.

2. Initial restore file selection.

   There are two levels of file selection in restore. Each level further qualifies files to be restored.

   At the first level, you indicate any pathname or filename wildcard entries to be used to select files to be restored. On the same display you can specify beginning and ending dates for files qualify for restore.

Press <F10> after entering the information. You are not required to enter any data at this point. Press <F10> to proceed to the next selection display.

3. Restore now or list specific files.

MegaBack now asks if you want to restore all files found in the backup indexes matching the selection criteria, or if you want to review a list of these files and select specific ones to restore.

If you have already entered enough information to have the proper files restored, you are ready to begin. Start restore by pressing <R>.

4. Selecting files from the selection list.

Selecting <L> for List will cause MegaBack to list all files that qualify your selection criteria. Files will be displayed in a scrollable selection list. You may mark any number of files to be restored. Use the <Space Bar> to toggle selection on or off.

Press <F1> key for other features of restore. You may sort the list, zoom it larger to fill the display and display alternate information about the backed up data. When finished with the selection list, press <F10> to begin restoring the selected files.

5. Restore processing.

The restore status display will be shown and you will immediately be asked to place a specific backup disk in the drive. Press <Enter> to indicate the disk is ready. Restore will begin and its status will be reported until all files are processed.

6. Restore termination.

When restore completes, MegaBack displays a message indicating it is done. Remove the backup volume from the drive.

That's all there is to basic MegaBack processing. There are several features that have not been mentioned in this quick start section. Use the help system or browse this manual to learn more about the system.

How MegaBack works

Different disk device types may be used to contain backup data. These devices may include 3 1/2 diskettes, 5 1/4 diskettes, removable hard disk devices, optical disk devices, and more. Due to this variety of backup storage devices, any backup storage media is referred to by MegaBack as a backup volume.

Backup Volumes

MegaBack backup processing takes the files you select and writes them on backup volumes. Each file is written to volume in a compressed format. Each MegaBack backup volume contains two files. The first file is a backup volume label file identifying the backup volume as well as information about other volumes written before and after the volume.

The second file on a backup volume contains all backup data written to the volume. This file contains any number of compressed backed up files and corresponding information needed to restore them. Since all files are written to a single output file, backup disk space is saved and backup performance is improved.

To use volumes efficiently, each volume is completely filled before a new volume is started. Whenever a new backup process is started, MegaBack asks for the last backup volume used for the previous backup. It then appends new data being backed up to the same volume.

A set of backup volumes is a series of numbered diskettes or disk volumes containing backup data. MegaBack uses only one set of backup data for any backup process. To use an alternative backup set you must start MegaBack with three-character set identifier. Use the /ID:xxx parameter on the MegaBack command line.

Backup Sets

Separate hard disk backup indexes are created for each backup volume set. Basically, backup sets let you keep track of multiple backups on the same system. A common reason for keeping multiple backup sets is to manage a backup set for your own system while still being able to examine and even restore files from secondary backup sets created on other systems.

To restore files from another user's backup set, start MegaBack with the /ID:xxx parameter to specify a secondary backup set name. Use MegaBack's index recovery utility to recover the user's backup index from their last backup diskette. Now you may list and restore the files as if they were backed up from your own system.

Backup File Index

As files are backed up, an entry for each file is placed in a backup index maintained in the MegaBack directory on your hard disk. This index is always maintained on the hard disk. The backup index record contains all information necessary for locating and restoring files. The backup index makes it possible for MegaBack to list backup files without having to read backup volumes.

When you restore a file, MegaBack uses its index to locate files. When files to be restored are selected, information in the index identifies the exact volumes needed to restore the file. MegaBack starts restore processing and asks you to place specific volumes in the drive as they are needed.

The Backup Volume Index

In addition to the backup file index, MegaBack also maintains an index about each backup volume. The backup volume index contains information about each volume and its status in the backup set. The index is maintained as a separate file in the MegaBack directory.

MegaBack reference

Before using MegaBack you will need to prepare a set of backup volumes. When using diskettes as backup volumes, start with a fresh box of the highest quality diskettes you can find. Of course, MegaBack can't tell the quality of your disks, but if your backup data is important to you, it is worth a few more cents per disk to avoid the problems and wasted time poor disks can cost you.

Take the labels provided with the disks and using a large felt marker, number the disks sequentially 1 through 10 (or whatever). If you plan on keeping multiple backup disk sets, you should mark all the disks in a set with a set identifier.

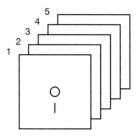

MegaBack can keep separate indexes for different sets of backup volumes. MegaBack only works with one backup set at a time and places secondary backup set names in the upper right corner of every display so you may be sure to use the correct disks. A good use for different backup sets is to use a secondary backup set name to restore files from another user's backup on your system.

MegaBack's Main Menus

The following are examples of MegaBack's main menu structure. The (...) following a menu item indicates the menu item takes you to another submenu. All other selections immediately take the action specified.

```
                  Main Menu

        Backup Processing
        Restore  Processing
        Specify Systems Options
        Utilities Menu...
        Help Index
        Print order form
        Exit to DOS
```

```
                  Utilities

        Exclude files from Backup
        Verify backup volume data
        Build indexes from backup volume
        Reinitialize backup indexes
        Set alternate display colors
        Synchronize hard disk with backup
        Quit to Main
```

The capitalized character on each menu line indicates the specific menu selection character that can be pressed to immediately select a menu item. You may use a mouse with a single click to select a menu option, or use the cursor up and down keys, followed by the <Enter> key, to select menu items.

Backup Processing

Backup begins by asking you to indicate the hard disk to be backed up. The following is an example:

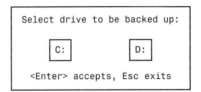

Use a mouse, the drive letter, or the left and right arrow keys followed by enter to specify the drive to be backed up.

MegaBack begins backup by scanning the selected drive to determine the number and size of files to be backed up in either Full or Incremental backup processing. Status lines at the bottom of the display show the progress during this scan.

Backup Type Selection Display

The following display is presented to let you select the type of backup to be done:

The Backup Type Selection Display shows you what files both types of backup will process, how many backup disks will be required for each, and the approximate amount of time that will be required.

The estimated backup time may be off considerably during your first run of MegaBack since it has no history of your computer's performance. After the first backup, MegaBack uses the previous backup's performance statistics to estimate required time for backup.

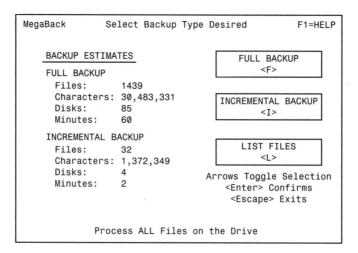

```
┌──────────────────────────────────────────────────────────────┐
│ MegaBack        Select Backup Type Desired        F1=HELP      │
│                                                                │
│    BACKUP ESTIMATES                    ┌──────────────────┐    │
│    ─────────────────                   │  FULL BACKUP     │    │
│    FULL BACKUP                         │      <F>         │    │
│      Files:       1439                 └──────────────────┘    │
│      Characters: 30,483,331                                    │
│      Disks:       85                   ┌──────────────────┐    │
│      Minutes:     60                   │ INCREMENTAL BACKUP│   │
│                                        │      <I>         │    │
│    INCREMENTAL BACKUP                  └──────────────────┘    │
│      Files:       32                                           │
│      Characters: 1,372,349             ┌──────────────────┐    │
│      Disks:       4                    │  LIST FILES      │    │
│      Minutes:     2                    │      <L>         │    │
│                                        └──────────────────┘    │
│                                        Arrows Toggle Selection │
│                                          <Enter> Confirms      │
│                                          <Escape> Exits        │
│                                                                │
│              Process ALL Files on the Drive                    │
└──────────────────────────────────────────────────────────────┘
```

Four actions are possible from this screen. Use the cursor arrow keys to select an option and then press enter, or press the letter associated with the selection you desire. The box represented by Patri-Soft, and the action selected will be highlighted; an explanatory line at the bottom of the display will confirm your selection.

Full Backup <F>

MegaBack will backup all files on your hard disk. If you have selected or excluded files for backup, only those files designated for processing will be backed up.

Full backup begins by asking if you want to start a new backup set, or to continue adding to an already existing one. Once this decision is made, backup processing will begin.

Incremental Backup <I>

Process only files marked with the DOS archive (file changed since backup) attribute. These will be added to an already existing backup set. If no full backup has been completed, MegaBack will warn you before starting Backup.

List Files <L>

You may obtain a scrollable list of all files to be backed up with Full or Incremental backup. After selecting this option, you will be asked if ALL files are to be listed, or if CHANGED files to be included in Incremental backup are to be shown.

The list files feature lets you verify what data is to be processed before starting backup. It is especially useful to verify Incremental Backup is processing only those files you desire to be backed up. You may want to review this list and then use MegaBack's exclude facility to exclude some files before backup begins.

Exit back to main menu <Escape>.

Press the <Escape> key to return back to MegaBack's main menu.

Backup Status Display

Backup Status Display

```
                      M E G A B A C K
  ··  100%        Copyright 1992 by Patri-Soft
  ··                  Backup processing
  ··
  ··
  ··
  ··                      Total      Completed   Remaining
  ··            Files:     43            0          43
  ··            Characters: 1,184,121    0        1,184,121
  ··
  ··
  ··            Path:      D:\BUD\
  XX            Filename:  FY1991.WKS
  XX            Size:      4,397
  XX            Date/Time: 31JUL91 / 5:31p
  XX
  XX                         Disk statistics for drive A:
  XX                                 Volume 1
  XX                      >>>>>>>>>>>>>>>>>>>XXXXXXXXX
  XX  0%                    Total bytes:
                            Bytes used:
Percent Complete            Bytes free:
```

The backup display keeps you informed of the progress of backup. It contains the following information:

➤ **Status Bar:** The status bar at the left side of the display gives a graphic status of the completion of MegaBack.

➤ **Totals:** The totals lines show the number of files and total characters to be processed, completed, and remaining to be processed.

➤ **Current File:** Shows information about the file currently being copied to diskette.

Disk Statistics

The disk statistics in the lower right portion of the display show the amount of space used on backup volumes and the space remaining. This is useful to help you to know when you will need another volume. For large backups you may want to wait to insert a new volume before going for that short break.

Request for Backup Volumes

Request for backup volumes Immediately upon starting backup you will be asked to insert a new volume in the drive. A message like the following one will be shown.

```
      Insert backup disk 1 into drive A.

Press Enter when ready, or ESC for other options

                Waiting
```

MegaBack has searched its volume indexes and found volume #1 to be the next volume to use. Place volume #1 in the drive and press <Enter> to continue processing.

Press <Escape> to be presented with additional options you have when mounting a volume.

MegaBack options indicate when you may safely quit processing. When a new volume is requested to hold the second part of a file that spans multiple volumes, you may not quit processing without having to restart backup for the file being processed.

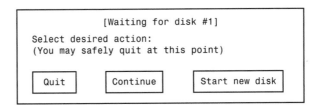

```
                  [Waiting for disk #1]
    Select desired action:
    (You may safely quit at this point)

     ┌──────────┐   ┌────────────┐   ┌─────────────────┐
     │   Quit   │   │  Continue  │   │  Start new disk │
     └──────────┘   └────────────┘   └─────────────────┘
```

Select Continue by pressing <C> and you will be returned to the display requesting the volume to be placed in the drive.

When MegaBack is requesting a volume from a previous backup, you may press <S> to start another new disk instead of appending new backup data to the last used volume. Use this feature when you do not have access to the previous backup volume. You might have stored the used disks of your backup set in another location, or temporarily loaned them to someone.

Recovering from Disk Write Errors

If DOS should encounter a disk write error when writing to the backup volume, you will be presented with messages and options to select to continue from the error. This only applies if the DOS VERIFY flag (see setup) is set on.

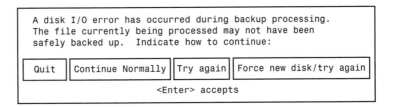

```
    A disk I/O error has occurred during backup processing.
    The file currently being processed may not have been
    safely backed up.  Indicate how to continue:

    ┌──────┐ ┌──────────────────┐ ┌───────────┐ ┌────────────────────┐
    │ Quit │ │ Continue Normally │ │ Try again │ │ Force new disk/try again │
    └──────┘ └──────────────────┘ └───────────┘ └────────────────────┘
                        <Enter> accepts
```

This message is presented after DOS issues its message to RETRY, FAIL, or ABORT after a disk I/O error. If you selected RETRY and processing continued successfully, the file was backed up successfully. If you selected FAIL or IGNORE, the file was not backed up correctly. Select one of the following responses to indicate how to proceed after the I/O error:

➤ Quit: Stop backing up immediately.

➤ Continue Normally: The retry was successful and you want to continue backing up. If the error was caused by a faulty volume, you may want to Try again, or Try a new volume to move the data for the file from the questionable volume area.

➤ Try again: Back up the file again on a new area of the same backup volume. This will skip over the faulty area of a volume. We recommend using Force New disk and trying again over this option since it is better not to try and back up more data on a potentially faulty volume.

➤ Force new disk and try again: (Recommended) Stop writing to the current volume. Ask for a new volume and start backing up for the same file again. The file will be written to the new volume and backup processing will continue.

➤ Interrupting/Resuming Backup: Both Full and Incremental backup may be interrupted by pressing ESC at any time during backup. MegaBack will remember its status, and continue when you restart backup.

➤ Completing backup: Before backup completes, the following message is presented on the display. This message is for your information only, you do not need to take any action. MegaBack is letting you know it is saving a copy of its backup indexes to the last output backup volume.

```
Saving Backup index backup to disk.  Please wait...
```

Once backup completes, the following message will be presented on the display. This is to give you a chance to examine backup statistics before leaving the status display. Press enter to indicate you are ready to continue.

The last message shown by backup reminds you to keep track of the last backup volume used as it contains a copy of the backup indexes for emergency recovery. Remove the volume from the drive and file it so you can identify it as the last disk used. Turn it sideways, upside-down, backwards, or just place it in front of all other volumes.

```
Backup complete.  Remove volume from the drive and
store so you may locate it if needed for recovery.

          Press <Enter> to continue...

            <Enter> to continue
```

An easy way to keep track of the last volume used is to store disk volumes with the used backup volumes behind the unused ones. Rotate the disks as they are used. Always keep the last disk used in the front of the set. In the following figure, assume volume 3 was the last backup volume used.

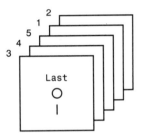

Once MegaBack has returned you back to its main menu you may start another backup or exit back to DOS.

Restore

Restore is the process of copying a backed up file back to normal disk storage. Restore is a copy, not a move. The backup copy remains intact exactly as before the restore. You may delete the restored copy and still have access to the data through the saved backup copy.

MegaBack makes locating and restoring files easy. Several features are included to help you organize backups and locate files they hold.

Backup data is stored in a special compressed form on consecutive disks of offline storage. The special compressed format obviously saves disk space but also increases backup performance. This compressed format requires you to use MegaBack to restore any file backed up by it.

MegaBack indexes all backed up files in a set of hard disk indexes. When you search for a file to be restored, MegaBack's hard disk indexes are used to locate information about the file.

MegaBack gets a disk location and a disk number from the index and asks you to place the disk in the drive. It then reads the data and writes it to your hard disk.

Restore begins by asking for specifications for files to be restored. There are two levels of restore file selection:

First you may optionally enter filename, pathname, and date ranges the file must fall within.

Files matching the first specification may be displayed in a scrollable selection list for your examination and processing selection.

Once files are selected, restore processing begins.

Entering Restore Criteria

After selecting the Restore option from MegaBack's main menu you will be presented with the following display which asks for file selection criteria. You may skip this selection level by pressing <F10> to select all files for restore.

```
Select files BACKED UP from:
            Drive   : *
            Path    : *_____
Pattern to restore  : *.*_____
Restore TO directory: _____
Overlay files on restore? (Y/N/Ask/Update): _
   Select files backed up AFTER this date : _____
   Select files backed up BEFORE this date: _____

                    Enter text
         Press F10 to begin or ESC to abort
```

Selection criteria specification

➤ **Drive : *:** Enter a drive letter indicating where the drive files were originally backed up from. '*' indicates to select files backed up from any drive.

➤ **Path : *:** Enter a pathname where files were backed up from. '*' indicates to select files backed up from any directory name. A directory specification may end with '*' to indicate the files are to be selected from any directory name beginning with the name specified up to the *. Valid specifications are:

```
\

\WP

\WP*

\WP\LETTERS

\WP\LETTERS\
```

➤ **Pattern to restore : *.*:** Enter a complete filename or wildcard pattern name of the backed up files. Extended wildcard capabilities allow you to enter multiple * in a name specification. The * indicates any number of characters may exist in this portion of the name. Valid specifications are:

```
AUTOEXEC.BAT

AUTO*.BAT

AUTO*.*

*.*

*TOEX*.BAT

*U*O*X*.BAT
```

➤ **Restore TO directory:** Optionally enter a target pathname where files are to be restored. This is a full pathname including drive letter. If no directory is specified, the files will be restored to their original drive and directories. Valid specifications are:

```
C:\WP

\WP

C:\WP\LETTERS\
```

➤ **Overlay files on restore? (Y/N/Ask/Update):** If during restore, MegaBack finds a file already defined on the hard disk with the same name as the file being restored, it must decide if the existing file is to be replaced, or to bypass restoring the file.

The following options to indicate what action MegaBack is to take when files of duplicate names are found.

➤ **Yes:** Replace the existing file with the new file.

➤ **No:** Don't overlay the existing file. Skip the restore for the file and continue restoring other files.

➤ **Ask Prompt:** When duplicate files are encountered, ask if the file is to be replaced, or the restore bypassed.

➤ **Update:** Replace files that are newer than the ones present on the disk. The DOS date of the file on the hard disk will be compared to the DOS date of the backup file recorded when the file was originally backed up.

➤ **Select files backed up AFTER this date:** Optionally enter a date to reject files last created or updated on or prior to the date.

➤ **Select files backed up BEFORE this date:** Optionally enter a date to reject files last created or updated on or after the date.

Listing Files to Restore

Once restore file selection has been made, you will be asked if you would like to view and further select files to be restored or immediately begin the restore process. The following display is presented as the last step prior to starting the restore process.

If you have already specified sufficient criteria to select all files to be restored, press <R> to restore all selected files. If you would like to list all files matching the selection criteria entered, press <L>. You will be presented with a scrollable selection list of files.

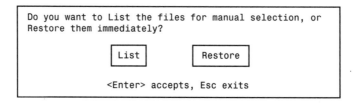

```
Do you want to List the files for manual selection, or
Restore them immediately?

          ┌─────────┐        ┌───────────┐
          │  List   │        │  Restore  │
          └─────────┘        └───────────┘

           <Enter> accepts, Esc exits
```

Restore File Select List Processing

Scrollable selection lists provide complete information about files maintained in MegaBack's backup indexes. Due to the amount of data stored about each file, MegaBack provides two different views of this list. Each view shows a different category of information about backed up files.

TABLE C.1.CONTENTS OF BACKUP LIST VIEWS

View # 1	View # 2
Filename	Filename
DOS File Date	Backup Date
DOS File Time	Backup Size
Original file Size	Original Size(again)
Original Pathname	Backup Volume Number

When the scrollable selection list is first displayed VIEW #1 is shown. To change between the two different views, press the <F6> key. As <F6> is repeatedly pressed the opposite view is shown.

The following keys are active when the restore selection list is displayed:

➤ <Space Bar>: Toggles selection - marks unmarked files to be selected for restore. Unmarks marked files to remove them from being selected.

➤ <Right Arrow>: Marks file to be selected for restore. Advances the file selection bar to the next file. Holding down the key will mark a series of files.

➤ <Left Arrow>: Unmarks file selected for restore. Advances the file selection bar to the next file. Holding down the key will unmark a series of files.

➤ <F1>: Help

➤ <F2>: Zoom. When first displayed, the scrollable list is shown in reduced size to make room for help text at the bottom of the display. Press <F2> to zoom the screen larger. The help text at the bottom of the screen will disappear. Press <F2> again to reduce the display and view the help at the bottom.

➤ <F3>: Enter a DOS Command

➤ <F6>: Show next VIEW. Toggles between the different views of the backup file list.

➤ <F7>: Sort the selection list. You will be presented with a sort selection menu as follows:

```
Change Sort order

Name order
Directory order
date order
Backup date order
Backup Volume Order
```

➤ Name order: Sort by filename.

➤ Directory order: Sort by filename within directory name.

➤ date order: Sort by the date the file was last updated or created (before it was backed up).

➤ Backup date: Sort files in sequence by the date they were backed up.

➤ Backup Volume: Sort files in the order they exist on the backup volumes.

➤ <F10>: Start restore. After you have marked one or more files to be restored, press <F10> to accept the selected items and start restore.

➤ <Escape>: Exit file selection list and quit restore processing.

Following are examples of the different views of the selection list. Select one or more files to be restored or press <Escape> to return to MegaBack's main menu. After selecting the desired files, press <F10> to start restoring the files.

VIEW #1

```
┌─────────────────────────────────────────────────────┐
│  Name          Date       Time     Size    Path      │
│                                                       │
│  AUTO.BAT      15JUN91    2:26p    134     C:\BAT\    │
│  B.BAT         15JUN91    2:39p    64      C:\BAT\    │
│  BC.BAT        7SEP91     2:39p    83      C:\BAT\    │
│  BCX.BAT       19MAY91    6:30p    144     C:\BAT\    │
│  BITFAX.BAT    27MAR91    4:01p    29      C:\BAT\    │
│  C.BAT         19AUG90    7:29p    99      C:\BAT\    │
│  C2.BAT        9MAR91     7:54a    56      C:\BAT\    │
│  DELA.BAT      20DEC90    7:48a    16      C:\BAT\    │
│  DELB.BAT      19JUL91    6:22a    23      C:\BAT\    │
│  DIRA.BAT      19NOV86    2:23p    11      C:\BAT\    │
│  DIRB.BAT      25APR91    6:59a    8       C:\BAT\    │
│                                                       │
│            F10 accepts, ESC exits                     │
└─────────────────────────────────────────────────────┘
```

VIEW #2

```
┌─────────────────────────────────────────────────────┐
│  Name         BakDate   BakTime  BakSize Ratio  Disk │
│                                                       │
│  AUTO.BAT     8OCT91    10:17a   134     1.00%    1   │
│  B.BAT        8OCT91    10:17a   64      1.00%    1   │
│  BC.BAT       8OCT91    10:17a   83      1.00%    1   │
│  BCX.BAT      8OCT91    10:17a   144     1.00%    1   │
│  BITFAX.BAT   8OCT91    10:17a   29      1.00%    1   │
│  C.BAT        8OCT91    10:17a   99      1.00%    1   │
│  C2.BAT       8OCT91    10:17a   56      1.00%    1   │
│  DELA.BAT     8OCT91    10:17a   16      1.00%    1   │
│  DELB.BAT     8OCT91    10:17a   23      1.00%    1   │
│  DIRA.BAT     8OCT91    10:17a   11      1.00%    1   │
│  DIRB.BAT     8OCT91    10:17a   8       1.00%    1   │
│                                                       │
│            F10 accepts, ESC exits                     │
└─────────────────────────────────────────────────────┘
```

Starting Restore

Starting Restore

After starting restore MegaBack determines the volumes needed to restore the files and immediately requests you place the first volume needed in the input drive. Following is an example of the volume mount message.

```
┌─────────────────────────────────────────────────────┐
│            Insert backup 1 into drive A.             │
│                                                       │
│   Press Enter when ready, or ESC for other options    │
│                    Waiting                            │
└─────────────────────────────────────────────────────┘
```

Locate the requested volume from your set of backup volumes and place it in the drive. You may terminate restore at any time by pressing <Escape>. All files restored to this point of processing are restored correctly. Other files selected will need to be selected again in a subsequent restore process to be restored.

Restore Processing

The restore display is presented throughout the restore process. It provides status of the restore.

Restore Status Display

```
                          M E G A B A C K
       ·· 100%        Copyright 1992 by Patri-Soft
        ··               Restore processing
        ··
        ··                  Total       Completed  Remaining
        ··           Files:     3
        ··           Characters: 219
        ··
        ··           Path:      C:\BAT\
        ··           Filename:  B.BAT
       XX            Size:      64
       XX            Date/Time: 15JUN91/2:39p
       XX
       XX                          Disk statistics for drive C:
       XX                          >>>>>>>>>>>>XXXXXXXXXXXXXX
       XX                          0%       freespace      100%
       XX  0%
                                 Total characters:
  Percent Complete                characters used:
                                  characters free:
```

The restore status display keeps you informed of the progress of restoring files. It has the following basic contents:

> **Status Bar:** The status bar at the left side of the display gives a graphic status of the completion of MegaBack.

> **Totals:** The totals lines show the number of files and total characters to be processed, completed, and remaining to be processed.

> **Current File:** Shows information about the file currently being restored.

> **Disk Statistics:** The disk stats shown in the lower right portion of the display show how much space is used on the target hard disk and how much freespace remains.

Overlaying Files with duplicate Names

If MegaBack finds that a file with the same name as the one being restored already exists in the target directory, it may overwrite the file with the backup version, bypass restoring the file, or compare the dates and times of the two files and restore the file only if it is a more recent copy than the version on disk.

MegaBack Setup options let you specify any of these alternatives as an action to automatically be taken during restore. A special restore option of "Ask" indicates restore processing is to ask what action to take each time a duplicate file name is found. The following question is asked:

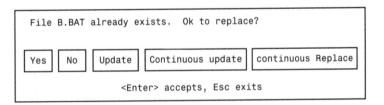

```
File B.BAT already exists.  Ok to replace?

┌─────┐ ┌────┐ ┌────────┐ ┌─────────────────┐ ┌───────────────────┐
│ Yes │ │ No │ │ Update │ │ Continuous update │ │ continuous Replace │
└─────┘ └────┘ └────────┘ └─────────────────┘ └───────────────────┘

              <Enter> accepts, Esc exits
```

Press Y, N, U, C, or R to indicate the action to take. <Escape> immediately terminates restore. Following are explanations of possible responses:

> <Yes>: Replace the file immediately. The backup file will overlay the already existing file.

> <No>: Do not restore the file. Leave the file on the hard disk.

> <Update>: Restore the file if it is a newer version than the file on the target drive. If the backup file is older than the disk file, bypass restoring this file.

> <Continuous update>: This is the same response as <Update> with the additional feature of indicating MegaBack is not to ask this question again if another duplicate file name is found. An

answer of <Update> will be assumed for all future instances of this situation during this restore process.

➤ <continuous Replace>: This is the same response as <Replace> with the additional feature that MegaBack is not to ask this question again if another duplicate file name is found. An answer of <Replace> will be assumed for all future instances of this situation during this restore process.

➤ Restore Complete: After all files have been restored, the following message will be presented over the Restore Status Display. It is an informational message to let you know the last action taken by MegaBack. Press <Enter> to acknowledge the message and return to MegaBack's main menu.

```
Restore Complete

<Enter> to continue
```

Restoring to an Empty System

Both DOS and MegaBack must first be present on a system to use MegaBack. If you lose your hard drive and want to restore your backup to it you should take the following steps:

1. Restore DOS to the system. Use procedures outlined in the DOS reference manual.

2. Install MegaBack on the system by using your original MegaBack installation diskette or a copy of it.

3. Use MegaBack index rebuild utility to regenerate the MegaBack indexes from your last backup diskette.

4. Use MegaBack restore to restore all files back to your system.

Making a System Recovery Boot Diskette

Some users choose to make a MegaBack system recovery boot diskette to use in the event their system is lost. The boot diskette contains a bootable version of DOS and the MegaBack system files. Take the following steps to make a recovery boot diskette:

1. Format a diskette using Format's DOS /S parameter. This will create a diskette that will boot your machine without DOS being on your system.

   ```
   FORMAT A:/S
   ```

2. Copy the following DOS files to the recovery diskette:

   ```
   FORMAT*.COM
   ```

   ```
   FDISK.EXE
   ```

3. Build a CONFIG.SYS file on the diskette that contains at least the following lines.

   ```
   FILES=30
   ```

   ```
   BUFFERS=30
   ```

4. Build an AUTOEXEC.BAT on the diskette to start MegaBack.

   ```
   PROMPT $P$G
   ```

   ```
   MD C:\MegaBack
   ```

   ```
   CD C:\MegaBack
   ```

   ```
   COPY A:MB.EXE
   ```

   ```
   COPY A:MegaBack.HLP
   ```

   ```
   MB
   ```

This recovery diskette will boot your system and start MegaBack if the system already has a formatted drive C:. If drive C: is not formatted, use DOS hard disk setup procedures to prepare the hard disk, and then boot your system again with the MegaBack recovery diskette.

Utility Functions

The utility menu of MegaBack's main menu provides access to functions supporting MegaBack backup and restore functions. Select Utilities from the main menu to access the following menu of options.

```
                    Utilities

      Advanced system options
      Exclude files from Backup
      Verify backup volume data
      Build indexes from backup volume
      Reinitialize backup indexes
      Set alternate display colors
      synchronize hard disk with backup
      Quit to Main
```

➤ Advanced system options: These options are available for further customization of MegaBack. These options are not necessary for normal operation and are set at the recommended defaults.

➤ Target Media Type: This indicates to MegaBack about the target media type. At this time, the only difference is MegaBack's disk mounts. For nonremovable media, MegaBack supresses a disk mount. MegaBack calls for a volume with all other settings.

➤ Directory to backup to: When backing up to a large capacity volume, it is sometimes desirable to put the backup data into a specific directory rather than the root directory. Set this directory here.

➤ Scan disk before backup: When backup is started, MegaBack scans the drives to gather the relevant statistics. This can take time on large hard disks, so you may skip this option if so desired.

➤ Maintain Activity Log: MegaBack may optionally keep an activity log of most of its actions. This log is maintained in the MegaBack directory, and is called MEGABACK.LOG. The log currently is somewhat cryptic, but Patri-Soft will soon provide a viewer.

➤ Is Activity Log to be Verbose: If you want a record of every file backed up or restored to be placed in the activity log, specify Y for this option.

➤ Backup zero byte files: If you do not want files of zero size to be backed up, specify N.

➤ Skip Stoaway AutoRestore files. Patri-Soft's Stowaway archival system can be configured to leave zero character empty files on hard disks. If these files are accessed, Stowaway's Auto Restore function will try to restore them so they can be backed up. Specify Y if you use Stowaway to archive data on your system. this option is ignored if you do not use Stowaway.

➤ Default restore sort: When a large number of files is selected for restore, MegaBack may take a while to sort it all. In the interest of efficiency, MegaBack will sort it in the way that YOU want it sorted in, so that you will not have to resort it.

Selection/Exclusion Processing

MegaBack can backup selected files, or all files on a disk except files excluded from the process. You may specify either select processing, or exclusion processing in MegaBack options.

The selection/exclusion facility displays lists of directories and files on your hard disk. While viewing these lists, you mark files to be selected or excluded from processing depending on your option selected.

While you are scrolling through the lists of files, you may view the contents of text and WordPerfect files using MegaBack's file viewers. You may sort file lists by file name, age, size, name, or extension.

Following is an example of a the file selection display area.

```
                   C:\WP

<PARENT>       26APR91    10:32p    <DIR>
<ROOT>         26APR91    10:32p    <DIR>
AGENDAS         5MAY91     4:10p    <DIR>
ARNOLD.LTR     10MAY91     8:15a    20430
BACKDAY.NOT    21JUN91    12:15p     3021
MONEY.GOT      19JUL91     7:32a    50583

           F10 accepts, ESC exits
```

The display shows files for one directory at a time. Entries for the current and root directory are always sorted to the top of the list along with other subdirectories defined in the listed directory.

The top border of the display indicates the drive and name of the directory being displayed. The bottom border gives brief help about keys used to terminate the selection process. The right-hand border of the display holds a scroll bar for mouse control of the list (not shown above). Also not shown is a highlighted selection bar that covers one entry at a time in the list. The selection bar's location is modified by using the UP, DOWN, LEFT, and RIGHT cursor control keys.

Backup File Selection Operation

The following keys are active during backup select/exclude processing:

➤ **<Space Bar>:** When positioned on a file name, it either marks the file to be selected or excluded, or if the file has already been marked, unmarks it. File names become highlighted in the list after they are marked. A small checkmark symbol is also displayed next to the file name to indicate it is selected.

➤ **<Right Arrow>:** Marks the file highlighted by the selection bar. If the file is already marked, it will remain marked. The file selection bar is also moved to the next file name in the list.

➤ **<Left Arrow>:** Unmarks the file highlighted by the selection bar. If the file is not marked it will remain unmarked. The file selection bar is also moved to the next file name in the list.

➤ **<Enter>:** When the file selection bar is placed over a directory name, changes the list to show the selected directory. Place the highlight bar on any directory name and press the <Enter> key to change to the directory.

Special file names of <PARENT> and <ROOT> are shown for any subdirectory listed. You may press <Enter> on the <PARENT> entry to list the files in the directory above the current directory listed. Pressing <Enter> on the <ROOT> entry lists the root directory of the currently selected drive.

➤ **<F1>:** At any time press the <F1> key for help on the current activity.

➤ **<F3>:** Press <F3> to bring up a temporary window to enter a DOS command or to exit to DOS.

➤ **<F10>:** The <F10> key signals the end of the file marking process. You will be returned back to the utilities menu.

➤ **<Escape>:** Use the <Escape> key to terminate file selection/ exclusion processing and return to the MegaBack main menu. The names of marked files are not saved.

➤ **<A>:** Press <A> when positioned on a directory name to mark the directory and all its subordinate directories.

➤ **<D>:** Press <D> to unmark any directory or file.

➤ **<S>:** Press <S> to activate a selection window to specify an alternate sort sequence for the file list.

```
Change List Order

Sort Date Descending
Sort Name Ascending
Sort Size Descending
```

➤ **<T>:** Tag all files in the currently displayed directory.

After tagging all files you can untag selected files to be omitted from processing.

➤ **<U>:** Untag all tagged files in the currently displayed directory.

➤ **<V>:** Press the <V> key to View text or WordPerfect files. The file viewer can examine up to 500 lines of a file. Use the cursor control keys to control the viewing of a file and press <Escape> from the viewer to return to the file list.

Marking a full directory

You may position the file selection bar over any subdirectory name and press the <Right Arrow> or <Space Bar> to mark it. MegaBack will immediately present the following question:

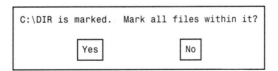

```
C:\DIR is marked.  Mark all files within it?

        Yes              No
```

This is a reminder that you will mark the entire directory as well as all directories below it. Press <Y> if this is correct. Press <N> to cancel the mark directory request.

Verify Backup Volume Data

Use verify to confirm backup has correctly backed up data. Sometimes you may be unsure of the validity of your backup data. This might happen if you suspect faulty backup volumes were used, or a drive might not be functioning properly. MegaBack provides this function to read backup data and verify it can be used to restore the files.

Volume verification is quick and easy as it only requires a quick read of each backup volume. No data is actually written to the hard disk.

Two verification processes actually occur. First, DOS verifies all the data can be read from the backup volumes. Second, a CRC check verifies data is accurate by arithmetically verifying the data on the volumes is the same as the data was on the hard disk before it was backed up.

Backup verification may verify selected backup files, or an entire backup volume set. Upon selecting the verify function you will be presented with a specification display similar to restore processing. Indicate the qualifications of all files to be verified.

```
Drive to verify    :*

Path to verify     :*

Pattern to verify :*.*

Select files backed up AFTER this date :

Select files Backed up BEFORE this date:

                 Enter text
     Press F10 to begin or ESC to abort
```

You are asked to fill in the following fields:

➤ **Drive to verify:** Enter the drive letter from where the files were originally backed up. (I.E. C, D)

➤ **Path to verify:** Optionally enter the pathname from where the files were backed up. If no path is specified, files from all paths will be selected. I.E. \LETTERS \PICTURES

➤ **Pattern to verify:** Enter a file name pattern to verify. When not specified, all file pattern will be selected.

➤ **Backed up before/after:** Select files by the date they were backed up. You may use one or both of the date specifications. Press <F10> to accept specifications and start verification. <Esc> to quit.

Like restore, you will be asked to place each volume in the input drive until all data is verified. You will be notified with error message displays if any errors are found in the data.

Build Index from Backup Volume

Since the hard disk backup indexes are critical to the system, they are backed up to the last backup volume at the end of every backup. This takes a little time and disk space but ensures indexes are always backed up and are kept with backup data.

Since the indexes are kept on backup volumes, each volume set becomes a portable set of files you may take to another computer for use.

To use any backup set, the indexes must exist on your hard disk. If they are somehow lost or not available on the computer where you want to restore files, you must first restore the index from the last backup volume. It is your responsibility to keep track of the last backup volume used since MegaBack does not know disk numbers without its indexes. During index recovery MegaBack will ask you to place the last used backup volume in the drive.

If you have lost track of the last backup volume, use the DOS directory command to display the files on each volume. The volume with the most recent file dates is the last disk used.

Place the last volume in the drive and press <Enter> after MegaBack asks for it. In some cases MegaBack may ask for a second volume if it determines part of the indexes backed up are stored on a previous volume.

```
┌─────────────────────────────────────────────────────┐
│              Restoring Backup Indexes                 │
│                                                       │
│   Attempting to restore indexes from backup diskettes.│
│                                                       │
│      Place the last backup disk used in drive A:      │
│                                                       │
│  Press <Enter> when volume is ready, <Escape> to exit.│
│                                                       │
│                 <Enter> to continue                   │
└─────────────────────────────────────────────────────┘
```

MegaBack will read the indexes and put them on the hard drive. You will be notified when the indexes are properly restored.

If the build of the index from the backup volume fails, Patri-Soft provides an emergency index rebuild utility. BACKRGEN will read individual backup volumes and recreate their index entries in an existing MegaBack index. You will find copies of BACKRGEN on the MegaBack distribution diskette. You may also always download it from the Patri-Soft BBS, or other popular BBS systems.

BACKRGEN is not always included in the BBS version of MegaBack to reduce the size of data to download. Contact us at Patri-Soft if you have any problems locating this utility. There is no fee for the BACKRGEN utility, it is free to anyone.

Reinitialize Backup Indexes

This function of MegaBack deletes the current set of backup indexes and create new empty ones. Use it before starting a new full backup for your system.

After selecting the index delete function you will be prompted to verify that you really do want to complete this process:

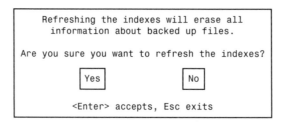

```
┌─────────────────────────────────────────────────────┐
│       Refreshing the indexes will erase all           │
│        information about backed up files.             │
│                                                       │
│   Are you sure you want to refresh the indexes?       │
│                                                       │
│          ┌─────┐              ┌────┐                   │
│          │ Yes │              │ No │                   │
│          └─────┘              └────┘                   │
│                                                       │
│            <Enter> accepts, Esc exits                 │
└─────────────────────────────────────────────────────┘
```

Respond <Yes> to continue the process and delete the current backup index set.

Respond <No> to cancel the index deletion process and return to MegaBack main menus.

Set Alternate Display Colors

MegaBack lets you change the colors of all its display windows to any colors of your choice. Setting alternate display colors involves setting NORMAL, REVERSE, HIGHLIGHT, and BORDER colors for each different type of window.

When changing colors, you are presented with a menu of each window type used by MegaBack. You may change colors on any or all window types.

Window colors are stored permanently on disk in the options file so they will be used each time you use MegaBack. When you are finished setting colors, press <Exit> to return to MegaBack's menus.

```
                    Select Colors

            Menus
            Pop-Ups
            User input
            Backup/Restore/Main
            Copyright Message
            Registration Message
            Disk statistics
            disk mounts
            Thermometers
            default colors
            Help Colors
            textured Background
            Exit to main

            Change all Menu colors

            Press <Enter> to select
```

You are presented with a screen with four major color types to pick across the top and with a screen full of color combinations below.

Use the <Space Bar> to move between each color type. Pressing the space bar indicates the current color selection for the active type is to be accepted.

Use the <Arrow Keys> to position the selection box on the color combination to be used for the current color type. When you are positioned on the desired color, press the <Space Bar>.

Press <Enter> to accept all colors and return to the window type menu. You can then change colors on another window type.

Press <Escape> to return to the window selection menu and leave the colors as they were originally defined.

Synchronize Indexes with Hard Disk

Since you may use Incremental backup for a long period of time before again needing to perform a Full backup, your backup sets will eventually contain copies of files that have been deleted from your hard disk. If you should ever need to recover your hard disk and restore all backup files, it is not desirable to recreate these deleted files.

MegaBack's synchronization feature compares the files stored in the backup indexes with the actual files on your hard disk and records files no longer on your hard disk as deleted.

MegaBack's restore processing provides options to include, or bypass these "deleted" files during restore. Your data is always available and you make sure not to accidently restore unwanted files.

You should perform the backup synchronization feature whenever you have deleted files from your hard drive.

Upon selecting synchronization from the menu, MegaBack will immediately begin comparing the indexes with the hard disk files. A status display will be presented to show you the progress of the activity. You may safely terminate the process at any time by pressing any key during the comparison. MegaBack will ask if processing is to terminate or continue.

Upon completing synchronization processing you will be returned to MegaBack's menus.

Command Line Operation

MegaBack is normally operated through its menu structure. This provides a simple technique for backing up files that reassures you at every step with displays and questions to let you make decisions.

More experienced users may want to use MegaBack's command line interface to backup their system. When the command line operation is used, MegaBack will take all its basic instructions from the command line and start the backup process. It will still require that the proper disks be placed in the drives and may ask for other decisions to be made based on your options. Although not totally automated, it provides a quick start to backing up specific data.

The MegaBack command line format is as follows:

```
MB  path /C  /EV:vol /F  /I /ID:xxx /S  /SV:vol/R /AF /NL /NS
/V
```

Command parameter explanations path Specify pathname to be restored. You must also specify the /R parameter.

➤ **/AF:** Assume Formatted. MegaBack will assume that all input backup disks are formatted.

➤ **/C:** Used by MegaBack's installation program to start MegaBack and proceed directly to setting system options.

➤ **/EV:vol:** During restore, it is sometimes desirable to only restore files in certain volumes. You may specify a range of disk volumes by using the /EV and /SV parameters. For example, to restore the files after volume 6 and before volume 9, the command line would be:

```
MB /SV:6 /EV:9
```

➤ **/F:** Start MegaBack and immediately start Full volume backup.

➤ **/I:** Start MegaBack and immediately start Incremental backup processing.

➤ **/ID:xxx:** Use alternative backup index set id. Specify any three characters to use an alternate index set. For more information about alternate index sets, see the heading about Backup Index

Sets in the manual. When not specified it is assumed the value will be "BAK".

```
/ID:TOM
```

➤ **/NL, /V:** No Log, Verbose. If you wish to suppress the log, use /NL. If you would like the log to be verbose, use the /V option.

➤ **/NS:** No Scan. This option supresses MegaBack's hard disk scan.

➤ **/R:** You may also accomplish restore from the command line. Specify a path and append /R to the command line.

➤ **/S:** If you already know the backup volume MegaBack will use, you may place it in the drive prior to starting MegaBack and specify this parameter to have MegaBack assume the volume is present. MegaBack will not ask you to place it in the drive during backup. This parameter is designed for those users backing up to huge capacity disk devices where volume mounting is not normally necessary.

➤ **/SV:vol:** To start the restore process with a certain diskette, use this command. For example, to restore only files on disk 6 and above, use the command:

```
MB  /SV:6
```

Specifying Options through DOS Environment Variables

Any MegaBack command line parameters may be placed in DOS environment variables to be effective each time MegaBack is started. Use the DOS SET command to add the parameter to the environment string. The environment variable name used by MegaBack is MegaBack. The following example demonstrates the most common use of the environment variable for MegaBack. In this example, the SET command is used to cause MegaBack to use an alternate index set identifier of TOM each time it is started.

```
SET MegaBack=/ID:TOM
```

See your DOS manual for more information about the SET command. The SET command is often placed in the AUTOEXEC.BAT file on a user's hard disk so it may automatically be issued each time your system is started.

Backup Maintenance

MegaBack lets you keep and use multiple backup sets on the same computer system. Although not often necessary, this feature is useful in many situations. Some examples are:

➤ To create a special backup set apart from your normal set to move files from one system to another.

➤ To create separate backup sets for multiple users of a system.

➤ To test your current backup set by restoring its indexes to a different backup set identifier.

A backup set consists of hard disk indexes and all backup volumes holding files referenced by those indexes. Backup sets are given three character set identifiers. This identifier is normally "BAK" but may be altered when starting MegaBack by using the /ID:xxx command parameter. An alternate set identifier may also be established by placing the /ID:xxx parameter in MegaBack's DOS environment variable.

Backup set indexes consist of a set of two index files and an options file. These files exist on the hard disk in MegaBack's directory. The normal files are named as follows:

```
BAKOPT.DAT

BAKVOLIX.DAT

BAKFILIX.DAT
```

Alternate backup sets are identical in function and usage to the normal index MegaBack uses. When using alternate index identifiers, be careful to use the correct index set for the files you are processing.

Making Copies of Backup Volumes

Each backup volume is in a normal DOS format. Backup volumes may be copied using DOS DISKCOPY, COPY, or XCOPY commands.

For safety reasons you may want to take a copy of backup information and store it at an offsite location. To do this, use the DISKCOPY command to copy the original volume to another volume. Store the original volume back with the backup set, and take the copied volumes to your offsite location.

When you only have a single drive to read and write a specific disk format use the DOS DISKCOPY command as follows. It will use memory to copy a volume to a new volume. The drive letters for the source and new volumes are the same. DOS will issue messages indicating what volumes to place in the drives and when.

```
DISKCOPY A: A:
```

If you have multiple drives able to read and write the same volume format, use the DISKCOPY command with different drive letters. The first drive identifier is for the source volume, the second letter is for the drive to hold the new volume.

```
DISKCOPY A: B:
```

Backup disks may be copied to different disk formats as long as the new disk has enough capacity to hold all information on the source volume. Once backed up, backup data cannot again be split across multiple volumes.

The Context-Sensitive Help System

MegaBack provides immediate help about its operation at every point of its processing. A comprehensive help system may be interrogated at any time by pressing the <F1> key. When <F1> is pressed, MegaBack automatically determines what function is active and what action is being requested. It will search a help index and retrieve information about your current activity. Help systems that bring up help about your current activity are referred to as "context sensitive" meaning they are aware of the context in which they are requested.

In addition to being context sensitive, MegaBack help system is layered to let you not only examine help about your current activity, but also browse through the help displays to learn about related topics or other aspects of MegaBack. Press the <Home> key any time you are in the help system to display the help menu.

The intelligent help system may be examined by using the following navigation keys.

➤ **<Enter>:** Takes you to the next related screen.

➤ **<Esc>:** Takes you back to the processing screen.

➤ **<Alt>:** Allows you to peek back at the processing screen to review what you are reading help about.

➤ **<PgUp>:** Will take you up to a more general topic in the help system.

➤ **<Home>:** Displays the main help menu The LEFT, RIGHT, UP, and DOWN keys are available when viewing screens smaller than the full page. Use them to move the help window around on the display to view areas hidden by the help window.

System Requirements

Operating system compatibilities: MegaBack must run on a 100% compatible PC, XT, or AT system and requires DOS 3.2 or above for its operation. MegaBack may operate on some other nonstandard systems, but we cannot guarantee its correct operation nor make any promises to make it compatible with those systems.

Backup device compatibilities: MegaBack uses only standard DOS disk devices for holding backup data. The obvious devices are various forms of 3 1/2 and 5 1/4 diskette systems.

MegaBack is also designed to use large format removable disk devices as backup media. These devices must have a standard DOS format and must appear to DOS as a normal disk device.

Troubleshooting

I/O errors on disks

If you should have a problem restoring data from a damaged or faulty volume take the following steps to attempt to circumvent the problem.

> ➤ Try turning the disk in the sleeve with your fingers to make sure it is loose and will spin. If 5 1/4 diskettes appear too tight, you can relieve some pressure placed on the magnetic media by drawing each edge of the diskette across the edge of a table applying a reasonable amount of pressure. This will expand the area inside the jacket for the media to move.

> ➤ Attempt to copy the diskette to another diskette. If the copy is successful, attempt to use the new disk to restore the data.

> ➤ Take the volume in error to another drive on another machine to attempt to restore the data.

> ➤ When all else fails, use the "FAIL" option during backup volume read error detection to indicate backup is to attempt to read as much data as possible.

Error Messages

MegaBack has comprehensive error and exception checking designed into every component of the system. MegaBack's help systems contain help about messages issued by MegaBack. Whenever an error message is displayed, press the <F1> key for a complete explanation of the error and suggested actions to take as a result of the error.

Technical Support

Patri-Soft may be reached for technical support through a variety of sources. Normal technical support hours are 8:30AM through 5:00 PM Monday through Friday (PST).

You may contact us through the following methods:

CompuServe:	76347,2477
Phone:	714-352-2820
BBS:	714-352-2825
FAX:	714-352-1527

Mail:

Patri-Soft
5225 Canyon Crest Drive, Suite 71-358
Riverside, CA 92507

A special order line is available if you would like to purchase using VISA or MasterCard or discuss other purchase options.

When calling for technical support please have the following information ready so we may serve you efficiently:

1. The exact version of MegaBack you are using. MegaBack main menu contains this data.

2. An exact problem description.

3. Screen print of the MegaBack directory and all files it contains.

4. The software configuration of your system including DOS version, AUTOEXEC.BAT contents as well as CONFIG.SYS contents.

5. The hardware configuration of your system.

A good problem description indicates exactly what you were doing when you encountered the error, and exactly what symptoms occurred as a result of the error. Please avoid the following problem descriptions. They are much too brief to begin to analyze.

Poor problem descriptions:

➤ Backup is not working.

➤ The machine will not read my disk.

➤ I can't restore my indexes.

➤ The system fails during backup or restore.

Following are examples of better problem descriptions:

➤ Backup is failing. MegaBack asks for a backup volume, and after I place it in the drive, the drive light comes on, goes off, and MegaBack indicates no disk is in the drive.

➤ I am attempting to restore indexes from a backup volume, and MegaBack indicates the indexes are not present. I have displayed the contents of the last used diskette, and it appears to be ok. Its contents are...

PCOPY Version 9.2B

June 1992
Copyright 1992 by Patri-Soft

The program author and sole proprietor of Patri-Soft, Norman Patriquin, is an active member of the Association of Shareware Professionals (ASP). The ASP wants to make sure that the Shareware principle works for you. If you are unable to resolve a Shareware related problem with an ASP member by contacting the member directly, ASP may be able to help. The ASP Ombudsman can help you resolve a dispute or problem with an ASP member, but does not provide technical support for members' products. Please write to the ASP Ombudsman at P.O. Box 5786, Bellevue, WA 98006 or send a Compuserve message via MAIL to ASP Ombudsman 70007,3536.

DISCLAIMER

Patri-Soft hereby disclaims all warranties relating to this product, whether express or implied, including without limitation any implied warranties of merchantability or fitness for a particular purpose. Patri-Soft cannot and will not be liable for any special, incidental, consequential, indirect or similar damages due to loss of data or any other reason, even if Patri-Soft or an authorized Patri-Soft agent has been advised of the possibility of such damages. In no event shall the liability for any damages ever exceed the price paid for the license to use software, regardless of the form and/or extent of the claim. The user of this program bears all risk as to the quality and performance of the software.

LICENSE

PCOPY is a Shareware product. As such, it is made available to the general computing public for evaluation. Users are licensed to operate PCOPY on their personal computers for the purpose of test and evaluation on a trial basis for a limited trial period. It is not possible to reasonably define any definitive limits of a fair and equitable time period for evaluation, therefore it is left to the user's judgment and sense of fair play as to the time required to make a decision as to its usefulness. If the user decides the program is not of sufficient merit to warrant purchase through registration with Patri-Soft, the program should be removed from their personal computer. Otherwise, if the program is deemed useful and is in regular use on the user's personal computer system, registration with Patri-Soft is required.

Registered users are those users that elect to pay for PCOPY and register by payment with Patri-Soft. By virtue of registration and payment for the program, registered users are granted a license to continue to utilize the program on their personal computer for as long as they choose. This license authorizes the user to use the program on any personal computer system he or she may own so long as the program is operated on only one computer system at a time.

Site licenses for use of PCOPY on multiple computers are available upon request at a reduced fee that is based upon the number of single machines licensed for use.

REGISTRATION

PCOPY is sole property of Patri-Soft Shareware products. The Shareware version, and ONLY that version, may be freely copied and transferred to individual parties for evaluation purposes. The

Shareware version, and ONLY that version, may be posted on Bulletin Board Systems (BBS) for electronic access as long as NO FEE is charged for its distribution except for private BBS operations that charge a regular user subscription fee. Computer information services such as Compuserve (CIS), Genie, etc., are authorized to post this product for subscriber access. The Shareware version of PCOPY may NOT be distributed on diskette by any disk distributor/vendor that charges more than $12.00 for the diskette upon which the program and attendant files are recorded without written consent from Patri-Soft.

PCOPY is a fully functional Shareware product. Shareware is a computer program distribution/marketing method that permits potential buyers to thoroughly try the program prior to purchase. It is NOT free and it is not in the Public Domain. If, after evaluating the program, you find it to be useful enough to use on a regular basis, you are expected to pay for it by registering with Patri-Soft. The registration fee is $20.00 and the registered version, which is NOT distributed as Shareware, will not contain the opening Shareware screen nor the closing messages.

You may register PCOPY in one of four ways:

1. By mail with check/money order/credit card (Visa/Mastercard only) to: Patri-Soft, P.O. Box 8263 San Bernardino, CA 92412. CALIFORNIA RESIDENTS MUST INCLUDE 7.75% STATE SALES TAX!

2. You may call Patri-Soft (714-352-2825 1200/14400, 24 hours a day) and order online using your credit card.

3. VISA/Mastercard orders are also accepted through telephone orders. Call Public Software Library: 800-242-4775 or 713-665-7017 to order.

4. FAX your order to us at (714) 352-1529, using your credit card.

The Patri-Soft Shareware Products BBS operates 24 hours per day, 7 days per week, open to all callers. For extended access, you MUST log on and leave a comment to the sysop to the effect that you are a registered user and desire access. The author can also be reached on CIS via PPN 76347,2477 (please use MAIL).

The Shareware version of PCOPY may be freely copied and passed onto other individual users for their evaluation.

We support our software. One of the great strengths of the Shareware concept is the interaction between the program's authors and its users. Many of the features contained in PCOPY are the result of user input. If you have a problem evaluating this program or want to make a suggestion, comment, or complaint, please contact us immediately. Even after registering PCOPY, if you later determine that it is unsuitable for your use, you may contact us for a refund. It is not necessary that you be a registered user to contact us for technical support. Technical support will be available through the U.S. mail, telephone, or the Patri-Soft BBS.

PCOPY

Copy and Move files intelligently and safely with a variety of options.

PCOPY is an advanced replacement for the DOS COPY command, one of the most used of the DOS commands. Unfortunately, the DOS COPY abilities are very limited and are not sufficient for many disk maintenance chores. PCOPY is similar to the DOS COPY command in that it copies file data between disks and hard disk directories. In addition, PCOPY provides intelligent file selection and processing options. PCOPY options allow you to use a single PCOPY command to perform a function that would require many complex DOS COPY commands.

PCOPY also provides a safer way to copy files than that provided by the DOS COPY command. It allows you to copy only newer files or update a directory with the contents of another. PCOPY will never allow you to overlay a file unknowingly.

PCOPY allows you to specify standard DOS wildcard pathnames in the source file specifications, and standard pathnames for the target directory specification.

PCOPY attempts to anticipate your needs and then help you accomplish your intent. For instance, if PCOPY determines that the target directory name does not exist, it will ask you if it is to be created. If you respond <YES>, PCOPY will create the directory. With the /SAVE option, if you are about to overlay a file with another file with the same name, you will be asked if the older duplicate file is to be re-named with a version number.

The PMOVE Option of PCOPY

PMOVE is an option of the PCOPY command you can use to move files between disks and directories on disks. PMOVE combines the functions of DOS COPY and DELETE commands to simplify the moving of files. In addition to just moving files, PMOVE also allows you to specify selection criteria to better qualify the files to be moved.

PMOVE automatically determines the environment in which the move is requested and determines if the data must be physically moved or if it can be moved by simply renaming it. The file will be moved by renaming it if the move is to another directory on the same disk device. This is much faster than physically moving the file. In addi-tion, it reduces free space fragmentation, and allows you to move very large files between directories when they could not otherwise be moved with DOS COPY because of insufficient space.

The only difference between PCOPY and PMOVE is that PMOVE removes the file from the source location after it has been successfully copied to the target location.

PMOVE is implemented as a .BAT file that invokes PCOPY with the /X parameter.

PCOPY Features

➤ Copies files to and from any disk or directory.

➤ Allows you to save older versions of files with new names before replacing them.

➤ Moves files by copying them or renaming them to the new location.

➤ Deletes the original file if /X is specified.

➤ Creates target directories if needed.

➤ Makes sure the DOS archive flag is set correctly for each file as it is moved.

➤ Preserves the DOS date and time for each file moved.

➤ Allows you to pause processing at any time by pressing any keyboard key. Once stopped, the program can be terminated by pressing <ESC>.

➤ Provides file selection and processing control options to tailor the move process to your own needs.

➤ Allows commands to be tested so you may be sure that commands are specified as you desire.

➤ Copies updated files to a special disk or directory.

➤ If there is not sufficient space on the current target disk, PCOPY allows you to place another disk in the drive and continue processing. This lets you copy groups of files larger than disk size to other computers.

➤ Start with a specific file in a directory.

➤ End with a specific file in a directory.

➤ Process files based on the date stored in the directory entry.

➤ Warns you before overlaying a file unless specific parameters indicating otherwise are specified.

➤ Checks target disk for available space before starting to copy files. This saves time when the copy will not be able to complete.

➤ Gives you constant status of the progress of the command.

➤ Runs with windows or using standard DOS screen output.

➤ Format new floppy disks as they are needed by pressing <F3> at any prompt.

➤ Process one directory, a single directory subtree or all directories on a disk (/S).

➤ Allows you to indicate that multiple input disks are to be used and prompts for the next one after each disk is processed.

➤ Create a series of output disks filled efficiently with files from the source location. DOS ERRORLEVEL set to indicate error conditions. PCOPY may be used in .BAT files to copy files and you may confirm results are good.

➤ Special wildcard matching allows you to select all files with specific text in filename.

PCOPY Command and Parameters

PCOPY lets you specify command parameters to qualify the copy criteria. These parameters are optional. If no parameters are specified, PCOPY performs in a manner similar to the DOS COPY command, except that it prompts you before overlaying files. The command format and parameters are described below.

```
PCOPY from_file [to_file] [(/ parameters)]
```

Enter the DOS file specification for the directory and file names to be moved. The filename portion of the file specification may contain wildcard characters documented by DOS (* and ?). You may also specify special pattern selection for text. For example, *DISK*.* would select all files that have the characters "DISK" anywhere in the first portion of the filename. *DI*S*K*.* type specification also works. You may optionally supply a file containing a list of input file names. Create a file containing a filename or complete pathname on each line. Specify the name of this file as the source filename to PCOPY and add the "@" character before the name. The list of files will be processed as if they were all specified on the input command line. For file list processing, PCOPY understands the output of the DOS DIR command. You may use the DOS redirection feature to direct DIR output to a file, edit the file to add or remove entries, and then provide this to PCOPY as input. For example:

```
DIR A: >DIRLIST    (edit dirlist)   PCOPY @DIRLIST B:
```

Enter the DOS file specification for the directory and filename to be copied to. If the "to" specification is not entered, files will be moved to the current directory. If a single level name is supplied as the last part of the target file specification, PCOPY will search for a directory that matches the specified name. If it does not exist, PCOPY will prompt you to determine if the name is a filename or a directory name. To avoid this prompt, append the name with a \ if it is a directory name, or a . to indicate it is a file name. For example:

```
PCOPY *.* C:\DIRNAME\   PCOPY *.* C:\FILENAME.
```

➤ **/4:** 4DOS support. PCOPY will copy and insert the appropriate 4DOS descriptions when copying files.

➤ **/A:** Archive. Selects only files that have been marked updated by DOS. This flag is updated by DOS whenever a file is processed with an intent to change or create new data.

➤ **/AF:** Assume that the target specified is a File. This will suppress PCOPY's prompt if the target does not exist.

➤ **/AD:** As above, except Assume Directory.

➤ **/AP:** APpend. All source files selected will be concatenated and placed together in a single output file. The output file will be given the name of the first or only selected input file, or the target filename specified.

If a target filename already exists when append is specified, all source files copied will be appended to the target file. To cause an already existing target file to be replaced by the copied files, also specify the /R parameter. To combine 3 files into one with /AP, use a command like the following:

```
PCOPY FILE1,FILE2,FILE3 NEWFILE /AP/R
```

➤ **/AZ:** Append text files removing CTRL-Z characters. Like /AP except CTRL-Z characters will be removed from the end of all but the last file copied.

➤ **/B:** Backup. When specified, the DOS ARCHIVE attribute is reset after a file has been copied.

➤ **/BA:** BAtch processing. Normally, PCOPY will pause if you press any key during processing. This can interfere with programs that store keystrokes in the keyboard buffer for subsequent activity. The /BA parameter sets "no-windows" mode and disables the "key press" check to leave stored keystrokes undisturbed.

> ➤ **/BW:** Black and white. Forces PCOPY to use monochrome colors even when it detects a color display environment.

> ➤ **/CD:xxx:** This parameter allows PCOPY to invoke any command of your choice for each file PCOPY selects. With this parameter, PCOPY will not copy your data. It simply becomes a file selection utility.

To use this parameter you must supply the command PCOPY is to execute. To be compatible with DOS command line option specifications, you must use special substitution characters to build a command to your specifications. The following special characters are used:

Is replaced with the full pathname of the file to be processed.

$ Is replaced with the filename of the file selected.

@ Is replaced with the target filename PCOPY would have copied the file to, if the COPY operation was active.

[Is replaced with a single-space character.

] Is replaced with a backslash character (\).

} Is replaced with a slash (/) character. This must be used to allow a command to include / parameters, since PCOPY will interpret a slash as one of its own parameters.

Example of /CD Parameter

The following example shows how PCOPY can be used to drive an EDIT command with variable parameters:

```
PCOPY *.c/d:)1jan89/cd:EDIT[#[}F[}pf:]log
```

Assuming file C:\COMP\TEST.C was selected, the following command would result:

```
EDIT C:\COMP\TEST.C /F /PF:\LOG
```

To execute the command, PCOPY invokes a second copy of the DOS command processor. When the /CD parameter is used, PCOPY forces operation without windows to eliminate screen flashing between commands.

➤ **/CF:path:** This parameter alters the meaning of the /CD parameter. When specified with a full DOS pathname (including the filename), it causes PCOPY to write all generated commands to the specified file. The commands will not be executed by PCOPY. This allows you to generate a .BAT file that can be modified and executed at a later time. For example, to generate commands and place them in batch file DOIT.BAT.

```
PCOPY *.c/d:)1jan89/cd:EDIT[#[}F[}pf:]log /CF:DOIT.BAT
```

➤ **/C2 /C3:** Specify /C2 or /C3 to use different colors when PCOPY is used with windows operation. To make this color change permanent, specify the parameter in the DOS environment variable.

➤ **/D:[(]xxx date:** Select files based on their last update date. This parameter may include a date or a number of days value, and optionally a condition modifier that changes the use of the date or number of days specified.

When xxx contains a valid date, the date is compared to the last update date of the file, contained in its directory entry. The file is selected if the condition specified by the condition modifier is met. The condition modifier meanings are:

(File date is older than that specified.

) File date is newer than that specified.

= File date is equal to that specified.

If the condition modifier is not specified,) is assumed. Date values may be specified in any of the following formats:

MM/DD/YY	MM-DD-YY	DDMMMYY
12/31/80	12-31-80	31DEC80

If xxx contains a numeric value instead of a valid date, that positive number is used to calculate a date value a number of days prior to the current date. Then that date is used as in the calculation above. The /D: parameter may be specified twice to select files between two dates (date ranges).

➤ **/D:(1FEB90/D:)1MAR90:** When two dates are specified, a file's date must qualify selection based on both date parameters. Specify the /DO parameter to indicate an OR condition between the dates. This will allow any file meeting either date parameter to be selected for processing.

➤ **/D-:** Delete all files on target drive before starting copy.

➤ **/D2:** Add files to those already on the first output disk. Then delete all files from subsequent disks provided before copying to them. Use /D2 when you want to append files to a set of already existing disks. This parameter allows you to continue backing up to a partially used disk and then reuse disks containing old unwanted backup files.

➤ **/DC & DCA:** Directory Copy. PCOPY will create a duplicate directory on the output disk for every directory processed on the source disk. Directories are only created when files are to be copied to them. See also the /S option. This is useful for copying all files and directories from one disk to another. Specify /DCA (Directory Copy-All) to copy all directories from source to target drive, even when no files will be moved to the new directory.

➤ **/DL:** Same as /DC except that only the last node of the source directory is copied to the target pathname specified.

➤ **/DO:** Specify when two /D: date parameters are used. Indicates either date parameter may be met to qualify a file for processing. See also the /D: parameter.

➤ **/DR:xxx:** Drive. Use to process multiple disk drives. /DR assumes the presence of the /S parameter, which indicates to process all directories on the source disks. If you are using PCOPY for backup, this lets you process all disk drives with a single command.

The following command will copy all modified files from hard drives C:, D:, and E:, to the floppy disk in drive A:. The /D2 parameter will ensure each new output disk is cleared of all files before it is written to.

```
PCOPY *.* A: /DR:CDE/A/D2
```

➤ **/DS:** Same as /DC except that only the current directory level, and all its subordinate levels, are copied to the target directory. The target directory may contain a pathname with multiple directory levels, so you can copy one directory structure below another directory structure.

➤ **/DX:** When target names are single level names with no extensions, PCOPY will ask you if the name refers to a directory or to a new file to be created. If you specify this parameter, PCOPY assumes names without extensions are new directory names.

➤ **/DY:** Synchronize source and target directory files. Before copying the first file to any directory, PCOPY will determine if any files exist in the target directory but not on the source directory. If so, PCOPY will remove those files from the target directory. Use this parameter when you want to update one directory or disk to be exactly like another.

IMPORTANT!!

PCOPY has the ability to synchronize an entire drive by traversing the directories, deleting directory trees and files that are on the target but not the source. This feature is utilitied by a careful combination of switches. Relevent switches are /S, /DC, and /U. Situations vary, so we have forced the /TF (Test First) on PCOPY when you use /DY. To override this Test, use the /TO paramter. BE SURE THE TEST PRODUCES THE DESIRED RESULTS BEFORE DOING IT FOR REAL! If you have any questions, or need a customized command line, feel free to call the Patri-Soft technical support line, (714) 352-2820. To synchronize two drives: PCOPY C:\ D:\ /DY/S/DC. To synchronize two directories: PCOPY C:\UT D:\UT /DY. To synchronize a drive and a target dir tree:

```
PCOPY C:\ D:\BACKUP /S/DC/DY
```

➤ **/E:** Select and move only files that exist in both the source and target directories. This allows you to replace all duplicate named files.

➤ **/EQ:** Designed for batch file operation. Use this parameter to prevent PCOPY from requiring you to press a key to terminate processing   (Exit Quick).   Note: Previous versions of PCOPY supported this option using the /EX. Parameter.

➤ **/EX:** Exclude files. The exclude facility allows you to provide a list of pathname and filename specifications that are to be excluded from PCOPY processing. Since searching through data on your hard disk requires extensive processing and disk read time, excluding files from the process will save you time, and will reduce the number of false matches displayed for your requests.

The exclude facility is implemented with two actions. First, you will need to create an exclude specification file and place it in the same directory where PCOPY is installed on your hard disk. This file will contain the names of all the files and paths to be excluded. Name the file PCOPY.EXC.

You may specify DOS pattern names to exclude groups of files with   a single specification. Like DOS, use the '*' to indicate the last part of a filename or filename extension may be any set of characters. Also like DOS, use the '?' to indicate that any single position of a filename may be any character.

In addition to DOS, two additional pattern features are available. You may place an '*' anywhere in the filename to indicate any set of characters may exist in this point in the name. For pathnames, you may place an '**' at the end of a directory path specification to indicate the specification applies to the specified directory and all subordinate directories. Using '**', you can exclude an entire path with a single specification. Following are examples:

1. *.EXE

2. *.COM

3. TEST*.*

4. *TEST*.*

5. DO?FIX.*

6. PC*XX.*

7. C:\DOS*.*

8. \TEST*.*

9. D:\GAMES***.*

Explanations for the above examples:

1. Excludes all filenames with the extension .EXE from processing.

2. Excludes all filenames ending with extension .COM.

3. Excludes all filenames beginning with the letters "TEST" from processing.

4. Excludes all filenames having the characters "TEST" anywhere in the first portion of the filename.

5. Excludes files having 'DO' as the first 2 characters of the filename, and 'FIX' as the 4th, 5th, and 6th filename characters. The 3rd character of the filename may be any character.

6. Excludes files having a name beginning with the 2 characters PC and where the first portion of the filename ends with the characters 'XX'. Any 0 to 4 characters may exist between the 'PC' and 'XX' in the first portion of the filename.

7. Excludes all files from the DOS directory on drive C:.

8. Excludes all files from the TEST directory existing on any drive searched.

9. Excludes all files from the D:\GAMES\ directory and also excludes all files and directories subordinate to the GAMES directory.

Activating Exclude

Exclude will only be functional when the /EX command parameter is specified. When /EX is specified, you must have a valid exclude file. PCOPY will not continue without one. If you wish exclude to be active during all executions, specify /EX as part of the PCOPY= DOS environment variable. See later in the documentation for a description of this feature.

➤ **/F:fileFirst:** Do not start processing until the specified filename is encountered in the source directory. This parameter is useful for restarting a move or copy that has been terminated. You may specify DOS pattern name characters * and ? to identify the file to begin processing.

➤ **/FI Fill:** Fill output disks as efficiently as possible. Normally files are copied in the sequence in which they are found in the source directory. If a large file cannot be copied onto the output disk, a new disk is requested even though there may be enough space left on the output disk to hold other smaller files.

The /FI parameter causes files to be copied in descending size sequence. When the next file will not fit on the output disk, PCOPY searches for another file that will fit on the disk before requesting a new output disk. When a new disk is placed in the drive, PCOPY begins processing the larger files again. Eventually, all files requested will be copied.

➤ **/FL:** PCOPY's automatic disk formatting senses the drive type and will format the disk if necessary accordingly. If you want to format a low density disk in a high density drive, use this parameter.

➤ **/FO:** Format Off. This turns off PCOPY's automatic disk formating/checking.

➤ **/IFA:pathname:** Check to determine that the source file does not already exist in an alternate directory before processing it. If it does not exist, processing will continue. Use just like IFP specified below.

➤ **/IFP:pathname:** Determine if the source file to be copied already exists in the pathname specified by IFP. If it does exist, process the file. If it does not exist, skip the file. For example, PCOPY *.BAT \newdir/IFP:\testdir copies files from the current directory to \NEWDIR only if each file already exists in \TESTDIR.

➤ **/L:fileLast:** Stop processing after the specified filename is encountered in the scan of the directory. The file specified will be processed if it matches selection criteria. You may specify DOS pattern name characters * and ? to identify the file to begin processing.

➤ **/LG:** LOG activities. PCOPY will create a disk log of all actions it takes. This is useful if you are using PCOPY as a backup system. The log will help you locate the disk on which a file has been backed up. The log file will be named PCOPY.LOG. For DOS versions 3.0 or later, the log will be created in the same directory from which PCOPY is executed. Other DOS versions will put the log in the current directory. If the log does not exist, PCOPY will create it. If the log does exist, PCOPY will add to it. To begin a new log, delete PCOPY.LOG before running PCOPY.

➤ **/M:** More. Stop the screen from scrolling past the end without user intervention.

➤ **/ME:** MErge. Works like using /U and /X parameter to move the most current files from one directory into another. In addition, it deletes all the files that are not moved. This effectively merges the most current files from two directories into a single directory.

➤ **/MU:** MUltiple. Process multiple input disks. After the first input disk is processed, PCOPY will prompt you for additional disks. Indicate <Y> to process more disks or <N> to terminate processing.

➤ **/N:** New files. Only move files that do not already exist on the target directory. If the file already exists, do not move it.

➤ **/NA:** No Archive. Only process files that do not have the DOS ARCHIVE attribute set in the directory entry. With this parameter specified, PCOPY will only process those files that have already been backed up. Files not backed up will not be processed.

➤ **/NP:** No Pause. Use when you have made the /P parameter the default action with the SET PCOPY=/P command in the DOS environment, and want to override it.

➤ **/NW:** No Windows. PCOPY will not use windows during processing. All screen output will be done through standard DOS facilities.

➤ **/O:filename-list:** Omit. Specify a list of filename patterns that are to be omitted (excluded) from PCOPY processing. If multiple filename patterns are specified, separate them with commas. For example:

`/O:*.BAK,*.EXE,TEST*.*`

➤ **/P:** Pause before each file is moved and ask for approval to process it.

➤ **/QA:x Quit:** After process x number of files. This can be useful if you only want to process a certain number of files.

➤ **/R:** Replace any duplicate files on the target disk or directory. PCOPY will replace files regardless of file dates and times.

➤ **/RD:** Reset Date. Normally PCOPY retains the original date and time of a file when copying it. With /RD specified, the copied file will have the current date.

➤ **/RE:** REgister the program. Use this option to register your copy of the PCOPY utility. You will need to have the registration number and code that is sent to you after you request registration. When you specify this parameter, part of the registration screen also allows you to modify the windows option permanently. If you do not want windows during processing, use this option to change the windows program option. You do not need to be registered to change this information.

➤ **/RO:** Read Only. PCOPY is just like DOS COPY when it enounters RO files. PCOPY will copy the file, but does not copy the Read Only attribute. Using /RO places the Read Only attribute on the target file.

➤ **/S:** System. If a source directory is supplied, that directory and all subordinate directories will be processed. If no source directory is specified, all directories on the disk will be processed.

➤ **/SA:** SAve. Instead of overlaying already existing files with duplicate names, PCOPY renames the file in the target directory with a version number before the new file is copied. This ensures that no data is lost. This facility can be used to save successive versions of a file in a directory. If the file has an extension name, the last two characters of the extension are replaced with a number from 01 to 99, depending on the next available number.

PCOPY determines the next available number by looking in the directory for other files with similar names. /SF System Files. Normally, PCOPY skips files marked with the DOS SYSTEM attribute. Using /SF causes SYSTEM files to be selected for processing.

➤ **/SHx:** File sharing options.

➤ **/SHA:** Ignores file sharing and copy all files. /SHR Allows files opened for read to be copied.

➤ **/SHN:** Disallows all file sharing.

➤ **/SP:** Splits files. /SP indicates PCOPY is to split a file onto another disk if there is insufficient room on the first disk.

➤ **/SP:nnn:** Splits a file nnn characters into the file. If disk space permits, both parts of the split file will remain in the target directory.

➤ **/SPL:nnn:** Splits a file at line number nnn. This can be useful for breaking a file into parts for editing.

➤ **Split File Parameters:** You may split a file into two or more parts with PCOPY. This is useful for copying files larger than a diskette will hold, or for dividing files into smaller parts for editing. PCOPY identifies the file parts by replacing the second character of the file's extension with a number. For example, PCOPY.EXE could be split into PCOPY.E1E and PCOPY.E2E. The time field of the first part of a split file holds the replaced extension character. For this reason, PCOPY can only automatically rejoin an unmodified split file. Just reference the first part of the split file and the rest will be copied. You may also rejoin files using DOS COPY or PCOPY explicit commands on each part of a split file, as follows:

Rejoining Split File with DOS COPY:

```
COPY /B FILENM.E1E+FILENM+E2E FILENM.EXE
```

Rejoining Split File with PCOPY:

```
PCOPY A:\FILENM.E1E,A:\FILENM.E2E FILENM.EXE/SP
```

!! IMPORTANT! PCOPY cannot split files into more than NINE parts !!

➤ **/SS:nnn:** Terminate processing when the source drive's free space reaches the value specified by the /SS parameter. Use when moving files from one drive to another using the /X parameter. The command PCOPY C:*.* D: /X/SS:1000000 will cause PCOPY to move files from drive C: to drive D: until the free space on source drive C: is greater than or equal to 1,000,000 characters.

➤ **/ST:nnn:** Terminate processing when the target drive's free space becomes less than or equal to the value specified by the /ST: parameter. The command PCOPY C:*.* d: /ST:500000 will cause PCOPY to copy files to target drive D: until drive D: has less than or equal to 500,000 characters free space.

➤ **/SZ: [(] [)] nnn:** Select a file based on its size. The (indicates that files less than the indicated size are to be selected. The) indicates to select files greater than the size. If neither is specified, (is assumed.

➤ **/T:** Test. Test the command without actually updating any files. Issue messages to indicate what will happen if the command is executed without the /T parameter.

➤ **/TO:** When using the /DY parameter, PCOPY forces /TF. Use this to override the test.

➤ **/T:[(][)][=]xxx:** Time. Select files based on the relationship between their last update time and the time specified in the command. The /T: parameter may also contain an operator that reverses or modifies the meaning of the time specified, just like the date parameter.

Examples of /T:xxx Parameter

1. Process files updated before 11:20 a.m.

   `/T:(11:20a or /T:(11:20`

2. Process files updated before 11:20 p.m.

   `/T:(11:20p or /T:(23:20  —> military time`

3. Process files updated after 11:20 p.m.

   `/T:)11:20p`

4. Process files updated within 60 seconds after 11:21 p.m.

   `/T:=11:21p`

5. Leading zeros in hour may be omitted.

   `/T:)1:20`

➤ **/TF:** Test First. Works similar to the /T parameter but after test processing is complete, PCOPY will ask you if you want to execute the command as if the /T parameter were not present. If you respond <Y>, the command will be executed and files will actually be processed.

➤ **/U:** Update files. Only copy files that do not exist on the target directory or duplicate filenames that are newer than their counterparts on the target directory or disk. Specifying this option results in the most current version of each selected file being in the target directory.

➤ **/V:** Verify. Use the DOS VERIFY option while copying data. This causes all data to be reread after it is written to disk to ensure it was written properly.

➤ **/WH:** WHy. Indicates why files are not selected for processing. Normally PCOPY will not show file names that are not selected for processing. Specifying /WH will cause PCOPY to display a message indicating why any file was not selected for processing.

➤ **/WT:** Wait. Wait for disk to be mounted before beginning processing. This parameter is intended primarily for systems with floppy disks. Before beginning the copy process, PCOPY will ask you to place the proper disks in the drives. This allows you to have PCOPY on a different disk than the disks being processed.

➤ **/X:** Move files. This parameter changes PCOPY's function to move files instead of copying them. After the file is copied, it will be deleted from the source location. If the file is moved to another directory on the same disk, the directory entry for the file is updated, but the actual data is not moved. This provides for the fastest move possible.

PCOPY Menu Operation

When you start PCOPY without command line specifications it displays a menu for entering copy specifications. Three menus are available for specification of options. You proceed forward and backwards through the menus by pressing the <PgUp> and <PgDn> keys. Once you have completed specifying options, press <F10> to start processing. Press <ESCape> at any time to exit from PCOPY. If you need PCOPY help for batch operation, press <F1>.

You may save a particular combination of menu specifications for use at a later time by assigning copy profile names to them. PCOPY saves up to four different copy profiles. To use these in a subsequent execution of PCOPY, simply select one of the saved names from the menu. All options on the menus will be set to reflect the contents of the saved profile options.

Menu options are specified in one of two ways. First, you may be asked to key specific parameter information into parameter fields. Second, you select toggle options by positioning the highlight bars over options specified and pressing the <Enter> key. PCOPY will only allow compatible options to be specified, so turning on some options may automatically deactivate others. You see this happen when watching highlighted options.

Use the up and down arrow keys, or the tab keys, to move from option to option. A short help line is provided at the bottom of the display to assist you in understanding each option. It changes as you move the cursor from option to option on the display.

PCOPY MENU (1 of 3)

Copy Profile

An area is provided for you to provide an optional copy profile name to be associated with these parameters. Provide a 1-8 character name. The parameters specified for this process will be saved and associated with this profile name. To the right of the name field are names for up to four copy profiles previously saved. To use the parameters of any one of these profiles, press <1>, <2>, <3>, or <4>. The menu will automatically change to reflect the saved specifications.

From Path

Enter the file specification for files to be copied. The same rules apply as for command line specifications. See that section of this document for details. Following are examples:

```
C:\DIRNAME\*.EXE

\DIRNAME\*.EXE

\DIRname

*.exe
```

Drives

Enter additional drives to be searched for the path specification in From Path above.

To Path

Specify the target location where files are to be copied. Following are examples:

```
C:

C:\DIRNAME

C:\DIRNAME\FILENAME
```

Process Options?

```
COPY

MOVE

TEST

VERIFY

WRITES
```

Highlight the MOVE or COPY action to take. TEST mode causes PCOPY to execute without really copying data. Use TEST to check that your parameters are correct (/TF ,/X, /V).

Multiple Directories?

ENTIRE DISK

ALL SUBORDINATE DIRECTORIES

Indicate what directories are to be read to find files to be processed. SUBORDINATE DIRECTORIES indicates to read the current directory and all of its subordinate directories to find files to process (/S, /DS).

Directory Actions?

CREATE NEW

CREATE ALL

CREATE/ADD

LASTNODE MERGE

SYNCHRONIZE

Specify actions to be taken at the directory level.

> ➤ **CREATE NEW:** Automatically create directories needed on the output disk (/DC).

> ➤ **CREATE ALL:** Automatically create directories for every directory read on the source disk (/DCA).

> ➤ **LASTNODE:** Use the last directory level from the source disk, and append it to the directory name on the target disk. This creates a new directory structure under the target directory specification (/DL).

> ➤ **MERGE:** Merge files from the source specification into the target directory. Delete old or exact duplicate files from the source location. Replace newer duplicate files on the target location (/ME).

File Filtering?

```
NEW & MORE RECENT FILES ONLY NEW

FILES PAUSE/ASK FOR EACH FILE

MARKED FOR BACKUP READONLY

HIDDEN SYSTEM

Indicate selection criteria for files to be  processed:
```

➤ **NEW:** Copy files that do not exist on the target directory and files that exist but are newer.

➤ **ONLY NEW:** Process files that do not already exist on the target directory (/N)>

➤ **PAUSE/ASK:** Stop and prompt for approval before processing each file (/P)/

➤ **MARKED BK:** Process files that have been modified since they were previously backed up (/A).

➤ **READONLY:** Process files that having their readonly attribute set (/RO).

➤ **HIDDEN:** Process files that have their hidden attribute set (/SF).

➤ **SYSTEM:** Process files that have their system attribute set (/SF). The second PCOPY menu. Access this menu by pressing <PgDn> from the first PCOPY menu.

The second menu of PCOPY options

LIST FILES NOT PROCESSED

Show filenames matching the filename criteria, but were not processed for other reasons. Indicates filename and the criteria that caused it to be skipped (/WH).

SET DOS FILE CHANGED INDICATOR AFTER COPY

After copying the file, reset the DOS attribute indicating the file needs backup (/BA).

SET DOS FILE DATE TO TODAY AFTER COPY

After copying the file, set the date and time on the file to the current date (/RD).

FILL OUTPUT DISKS EFFICIENTLY WITH BEST FIT

Process files in a sequence that will allow them to efficiently fit on output diskettes. PCOPY will find files to completely fill a disk before going on to additional disks (/FI).

ERASE OUTPUT DISKS BEFORE USING ERASE ON ALL BUT FIRST

Erase all files on target disks before copying files to them. 'ALL BUT FIRST' is normally used during backup to add files to the first backup disk used (the last one used for the previous backup run), and then erase all subsequent disks before copying to them (/D- , /D2).

APPEND COPIED FILES TOGETHER IN ONE OUTPUT FILE

All files being copied are to be merged into one output file. The output file is the filename specified on the target specification (/AP).

FILES MAY BE DIVIDED INTO PARTS ACROSS DISKS

Split files onto multiple disks if there is not enough room on the target diskette for the entire file to fit. See the /SP command line parameter.

ASK FOR MULTIPLE INPUT DISKETTES

Causes PCOPY to ask for more input diskettes after the first diskette is processed. Great when reading from a series of diskettes (/MU).

DISABLE SOUNDS DURING PROCESSING

Disables speaker beeps normally sounded to inform the user some action is needed (/SO).

The third and last PCOPY menu

Select files by size ===>

If a numeric value is specified, only files larger than (>), or smaller than (<) the value are processed. The numeric value must be preceded by < or > (/SZ:).

Select by date From Date: to Date:

If one or more dates are specified, only files having a date less than or greater than the dates specified will be selected for processing (/D:).

Stop when Source Drives freespace >

If a numeric value is specified, PCOPY will check the source drive free space before copying each file. If the drives free space is greater than the value specified, processing will stop. Use with MOVE option to empty a disk up to a specified level of free space (/SS:).

Stop when Target Drives freespace <

If a numeric value is specified, PCOPY will check the target drive's free space before copying each file. If the free space is less than the value specified, processing will stop. Use to copy files to a disk until it has less than n characters free (/ST:).

Duplicate Files:

REPLACE

SAVE OLD COPY

ONLY DUPLICATES

Indicate how to process files that already exist on the target directory.

➤ **REPLACE:** Overlay files regardless of date/time (/R).

➤ **SAVE OLD:** Rename the target file and then copy the source file to the directory. The new name will have a number placed in the files extension to indicate the version of the file (/SA).

➤ **ONLY DUPs:** Select duplicate filenames for processing. Ignore all other files (/E).

Networks

```
NO FILE SHARING

COPY FILE BEING READ

COPY ALL IN USE
```

When using PCOPY in network environments, indicate how PCOPY is to proceed when files are found to be in use by other tasks in progress.

➤ **NO SHARE:** Skip files in use (/SHN).

➤ **READ:** Process files being read by another task (/SHR).

➤ **ALL:** Continue to process any file already in use (/SHA).

Process files in date sequence

```
ASCENDING

DESCENDING
```

Process files in date sequence. Use to copy the most recent files, or the oldest files to a target location (/SN, /SO).

WAYS TO USE PCOPY

1. Copy files from floppy disk to hard disk

   PCOPY is safer than DOS COPY when copying files to your system. It prevents you from accidently replacing a file with another of the same name.

When PCOPY encounters a duplicate file, it will stop and ask if the file is to overlay the already existing one. You can tell PCOPY to REPLACE or UPDATE files with /R and /U command line parameters.

Following are samples of the simplest copy commands using PCOPY:

If you are copying to the current directory on the hard disk:

```
PCOPY A:*.*
```

To copy to a specific directory:

```
PCOPY A:*.* \SPECDIR
```

2. Taking changed files from work to home.

It is common to need to take files from home to work or vice-versa. Since it is difficult to keep track of all the files you may have updated, it is convenient to let PCOPY find the updated files by copying all files updated within the last n days to a diskette. You reduce copy time by not copying an entire directory and are sure to get all newly changed files.

```
PCOPY *.* A:/d:3 <== updated last 3 days
```

```
PCOPY *.* A:/D:)1DEC90 <== After date
```

3. Copy files modified before/after a time.

Sometimes the only way to identify recently changed files is by using the time they were updated. PCOPY can select files by time of day. You might use this option to determine what files were updated after 5:00PM. Remember, with the /T TEST option, PCOPY serves as a unique facility to locate and list files matching your selection criteria. PCOPY's unique selection facilities can be used to locate and list files. The /T option indicates to scan disks and simulate processing but do not actually move or change any data.

4. Quick moves files to a new directory on the same hard disk.

Moving files with DOS requires two commands. COPY the data, then DEL the files from their original location. In addition to requiring two commands it forces DOS to copy the data. If the file is larger than the available free space on the hard disk, a copy of the data is not possible. PCOPY moves files to new directories on the same disk without having to physically copy the data. It simply moves the file reference to a new directory. Even huge files move in an instant!

```
PCOPY \OLDDIR\*.DAT \NEWDIR /X
```

5. Copy only duplicate files. To update a directory with duplicate files from another directory or disk:

```
PCOPY \FROMDIR1 A:*.* /E
```

6. Copy multiple groups of file by extension names. Use PCOPY to process multiple file selection specifications with a single copy command. Separate each with a comma.

```
PCOPY *.BAT,*.EXE,*.COM \EXEDIR
```

7. Copy files excluding files of one or more extension names. The OMIT feature lets you exclude files from processing using command line specifications. It is commonly used to exclude program files when copying to diskettes.

```
PCOPY *.* A: /O:*.EXE,*.BAT,*.COM
```

8. Copy files containing specific characters in their name. When you need to select or find files having a specific word in their names, but the filenames do not begin with the word, PCOPY can locate them. Copy all files having names containing the 3 consecutive characters.

```
"ZIP".   PCOPY *ZIP*.* \ZIPFILES
```

9. Display files having specific name.

   Use PCOPY to find all occurrences of files by name on a disk. PCOPY can scan a disk and display or process files from multiple directories. The /S (SCAN) parameter causes PCOPY to search all directories.

```
PCOPY *.DOC \TEST /S/T
```

10. Copy only newer files between disks and directories.

One of the most common uses of PCOPY is to copy data between diskettes and hard disks. Use the update (/U) parameter to make sure only newer files are updated. Add the "WHY" (/WH) parameter to cause PCOPY to show any files that were not processed. Note that you can specify the target directory name without trailing \.

```
PCOPY A:*.* C:\NEWDIR /U/WH
```

11. Copy a disk including all directories to a new disk.

PCOPY copies directories too. Simply specify the Directory Copy parameter (/DC). The file will be copied to the same directory name on the target drive. If the directory does not exist, it will automatically be created for you. Adding the Scan (/S) parameter causes PCOPY to scan all disks on the source drive. Using a combination of /S/DC, you can copy all files and directories from one disk to another. Note, /DC only copies directories when files are to be copied into them. This insures that unneeded directories are not also copied. To copy every directory even if no files are copied, specify the All Directory Copy (/DCA) parameter instead of /DC.

```
PCOPY A:*.* F: /DC/S
```

12. Copy a directory and all subordinate directories.

To copy or move files from a directory and all its subordinate directories use PCOPY's /DS parameter. The following example scans the directory C:\WP and any subordinate directories to copy all files having the extension name .TOM to a diskette.

```
PCOPY \WP\*.TOM A: /DS
```

13. Fill one or more diskettes from hard disk files. DOS COPY and XCOPY are unable to copy a set of files to multiple diskettes. When the first diskette is full, they stop. PCOPY is not limited to copying to a single diskette. It detects when a disk is full and asks if the copy is to continue on to additional output diskettes. PCOPY also makes maximum use of diskette space. When you are attempting to copy many files to diskettes for backup or transporting, you want to use as few diskettes as possible. The PCOPY Fill (/FI) parameter causes PCOPY to fill output diskettes

without wasting space. With the /FI parameter,PCOPY when PCOPY is unable to fit a file on an output diskette, it saves that filename for later processing and searches for another file that will fit on the disk. This results in significant savings in diskettes and time to process them.

```
PCOPY C:\WP\*.* A: /FI
```

14. Copy files larger than a floppy disk to multiple diskettes.

    Unlike DOS COPY and XCOPY, PCOPY can copy files larger than a diskette to multiple diskettes. This is accomplished by splitting large files into multiple parts. PCOPY only splits files when there is insufficient space on the output disk and when the split parameter is specified. The Split (/SP) parameter tells PCOPY it is OK to split large files. Following is an example:

    ```
    PCOPY C:\WP\*.* A: /SP/FI
    ```

    To restore split files, simply use PCOPY to copy the files back to a disk large enough to contain the entire file. PCOPY will find the split files and automatically recombine them.

    ```
    PCOPY A:*.* C:\WP /MU
    ```

15. Backup from hard disk to floppy disks.

    PCOPY is not a full backup system but its features allow it to be used for backup processing. It is very effective for backing up one hard disk to another. Following is a basic explanation of backup procedures.

    The most common backup technique is referred to as Incremental Backup. This technique uses two different backup commands to implement initial full backup, and daily incremental backup.

    Incremental backup lets you avoid repeatedly backing up your entire system each time you want to backup. Instead, the first time you backup, you copy your entire system to disks. Then, each subsequent day (or other backup period) you only backup the files that have changed since the previous backup. If you are like most users, your "daily" backups will require only a couple of minutes because you only modified a small portion of your files since you last backed up.

A special DOS maintained file archive attribute supports incremental backup. The flag is an indicator field that is kept by DOS in each files directory entry. It is stored along with file date, time and size information. Whenever DOS, or an application, creates or changes a file, this archive attribute flag is set to indicate the file needs to be backed up. Programs that support backup use this flag to distinguish between files that need backup, and those that have already been backed up.

Whenever a program backs up a file, it should reset the flag to indicate backup has been done. Then, incremental backup processing will know to skip the file and not back it up again until it has changed.

Following is an example of using PCOPY to backup hard disk C: to diskettes in drive A:.

Full Backup

First we will show the PCOPY command to make the first backup.

```
PCOPY C:*.* A: /DC/S/D-/A/LG/FI
```

The above command causes PCOPY to copy all files on drive C: to drive A:. /DC and /S causes directory names to be copied to the target drive and makes PCOPY backup from all directories. Since this is the first backup, /D- is included to force all files on drive A; to be deleted prior to the copy. /A causes PCOPY to reset the DOS archive flag on each processed file to show the files were backed up. The /LG parameter asks PCOPY to write a log record to PCOPY.LOG for each file written. The log file can be used to locate the diskette containing a file to be restored. /FI causes PCOPY to fill all disks efficiently and make optimum use of diskette space. This command should only be run for the first backup.

INCREMENTAL BACKUP (Daily backup)

The following command causes PCOPY to scan your disk to find files that have changed since your previous backup, and add them to your already started set of backup diskettes.

```
PCOPY C:*.* A: /DC/S/D2/A/LG/FI/B
```

The incremental backup command is almost the same as the full backup except for two parameters. The /B parameter causes PCOPY to only process files that have the archive (backup) attribute set. Processing will be confined to changed files. /D2 is used in place of /D-. /D2 indicates that PCOPY is to append files to the first backup disk and then to erase all files before reusing any additional diskettes. After running your full backup, keep track of the last diskette written to. This will be the first disk provided for the next Incremental Backup. Label a set of backup disks and number them sequentially. Use a specially marked diskette sleeve for storing the last disk used. This will make it easy to identify when running backup again.

Restoring files from backup disks. Use PCOPY to restore any file from the backup disks. The PCOPY.LOG file contains a complete list of all backups done. You can examine this file to determine if and when a file was backed up. Then use the following PCOPY command to restore any files.

```
PCOPY A:filename.ext C: /MU/DC/S
```

16. Combine one or more files to a single new file.

Use PCOPY to combine two DOS text files into a single output file. The following command copies two files to a single file, DOS.TXT. The append parameter causes them to be concatenated together.

```
PCOPY DOC.TX1,DOS.TX2 DOS.TXT /AP
```

17. Copy and save duplicate files with a new generated name.

Use PCOPY when you need to copy updated files to diskettes that already contain previous versions of the same files. The /SA parameter indicates PCOPY is to save old versions of files by renaming them with version numbers in their extension names. PCOPY.C would be renamed to PCOPY.C01 before a new PCOPY.C is copied to the same diskette.

```
PCOPY \UPDATES \CSOURCE /R/SA
```

18. Merge two directories.

Use PCOPY to move all files from one directory to another making sure the most current version of files in both directories are kept. Merging files from one directory into another involves three actions. First PCOPY moves files from the source directory that do not already exist on the target directory. Second, it moves newer duplicate files to the target directory. Third, it deletes files from the source directory that were not copied to the target directory.

```
PCOPY \fromdir \todir /ME
```

19. Execute any command with selected files as parameters.

    Since PCOPY has file selection capabilities not available in other programs it can be used to select files to be processed by other commands and applications. For example, the following command will start an EDIT command for all P*.C files found by PCOPY. With the /CD parameter, PCOPY only starts other commands. It does not copy or move data.

    ```
    PCOPY P*.C /CD:EDIT[#
    ```

20. Search multiple directories for files to copy.

    Use PCOPY to scan a set of directories and copy files to a new location. This is useful if you are not sure of exactly what directory a file name exists in or if files from multiple directories are to be copied. Use the /S or /DS parameter. Here is a sample command:

    ```
    PCOPY LOOKFOR.ZIP A: /S/DR:CDE
    ```

21. Delete files on target disk and copy files to it.

    You may keep a work diskette handy by your machine to use to transport files between home and office. Use the /D- command with PCOPY to erase any old files on the disk before copying new files to it. This saves you from having to use a delete command and press Y to delete all files. The following command will erase the disk in drive A: and then copy files to it.

    ```
    PCOPY PW*.C A:/D-
    ```

22. Restarting a previously incomplete copy.

    Sometimes it is necessary to stop a copy and start again at a later time. Even with a single diskette the DOS COPY command is unable to resume processing from a specific filename. The PCOPY /F:filename.ext parameter provides PCOPY with a starting filename. The following command copies all files from PCOPY.C in a directory to diskette drive A:

```
PCOPY *.* A: /F:PCOPY.C
```

If you are referring to a hard disk, you do not need the /F command to resume processing. Simply specify the /U parameter. PCOPY will skip all files previously copied and start when the first uncopied file is reached.

23. Freeing disk space by copying files to archive disks.

When your hard disk becomes full, you can use PCOPY to locate old files and move them to diskettes for archival storage. The following command finds files in the ARCHIVE directory that are older than a specified date, and move them to diskette. Include the /SS:nnn command to stop processing when sufficient free space is available on the hard disk.

```
PCOPY \ARCHIVE A: /X /D:(1jan89 /ss:1000000
```

24. Transporting an entire disk to another computer.

Copying one disk and all its subdirectories to another disk is easy. The first command copies all files to diskettes. The second command copies the files and directories from the diskettes back to any hard disk.

```
PCOPY C:*.* A: /DC /S /FI    PCOPY A:*.* C: /DC /S
```

25. Determine differences between files in two disks.

One of the most useful functions of PCOPY does not copy files at all. To compare and report the differences between files on a diskette and the files on a hard disk directory, use the PCOPY command in test mode.

```
PCOPY A:*.* \DIRNAME /U/WH/T
```

The /T parameter indicates test mode, no copy or move is to be done. The /U indicates to update any newer files. The /WH indicates to show why any files would not be copied. The resulting display shows the new files, which are newer versions, and what files are already on the drive as duplicates. It will also indicate what files are older copies of the same filenames.

26. Keeping files on two computers in synchronization.

    The /DY synchronization parameter indicates PCOPY is to make the target directory contain the same files as the source specification. It saves time by only copying files needed. An important feature is its ability to remove any files from the target drive that are not on the source drive being copied from. This command is especially useful for transporting files from work to home and home to work using diskettes. A quick command at the end of each day will copy the files and remove deleted ones.

    ```
    PCOPY \WORDPROC\*.* A: /DY  Work to diskette

    PCOPY A:*.* C:\WORDPROC /DY disk to home
    ```

27. Saving generation backup copies of a files.

    Products that backup files before changing them often do not consider situations when a user stops and starts an application many times between backups. Unless multiple backup files are maintained, good versions of a file can be lost when good backup versions are replaced with bad versions. Since PCOPY can create backup files with consecutively numbered names, you never lose a backup version. Just use PCOPY to make a copy of the file(s) to a backup directory before starting your application.

    ```
    PCOPY %1 \BACKUP/SA/NW/U Make backup

    123 %1  <=== Start application
    ```

    After you backup your system, delete the PCOPY backup versions to free space on your hard disk. Use PDEL delete utility to delete all files in the BACKUP directory without being prompted to confirm the delete request. After Backup:

    ```
    PDEL \BACKUP\*.*/NC  Erase backup directory
    ```

28. Quickly copying files from one diskette to another. Since multiple floppy drives on a system cannot be accessed at the same time, it is very inefficient to copy files from one floppy disk to another. Instead, create a temporary directory on your hard disk

and first copy the files to the hard disk directory. Then move
them from the hard disk directory to the output diskette. This
greatly reduces copy time by avoiding multiple stopping and
starting of floppy drives. If you can use a ram disk as an intermediate drive, the copy will be very fast.

```
MD  C:\TEMP

PCOPY  A:*.*/NW

PCOPY  C:\TEMP B:/X/NW

RD  C:\TEMP
```

Site licensing plans for one or more Patriquin utilities:

Site licensing fees are as follows:

➤ The first five copies of any or all utilities are purchased at full
price. If all utilities are purchased, printed documentation is
included for these first 5 copies. All additional copies of any
utility or complete package are 1/3 off the normal price.

➤ You pay a maximum of $2000.00 to register any individual
utility or $4500.00 for all utilities, for an entire site. This gives
your installation rights to copy and distribute the utilities to
anyone at your site. This also allows "at-home" use of any utility
for any person at the site.

➤ A site is a company location in one city. A location in another
city is considered a second site.

➤ If a utility is placed on a LAN, each regular user of a utility placed
on the LAN should be registered. Use your own good judgement
here.

Stowaway:
True Archival System for
PC Systems

Stowaway User's Guide

Copyright 1992 by Patri-Soft

IMPORTANT WARRANTY INFORMATION

REGISTERED VERSION ONLY WARRANTY:

Patri-Soft warrants the physical diskette(s) and physical documentation provided with registered versions to be free of defects in materials and workmanship for a period of ninety days from the date of registration. If Patri-Soft receives notification within the warranty period of defects in materials or workmanship, and such notification is determined by Patri-Soft to be correct, Patri-Soft will replace the defective diskette(s) or documentation.

The entire and exclusive liability and remedy for breach of this Limited Warranty shall be limited to replacement of defective diskette(s) or documentation and shall not include or extend to any claim for the right to recover any other damages, including but not limited to, loss of profit, data, or use of the software, or special, incidental, or consequential damages or other similar claims, even if Patri-Soft has been specifically advised of the possibility of such damages. In no event will Patri-Soft's liability for any damages to you or any other person ever exceed the lower of suggested list price or actual price paid for the license to use the software, regardless of any form of the claim.

Patri-Soft SPECIFICALLY DISCLAIMS ALL OTHER WARRANTIES, EXPRESSED OR IMPLIED, INCLUDING BUT NOT LIMITED TO, ANY IMPLIED WARRANTY OF MERCHANTABILITY AND/OR FITNESS FOR A PARTICULAR PURPOSE.

Important Information About This Manual

This manual for Stowaway is distributed as machine readable text with the Shareware version of Stowaway. It is different from the bound, printed manual for the registered version of Stowaway. The bound version is in a 5 1/2 by 8 1/2 format, spiral bound, and is professionally formatted with figures to describe Stowaway's features.

This manual is designed to print on any printer. It describes all features in Stowaway and basically has the same text as the bound manual. You will receive the bound manual when you register Stowaway.

About Stowaway

Stowaway is a personal archival system for your computer. Stowaway releases space on your hard disk by archiving inactive files to offline storage media such as diskettes.

The files and software on our PC systems are changing at a rapid pace. We are constantly creating new data, trying new software, and updating old systems. Our hard disks become vessels holding massive amounts of information we want to keep at our fingertips. In our fast paced world, much of what we use today is old tomorrow! Old data and software clutter our hard disks files and do little more than take up space. These files get in our way when we search for the files we need.

Deleting old files is not a solution, as we may have use for them in the future, so we end up purchasing more hard disk space to increase our storage capacity.

Although we do have need for larger hard disks to accommodate today's larger software and more complex systems, we can also use what space we have more efficiently. Hard disks are expensive storage locations for inactive data. Based on disk storage prices in 1992, it costs about $5.00 to store 1,000,000 characters of data on a hard disk. You can store the same amount of data in archive format on diskette for less than $0.50. This example shows a substantial savings to be gained by archiving data. Inactive data should be stored on inexpensive media and in a place where we no longer have to deal with it each day.

Stowaway is a solution to the storage and maintenance of your inactive files. It manages the process of storing and tracking inactive data on less expensive storage media such as diskettes.

Stowaway automates the task of moving files to offline storage and cataloging them so they may be quickly located and restored when you need them. Stowaway is a data and software archival system for your personal computer.

Stowaway Features

➤ Age and select files for archival automatically based on your specification criteria.

➤ Select files to be archived from optional scrollable selection lists.

➤ Locate archived files quickly using hard disk archive indexes maintained by Stowaway.

➤ Formats new diskettes automatically.

➤ Compressed data over 50%.

➤ Recover files to their original or new location.

➤ Archive to diskette, removable hard disks, or optical disks.

➤ Transport archives to other systems.

➤ Create multiple archive sets to keep archives for different users on the same system.

➤ Categorize archive files into groups.

➤ Add descriptive text to archive files.

➤ Archive and restore directories or trees.

➤ View WordPerfect and text files.

➤ Assign expiration dates to archived files.

➤ Run with command line parameters or menus.

➤ Examine context sensitive help at any time.

➤ Copy archive volumes easily to offsite storage.

➤ Archive files in a network environment.

Archiving with Stowaway

Stowaway moves files to offline disk volumes and keeps indexes of them on your hard drive. You retain the same access to inactive files that you had when they were on your hard disk. The index is instantly accessible to let you locate files. When you need a file again, Stowaway will bring it back from storage for you.

Stowaway organizes your archives volumes in simple numerical order so it is easy to file and locate archive volumes. All archive volumes are numbered sequentially starting at 1. Newly archived files are stored in the next available space on archive volumes. Volumes are completely used before new volumes are started. Stowaway tracks volumes by number and records information about the exact location of every stored file in its hard disk index.

Archive volumes are stored in numeric order. During restore processing, Stowaway determines where the archived file is stored, and requests archive volumes by number.

This organization lets you keep hundreds of volumes of archive data while still maintaining easy access to any file.

Use Stowaway to save all your old and seldom used files. Archive:

1. Old versions of software

2. Old documentation

3. Old data files

4. Old system configuration information

5. Picture and graphic files

System Setup

Installation from the distribution diskette.

To install Stowaway take the following steps.

1. Place distribution diskette in any diskette drive.

2. Enter the following INSTALL command. (If you are not using drive A, substitute the appropriate drive letter as the first letter in the command.)

    A:INSTALL

Once the installation is complete, you will find the following files installed in the selected directory on your hard disk:

STOW.EXE: The Stowaway program file.

STOW.HLP: Contains the context sensitive help.

The first time Stowaway is started it builds files it needs for its general operation. They are:

STOSAWAY.DAT: The options file. These options are set using the Setup option from the Stowaway menu.

STOVOLIX.DAT: Stowaway's index containing information about each archive volume it maintains.

STOGRPIX.DAT: Stowaway's index containing information about each archive group defined.

STOFILIX.DAT: Stowaway's index containing information about each file maintained in the archives.

NOTE

Each of the installed file names begin with the letters "STO". Stowaway allows multiple archive sets to be created. Each set is assigned a three letter identification. Stowaway's index and option file names will be prefixed with the three letter identifier on secondary archive sets so archive set data is maintained independently. Alternate archive sets will be discussed further in subsequent sections of this manual.

Setting system options

Stowaway is installed with default system options. Verify these options before using Stowaway. Enter the STOW command from the DOS command line:

C> STOW<Enter>

From Stowaway's Main Menu, select the SetUp function by pressing 'S' or by using the menu selection bar.

Stowaway's options will be displayed. Examine and modify the options as they are appropriate for you. The following descriptions will help you decide what options to choose. Help is always available by pressing <F1> at any time.

Drive to archive to/from?

Enter the letter of the DOS device you will use to write archive data. This may be the drive letter of any valid DOS mountable disk device. You may use 5 1/4 or 3 1/2 diskette formats or large capacity demountable hard disk type devices.

Level of compression desired?

Use the Right and Left cursor positioning keys to select the level of compression desired for data written to the archives.

➤ **NONE:** Do not compress archive data. Will provide the fastest possible archiving but you will use many archive disks.

➤ **MINIMUM:** Provides about 40% compression of data but is not as slow as higher compression levels. This is the recommended level of compression.

➤ **STANDARD:** Provides about 45% compression on data but is not as slow as MAXIMUM compression.

➤ **MAXIMUM:** Provides 50-60% compression but is slower than other compression.

Disk capacity?

Specify the size of disk you will be using for archival. Each archival disk should be the same size. This size is used when Stowaway formats new diskettes for the archives.

If you incorrectly specify a size of a high-density disk and place a low-density disk in the drive, Stowaway will format the disk as a high-density disk and format errors will be encountered.

Enter descriptions when archiving (Y/N/Ask)

Since filenames are often not descriptive enough to help locate a file, you can optionally enter descriptive text for each file archived. Descriptions are entered when files are selected for archival.

Enter 'Y' if Stowaway is to prompt for descriptive text for each file to be archived. When 'N' is specified Stowaway will not prompt for descriptions.

Enter 'A' to make Stowaway <A>sk if descriptions are to be entered before archive selection is started.

A value of <Yes> assumes descriptions are to be asked for. Even with a value of <Yes>, you may temporarily suspend entering descriptions for each file by pressing <Escape> when the description is requested. You will not be asked for descriptions for subsequent files.

Perform a group archive? (Y/N/Ask)

After selecting files for archival, you may assign a group name to the set of files. This group name lets you categorize files stored in the archives. During restore, you can list or select files by group name, as well as filename or directory name.

Groups and their descriptions are saved by Stowaway in its indexes. New groups may be added at any time. When prompted for a group name, you are presented with a scrollable selection list of existing groups. You may select one of the previously defined groups, or a new group to store the files under.

Typical groups might be SPREADSHEET, GRAPHICS, SMITHS, LETTERS, MEMOS, HOME, CORPORATE, etc.

Enter 'Y' to be prompted to enter group information for sets of files to be archived. Specify 'A' to have Stowaway <A>sk if you want to enter group names before each archive process.

Enter 'N' to indicate group names are not to be associated with archived files.

Enter an expiration date for files archived? (Y/N)

Expiration dates may be optionally specified for each set of files archived. When 'N' is specified to bypass the prompt for expiration dates during archive file selection, you may still specify expiration dates by pressing <F8> while selecting files for archival. Enter 'Y' if you want Stowaway to prompt for an expiration date during archive file selection.

Verify archive data after it is written? (Y/N)

For data integrity, Stowaway can verify archive volume contents before deleting archived files from your hard disk.

The verify process is performed just before you are asked to remove an archive volume from the drive. Verification rereads the entire disk to make sure the data is accessible.

Use DOS Verify feature? (Y/N)

DOS provides a Verify feature to check that data is properly written during disk write processing. This feature adds additional time to verify disk data during processing, but provides an additional level of assurance that archive data is properly written to disk and can later be accessed. This verification may also be activated through the DOS VERIFY command, Documentation about it may be found in DOS reference manuals.

Enter 'Y' to have Stowaway activate the DOS VERIFY feature during its operation. We recommend you use this feature.

Sound speaker tones when action needed? (Y/N)

If you dislike the speaker sounds Stowaway makes during processing, specify <N> to have Stowaway disable all sounds during its operation.

When <Y> is specified, you will hear a quiet tic as each file is archived. This gives you an audible signal that archive is currently working. You will also be beeped whenever Stowaway is waiting for you to take an action, such as placing another volume in the drive.

Action to perform on archived files?

Normally archival is the process of copying files to another storage location and then deleting them from your hard disk. If you want to retain the files on your hard disk after archiving them, specify "Keep."

Specify <Ask> to indicate you desire to be prompted before Stowaway processes the files after archival. At the prompt you may decide if the files are to be deleted or not.

Stowaway may also ready the archived files for Auto Restore by setting this entry to "Auto Restore." Auto Restore is a unique way to manage your archived files. For more details about AR, see the file, AUTOREST.INF.

When experimenting with Stowaway, set this value to "Keep." You may then practice archival without actually removing files from your system. Stowaway comes with this option set to "None." When you are ready to start archiving, set this value to the desired setting.

A potential reason for archiving without deleting is to use Stowaway to copy selected files to diskette to take to another location. You still want to keep the files on your current drive. Another use of archival without deletion is to take a copy of files to place in the archives for historical reasons. You may store multiple files in the archives with the same name. This lets you keep copies of the same file at different points in its life.

Overlay files when restoring? (Y/N/Ask)

If during restore, Stowaway finds a file already defined on the hard disk with the same name as the file being restored, it must decide if the existing file is to be replaced, or to bypass restoring the file.

The following options indicate what action Stowaway is to take when files of duplicate names are found during restore processing.

➤ **Yes:** Replace the existing file with the new file.

➤ **No:** Don't overlay the existing file. Skip the restore for the file and continue restoring other files.

➤ **Ask:** Prompt when duplicate files are encountered and ask if the file is to be replaced, or the restore bypassed.

➤ **Update:** Replace files that are newer than the ones present on the disk. The DOS date of the file on the hard disk will be compared to the DOS date of the archive file recorded when the file was originally archived.

Test to verify installation

After Stowaway is successfully installed you will want to take a few minutes to learn how it works and develop some confidence in it. You may test Stowaway without actually archiving any data from your hard disk by setting the "Delete files after archival" Setup option to <N>.

Explore Stowaway's features by archiving and restoring files and directories. When restoring files, always specify an alternate restore target pathname so you will not replace the files on your hard disk during your evaluation.

Since Stowaway allows multiple archive sets to be created, you can create a special archive set to test or demonstrate Stowaway. If you would like to use this feature specify /ID:TMP on the Stowaway command line or set a DOS environment variable with the archive set desired.

SET STOW=/ID:TMP

You may delete the test archive set by using the Clean option from Stowaway's utility menu.

Archive volumes used for the test archive set may be reused for any other archive set. You do not need to delete the files on the disk before reusing them as Stowaway will do this for you.

Quick Start guide

If you dislike reading manuals and want to get right to the action, this section will get you started using Stowaway. Remember the <F1> key provides direct access to information about your current action in Stowaway. The context sensitive help system provides complete information for using the system.

Starting Stowaway

Use the STOW command to start Stowaway. Stowaway may be started from any directory or disk. Stowaway uses indexes and options from the directory \STOWAWAY.

You may place the STOWAWAY directory in your PATH environment variable (see your DOS manual) or may specify the pathname where the STOW command exists as the command prefix. Following are some command examples:

```
STOW

\STOW\STOW

D:\STOW\STOW
```

Stowaway can be run from the DOS command line using command line parameters. Command line parameters are documented later in this manual. This section assumes you are using menus to direct Stowaway's operation.

We assume you have already used the Setup of the Main Menu to specify system options. If you have not done this yet, do it now.

Archiving files

1. Starting from the menu.

   Select the Archive function from Stowaway's main menu. You will be presented with a second menu to select how files are to be archived. Files can be automatically selected based on entered specifications, or manually select files from scrollable directory lists. Choose the manual selection option for your evaluation. This will give you a good idea of how Stowaway works.

   Depending on Setup options specified, you may be asked the following question.

   Do you want to enter descriptions for files to be archived? (Y/N)

   Answer 'Y' if you want to manually enter a description for one or more files to be archived.

2. Selecting files.

   Next you will be presented with a display of files from the current directory. This is a selection list to let you mark files for archival. Press the <Space Bar> to toggle your selection on or off.

Depending on your options, Stowaway may ask you to enter a description for any files you mark to be archived. To ignore the description for a single file, press <Enter> without entering any data. To ignore entering descriptions for this and all subsequent files, press the <Escape> key.

File descriptions will assist you in locating files at restore time. You will be able to browse through description data as well as file names, and directory names.

3. Changing directories to select from.

At the top of the scrollable list of files are subdirectories defined within the directory. These serve two purposes. First they can be selected like files to mark an entire directory or directory tree for archiving. Second, you can position the selection bar on a directory name and press <Enter> to change the list displayed to a new directory.

Stowaway remembers all selected files even though you may change directories. The upper right hand portion of the display shows the total number of files and amount of disk space to be freed as a result of archival.

4. Viewing files.

Press <F1> for help with all the functions of the selection screen. You can View WordPerfect or text files by positioning the selection bar on them and pressing <V>.

When you have marked some files for archival and are ready to move to the next step press <F10>.

5. Associating a group name with files.

Depending on setup options specified, you may be asked if you want to assign a group name to the files to be archived. If you respond 'Y' Stowaway will present you with a group selection display.

Archive groups are a feature provided to help you categorize your archive data more effectively. Locating files by name may not seem difficult at archival time, but after a few months you will appreciate any additional comments you may have attached to file names.

Enter any group name to be associated with the set of files to be archived, and enter a description to help explain the purpose of the group.

6. Archive processing.

Stowaway will present an archive status display. You will immediately be asked to place an archive volume in the output drive. Place any formatted or unformatted disk in the drive. IF THE DISK CONTAINS DATA IT WILL BE ERASED! Press <Enter> to indicate the volume is ready.

Archive processing will progress while continually updating the status on the display. You will be asked for additional disk volumes as they are needed. Label each archive volume with the number indicated by Stowaway. It is usually sufficient to place a label with a large number on it.

7. Archive termination.

When archive processing ends, Stowaway saves its own indexes and options at the end of the archived data on the archive volume. This may be used if you need to recover the indexes on another machine.

Restoring files

1. Restoring files.

Restore processing is very similar to archive processing except you select files to be restored from Stowaway's index of archived files. From the Stowaway Main Menu, select restore to begin processing.

2. Initial restore file selection.

There are three levels of file selection in restore. Each successive level further qualifies files to be restored.

At the first level, you indicate any pathname or filename wildcard entries to be used to select files to be restored. On the same display you can specify beginning and ending dates for files that qualify for restore.

Press <F10> after entering the information. You are not required to enter any data at this point. Press <F10> to proceed to the next selection display.

3. Selecting a group.

If you have associated group names with files you archived, you will be presented with a selection display of all defined groups and asked if you want to restore files from any particular group.

The first entry in this list is a generic entry indicating to select files from all groups. Other entries are for specific groups. Selecting a specific group at this point will isolate the files to be restored to files associated with that group. Pressing <Enter> from this display will move you to the next step in restore selection.

4. Restore now or list specific files.

Stowaway now asks if you want to restore all found in the archive indexes matching level 1 and level 2 selection criteria, or if you want to review a list of these files and select specific ones to restore.

If you have already entered enough information to have the proper files restored, you are ready to begin. Start restore by pressing <R>.

5. Selecting files from the selection list.

Selecting <L> for List will cause Stowaway to locate all files that qualify your selection criteria. Files will be displayed in a scrollable selection list. You may mark any number of files to be restored. Use the <Space Bar> to toggle selection on or off.

Use the <F1> key to see other features of the restore selection display. You may sort the list, zoom it larger to fill the display and display alternate information about the archived data.

When finished with the selection list, press <F10> to begin restoring the selected files.

6. Restore processing.

The restore status display will be shown and you will immediately be asked to place a specific archive disk in the drive. Press

<Enter> to indicate the disk is ready. Restore will begin and its status will be reported until all files are processed.

7. Restore termination.

When restore completes Stowaway will display a message indicating it is done. Remove the archive volume from the drive and file it in your archive set.

That is all there is to basic Stowaway processing. There are several features we have not mentioned in this quick start section. Use the help system or browse this manual to learn more about the system.

Archival Concepts

Hard disks are not intended to be repositories for a lifetime of information. When we get a larger hard disk it enables us to store more files, but does not solve our problem of managing inactive files. We often keep old and obsolete files on our hard disks just in case we might someday need them. It becomes convenient to save old copies of data just in case we might need them.

Unfortunately, we gradually consume the space on the disk and begin looking for ways to release disk space. We can immediately delete some files. Others we may compress to keep around while reducing the disk space they require. When all else fails, we look for files to copy to diskette for safe keeping.

This scenario demonstrates some of the basic parts of computer disk storage management. They are:

1. Remove unneeded data by deleting it.

2. Compress data on primary storage when practical.

3. Move old or archive copies of data to less expensive storage.

4. Purchase new primary storage only when necessary.

You might think that hard disks are not expensive, why not just keep buying bigger ones? Purchasing additional disk space might work for a while but there are other costs to keeping data than just hard disk space.

Every file on your hard disk must be managed. It must be kept track of, as well as regularly backed up. The more files we keep on our hard disk, the more work we have to do to manage them. Archival is a procedure for moving data to a special offline location where the cost of management and storage is much less than on our hard disk. Archived data is stored away so we do not have to work with it on a day-to-day basis. Archived files no longer require repeated backup, and they are filed properly once, so they may be easily found when needed.

One common use of archiving is to save old generations of data. For instance, you might want to keep a copy of a customer database on a monthly basis. This lets you go back and restore the database from any monthly copy. Backup systems don't provide this capability as they only keep one or two old copies of data.

The concept of archival is not new to us, we use archival techniques in our everyday lives. For example, the federal government requires us to keep years of tax receipts for proof in case we are eventually audited. We may keep our current years tax receipts and data in our desk, but we typically don't have enough desk space to hold several years of information. It is instead "archived" to the closet or garage for storage. The garage holds more information than the desk, and is a less costly storage area. It is the same concept for hard disk management.

Many computer users have implemented simple archival systems of their own. They usually consist of using the DOS COPY command to copy old files to diskette. Then they store the disks in a safe location. This technique is valid but is often incomplete because we do not take the time and effort to properly catalog and organize the disks as we create them. We quickly discover this when we go looking for a file we once saved to diskette and cannot locate it.

Stowaway's archival system provides the proven methodology and software to create and manage our archives for us. It is implemented to make archiving data almost effortless. You don't need to worry about how to label or store archive diskettes. When a file is needed, Stowaway helps locate it quickly. Stowaway puts your computer to work for you to manage your archive data.

Archival vs Compression Systems

Since modems were introduced and PC users began transmitting files to other systems, file compression utilities were developed to reduce the number of characters transmitted over phone lines between two computers. They also served to group files together for transmission.

These same compression utilities were quickly found useful for compressing and storing data in a format that used less disk space.

Over the years different compression utilities have proliferated. They have greatly improved in their compression ability and performance, but still provide the same basic function of compression and grouping data.

Some of these utilities become known as archival system seven though they only archive data in a crude sense. They do not automate the storage and cataloging of data for a user. They rely on the user to "archive" the compressed files to offline storage using the DOS COPY command.

Compression systems provide valuable capabilities to the PC user and allow for much more efficient use of hard disk space, but their archival capabilities are limited and should not substitute for a good archival system.

How Stowaway works

Archive Volumes

Different disk device types may be used to contain archival data. These devices may include 3 1/2 diskettes, 5 1/4 diskettes, removable hard disk devices, optical disk devices, and more. Due to this variety of archival storage devices, any archive storage media is referred to by Stowaway as an archive volume.

Stowaway archival processing takes the files you select and writes them on archive volumes. Each file is written to volume in a compressed format. Each Stowaway archive volume contains two files. The first file is an archive volume label file identifying the archive volume as well as information about other volumes written before and after the volume.

The second file on an archive volume contains all archive data written to the volume. This file contains any number of compressed archived files and corresponding information needed to restore them. Since all files are written to a single output file, archive disk space is saved and archive performance is improved.

To use volumes efficiently, each volume is completely filled before a new volume is started. Whenever a new archive process is started, Stowaway asks for the last archive volume used for the previous archive. It then appends new data being archived to the same volume.

Archive Sets

A set of archive volumes is a series of numbered diskettes or disk volumes containing archive data. Stowaway uses only one set of archive data for any archive process. To use an alternative archive set you start Stowaway with 3 character set identifiers.

Use the /ID:xxx parameter on the stowaway command line.

Separate hard disk archive indexes are created for each archive volume set. Basically, archive sets let you keep track of multiple archives with Stowaway. A common reason for keeping multiple archive sets is to keep separate archives for different people using the same machine. For example, different users on a network.

Archive File Index

As files are archived, an entry for each file is placed in an archive index maintained in the Stowaway directory on your hard disk. This index is always maintained on the hard disk and may grow to be fairly large. About 80 characters of hard disk space is used for each file archived. The archive index record contains all information necessary for locating and restoring files. The archive index makes it possible for Stowaway to list archive files at your request without having to read archive volumes.

When you restore a file, Stowaway uses its index to locate files. When the exact files to be restored are selected, information in the index identifies the exact volumes needed to restore the file. Stowaway starts restore processing and asks you to place specific volumes in the drive as they are needed.

As you archive more and more data, the archives continue to grow. Archive volumes are inexpensive as compared to hard disk space; so, adding new volumes to the archives is not costly. To preserve hard disk space used by the archive indexes, you may delete index entries from the archive index. Future versions of Stowaway will let you reuse archive volumes as the data on them is released.

Archive File Expiration Dates

You may assign expiration dates to sets of files archived. An expiration date is a date in the future when the archived files can automatically be deleted from the archives. Expiration dates are part of automated archival management.

When you specify expiration dates for archive files, you are giving Stowaway information that lets it automatically manage archive files and are freeing yourself from the burden of having to again examine the file at some later time to determine if it is still needed. When the day of the expiration date arrives, Stowaway can automatically remove files from the archives.

To remove expired archive files, use the Pack Archive Index utility. This is accessed through the Utility option from the main menu. If you do not pack your archives using this utility, expired index entries will remain in the archives.

Not all files will have expiration dates. Files with no expiration dates will be kept indefinitely. It is a good idea to assign expiration dates whenever possible as they help to keep the archives uncluttered.

Other Archive Indexes

In addition to the archive file index, Stowaway also maintains indexes about each archive volume and archive group defined. The archive volume index contains information about each volume and its status in the archives. The group index keeps all group names defined to

Stowaway and their associated descriptions. These indexes are maintained as separate files in the Stowaway directory. Separate indexes are maintained for each archive set.

Stowaway reference

Preparing archive volume sets

Before using Stowaway you will need to prepare a set of archive volumes. When using diskettes as archive volumes, start with a fresh box of the highest quality diskettes you can find. Of course, Stowaway can't tell the quality of your disks, but if your archives are important to you, it is worth a few more cents per disk to avoid the problems and wasted time poor disks can cost you.

Take the labels provided with the disks and using a large felt marker, number the disks sequentially 1 through 10 (or whatever). If you plan on keeping multiple archive disk sets, you should mark all the disks in a set with a set identifier.

Stowaway can keep separate indexes for different sets of archive volumes. Stowaway only works with one archive set at a time. A good use for different archive sets is to let multiple users keep separate archive sets on a single computer. Each user can then have their own set of archive disks. For most users only one set of archive volumes are used.

Stowaway's Main Menus

Following are examples of Stowaway's main menu structure. The (...) indicate where a menu selection takes you to another submenu. All other selections immediately take the action specified.

The capitalized character on each menu line indicates the menu selection character that can be pressed to immediately select a menu item. You may also use a mouse with a single click to select a menu option, or use the cursor up and down keys to position a menu selection bar and then press <Enter> to select any menu item.

Main Menu Archive files to diskette Restore files from diskette Set up Utilities Help Print order form Exit. ArchivSelect files manually Scan files automatically Quit to main menu.

UtilitieAdvanced system options. Remove files after archival. Prepare files for auto-restore. Delete files from archives. Verify archived files. Pack the archive index. Build index from archive volume. Clean archive indexes. Set alternate display colors. Archive Summary Statistics Quit to Main.

Manual Archive Processing

The manual archive selection process lists all the files and directories on your hard disk and lets you individually select files for archival. While you are scrolling through the lists of files, you may view the contents of text and WordPerfect files using Stowaway's file viewers. You may sort file lists by file name, age, size, name or extension.

Depending on your setup options, you may enter a description for each file to be archived. File descriptions are stored in the archive index and are used to locate files to be restored.

Start manual archive processing by selecting <A> from the Main Menu followed by <S> from the Archive submenu.

Entering archive file descriptions

When you mark a file for archival, Stowaway may ask the following question:

```
Do you want to enter descriptions for the files to be
archived? (Y/N)
```

Stowaway asks this question when setup options indicate descriptions are to be entered for archived files. If you want to take the time to enter descriptions for each file selected for archival, answer YES to this question. You will be prompted for a description each time you mark a file for archival. If you mark an entire directory for archival, you will be asked for a description for each file in the directory.

Request window for file description

The following description entry message is displayed to accept description data:

```
Enter description for C:\WP\REQUEST.LTR<Enter> accepts, <Esc>
Cancels
```

Even though you are asked to enter a description for every file, you can press the <Enter> key without entering descriptive text to indicate no description is to be maintained for the file.

To stop the prompting for descriptions, press the <Escape> key without entering any description data. You will not be prompted again during this archive process.

The Archive File Selection Display

Manual archiving involves scrolling through file names on your hard disk and marking specific ones to be archived.

The display shows files for one directory at a time. Entries for the current and root directory are always sorted to the top of the list along with other subdirectories defined in the listed directory.

The top border of the display indicates the drive and name of the directory being displayed. The bottom border gives brief help about keys used to terminate the selection process. The right-hand border of the display holds a scroll bar for mouse control of the list (not shown above). Also not shown is a highlighted selection bar that covers one entry at a time in the list. The selection bar's location is modified by using the UP, DOWN, LEFT, and RIGHT cursor control keys.

As files are selected, a status window in the upper right portion of the display shows the number of files selected as well as the number of characters to be archived. This helps you to know when you have archived enough data to free up a desired amount of disk space.

The Drive Statistics window Total field shows space available on your hard drive. The Used value shows the amount of hard disk space currently in use. The Free space value shows the amount of hard disk space currently available for use.

The Projected free space field shows the amount of space that will be available on your hard disk after archive processing is complete. This field is incremented as files are tagged for archival. The Space Tagged and Files Tagged fields are also incremented to show how much data you have marked for archival.

Selecting Groups of Files for Archival

If you plan to assign group names to files to be archived, you must select and archive only one group of files at a time. Group names are assigned to all files selected for an archive process. Group names are selected after all files have been marked.

Group names are categories for keeping track of archive files. See the information about group names documented later in this manual for a complete explanation of archive groups.

Archive File Selection Operation

The following keys are active during the manual archive selection process:

➤ **<Space Bar>:** When positioned on a file name, it either marks the file to be archived, or if the file has already been marked, unmarks it. File names become highlighted in the list after they are selected for archival. A small checkmark symbol is also displayed next to the file name to indicate it is selected.

➤ **<Right Arrow>:** Marks the file highlighted by the selection bar for archival. If the file is already marked for archival, it will remain marked. The file selection bar is also moved to the next filename in the list.

➤ **<Left Arrow>:** Unmarks the file highlighted by the selection bar. If the file is not marked for archival it will remain unmarked. The file selection bar is also moved to the next filename in the list.

➤ **<Enter>:** When the file selection bar is placed over a directory name, changes the list to show the selected directory. Place the highlight bar on any directory name and press the <Enter> key to change to the directory.

Stowaway remembers files marked for archival from multiple directories so you may mark files from several directories before starting archive.

Special file names of <PARENT> and <ROOT> are shown for any subdirectory listed. You may press <Enter> on the <PARENT> entry to list the files in the directory above the current directory listed. Pressing <Enter> on the <ROOT> entry lists the root directory of the currently selected drive.

➤ **<F1>:** At anytime press the <F1> key for help on the current activity.

➤ **<F3>:** Press <F3> to bring up a temporary window to enter a DOS command or to exit to DOS.

➤ **<F4>:** Press <F4> to bring up a window to let you change the hard disk drive to list files from.

➤ **<F10>:** The <F10> key signals the end of file selection processing and starts the archive process.

➤ **<Escape>:** Use the <Escape> key to terminate the manual file selection process and return to the Stowaway main menu. The names of marked files are not saved.

➤ **<S>:** Press the <S> key to activate a selection window to specify an alternate sort sequence for the file list.

Sorting by date lets you quickly find the old files that are good candidates for archival.

Sorting by size lets you quickly identify the largest files that will free more disk space when archived.

➤ **<T>:** Tag all files in the currently displayed directory. After tagging all files you can untag selected files to be omitted from processing.

➤ **<U>:** Untag all tagged files in the currently displayed directory.

➤ <V>: Press the <V> key to View text or WordPerfect files.The file viewer can examine up to 500 lines of a file. Use the viewer to confirm the content sofa file before deciding to archive it.

Use the cursor control keys to control the viewing of a file and press <Escape> from the viewer to return to the file list.

Archiving a full directory

You may position the file selection bar over any subdirectory name and press the <Right Arrow> or <Space Bar> to mark it to be archived. Stowaway will immediately present the following question:

```
C:\DIR is marked.Process all files within it?
```

This is a reminder that you will mark the entire directory for archival as well as all directories below it. Press <Y> if this is correct. Press <N> to cancel the mark directory request.

If you mark a directory for processing and are also entering file descriptions, you will be prompted to enter descriptions for all files in the directory.

Completing file selection

Once you have selected one or more files for archival, press the <F10> key to exit the file selection display and proceed to start the archive process.

Automatic Archive Processing

Stowaway can automatically select files to be archived with your parameter specifications. The Automatic Scanning archive process lets you enter a set of archive specifications and then start archive. Files will be selected that meet your archive criteria. When you select Scan Automatic from the Stowaway menus the an form will be presented for you to complete.

Complete the automatic archive specification form as follows:

Path to archive:

Enter a directory name files are to be archived from. If this is a parent directory to other directories, files may be archived from this directory and all its subordinate directories.

Pattern to archive:

Enter a file pattern to be archived. *.* will select all files from the selected directories. You may specify normal DOS wildcard characters or extended wildcard specifications like *TIM*.*. This would select all files having TIM as any part of the filename. An extended wildcard specification of *T*I*M*.* indicates to select all files having the three characters T, I, M in the filename in the specified sequence.

Process all subdirectories (Y/N):

Specify <Y> if all subdirectories of the directory specified are also to be searched for matching filenames. Specify <N> if only the specified directory is to be searched.

Files Older than:

To delete files by their age, specify a date. Stowaway will only select files older than this date for archival. You may enter dates' information in the following formats:

1. Number of days old. Enter a number of days. This number of days will be subtracted from the current date. Any files older than this date will be considered candidates for archival.

2. Gregorian Date formats - The following date formats are supported.

3. JAN 91 01/31/91 01-31-91

Archive until this amount of free space met:

To archive files until a specified amount of hard disk space is available, enter a desired amount of hard disk free space. Archive file selection will automatically attempt to archive enough files to satisfy the desired free space and then stop.

The value can be entered as a total number of characters, or 1000's of characters (K), or 1,000,000's of characters (M). The following three examples all indicate to archive until two million characters of free space are available on a hard disk.

2000000 2000K 2M

Select only files needing backup?

Each DOS file has an attribute in its directory entry indicating if it has been changed since it was last backed up. Backup programs reset this indicator after backing up the file. DOS sets the indicator when the file is created and whenever it is updated.

To archive files that have changed enter <Y> for this value. Only files with this indicator set will be selected for archival.

Reset ARCHIVE attribute after archival?

If you want Stowaway to reset the backup indicator in a file's directory entry after archival specify <Y>. If <N> is specified, the backup indicator will be left in its same condition after archival. A value of <Y> is only effective if files are not deleted after the archival process.

After completing the form presented on the display, press <F10> to begin the archival process. Stowaway will scan directories selecting files for archival. If you want to terminate archive processing before starting, press <Escape> to return to Stowaway's main menu.

Specifying Archive Groups

Archive groups...

After selecting files for archival, you may assign the main group name. Group names let you categorize files in the archives. At restore time the group name becomes one of the criteria you can specify when selecting files.

There is no limit to the number of groups you may define to Stowaway. New groups may be created at any time. When Stowaway prompts you for a group name, you are presented with a scrollable list of existing groups to select from. You may select any previously defined group or add a new one.

To select a group to be associated with the archive set, use the UP and DOWN arrow keys to position the scroll bar on any desired group and press <Enter>.

Adding an archive group

New groups may be defined when examining the group name selection list. To define a new group, select the top item on the display <add a new group>. You will be prompted to enter a new group name and description. After entering the group information press <F10> to accept the new group definition. Press <Escape> to cancel the group definition request.

Group names may contain any alphanumeric characters. Groups are sorted by name when listed so, selecting a good scheme for naming groups will cause them to be displayed in a manner where they can be quickly identified and selected. Consider a scheme like the following:

```
DOS_UTILITIESDOS_SHAREWAREDOS_SHELLSWP_LETTERSWP_MEMOSHOME_FINANCEHOME_GAMES

Press <F10> to accept the group.Press <Escape> to cancel.
```

Archive Processing

When all file and group selection processing is complete, archive processing starts. Archive begins by displaying an Archive Status display.

The archive status display keeps you informed of the progress of archival. It contains the following information:

➤ **Status Bar:** The status bar at the left side of the display gives a graphic status of the completion of Stowaway.

➤ **Totals:** The totals lines show the number of files and total characters to be processed, completed, and remaining to be processed.

➤ **Current File:** Shows information about the file currently being copied to diskette.

➤ **Disk Statistics:** The disk statistics in the lower right portion of the display show the amount of space used on the archive volume and the space remaining. This is useful to help you to know when you will need another archive volume. For large archive tasks you might want to wait to insert a new volume before going for that short break.

➤ **Request for archive volumes:** Immediately upon starting archive you will be asked to insert a new archive volume in the drive. Stowaway has search edits volume indexes and found volume one to be the next archive volume to use. Place the volume in the drive and press <Enter> to start the archive processing.

Press <Escape> to the volume request message to be presented with additional options you have when mounting a volume.

Stowaway options indicate when you may safely quit processing. When a new volume is requested to hold the second part of a file that spans multiple volumes, you may not quit processing without having to restart archive for the file being processed.

Select Continue by pressing <C> and you will be returned to the display requesting the volume to be placed in the drive.

When Stowaway is requesting a volume from a previous archive process, you may press <S> to start another new disk instead of appending the new archive data to the last used volume. Use this feature when you do not have access to the previous archive volume. You might have stored the used disks of your archive set in another location, or loaned them to someone.

Recovering from disk write errors

If DOS should encounter a disk write error when writing to the archive volume, you will be presented with messages and options to select to continue from the error. This only applies if the DOS VERIFY flag (see setup) is set on.

A message is presented after DOS issues its message to RETRY, FAIL, or ABORT after a disk I/O error. If you selected RETRY and processing continued successfully, the file was archived successfully. If you selected FAIL or IGNORE, the file was not archived correctly. Select one of the following responses to indicate how to proceed after the I/O error:

QuitStop archiving immediately.

➤ **Continue Normally:** Try was successful and you want to continue archiving. If the error was caused by a faulty volume, you may want to Try again, or Try a new volume to move the data for the file from the questionable volume area.

➤ **Try again:** Archive the file again on a new area of the same archive volume. This will skip over the faulty area of a volume. We recommend using Force New disk and try again over this option since it is better not to try and archive any more data on a potentially faulty volume.

Force new disk and try again

(Recommended) Stop writing to the current volume. Ask for a new volume and start archiving for the same file again. The file will be written to the new volume and archive processing will continue.

Completing archive

Before archive completes you will see the following message presented on the display. This message is for your information only. You do not need to take any action. Stowaway is letting you know it is backing up its archive indexes to the output archive volume.

Saving Archive index backup to disk. Please wait

Once archival completes the following message will be presented on the display. This is to give you a chance to examine archive statistics before leaving the archive status display. Press enter to indicate you are ready to continue.

The last message shown by archive relates to your archive volume. Since Stowaway has saved its indexes on the last volume it used, you should always keep track of this volume. Remove the archive volume from the drive and file it so you know it was the last disk used. Turn it sideways, upside-down, backwards, or just place it in front of all other volumes.

An easy way to keep track of the last archive volume used is to store volumes with the used volumes behind the unused volumes.

Keep rotating the disks as they are used. Always keep the last disk used in the front of the set. In the following figure, assume volume 3 was the last archive volume data was archived to.

Once Stowaway has returned you back to its main menu you may start another archive or end Stowaway to return back to your operating system.

Restore

Restore is the process of copying an archived file back to normal disk storage. Restore is a copy, not a move. The archive copy remains intact exactly as before the restore. You may delete the stored copy and still have access to the data through the archives.

Restore brings a file back to your hard disk from the "archives." Stowaway makes locating and restoring files easy. Several features are included to help you organize the archives and locate files in them.

Archive data is stored in a special compressed form on consecutive disks of offline storage. The special compressed format obviously saves disk space but also increases archive performance. Stowaway is needed to restore any file archived by it.

Stowaway indexes all archived files in a set of hard disk indexes. When you search for a file to be restored, Stowaway's hard disk indexes are used to locate information about the file.

Stowaway gets a disk location and a disk number from the index and asks you to place the disk in the drive. It then reads the data and writes it back to your hard disk.

Restore begins by asking for specifications for files to be restored. There are three levels of file selection:

1. First you may optionally enter file name, path name, text to find in file descriptions and date ranges the file must fall within.

2. Optionally specify a group name files are to be selected from. This will help isolate selection to a category of files in the archives.

3. Files matching the first two specifications may be displayed in a scrollable list for your examination and manual selection.

Once files are selected, restore processing begins.

Entering Restore Criteria (level 1)

After selecting the Restore option from Stowaway's main menu you will be presented with the following display which asks for the first level of file selection criteria. You may skip this selection level by pressing <F10>. Stowaway will assume all files qualify this selection level.

Drive: *

Enter a drive letter indicating the drive files were originally archived from. '*' indicates to select files archived from any drive.

Path : *

Enter a path name where files were archived from. '*' indicates to select files archived from any directory name. A directory specification may end with '*' to indicate the files are to be selected from any directory name beginning with the name specified up to the *. Valid specifications are:

    \\WP\WP*\WP\LETTERS\WP\LETTERS\

Pattern to restore: *.*

Enter a complete file name or wildcard pattern name of the archived files. Extended wildcard capabilities allow you to enter multiple * in a name specification. The * indicates any number of characters may exist in this portion of the name. Valid specifications are:

```
AUTOEXEC.BATAUTO*.BATAUTO*.**.**TOEX*.BAT

*U*O*X*.BAT
```

Restore TO directory:

Optionally enter a target path name where files are to be restored. This is a full path name including drive letter. If no directory is specified, the files will be restored to their original directories and drive. Valid specifications are:

```
C:\WP\WPC:\WP\LETTERS\
```

Select files where description contains:

If you have entered descriptive text for files archived, you may select files based on the contents of descriptive text. Enter any word or phrase to be found in descriptive text. Only files with descriptive information containing this text will be selected for restore. The text will be searched ignoring upper/lower case.

Select files archived AFTER this date :

Optionally enter a date to reject files last created or updated on or prior to the date.

Select files archived BEFORE this date:

Optionally enter a date to reject files last created or updated on or after the date.

Selecting Group to Restore (level 2)

If you would like to further qualify your file selection by selecting only files archived under a group name, scroll through the group list and chose a group.

To select a group to restore files from, use the UP and DOWN arrow keys to position the scroll bar on any desired group and press <Enter>. To ignore groups and select files from all groups, select the top item (all groups) and press <Enter>.

Listing Files to Restore (level 3)

The third level of restore file selection is manual selection of exact files to be restored. Manual selection is an optional step.

If you have already specified sufficient criteria to select all files to be restored, press <R> to restore all selected files. If you would like to list all files matching the selection criteria entered, press <L>. You will be presented with a scrollable selection list of files.

Restore File Select List Processing

Scrollable selection lists provide complete information about files maintained in Stowaway's archives. Due to the amount of data stored about each file, Stowaway provides four different views of this list. Each view shows a different category of information about archived files.

Contents of archive list views

➤ **View # 1:** Filename DOS File Date DOS File Time Original file Size Original Pathname.

➤ **View # 2:** Filename Archive Date Archive Time Archive Size Compression Percent Archive Volume ID.

➤ **View # 3:** Filename File Description.

➤ **View # 4:** Filename Group Name Expiration Date Starting archive volume Ending Archive volume Offset where data stored on volume.

When the scrollable selection list is first displayed VIEW #1 is shown. To change between the three different views, press the <F6> key. As <F6> is repeatedly pressed the next view is shown. VIEW #1 is shown again after VIEW #4.

The following keys are active when their store selection list is displayed:

➤ **<Space Bar>:** Toggles selection—marks unmarked files to be selected for restore. Unmarks marked files to remove them from being selected.

➤ **<Right Arrow>:** Marks file to be selected for restore. Advances the file selection bar to the next file. Holding down the key will mark a series of files.

➤ **<Left Arrow>:** Unmarks file selected for restore. Advances the file selection bar to the next file. Holding down the key will unmark a series of files.

➤ **<F1>:** Help.

➤ **<F2>:** Zoom.When first displayed, the scrollable list is shown in reduced size to make room for help text at the bottom of the display. Press <F2> to zoom the screen larger. The help text at the bottom of the screen will disappear. Press <F2> again to reduce the display and view the help at the bottom.

➤ **<F3>:** Enter a DOS Command.

➤ **<F5>:** Locate text. If you have entered descriptive text for archived files, you may search for words or phrases in the text. Press <F5> to request a window to enter the text to be found. Stowaway will search all displayed files for the entered text. Only files containing the text will be displayed.

➤ **<F6>:** Show next VIEW. Toggles between the three different views of the archive file list.

➤ **<F10>:** Start restore. After you have marked one or more files to be restored, press <F10> to accept the selected items and start restore.

➤ **<Escape>:** Exit file selection list and quit restore processing.

➤ **<S>:** Sort the list. Press <S> to display a selection menu of alternate sort sequences for the restore selection list.

➤ **Name order:** Sorts by filename.

➤ **Directory order:** Sort by file name within directory name.

➤ **daTe order:** Sort by the date the file was last updated or created (before it was archived).

➤ **Archive date:** Sort files in sequence by the date they were archived.

Starting Restore

After starting restore Stowaway determines the volumes needed to restore the files and immediately requests you place the first volume needed in the input drive.

Locate the requested volume from your set of archive volumes and place it in the drive. You may terminate restore at any time by pressing <Escape> when Stowaway is requesting an input volume. All files restored to this point of processing are restored correctly. Other files selected will need to be selected again in a subsequent restore process to be restored.

➤ **Restore Processing:** The restore status display keeps you informed of the progress of restoring files. It has the following basic contents:

➤ **Status Bar:** The status bar at the left side of the display gives a graphic status of the completion of Stowaway.

➤ **Totals:** The totals lines show the number of files and total characters to be processed, completed, and remaining to be processed.

➤ **Current File:** Shows information about the file currently being restored.

➤ **Disk Statistics:** The disk stats shown in the lower right portion of the display show how much space is used on the target hard disk and how much free space remains.

Overlaying Files with duplicate Names

If Stowaway finds that a file with the same name as the one being restored already exists in the target directory, it may overwrite the file with the archive version, by pass restoring the file, or compare the dates and times of the two files and restore the file only if it is a more recent copy than the version on disk.

Stowaway Setup options let you specify any of these alternatives as an action to automatically be taken during restore. A special setup option of "Ask" indicates restore processing is to ask what action to take each time a duplicate file name is found. The following question is asked.

```
File B.BAT already exists.Ok to replace?
```

Yes/No/Update/Continuous update/continuous Replace

Press Y, N,U, C, or R to indicate the action to take. <Escape> immediately terminates restore. Following are explanations of possible responses:

➤ **<Yes>:** Replace the file immediately. The archive file will overlay the already existing file.

➤ **<No>:** Do not restore the file. Leave the file on the hard disk.

➤ **<Update>:** Restore the file if it is a newer version than the file on the target drive. If the archive file is older than the disk file, bypass restoring this file.

➤ **<Continuous update>:** This is the same response as <Update> with the additional feature of indicating Stowaway is not to ask this question again if another duplicate filename is found. An answer of <Update> will be assumed for all future instances of this situation during this restore process.

➤ **<continuous Replace>:** This is the same response as <Replace> with the additional feature that Stowaway is not to ask this question again if another duplicate file name is found. An answer of <Replace> will be assumed for all future instances of this situation during this restore process.

Completing Restore

After all files have been restored the following message will be presented over the Restore Status Display. It is an informational message to let you know the last action taken by Stowaway. Press <Enter> to acknowledge the message and return to Stowaway's main menu.

Utility Functions

The utility menu off Stowaway's main menu provides access to functions supporting Stowaway archive and restore functions. Select Utilities from the main menu to access the following menu of options.

Utilities- Specify system options

Remove files after archival. Prepare files for Auto-Restore. Delete files from archives. Verify archived files. Pack the archive index. Build index from archive volume. Clean archive indexes. Set alternate display colors. Archive summary statistics. Quit to Main.

Stowaway has a number of advanced options that are not necessary to set for normal operation. These options are discussed in the help screens, so to learn more about these, press F1 from the utilities menu.

Utilities - Remove files after archival

Stowaway options let you archive files without deleting files after archival is complete. When you use this feature Stowaway keeps a list of the files archived. This list may be used to later delete the files from the original hard disk. The purpose of this feature is to provide an optional capability to let you archive data and verify archive disks before deleting the original files.

Use this utility option to delete the last set of files archived from your system. A message will appear indicating files are being deleted. Once all files are deleted you will be presented with a message indicating all files have been successfully deleted.

Utilities - Prepare files for Auto Restore

If you want to use the Auto Restore package (see AUTOREST.INF for information about Auto Restore), then you might want to take a number of previously archived files and prepare them for use with Auto Restore. This operation is similar to the above operation, with the exeception that it does not physically delete the files, it sets them to 0 bytes and a time of 12:00 am. This is an indication to Auto Restore that the file has been archived. See the above for instructions.

Utilities - Delete files from archives

When you no longer need to keep files in the archives the Delete Archive File function will find selected archive file index entries and remove them.

The Delete Archive File function selects the files to be deleted in the same way restore processing selects files. You will be presented with a display asking for specifications for files to be deleted. Complete the form and press <F10> accept the specifications.

Stowaway will search the archive indexes for all files matching the selection criteria. You will be presented with a selection list similar to the one presented during restore processing. Select the specific files to be removed from the archives. When done with specific file selection press <F10>.

Stowaway will remove each index entry from the archives. You will no longer be able to restore the files with Stowaway. Archive index size will be reduced and future archive index lists will not show these files.

NOTE

This process only logically removes the files from the archive index. To actually release the space they occupy in the archive index you must use the PACK ARCHIVE INDEX utility provided.

Utilities - Verify archived files

Use verify to confirm archival has correctly archived data. Sometimes you may be unsure of the validity of your archives. This might happen if you suspect faulty archive volumes were used, or a drive might not be functioning properly. Stowaway provides this function to read archive data and verify it can be used to restore the files.

Volume verification is quick and easy as it only requires a quick read of archive volume data. No data is actually written to the hard disk.

Two verification processes actually happen. First, DOS verifies that all the data can be read from the archive disk. Second, a CRC check verifies that the data is accurate by arithmetically verifying the data in the archives is the same as the data was on the hard disk before it was archived.

Archive verification may verify a part of the archives, or an entire archive set. Upon selecting the verify function you will be presented with a specification display similar to restore processing. Indicate the qualifications of all files to be verified.

You are asked to fill in the following fields:

➤ **Drive to verify:** Enter the drive letter where the files were originally archived from. (I.E. C, D)

➤ **Path to verify:** Optionally enter the path name where the files were archived from. If no path is specified, files from all paths will be selected. (I.E. \LETTERS\PICTURES)

➤ **Pattern to verify:** Enter a file name pattern to verify. When not specified, all file patterns will be selected.

➤ **Archived before/after:** Select files by the date they were archived. You may use one or both of the date specifications.

Press <F10> to accept specifications and start verification. <Esc> to quit.

Like restore, you will be asked to place each archive volume in the input drive until all data is verified. You will be notified with error message displays if any errors are found in the data.

Utilities - Pack the archive index

Stowaway archive indexes periodically need reorganization to recover space released by expired of deleted archive files. Packing of the archive indexes performs two functions. First, it examines expiration dates assigned to each archived file, and deletes expired files from the archives. Second, it reorganizes the archive index to recover space from deleted file index records.

Although the packing process will always attempt to release space left by deleted file index records, you may optionally decide if you want expired files released from the archives. You may want to bypass releasing expired files if there is no real need to release the space their index records occupy. The biggest reason to remove expired data is to unclutter the archives. If this is not a problem, you can defer removing expired files in case their data is needed at some later time.

Immediately after selecting the Pack option from the utilities menu you will be presented with the following question and options:

```
Do you want to pack the archive index file?Yes / No / Expired
files / Escape
```

Respond <Yes> to recover space released by deleted archive index records. Expired archive index entries will not be processed and will remain in the archives.

Respond <No> to cancel the request to pack the files without taking any further action.

Respond <Expired files> to delete expired archive index entries and to recover space released by deleted archive index records.

Once your response is entered, the following message will appear indicating the index pack process is active.

```
Now removing deleted records from archive index
```

When index packing is complete you will be returned to Stowaway main menus.

Utilities - Build index from archive volume

As Stowaway archives files, it saves information about each file in a set of indexes on the hard disk.

Since the indexes are critical to the system, they are backed up to the last archive disk at the end of each archive process. This takes a little time and disk space but ensures indexes are always backed up and are kept with archives. Since the archive indexes are kept on archive volumes, each archive set becomes a portable set of files you may take to another computer for use.

To use any archive set, the archive indexes must exist on your hard disk. If they are somehow lost or not available on the computer where you want to restore files, you must first restore the index from the archive volumes. The indexes are always found on the last one or two volumes of the archive set. It is your responsibility to keep track of these disks since Stowaway does not know disk numbers without its indexes. During index recovery Stowaway will ask you to place the last used archive volume in the drive. It is always important to keep track of the last archive volume you use.

If you have lost track of the last archive volume, use the DOS directory command to display the files on each archive volume. The volume with the most recent file dates is the last disk used.

Stowaway immediately asks for the last archive volume when index restore is started. Place the volume in the drive and press <Enter>. In some cases Stowaway may ask for a second volume if it determines part of the indexes backed up are split from a previous volume.

Stowaway will read the indexes and put them on the hard drive. You will be notified when the indexes are properly restored.

If for some reason you lose your archive indexes, Patri-Soft does include a utility which can "regenerate" the indexes by scanning the disk. Call Patri-Soft or register Stowaway to obtain this program.

Utilities - Clean archive indexes

This function of Stowaway deletes the current set of archive indexes. Its purpose is to delete test versions of archive index sets before reusing them. Your primary set of indexes should never be deleted as they are required for restoring data.

After an archive index set is deleted, you will no longer be able to restore files from the archive set. You can use the restore archive index function to replace the indexes on the hard disk.

After selecting the index delete function you will be prompted to verify you really do want to complete this process:

Respond <Yes> to continue the process and delete the current archive index set.

Respond <No> to cancel the index deletion process and return to page 52 Stowaway main menus.

Once the indexes have been deleted, you may create them again by archiving more data with Stowaway.

Utilities - Set alternate display colors

Stowaway lets you change the colors of all its display windows to any colors of your choice. Setting alternate display colors involves setting NORMAL, REVERSE, HIGHLIGHT, and BORDER colors for each different type of window.

When changing colors, you are presented with a menu of each window type used by Stowaway. You may change colors on any or all window types.

Window colors are stored permanently on disk in the options file so they will be used each time you use Stowaway. When you are finished setting colors, press <Exit> to return to Stowaway's menus.

You are presented with a screen with four major color types to pick across the top and with a screen full of color combinations below.

Use the <Space Bar> to move between each color type. Pressing the space bar indicates the current color selection for the active type is to be accepted.

Use the <ArrowKeys> to position the selection box on the color combination to be used for the current color type. When you are positioned on the desired color, press the <Space Bar>.

Press <Enter> to accept all colors and return to the window type menu. You can then change colors on another window type.

Press <Escape> to return to the window selection menu and leave the colors as they were originally defined.

Utilities - Archive summary statistics

This option displays statistical information about archived data. Upon selecting this option, Stowaway will scan the archive indexes and show archive statistical information.

Command Line operation

Stowaway is normally operated through its menu structure. This provides a simple technique for archiving files that reassures you at every step with displays and questions to let you make decisions.

More experienced users may want to use Stowaway's command line interface to archive files. When the commandline operation is used, Stowaway will take all its basic instructions from the command line and start the archival process. It will still require the proper disks be placed in the drives and may ask for other decisions to be made based on your options. Although not totally automated it provides a quick start to archiving specific data.

A typical use of command line operation is to start Stowaway to archive specific files. Following is a sample command to archive all files in the directory named \TESTDIR\..:

```
STOW \TESTDIR\*.*
```

The Stowaway command line format:

```
STOW path/B/BA/D:01-01-91/DEL /EV:vol/EX:date/F:space/ID:xxx/
ND/P/S/SV:vol/RA/R
```

Command parameter explanations path Specify pathname to be archived.

```
STOW C:\LETTERS\*.* STOW \LETTERS
```

➤ **/B:** Select only files with the DOS ARCHIVE (BACKUP) indicator set.

➤ **/BA:** Batch file operation. This parameter indicates Stowaway is to attempt to complete processing without prompting the user. ARCHIVE COMPLETE and other such messages will not wait for a user response. Stowaway menus will not be used. You still may be prompted for volumes to be placed in drives and to decide how to handle error or exception conditions.

➤ **/D:xxx:** Stowaway is to limit its file selection to files older than the specified date. Use to free hard disk space by scanning a directory and archiving "old" files. Dates can have multiple formats. See information in the archive section of this manual for more information about different date formats.

```
/D:31DEC91 /D:01/01/91 /D:60 <== over 60 days old
```

➤ **/DEL:** If your Stowaway options are set to NOT delete files after they have been archived, this parameter will let you override that specification and force Stowaway to delete files after they have been successfully archived.

➤ **/EV:vol:** During restore, it is sometimes desirable to only restore files in certain volumes. You may specify a range of disk volumes by using the/EV and /SV parameters. For example, to restore the files after volume 6 and before volume 9, the command line would be:

```
STOW /SV:6 /EV:9
```

➤ **/EX:date:** Specify an expiration date to give to files selected for archival.

➤ **/F:nnn:** Archive until nnn characters of hard disk space available. Use this parameter to stop archiving files when the hard disk being processed has a specified amount of free space available.

The freespace parameter has three different forms (characters, K=1000's of characters, M=1,000,000s of characters). Each of the following examples will stop archiving when 1,000,000 characters of hard disk free space exist.

```
/F:1000000  /F:100K  /F:1M
```

➤ **/ID:xxx:** Alternative archive index setting. Specify any three characters to use an alternate index set. For more information about alternate archive index sets, see the heading about Archive Index Sets in the manual. When not specified it is assumed the value will be "STO".

```
/ID:TOM
```

➤ **/ND:** Normally options are set to delete files after they have been archived. Use this parameter to prevent the archived files from being deleted.

➤ **/R:** You may also accomplish restore from the command line. Specify a path as if you were archiving, and append /R to the command line.

➤ **/RA:** After archiving files, if you want Stowaway to reset the Archive attribute, select this option

➤ **/S:** If you already know the archive volume Stowaway will use, you may place it in the drive prior to starting Stowaway and specify this parameter to have Stowaway assume the volume is present. Stowaway will not ask you to place it in the drive during archival.

This parameter is designed for those users archiving to huge capacity disk devices where volume mounting is not normally necessary.

➤ **/SV:vol:** To start the restore process with a certain diskette, use this command. For example, to restore only files on disk 6 and above, use the command:

```
STOW /SV:6
```

Specifying options through DOS environment variables

Any Stowaway command line parameters may be placed in DOS environment variables to be effective each time Stowaway is started. Use the DOSSET command to add the parameter to the environment string. The environment variable name used by Stowaway is STOW. The following example demonstrates the most common use of the environment variable for Stowaway. In this example, the SET command is used to cause Stowaway to use an alternate index set identifier of TOM each time it is started.

```
SET STOW=/ID:TOM
```

See your DOS manual for more information about the SET command. The SET command is often placed in the AUTOEXEC.BAT file on a user's hard disk so it may automatically be issued each time your system is started.

Archive Maintenance

Multiple Archive sets

Stowaway lets you keep and use multiple archive sets on the same computer system. Although not often necessary, this feature is useful in many situations. Some examples are:

➤ To create a special archive set apart from your normal set to move files from one system to another.

➤ To create separate archive sets for multiple users of a system.

➤ To test your current archive set by restoring its indexes to a different archive set identifier.

An archive set consists of hard disk archive indexes and all archive volumes holding files referenced by those indexes. Archive sets are given three character set identifiers. This identifier is normally "STO" but may be altered when starting Stowaway by using the /ID:xxx command parameter. An alternate archive set identifier may also be established by placing the /ID:xxx parameter in Stowaway's DOS environment variable.

Archive set indexes consist of a set of three index files and a Stowaway options file. These files exist on the hard disk in Stowaway's directory. The normal files are named as follows:

```
STOSAWAY.DAT

STOVOLIX.DAT

STOGRPIX.DAT

STOFILIX.DAT
```

Notice that each file name begins with the three characters "STO". These identify this as the main archive set for Stowaway. When you start Stowaway with an alternative archive set identifier using the /ID:xxx parameter, a new archive set is created with the names changed to begin with the alternative set id.

Alternate archive indexes may be created new by starting Stowaway with the /ID:xxx parameter and then archiving files. They may also be created by starting Stowaway with the /ID:xxx parameter and restoring archive indexes from archive volumes. The indexes from the archive volume will be assigned the archive set identifier used to start Stowaway.

Alternate archive sets are identical in function and usage to the normal index Stowaway uses. When using alternate index identifiers, be careful to use the correct index set for the files you are processing.

Backing up the indexes

The archive indexes are backed up to archive volumes after each archive process. This insures the archive set is always complete. Your system backup procedures may also backup the archive indexes each time it processes. This provides redundant backups of archive indexes. Each backup is valid and useful when needing to recover archive indexes.

It is recommended to let your backup system continue to backup the archive indexes as full hard disk recovery procedures will be simplified. If you do not backup archive indexes with your normal backup system and need to recover your entire hard disk, you will also separately be required to recover the archive indexes.

Making copies of archive data

Each archive volume is in a normal DOS format. Archive volumes may be copied using DOS DISKCOPY, COPY, or XCOPY commands.

For safety reasons you may want to take a copy of archive information and store it at an off site location. To do this, use the DISKCOPY command to copy an archive volume to another volume. Store the original archive volume back with the archive set, and take the copied volumes to your off site location.

When you only have a single drive to read and write a specific disk format use the DOS DISKCOPY command as follows. It will use memory to copy a volume to a new volume. The drive letters for the source and new volumes are the same. DOS will issue messages indicating what volumes to place in the drives and when.

```
DISKCOPY A: A:
```

If you have multiple drives able to read and write the same volume format, use the DISKCOPY command with different drive letters. The first drive identifier is for the source volume, the second letter is for the drive to hold the new volume.

```
DISKCOPY A: B:
```

Archive disks may be copied to different disk formats as long as the new disk has enough capacity to hold all information on the source volume. Once archived, the archive data cannot again be split across multiple archive volumes.

The Context Sensitive Help System

Stowaway provides immediate help about its operation at every point of its processing. A comprehensive help system may be interrogated at any time by pressing the <F1> key. When <F1> is pressed, Stowaway automatically determines what function is active and action is being requested. It will search a help index and retrieve information about your current activity. Help systems that being up help about your current activity are referred to as "context sensitive" meaning they are aware of the context in which they are requested.

In addition to being context sensitive, Stowaway help system is layered to let you not only examine help about your current activity, but also lets you browse through the help displays to learn about related topics or other aspects of Stowaway. Press the <Home> key any time you are in the help system to display the help menu.

The intelligent help system may be examined by using the following navigation keys:

➤ **<Enter>:** Takes you to the next related screen.

➤ **<Esc>:** Takes you back to the processing screen.

➤ **<Alt>:** Allows you to peek back at the processing screen to review what you are reading help about.

➤ **<PgUp>:** Will take you up to a more general topic in the help system.

➤ **<Home>:** Displays the main help menu.

The LEFT, RIGHT, UP, and DOWN keys are available when viewing screens smaller than the full page. Use them to move the help window around on the display to view areas hidden by the help window.

System Requirements

Operating system compatibilities

Stowaway must run on a 100% compatible PC, XT, or AT system and requires DOS 3.2 or above for its operation. Stowaway may operate on some other nonstandard systems but we cannot guarantee its correct operation nor make any promises to make it compatible with those systems.

Archive device compatibilities

Stowaway uses only standard DOS disk devices for holding archive data. The obvious devices are various forms of 3 1/2 and 5 1/4 diskette systems.

Stowaway is also designed to use large format removable disk devices as archive media. These devices must have a standard DOS format and must appear to DOS as a normal disk device.

Troubleshooting

I/O errors on disks

If you should have a problem restoring data from a damaged or faulty archive volume take the following steps to attempt to circumvent the problem.

➤ Try turning the disk in the sleeve with your fingers to make sure it is loose and will spin. If 5 1/4 diskettes appear too tight, you can relieve some pressure placed on the magnetic media by drawing each edge of the diskette across the edge of a table applying a reasonable amount of pressure. This will expand the area inside the jacket for the media to move.

➤ Attempt to copy the diskette to another diskette. If the copy is successful, attempt to use the new disk to restore the data.

➤ Take the volume in error to another drive on another machine to attempt to restore the data.

➤ When all else fails, use the "FAIL" option during archive volume read error detection to indicate that archive is to read as much data as possible.

Error Messages

Stowaway has comprehensive error and exception checking designed into every component of the system. Stowaway's help systems contains help about messages issued by Stowaway. Whenever an error message is displayed, press the <F1> key for a complete explanation of the error and suggested actions to take as a result of the error.

Technical Support

Patri-Soft may be reached for technical support through a variety of sources. Normal technical support hours are 8:30 AM through 5:00 PM Monday through Friday (PST).

You may contact us through the following methods:

CompuServe:	76347,2477
Phone:	714-352-2820
BBS:	714-352-2825
FAX:	714-352-1527
Mail:	Patri-Soft
	5225 Canyon Crest Drive
	Suite 71-358
	Riverside, CA 92507

A special orderline is available if you would like to purchase using VISA or MasterCard or discuss other purchase options.

When calling for technical support please have the following information ready so we may serve you efficiently:

1. The exact version of Stowaway you are using. Stowaway main menu contains this data.

2. An exact problem description.

3. A screen print of the Stowaway directory and all files it contains.

4. The software configuration of your system including DOS version, AUTOEXEC.BAT contents as well as CONFIG.SYS contents.

5. The hardware configuration of your system.

A good problem description indicates exactly what you were doing when you encountered the error, and exactly what symptoms occurred as a result of the error. Please avoid the following problem descriptions. They are much too brief to begin to analyze.

Poor problem descriptions

1. Archive is not working.

2. The machine will not read my disk.

3. I can't restore my indexes.

4. The system fails during archive or restore.

Following are examples of better problem descriptions:

1. Archive is failing. Stowaway asks for an archive volume and after I place it in the drive, the drive light comes on, goes off, and Stowaway indicates no disk is in the drive.

2. I am attempting to restore indexes from an archive volume and Stowaway indicates the indexes are not present. I have displayed the contents of the last used diskette and it appears to be ok.

Glossary

.	A code used in a path to represent the current directory. Always the first entry in a subdirectory.
..	A code that represents the parent of the current directory. Always the second entry in a subdirectory.
Absolute path	A path that starts from the root directory.
Address	A number that identifies a location in memory.
Allocation unit	The smallest unit in which DOS stores a file or part of a file. Also referred to as a cluster. An allocation unit can be 1,2,4, or 8 consecutive sectors.
Alphanumeric data	Data made up of letters, digits, and printable special characters.

ANSI	American National Standards Institute, which has established standards for data storage and communication. The standard 256-character ANSI code includes ASCII characters and others.
Antivirus	A program designed to detect the presence of a computer virus in a system. See *Virus*.
Archive	To make a copy of a file for safekeeping in a different location, usually on removable media. Same as *Back up*.
Archive attribute	A directory attribute indicating whether a file has changed since it was last backed up. The archive attribute is turned on when a file is first created and when it is modified. Backup programs turn the archive attribute off when the file is backed up.
ASCII	American Standard Code for Information Interchange. A standard 127-character code that represents letters, digits, printable special characters, and some control codes. IBM Extended ASCII includes 128 additional character codes.
Associated file	A data file with an extension that DOS associates with a particular program. If an associated file is selected in the DOS Shell, the program starts using that file for data.

Attribute
One of six characteristics that can be assigned to a file or directory and recorded in its directory entry. They include the archive, hidden, read-only, system, volume label, and diretory attributes.

AUTOEXEC.BAT
A batch file that is executed when the system boots, immediately after CONFIG.SYS is processed.

Back up
To copy a file for safekeeping to another location, often on removable media. The copy itself also is called a *backup*.

BAT
An extension that indicates a batch file.

Batch file
A text file that contains a series of DOS commands.

Baud rate
Technically, the maximum number of changes in electrical state per second of a communications circuit. Not to be confused with *Bits Per Second* which is often greater than the baud rate.

BBS
See *Bulletin board system*.

Binary
A numbering system that uses only two digits, 0 and 1. All internal data in a computer or on a disk is handled and stored in binary.

BIOS
Basic Input Output System. See *ROM BIOS*.

BIOS Parameter Block
A data structure containing information about a particular drive such as the number of sides, cylinders and sectors.

Bit	The smallest unit of information handled by a computer. A bit can have one of two values, usually represented by 0 and 1. Bit stands for Binary digit.
Bits Per Second	In communications, the data transfer rate.
Boot	To start up a computer system.
Boot record	A program found in the boot sector. The boot record on the boot drive loads the operating system when you start up the computer or reboot.
Boot sector	The first sector of a disk. On diskettes the boot sector is the DOS Boot Record. On hard disks, the first sector is the *Master Boot Record*.
BPS	See *Bits Per Second*.
Buffer	A memory area that holds data temporarily.
Bulletin board system	A computer system running software that allows access to many people at one time through their modems. Such systems typically enable you to carry on a "conversation" by reading and posting messages and to send and receive files. Abbreviated as BBS.
Byte	A series of eight bits, which can form 256 unique combinations. The term *byte* is often used as the equivalent to one character.
Cache	A memory location used to store data for rapid access. A disk

	cache holds data read from or written to a disk. It is similar to, but more intelligent and efficient than, a read-write buffer.
CD-ROM	A drive that holds read-only data on a medium similar to that of an audio CD.
Checksum	The sum of all the bytes in a sector or a file. Checksum is usually used to validate the data.
Click	To press and release a mouse button without moving the mouse.
Cluster	See *Allocation unit*.
COM	An extension used to identify a file as an executable program file. COM is short for COMMAND and indicates a file which is a binary image of memory. See also *EXE* and *BAT*.
Command	An instruction processed by DOS's command interpreter (or perhaps an alternative command interpreter).
Command button	A dialog box item that initiates an immediate action when you press it. Examples may be an OK button to proceed with a program or a Cancel button to cancel the dialog.
Command processor	A program that can interpret commands entered from a command prompt or a batch file. The command processor carries out internal commands and passes external commands to the proper program.

COMMAND.COM	The command processor included in DOS.
Compressed drive	See *Compressed volume file*.
Compressed volume file	(CVF or compressed drive) A file that acts like a drive. The CVF is created and managed by a disk compression program such as DoubleSpace to contain compressed files.
Compression	Reducing the size of a file or files by eliminating repetition and/or waste space.
CONFIG.SYS	A text file that contains commands necessary to configure the system and load device drivers. CONFIG.SYS is executed immediately after the operating system files are loaded during booting.
Conventional memory	RAM in the range of 0K to 640K. In versions of DOS before DOS 5, programs had to be loaded into conventional memory for execution.
CMOS	(Complementary Metal-Oxide Semiconductor) In 286 and higher machines, a battery-powered module that retains information about the computer's hardware for booting purposes.
Cross-linked allocation unit	An allocation unit, or cluster, that appears to belong to two files in the FAT.
CVF	See *Compressed volume file*.
Cylinder	In disk drives, a set of tracks all occupying the same relative

position. On double-sided disks, a cylinder includes track 1 on both the top and bottom sides. Hard disks may have many sides.

DBLSPACE.BIN
One of DOS's system files. DBLSPACE.BIN manages DoubleSpace CVFs.

Default
An item, option, or value used if you don't specify otherwise.

Deletion protecton
A program that tracks deleted files to assist in undeleting them.

Device driver
A file that contains information used to control hardware devices such as memory, a monitor, a keyboard, a printer, and so on. Some device drivers create and control logical devices such as RAM drives.

Directory
A DOS data structure that contains information about the locations, sizes, attributes, and so on of files and other directories. Any directory that is not a root directory is a subdirectory.

Directory tree
The entire set of directories on a drive, from the root directory down through its children and their children to the lowest level on the drive.

Disk
See *floppy disk* and *hard disk*.

DOS
The Disk Operating System; an operating system designed for the IBM line of personal computers and their compatibles.

DOS Boot Record	This first sector of a logical partition of a hard disk. The DOS Boot Record contains the drive's BIOS Parameter Block.
Drag	To hold down a mouse button while moving the mouse.
Drive name	A letter assigned to a physical or logical drive followed by a colon.
EXE	An extension used to identify a file as an executable program file. EXE program files must be loaded by a special section of DOS since they are not memrory images like COM files. See also *COM* and *BAT*.
Executable file	A file containing instructions that control the computer. Also known as a program file. Executable files usually have the extension EXE or COM.
Expanded memory	Also called EMS. An external memory device managed by an expanded memory manager in accordance with LIM EMS standards.
Extended memory	Also called XMS. In a 286 or higher-level machine, RAM at addresses beyond 1M.
Extension	A suffix for a filename. An extension can be one to three characters. Extensions are connected to the filename by a period.
FAT	See *File allocation table*.

Field	A data item in a dialog box or database record; for example, a ZIP code or a name.
File	A collection of related data stored and handled as a single entity by DOS.
File allocation table	A table maintained by DOS on every floppy disk or hard drive, used to track the locations of files and empty space.
Filespec	The complete description of a file's location including drive letter, path, filename, and extension.
Floppy disk	A small removable magnetic disk. The most common are 5.25-inch flexible disks and 3.25-inch hard-body disks.
Floppy drive	A device that uses floppy disks.
Fragmentation	Storing a file in nonadjacent clusters.
Global filespec	A filespec containing wildcard characters in the filename and/or extension.
Hard disk	A nonremoveable storage medium.
Hard drive	A logical drive on a hard disk.
Hardware	The physical equipment that makes up a computer system, including boards, monitor, keyboard, disk drives, printer, modem, mouse, and other possible items.
Head	See *Read/Write Head*.

Hexadecimal	(Hex) A number system based on the number 16; hexadecimal numbers have 16 digits, from 0 through F. Computers often turn the binary numbers used internally into hexadecimal numbers for display purposes.
Hidden attribute	An attribute that, when turned on, indicates that a file or directory should not be casually accessible by Dir or other commands.
Hidden file	A file with the hidden attribute turned on.
High memory area	The first 65,520 bytes of extended memory.
HMA	See *High memory area*.
Host drive	The drive on which a compressed volume file resides.
Hotkey	A key or key combination that activates a TSR or command.
I/O	See *Input/Output*.
IBMBIO.COM	One of the DOS system files. See *IO.SYS*.
IBMDOS.COM	The DOS system file. *See MSDOS.SYS*.
Icon	A small drawing used instead of words by a graphical program to label an item's type or to represent a command or function that can be invoked by clicking the icon.
Input	Information entered into a computer by a keyboard, mouse, modem or other input device.

Input/Output	(Often abbreviated I/O.) Input and output operations or devices.
Interface	A connection between any two parts of a system; for example between a computer user and a program.
Interrupt	An interrupt is a signal sent to a microprocessor to interrupt its current activity and request immediate processing. An *external interrupt* is from the outside world, such as a disk drive. A *processor interrupt* reports that an unusual situation has arisen, usually an error condition. A *software interrupt* is a request from a program for a service.
IO.SYS	One of DOS's system files, which contains the core of the DOS program. See *IBMBIO.COM*.
K or Kb	See *Kilobyte*.
Kilobyte	1024 bytes. Abbreviated as K or Kb.
Logical drive	An area of memory or part of a disk treated as a separate drive although it has no separate physical existence.
Lost allocation unit	An allocation unit that is marked in the FAT as unused but does not seem to belong to a file.
M or Mb	See *Megabyte*.
Master Boot Record	The first sector of a hard disk containing a short program which loads the DOS Boot Record, and the Master Partition Table.

Megabyte	A kilobyte squared (1,048,576 bytes). Abbreviated as M or Mb.
Memory	An internal storage device used to store the programs currently being executed and their data.
Memory-resident	Also called TSR programs. A program that remains loaded in memory until the end of the session (or until you specifically unload it). It usually monitors input and/or processing, looking for specific events that it is designed to handle.
Menu	A list of commands for you to choose from. Menus usually appear in graphical programs, which enable you to select items by using the mouse or the keyboard.
Modem	A hardware device that enables communication between two computers over a telephone line. Short for Modulation/Demodulation.
MSDOS.SYS	One of DOS's system files, which contains the core of the DOS program. See *IBMDOS.COM*.
Numeric keypad	A set of keys arranged like those on a 10-key adder and used to enter numeric data. The numeric keypad often shares the same functions as the cursor-movement keys, with the Shift and NumLock keys used to select between the two functions.
Operating system	A program that manages all of a computer's operations, controlling

other programs' access to the computer's basic resources such as memory and the disk drives. The operating system also provides the user interface.

Output
Data sent from a program to a storage or output device, such as a printer, a monitor, a disk, and so on.

Parallel port
A port through which data passes eight bits (one byte) at a time. Frequently used to communicate with printers.

Parameter
A variable data item entered as part of a command. The parameter provides information to a program, such as a filespec that tells a copy command what files to copy.

Partition
A division of a hard disk.

Partition table
A table stored at the beginning of a hard disk that identifies the partitions on the disk.

Path
A list of directories that DOS must go through to find a directory or file.

Port
An address used to communicate with another device such as a printer, modem, or mouse.

Processor
The hardware device that carries out program instructions.

Program
See *executable file*.

Program search path
See *Search path*.

Prompt
A message from a program requesting input from a user.

RAM	(Random access memory.) Memory that can be written to and read from. Data stored in RAM is not permanent but disappears when the system is turned off or rebooted.
RAM Disk	A logical drive created in RAM to provide rapid access to data that would otherwise require disk access. Data in a RAM drive disappears when the system is turned off or rebooted.
Read-only attribute	An attribute that indicates whether a file or directory can be written to. When the read-only attribute is turned on, programs are not supposed to modify or delete the file.
Read-only file	A file with the read-only attribute turned on.
Read/write head	The physical device that reads and writes data on a disk or tape drive.
Reboot	To reload the operating system; in DOS, you normally reboot by pressing Ctrl-Alt-Del.
ROM	(Read-only memory.) A type of memory in which data is permanently stored; the data cannot be erased or replaced. ROM retains its data even when the power goes out.
ROM-BIOS	A collection of programs stored in ROM that DOS uses to perform the basic input and output operations of the computer.

Root directory	The primary directory on a disk; the top level of the directory tree.
Scroll	To move data on the screen or within a box or window.
Search path	A list of directories that DOS should scan when looking for a program file that is not in the current directory. Some newer DOS programs also use the search path to look for data files.
Sector	A portion of a track on a disk, usually 512 bytes. A sector is the smallest amount that can be read or written at one time.
Serial Port	A port through which data passes one bit at a time. Usually used to connect with a modem, a mouse, or some special type of printer.
Shell	A program that replaces DOS's basic command prompt and command processor. DOS's Shell program provides a graphic interface from which you can perform many DOS functions.
Stack	A memory area used to store temporary information. Stacks often hold information needed to return to a program after an interrupt.
Software	Computer programs.
Subdirectory	Any directory on a disk except the root directory.

Switch	A parameter included in a command to turn a program feature on or off. Most switches begin with a slash (/) although some may also use a dash (-).
SYS	An extension often used for device drivers and other programs loaded in CONFIG.SYS.
System attribute	An attribute that tells DOS whether a file or directory should be both hidden and read-only.
System file	A file with the system attribute turned on; one of the files that contain DOS's core program—IO.SYS, MSDOS.SYS, and DBLSPACE.BIN. Some older versions of MS-DOS and all versions of PC-DOS use the names IBMBIO.COM and IBMDOS.COM.
Telecommunications	Communication between two computers over a phone line.
Track	On a disk, one of the set of concentric circles on which the drive writes data. See *Cylinder*.
Trojan Horse	A program that intentionally destroys data.
TSR	See *Memory-resident*.
Undelete	To recover data that has been deleted.
Unformat	To restore data removed from a disk by the Format command.
Upper memory	The area of memory from 640K to 1024K (1M). In earlier versions of DOS, upper memory was reserved

	for DOS's system use, but it now can be used to load and execute programs in 386 and higher-level machines.
User interface	The way in which a user and a program communicate with each other. DOS provides two interfaces, the command prompt and the graphical DOS Shell.
Utility program	A program that helps to manage the computer and its data. AntiVirus, Undelete, and Backup are examples of utility programs provided with DOS 6.
Virtual disk	See *RAM Disk*.
Virus	A computer program that replicates itself.
Wildcard character	A nonspecific character in a filespec. The question mark (?) is matched by any single character. The asterisk (*) is matched by any number of characters or even no characters.
Window	A rectanglular area on a screen that displays program output independent of that displayed in other areas of the screen.
WORM	(Write Once, Read Many.) Similar to a CD-ROM except that the user may write the original data on the disk. Once written, it cannot be overwritten, only read.
Worm	Common term for a destructive program such as the Internet Worm.

Write-delayed cache	A caching system that delays writing data to a disk until system resources are not otherwise occupied so that reading and other processing have priority.
Write protection	A physical mechanism that prevents a disk from being modified. On a 5.25-inch disk, activating this protection usually involves placing a tab over a notch. On a 3.5-inch disk, it usually involves sliding a tab to unblock a cutout on the disk.

Index

Symbols

. (Dot) subdirectory name,
230, 509
.. (Double Dot) parent
directory name, 230, 509
/4 switch, PCOPY
command, 424
... (ellipsis) in MegaBack
program menus, 382
xxxx 201 error message, 141
1701 error message, 29, 142
17xx error message, 188
300bps subcarrier of
viruses, 343
301 error message, 29, 35,
141-142
601 error message, 142
80186 chips, 28
80286 chips, 28
80386 chips, 27-28
80486 chips, 27-28
8086 chips, 28

A

/A switch
DIR command, 199
PCOPY command, 424
XCOPY command,
116-117
abnormal program termina-
tion, guidelines, 186
Abort, Retry, Fail
message, 387-388
Abort, Retry, Ignore,
Fail? message, 196
absolute paths, 509
Access denied message, 197
/AD switch, PCOPY
command, 424
address marks, 156
address ports, Input/Output,
166
addresses, 509
/AF switch
MB command, 409
PCOPY command, 424
allocating memory, 287-288

allocation errors, 227-228
allocation units (clusters),
173, 206, 218, 509
cross-linked, 514
lost, 219-222, 519
alphanumeric data, 509
Alt-Ctrl-Del (warm boot)
keyboard shortcut, 149
amperes, 25
animals, disasters caused by,
94-95, 102
ANSI (American National
Standards Institute),
14, 510
anti-virus programs, 68, 510
behavior blockers, 70
BOMBSQAD, 63
CHK4BOMB, 63
foolproof protection, 347
integrity checkers, 69-70
MONITOR, 315-316
restoration programs,
71-72
scanners, 68-69
/AP switch, PCOPY
command, 424

applications, 5, 8
see also programs
archive attribute, 510
    copying files with,
        116-117
archive groups, 482-483
archive indexes
    backing up, 503
    building, 496-497
    deleting, 497
    for files, 473-474
    for volumes, groups, and
        sets, 474-475
    packing, 495-496
archive sets, 473
    multiple, 501-502
    preparing, 475
archive volumes, 472-473
    copying, 503-504
archiving, 510
    backups, 132-133
    files, 451, 458-459,
        466-468
        automating, 324-327
        deleting files after, 493
        expiration dates, 474
        manually, 476-484
        reasons, 457, 470-471
        restoring, 468-470,
            486-492
        verifying, 494-495
        versus compressing,
            472
arguments, 44
ASCII (American Standard
    Code for Information
    Interchange), 510
    codes, 14-24
ASP (Association of
    Shareware Professionals),
    taking problems to, 417
associated files, 510
AT Class PCs, saving and
    restoring setup informa-
    tion, 333-334

atoms, 24
ATTRIB command, 197,
    208, 347
attributes, 511
    archive, 510
        copying files with,
            116-117
    hidden, 518
    in directory entries,
        176-177
    read-only, 522
    system, 524
Auto Restore, preparing files
    for, 493
AUTOEXEC.BAT file, 31, 511
    installation programs
        rewriting, 51-52
    losing to DOSSHELL
        Select Across Directories
        option, 102
    testing for hanging
        system, 189-190
Automatic File Selection
    screen, STOWAWAY
    program, 326
AUX file, 180
/AZ switch, PCOPY
    command, 424

B

/B switch
    PCOPY command, 424
    STOW command, 499
/BA switch
    PCOPY command, 424
    STOW command, 499
back doors, 151
BACKUP command, 114-115
backup file indexes, 381
backup indexes, 381
    keeping updated with
        hard drives, 408

rebuilding from backup
    volumes, 405-406
    reinitializing, 406-407
Backup Processing com-
    mand, MegaBack program,
    383-389
backup sets, 380-381
    uses, 411
backup volume indexes, 381
backup volumes, 380
    copying, 412
    preparing, 381-382
    rebuilding indexes from,
        405-406
    verifying data, 404-405
backups, 511
    archive indexes, 503
    archiving, 132-133
    automating, 320-324,
        365-367
    backups gone wrong,
        97-102
    data, 9
    data integrity, MegaBack
        program, 370-371,
        404-405
    deciding what to back up,
        110, 123-125
    deciding when to back
        up, 125-126
    discrete, 126
    DOS Boot Sector, 243-244
    DOS methods, 113-121
    DOS process, 118-121
    files, 115-116, 376-378,
        383-389
    floppy disks, 117-118
    full, 110-111, 114-115,
        367-368
    grandfathering, 125
    hard drives, 114-115,
        447-449
        multiple, 368-369
    hardware versus software
        methods, 126-128

incremental, 111,
116-117, 367-368
information about,
displaying, 335
off-site, 128
problems caused by not
having, 97, 102
reasons for, 107-110
remote, 130-131
restoring, 367, 378-379,
389-398
to lost hard drives, 398
saving generation backup
copies, 452
selecting files for, 369,
401-404
tape, using MegaBack
program with, 369
using file extensions and
wildcards, 112
using telecommunica-
tions, 129-130
viruses, 347
Bad command or file name
message, 144, 197
Bad or missing command
interpreter message, 102,
197-198
Bad Sector mark, 174
bases, electrical, 26
Basic Input Output (BIO)
file, 166
Basic Input Output System,
see BIOS
.BAT file extension, 31,
144-145, 511
batch files, 511
improving performance,
283-284
recursive, 143-144
baud rate, 511
BBSs (bulletin board
systems), 62-63, 338, 512
as sources of viruses,
343-344

behavior blockers, 70
.BIN files versus .EXE files,
284-286
binary multiplication
table, 13
binary numbering system, 4,
235-238, 511
versus decimal system,
12-13
BIO (Basic Input Output)
file, 166
BIOS (Basic Input Output
System), 166
checking for mismatched
information with
partition table, 319-320
ROM-BIOS, 522
BIOS Parameter Block (BPB),
172, 239-240, 511
information about,
displaying, 309-310
BIPS (billion instructions per
second), 28
bits, 13, 236, 512
parity, 142
bits per second (bps), 512
boards, adding to hard
drives and broadcasting
radio spectrum radiation,
94
Bologna, Jack, 74-75
bombed programs, 149-152
see also crashes
BOMBSQAD anti-virus
program, 63
boot disks
creating, 398-399
problems caused by not
having, 101
boot records, 209, 512
Boot Sector Infectors (BSI)
infectors, 60
boot sectors, 30, 64, 512
bad, causing endless
loops, 140

BIOS Parameter Block
(BPB) information,
309-310
checking for mismatched
information with
partition table, 319-320
DOS Boot Sector,
239-267, 516
MBR (Master Boot
Record), 239, 246-267,
519
viruses, 53, 60, 64-65
in DOS Boot Sectors,
241-242
in Master Boot Records
(MBRs), 253-255
sources, 344
stealth techniques, 67
BOOTINFO program
(PANDA Systems), 188,
207, 306, 309-310
booting, 28-30, 240-241, 512
from hard drives, troubleshooting, 187-189, 190
warm, 149
bootstrap loader program,
28-29
BPB (BIOS Parameter Block),
172, 239-240, 511
information about,
displaying, 309-310
BRAIN virus, 60
BROWSE program (PANDA
Systems), 306, 310-311
BSI (Boot Sector Infectors)
infectors, 60
buffers, 48-51, 512
bugs, 232, 338
bulletin board systems
(BBSs), 62-63, 338, 512
as sources of viruses,
343-344
Burleson, Donald, 344-345
buying
at flea markets, 281-282

from mail-order houses, 281
from unknowledgable salespeople, 100-101, 275-276
"new" hardware or software, 273-274
/BW switch, PCOPY command, 425
bytes, 13, 164, 236, 512
media descriptor, 178, 267-268

C

/C switch, MB command, 409
/C2 switch, PCOPY command, 426
/C3 switch, PCOPY command, 426
caches, 512-513
non-write through, losing data, 145-146
write-delayed, 526
Calibrate (Norton Utilities), 200
Cannot find system files message, 198-199
Cannot load COMMAND, system halted message, 199
capacities
floppy disks, 158-159
matching, 146-148
hard drives, 162
logical sectors, 170
CARO (Computer Anti-Virus Research Organization), 60
cats, disasters caused by, 95, 102
/CD switch, PCOPY command, 425

CD-ROM drives, 513
Central Point virus signature updates, 69
central processing units (CPUs), 6, 27-28, 239
/CF switch, PCOPY command, 426
characters
control, 15
wild card, 112, 525
Check Disk (CHKDSK) program
allocation errors, 227-228
cross-linked files
directory entries, 222-224
FAT entries, 224-226
invalid subdirectory entries, 228-231
lost allocation units, 219-222
report areas, 217-219
risks of repairing directory errors, 219
checksums, 69, 513
chips, 6, 27-28
CHK4BOMB anti-virus program, 63
CHKDIR program, 307, 334-335
CHKDSK command, 186, 193, 206, 219-223, 228-230
circuits
flip-flop, 26
ICs (integrated circuits), 27
cleaning
floppy drives, 38
keyboards, 34
see also maintenance
clicking, 513
closing files, 182
clusters, see allocation units
CMOS (Complementary Metal-Oxide Semiconductor), 514

CMOS program, 307, 333-334
Code Segment (CS) register, 28
at startup, 29
Cohen, Dr. Fred, 59
cold, effects on magnetic media, 83-84
collectors, 26
colors, screen display
MegaBack program, 407-408
Stowaway program, 498
.COM file extension, 5, 31, 144-145, 513
.COM files versus .EXE files, 284-286
command buttons, 513
command line, protecting against deletions, 317-318
command processors, 513
COMMAND.COM
command processor, 30-31, 167-168, 514
mismatching with hidden files, 102
precedence for running programs, 144-145
commands, 513
ATTRIB, 197, 208, 347
BACKUP, 114-115
CHKDSK, 186, 193, 206, 219-223, 228-230
COPY, 115-116
DEBUG, 195, 209-210, 232
DEBUG.COM (DEBUG.EXE) program, 232-234
DEL . (period), 94
DELTREE, 191
DIR, 46-47, 145, 199
DISKCOPY, 117-118, 203
DOSSHELL Select Across Directories option, 102

FASTOPEN, 185-186
FDISK, 250, 255-259
FILECOMP, 151
FORMAT, 32, 192, 211
INSTALL, 459
MB, 376, 380-381, 409-410
MD, 191
MegaBack program (Patri-Soft Utilities), 382-383
    Backup Processing, 383-389
    Restore Processing, 389-398
    Utilities menu, 399-408
MEM, 287
MIRROR, 184, 192, 243-244
parameters, 521
    files as, 450
PATH, 145
PCOPY, 423-436
PCOPY program, copy-specification menus, 437-443
PRINT SCREEN, 36
RAMDRIVE, 283-284
RESTORE, 114-115
SMARTDRV, 145-146
STOW, 460, 465-466, 499-501
SUBST, 169
switches, see switches
SYS, 199-201
TRUENAME, 179
UNDELETE, 184-185, 190-191, 195
UNFORMAT, 192
XCOPY, 116-117
companion viruses, 61, 286
comparing files and report-ing differences, 451-452
complete redundancy, 41-42
compressed volume files (CVFs), 514

compressing
    disks, 282-283
    files, 332-333, 514
        versus archiving, 472
Computer Anti-Virus Research Organization (CARO), 60
computers, see PCs
CON file, 180
conductors, 25
CONFIG.SYS file, 30, 514
    installation programs rewriting, 48-51
    testing for hanging system, 189-190
context sensitive help
    MegaBack program, 412-413
    Stowaway program, 504
control characters, 15
conventional memory, 514
conversion programs, 45-46
COPY command, 115-116
copy-specification menus, PCOPY program, 437-443
copying
    archive volumes, 503-504
    backup volumes, 412
    directories with all subdirectories, 446
    disks to new disks, including directories, 446
    files
        advanced options, 327-332, 423-436
        between floppy disks, 452-453
        by parts of names, 445
        duplicates only, 445
        duplicates with new names, 449
        from floppy disks to hard drives, 443-444

    hard disk sets to multiple floppy disks, 446-447
    larger than floppy disks, to multiple floppy disks, 447
    multiple groups by extensions, 445
    newer, between disks, 445-446
    newly changed only, 444
    selecting by time of day, 444
    with archive attribute, 116-117
    restarting incompleted copies, 450-451
Core Wars, 58-59
cost
    PCOPY program registration, 419
        site licensing fees, 453
    reconditioned keyboards, 34
    remote backup systems, 131
    storing data on hard drives, 325
    tape backup units, 127
Cost Benefit Analysis, 41-42
CPUs (central processing units), 6, 27-28, 239
crashes, 39, 149-152
    caused by
        changing interrupt vector addresses, 286
        TSRs, 288-289
    troubleshooting, 186
CRC (Cyclical Redundancy Check), 69
creating
    files, 178-179
    system recovery boot disks, 398-399

cross-linked allocation
units, 514
cross-linked files
directory entries, 222-224
FAT entries, 224-226
CRTs (Cathode Ray Tube), 6
CS (Code Segment)
register, 28
at startup, 29
current, electrical, 25
CVFs (compressed volume
files), 514
Cyclical Redundancy Check
(CRC), 69
cylinders, 514-515

D

/D switch
HOWBAD program, 335
NODEL program, 317
PCOPY command,
426-427
STOW command, 499
/D- switch, PCOPY
command, 427
/D2 switch, PCOPY
command, 427
damaged files, causes, 344
data, 4-5
alphanumeric, 509
backing up, 9
destroyed, causes, 344
encoding schemes, 154
entering in files, 180-181
formatting, 43-44
importing, 45-46
process, 5
reasons for backups,
107-110
semantic, 5
data area, 178

Data error reading/
writing drive x message,
199-200
data files
leaving open versus
opening as needed,
185-186
viruses in, 342
data integrity
MegaBack program,
370-371, 404-405
Stowaway program,
494-495
data ports, 6
database programs, 44
dates, file stamps in
directory entries, 177
DBLSPACE.BIN file, 515
/DC switch, PCOPY
command, 427
/DCA switch, PCOPY
command, 427
DEBUG command, 195,
209-210, 232
DEBUG.COM (DEBUG.EXE)
program, 232-234
Master Boot Records,
246-247
replacing startup code,
250-253
recovering damaged DOS
Boot Sectors, 242-243,
245-246
repairing
FAT, 267-268
root directories,
268-269
subdirectories, 270
decimal numbering system,
237-238
ASCII codes, 16-24
versus binary system,
12-13
default, 515
file and buffer settings, 49

defragmenting disks,
282-283
DEL . (period) command, 94
/DEL switch, STOW
command, 499
DELALL program (PANDA
Systems), 306, 319
DELBUT program, 307, 334
DELETE SENTRY, 184-185
DELETE TRACKING, 184
deleting
archive indexes, 497
files, 182
accidentally, 98-99
after archiving, 493
all but those to be
saved, 334
from archives, 494
from target disks
before copying files
to, 450
in any subdirectory,
319
protecting against
at command line,
317-318
recovering, 190
read-only designation
from files, 197
subdirectories, recovering
files from, 191
deletion protecton, 515
delimited files, 45
DELPHI on-line service,
exiting E-mail service by
back door, 90
DELTREE command, 191
destination disks, 114
deleting files from, before
copying files to, 450
device drivers, 515
device ROM, 29
devices
logical, 168-169
naming, 168, 289-290

dialog boxes, answering non-understood questions, 90

DIR command
/A switch, 199
/O switch, 47
/S switch, 46, 145

direct infectors, 66-67

directories, 515
copying, with all subdirectories, 446
cross-linked files, 222-224
entry offsets, 174-178
merging, 449-450
parent, .. (Double Dot) name, 230, 509
paths, 521
root, 523
repairing, 268-269
troubleshooting, 195
searching for files, 46-47
in multiple, 450
sorting files, 47
subdirectories, 523
. (Dot) name, 230, 509
deleted, recovering files from, 191
information about, 334-335
invalid entries, 228-231
lost or damaged, 193-194
repairing, 270

Directory Sort (DS) program (Norton Utilities), 47

directory trees, 515

disasters
caused by
accidentally deleting files, 98-99
answering non-understood questions, 90

attempting to outsmart installation programs, 93-94
auto-pilot reflexes for keyboard shortcuts, 88-89
backups gone wrong, 97-102
DEL . (period) command, 94
dropping propped books onto keyboard, 96
exit shortcuts, 89-90
formatting unlabelled floppy disks, 88
message sources and meanings, determining, 92-93
mismatching COMMAND.COM and hidden files, 102
misnaming files, 97
no boot disks, 101
not backing up, 97, 102
not checking about vendor support, 100-101, 275-276
not planning for enough memory, 100
not understanding programs before using, 92
overloading memory at startup, 99
pets, 94-95, 102
program piracy, 91
radio spectrum radiation, 94
running unknown/untested programs, 93
speakers, 101

trusting "knowledgable" friends, 276
using keyboard shortcuts without reading documenta, 96
planning for
assessing vulnerability, 77-79
determining levels of planning, 74-75
DOS-upgrade support, 80-81
hardware, 79
installing and using software, 81-82
management considerations, 75-76
program documentation, 82-83
site security preventive maintenance, 85-86
software, 79-80
storage media maintenance, 83-85

disclaimers, PCOPY program, 417-418

discrete backups, 126

Disk Base Table, 240

Disk boot failure message, 200

Disk Doctor (Norton Utilities), 188, 194-195, 200, 202-203, 205, 207, 209, 212

disk drives, see drives

DISK EDIT (Norton Utilities), 268, 270

Disk Fix (PC Tools), 188, 194-195, 200, 202-203, 205, 209, 212

disk write errors, recovering from when archiving, 484-486

DISKCOPY command, 117-118, 203

diskettes, *see* floppy disks

DISKINFO program (PANDA Systems), 305, 311-312

disks
BPB (BIOS Parameter Block), 172
comparing files and reporting differences, 451-452
copying to new disks, including directories, 446
data area, 178
defragmenting, 282-283
directories, 174-178
FAT (File Allocation Table), 172-174
finding and correcting errors, 219-231
floppy, *see* floppy disks
hard, *see* hard disks
source, 114
target (destination), 114
deleting files from before copying to, 450
transporting to other computers, 451

distinctive ringing, 131

Divide overflow message, 200

/DL switch, PCOPY command, 427

/DO switch, PCOPY command, 427

documentation, 82-83

dogs, disasters caused by, 95

DOS (Disk Operating System), 6-8, 153, 515
backup methods, 113-121
BIO (Basic Input Output) file, 166
BIOS (Basic Input Output System), 166

COMMAND.COM shell program, 167-168
environment variables
MegaBack command line parameters in, 410
Stowaway command line parameters in, 501
file retrieval system, 170-172
history, 163-166
interaction with programs, 167
upgrading
backwards compatibility, 164-166
support by data recovery utilities, 80-81
versions, determining, 188

DOS Boot Sector, 239-240, 516
backing up, 243-244
recovering
floppy disks, 242-243
hard disks, 243-246

DOSSHELL Select Across Directories option, 102

Dot (.) subdirectory name, 230, 509

Double Dot (..) parent directory name, 230, 509

downloading, 62

downward compatibility, 81

DPB (Drive Parameter Block), displaying information about, 311-312

/DR switch, PCOPY command, 427

DR. PANDA UTILITIES, 336

Dr. Solomon's Anti-Virus ToolKit, virus signature updates, 69

dragging, 516

DRHOOK program (PANDA Systems), 282, 287, 289, 305, 312-313
Device Driver screen, 313
DOS Memory Usage screen, 312

Drive not ready error reading/writing drive x message, 201

Drive Parameter Block (DPB), displaying information about, 311-312

drives, 6
CD-ROM, 513
host, 518
logical, 519
names, 516
RAM disks, 522
searching for files, 46-47
WORM (Write Once, Read Many), 525

dropper programs, 344

/DS switch, PCOPY command, 428

/DT switch, MIRROR command, 184

/DX switch, PCOPY command, 428

/DY switch, PCOPY command, 428

E

/E switch, PCOPY command, 428

EGABTR Trojan Horse, 63

electricity, 24-27

electromotive force (EMF), 25

electrons, 24-25

Elk Cloner virus, 60-61

ellipsis (...) in MegaBack program menus, 382

Emergency Disk
(PC Tools), 207
emitters, 26
encoding schemes, 154
End Of File <EOF>
marker, 174
environment variables
MegaBack command line
parameters in, 410
Stowaway command line
parameters in, 501
environments, 8
/EQ switch, PCOPY
command, 428-429
ERASE PROTECT (Norton
Utilities), 195
Error in EXE file
message, 201
Error loading operating
system message, 201, 248
Error reading drive A:.
Abort, Retry, Fail
message, 243
Error writing directory
message, 202
Error writing FAT
message, 202
Error writing fixed disk
message, 201-202
Error writing partition
table message, 203
errors
disk write, recovering
from when archiving,
484-486
messages, see messages
/EV switch
MB command, 409
STOW command, 500
/EX switch
PCOPY command,
429-430
STOW command, 500
.EXE file extension, 5, 31,
144-145, 516

.EXE files versus .COM files,
284-286
executable files, 516
exiting programs
BROWSE, 311
disasterous shortcuts,
89-90
DRHOOK, 313
FINDPART, 320
PARTINFO, 314
expanded memory, 516
extended DOS partitions,
169
extended memory, 516
extensions, 112, 516
.BAT, 31, 144-145, 511
.COM, 5, 31, 144-145,
513
copying multiple groups
of files by, 445
.EXE, 5, 31, 144-145, 516
in directory entries,
175-176
.SYS, 524
external interrupts, 519

F

/F switch
BACKUP command, 115
CHKDSK command,
219-223, 228-230
MB command, 409
MONITOR program, 316
PCOPY command,
430-431
STOW command, 500
Fastback Plus (Fifth
Generation), 126
FASTOPEN command,
185-186
FAT (File Allocation Table),
172-174, 218-219, 517

cross-linked files, 224-226
of floppy disks, overwriting, 47-48
reading, 270-272
repairing, 267-268
troubleshooting, 191-192
Fatal Error. Reboot Now!
message, 93
FDISK program
reconstructing partition
tables, 255-259
replacing Master Boot
Record (MBR) startup
code, 250
/FI switch, PCOPY
command, 431
fields, 44, 517
key, 44
Fifth Generation's Fastback
Plus, 126
File Allocation Table,
see FAT
File allocation table
bad, drive x message,
203
File Allocation Units, see
allocation units
File creation error
message, 203-204
file handles, 179-180
File not found
message, 204
FILECOMP command, 151
FILENAME.EXT already
exists. Replace it? Y/
N? message, 55
files, 517
archived, verifying,
494-495
archiving, 451, 458-459,
466-468, 510
automating, 324-327
expiration dates, 474
manually, 476-484
reasons, 457, 470-471

versus compressing, 472

as command parameters, 450

associated, 510

AUTOEXEC.BAT, 31, 511
  installation programs rewriting, 51-52
  losing to DOSSHELL Select Across Directories option, 102
  testing for hanging system, 189-190

AUX, 180

backups, 115-116, 376-378, 383-389
  indexes, 381
  restoring, 367, 378-379, 389-398
  saving generation backup copies, 452

batch, 511
  improving performance, 283-284
  recursive, 143-144

BIO (Basic Input Output), 166

closing, 182

combining into single output file, 449

comparing and reporting differences, 451-452

compressed volume (CVFs), 514

compressing, 332-333, 514

CON, 180

CONFIG.SYS, 30, 514
  installation programs rewriting, 48-51
  testing for hanging system, 189-190

copying
  advanced options, 327-332, 423-436

between floppy disks, 452-453
by parts of names, 445
duplicates only, 445
duplicates with new names, 449
hard disk sets to multiple floppy disks, 446-447
larger than floppy disks, to multiple floppy disks, 447
multiple groups by extensions, 445
newer, between disks, 445-446
newly changed only, 444
selecting by time of day, 444
with archive attribute, 116-117

creating, 178-179

cross-linked
  directory entries, 222-224
  FAT entries, 224-226

damaged, causes, 344

data
  leaving open versus opening as needed, 185-186
  viruses in, 342

DBLSPACE.BIN, 515

deleting, 182
  accidentally, 98-99
  after archiving, 493
  all but those to be saved, 334
  from archives, 494
  from target disks before copying files to, 450
  in any subdirectory, 319
  recovering, 190

deletion protecton, 515
  at command line, 317-318

delimited, 45

displaying with specific names, 445

DOS retrieval system, 170-172

downloading, 62

EXE, versus COM/BIN files, 284-286

executable, 516

extensions, 112, 516
  .BAT, 31, 144-145, 511
  .COM, 5, 31, 144-145, 513
  copying multiple groups of files by, 445
  .EXE, 5, 31, 144-145, 516
  in directory entries, 175-176
  .SYS, 524

fragmentation, 517

hidden, 7-8, 518
  mismatching with COMMAND.COM, 102

HOWBAD.EXE, 307

IBMBIO.COM, 30, 166, 198-199, 239, 518

IBMDOS.COM, 166, 198-199, 239, 518

INSTALL.BAT, 307-308

IO.SYS, 30, 166, 199, 519

LHA.EXE, 307

LHARC.LZH, 307

locations, in directory entries, 177

lost from non-write through caches, 145-146

MBACK.LZH, 307

misnaming, 97

missing, 194
moving, 444-445
 advanced options,
  329-330
MSDOS.SYS, 166,
 199, 520
naming, 112-113, 208
 in directory entries,
  175-176
 viewing full paths, 179
NUL, 180
opening, 179-180
overwriting, 55, 117, 195
PANDA93.LZH, 307
PCOPY93.LZH, 307
preparing for Auto
 Restore, 493
PRN, 180
program, viruses in, 342
PUBDOM93.LZH, 308
read-only, 522
 removing designation,
  197
 virus infections, 347
reading from, 181-182
restoring
 archived, 468-470,
  486-492
 virus-infected, 71-72
searching for, 46-47, 145
 in multiple
  directories, 450
 through all
  subdirectories,
  314-315
selecting for backup, 369,
 401-404
sizes, 178
sorting in directory
 listings, 47
split
 copying to multiple
  floppy disks, 447
 parameters, 434
STOW93.LZH, 308

synchronizing between
 computers, 452
system, 524
undeleting, 182-185
uploading, 62
writing to, 180-181
filespecs, 517
 global, 517
FINDPART program (PANDA
 Systems), 306, 319-320
fire, protecting against,
 85-86
/FL switch, PCOPY
 command, 431
flat databases, 44
flea markets, 281-282
flip-flop circuits, 26
floppy disks, 517
 backing up hard drives
  to, 447-449
 backups, 117-118
 boot
  problems caused by
   not having, 101
  system recovery,
   creating, 398-399
 booting from, 188
 capacities, 158-159
 components, 154
 copying files between,
  452-453
 DOS Boot Sector, 239-267
  recovering, 242-243
  viruses, 241-242
 formatting, 31-32,
  156-157
  accidentally, 192
 labeling, 88
 matching sizes and
  capacities, 146-148
 swapping overwriting
  FATs, 47-48
 write protection, 155, 526
  virus infection, 348

floppy drives, 517
 troubleshooting, 36-38
/FO switch, PCOPY
 command, 431
FORMAT program
 (PC-Tools), 192
FORMAT command, 32
 /S switch, 211
 /U switch, 192
formatting, 31-32
 data, 43-44
 floppy disks, 156-157
  accidentally, 192
 hard drives, accidentally,
  192-193
 unlabelled disks, 88
fragmentation, 517
freeing hard drive space, 451
frozen programs, 149-152
 troubleshooting, 186
full backups, 110-111,
 114-115
 in MegaBack program,
  367-368

G

games, Core Wars, 58-59
Gates, Bill, 164-165
General failure reading/
 writing drive x message,
 204-205
gigabytes, 14
global filespecs, 517
grandfathering backups, 125
graphic ASCII character
 codes, 16-24
Greenberg, Ross, 337
GUIs (graphical user
 interfaces), 8, 167
Gulf War virus plant,
 346-347

H

hackers, 338
 writing viruses, 340
handles, file, 179-180
hard disks, 517
 archiving files
  freeing space by, 451
  reasons, 457, 470-471
  versus compressing,
   472
 backing up, 114-115,
  447-449
  multiple, 368-369
  saving generation
   backup copies, 452
 booting from, trouble-
  shooting, 187-190
 capacities, 162
 components, 159-160
 DOS Boot Sector,
  recovering, 243-246
 files, copying sets to
  multiple floppy disks,
  446-447
 formatting, 32
  accidentally, 192-193
 interleaving, 161-162
 lost, restoring files to, 398
 MBR (Master Boot
  Record), 239, 246-267
 partitions, 169, 521
  information about,
   313-314
 repartitioning, 258-267
hard drives, 6, 517
 adding boards and
  broadcasting radio
  spectrum radiation, 94
 crashes, see crashes
 troubleshooting, 38-39
hardware, 5-6, 517
 assessing vulnerability, 77
 backup, 127-128
 buying "new", 273-274

latest technology,
 277-279
MegaBack program
 requirements, 413
planning for disasters, 79
Stowaway program
 requirements, 505
Weirdware, 279
headers, 284
heads, see read/write heads
heat, effects on magnetic
 media, 83-84
Help
 MegaBack program,
  412-413
 Stowaway program, 504
hexadecimal numbering
 system, 13-14, 237-238,
 518
 ASCII codes, 16-24
hidden attribute, 518
hidden files, 7-8, 518
 mismatching with
  COMMAND.COM, 102
HMA (high memory
 area), 518
Hopkins, Andy, 63
Hopper, Grace, 232
host drives, 518
hotkeys, 52, 518
HOWBAD program,
 307, 335
HOWBAD.EXE file, 307
human error
 accidentally deleting files,
  98-99
 adding boards to hard
  drives and broadcasting
  radio spectrum radia-
  tion, 94
 answering non-under-
  stood questions, 90
 attempting to outsmart
  installation programs,
  93-94

auto-pilot reflexes for
 keyboard shortcuts,
 88-89
backups gone wrong,
 97-102
DEL . (period)
 command, 94
dropping propped books
 onto keyboard, 96
exit shortcuts, 89-90
formatting unlabelled
 floppy disks, 88
leaving disks on
 speakers, 101
mismatching
 COMMAND.COM and
 hidden files, 102
misnaming files, 97
no boot disks, 101
not backing up, 97, 102
not checking about
 vendor support,
 100-101, 275-276
not determining message
 sources and meanings,
 92-93
not planning for enough
 memory, 100
not understanding
 programs before
 using, 92
overloading memory at
 startup, 99
running unknown/
 untested programs, 93
software piracy, 91
trusting
 "knowledgable"
  friends, 276
 reviews, 277
using keyboard shortcuts
 without reading
 documentation, 96
hung programs, trouble-
 shooting, 186
 see also crashes

I

/I switch, MB
command, 409
I/O (input/output), 519
IBM PCs, history, 3-4
IBMBIO.COM file, 30, 166,
198-199, 239, 518
IBMDOS.COM file, 166,
198-199, 239, 518
icons, 518
ICs (integrated circuits), 27
/ID switch
MB command, 380-381,
409-410
STOW command, 500
/IFA switch, PCOPY
command, 431
/IFP switch, PCOPY
command, 431
IMAGE (Norton
Utilities), 192
importing data, 45-46
Incorrect DOS version
message, 205
incremental backups, 111,
116-117
in MegaBack program,
367-368
indexes
archive
backing up, 503
building, 496-497
deleting, 497
files, 473-474
packing, 495-496
volumes, groups, and
sets, 474-475
backup
file, 381
keeping updated with
hard drives, 408
rebuilding from
backup volumes,
405-406

reinitializing, 406-407
volume, 381
indirect infectors, 66-67
input, 518
input/output (I/O), 519
Input/Output Address
Ports, 166
Insert disk with
\COMMAND.COM in drive x
message, 205-206
INSTALL command, 459
INSTALL.BAT file, 307, 308
installing programs
disasters caused by
outsmart attempts,
93-94
MegaBack, 371-375
planning for disasters, 81
rewriting
AUTOEXEC.BAT file,
51-52
rewriting CONFIG.SYS
file, 48-51
Stowaway, 459-460
Instruction Pointer (IP)
register, 28
at startup, 29
Insufficient disk space
message, 206
integrated circuits (ICs), 27
integrity checkers, 69-70
interfaces, 519
user, 525
interleaving, 161-162
InterNet worm, 58, 345-346
Interrupt Vector Table, 286
interrupt vectors, displaying
associations with TSRs,
312-313
interrupts, 519
hooked by
MONITOR program,
316
NODEL program, 317

Invalid drive
specification message,
188, 206-207, 246,
249, 255
Invalid partition table
message, 207, 248
Invalid path, not
directory, dir not
empty message, 207-208
invalid subdirectory entries,
228-231
IO.SYS file, 30, 166,
199, 519
IP (Instruction Pointer)
register, 28
at startup, 29

J-K

Jerusalem B virus, 66
JFT (Job File Table), 49
key fields, 44
keyboard input routines, 31
keyboard shortcuts
auto-pilot disasters, 88-89
hotkeys, 52, 518
using without reading
documentation, 96
warm boot (Alt-Ctrl-Del),
149
keyboards, 6
dropping propped books
onto, 96
troubleshooting, 33-35
keys
BROWSE movement, 311
DRHOOK movement,
313
kilobytes (K or Kb), 14,
158, 519

L

/L switch, PCOPY command, 431

labeling floppy disks, 88

laptop/notebook computers, troubleshooting, 41

/LG switch, PCOPY command, 432

LHA.EXE file, 307

LHARC program, 307, 332-333

LHARC.LZH file, 307

licenses, PCOPY program, 418
  site fees, 453

locked programs, 149-152

locking up system, TSR problems, 53-54
  see also crashes

logic gates, 26-27

logical devices, 168-169

logical drives, 519
  RAM disks, 522

logical sectors, 170
  capacities, 170

loops, endless
  bad boot sectors, 140
  recursive
    batch files causing repeating lines of text, 143-144
    partition tables, 140-141

lost allocation units, 219-222, 519

M

/M switch
  PCOPY command, 432
  XCOPY command, 117

Machrone, Bill, 343

magnetic media
  assessing vulnerability, 77-78
  maintenance, 83-85

magnets, effects on magnetic media, 83

mail-order houses, 281

maintenance
  floppy drives, 37
  keyboards, 35
  monitors, 36
  power supply, 40
  preventive, site security, 85-86
  saving hard drives from batch files, 283-284
  spare parts, shopping list for, 41-42
  storage media, 83-85
  see also cleaning

malicious software (malware), 57
  defining, 61-62
  history, 62-63
  naming, 63-64

manuals, Stowaway program, 456

Master Boot Record (MBR), 239, 246-249, 519
  boot sector viruses, 60, 253-255
  replacing startup code, 250-253

MB command, 376, 409-410
  /ID switch, 380-381

MBACK.LZH file, 307

McAfee, John, 341-342, 345-346

McIlroy, H. Douglas, 58

MD command, 191

/ME switch, PCOPY command, 432

media descriptor byte, 178, 267-268

MegaBack program (Patri-Soft Utilities), 126-127, 306, 320-324, 364
  backing up files, 365-367, 376-378, 383-389
  backup indexes
    file, 381
    keeping updated with hard drives, 408
    rebuilding from backup volumes, 405-406
    reinitializing, 406-407
    volume, 381
  backup sets, 380-381
    uses, 411
  backup volumes, 380
    copying, 412
    preparing, 381-382
    verifying data, 404-405
  backups
    full versus incremental, 367-368
    multiple hard drives, 368-369
    selecting files for, 369, 401-404
  command line structure, 409-410
  data integrity, 370-371, 404-405
  display colors, changing, 407-408
  features, 364-365
  hardware/software requirements, 413
  help system, 412-413
  installing, 371-375
  menu commands, 382-383
    Backup Processing, 383-389
    Restore Processing, 389-398
    Utilities menu, 399-408

restoring backup files,
367, 378-379, 389-398
to lost hard drives, 398
starting, 376
setting switches
automatically, 410
system recovery boot
disks, creating, 398-399
technical support,
414-416
troubleshooting, 414
using with tape
backups, 369
warranty information,
363-364
megabytes (M or Mb or
meg), 14, 158-159, 520
MEM command, 287
memory, 520
allocating, 287-288
buffers, 48-51, 512
caches, 512-513
control block informa-
tion, 209
conventional, 514
expanded, 516
extended, 516
HMA (high memory
area), 518
not planning for
enough, 100
overloading at startup, 99
RAM (random access
memory), 27, 522
ROM (read-only
memory), 27, 239, 522
stacks, 523
TSR usage, displaying,
312-313
upper, 524-525
Memory allocation error
message, 199, 209
memory-resident programs,
see TSRs

menus, 520
copy-specification,
PCOPY program,
437-443
Stowaway program,
475-476
merging directories, 449-450
messages, 148
xxxx 201, 141
1701, 29, 142
17xx, 188
301, 29, 35, 141-142
601, 142
Abort, Retry, Fail,
387-388
Abort, Retry, Ignore,
Fail?, 196
Access denied, 197
Bad command or file
name, 144, 197
Bad or missing
command interpreter,
102, 197-198
Cannot find system
files, 198-199
Cannot load COMMAND,
system halted, 199
Data error reading/
writing drive x,
199-200
Disk boot failure, 200
Divide overflow, 200
Drive not ready error
reading/writing drive
x, 201
Error in EXE file, 201
Error loading operat-
ing system, 201, 248
Error reading drive
A:. Abort, Retry,
Fail, 243
Error writing
directory, 202
Error writing FAT, 202
Error writing fixed
disk, 201-202

Error writing parti-
tion table, 203
Fatal Error. Reboot
Now!, 93
File allocation table
bad, drive x, 203
File creation error,
203-204
File not found, 204
FILENAME.EXT already
exists. Replace it?
Y/N?, 55
General failure read-
ing/writing drive x,
204-205
Incorrect DOS version,
205
Insert disk with
\COMMAND.COM in drive
x, 205-206
Insufficient disk
space, 206
Invalid drive specifi-
cation, 188, 206-207,
246, 249, 255
Invalid partition
table, 207, 248
Invalid path, not
directory, dir not
empty, 207-208
Memory allocation
error, 199, 209
Missing operating
system, 209, 248
No room for system
on destination disk,
210-211
Non-DOS disk error
reading/writing drive
x, 209-210
Non-system disk or
disk error. Replace
and press any key
when ready, 29-30, 65,
210, 241

Not ready error
reading/writing drive
x, 210
Parity Check, 142
Path not found, 211
Read fault error
reading drive x,
211-212
Sector not found error
reading/writing drive
x, 212
Seek error reading/
writing drive x, 212
source and meaning,
determining, 92-93
Starting MS-DOS, 190
Write protect error
writing drive x,
212-213
Your PC is stoned,
legalize marijuana,
148
MFM (Modified Frequency
Modulation) encoding, 154
Michelangelo virus, 64, 71,
107-108, 341-342
MIPS (million instructions
per second), 28
MIRROR command, 192
/DT switch, 184
MIRROR program
(PC-Tools), 192, 243-244
missing files, 194
Missing operating system
message, 209, 248
modems, 520
Modified Frequency
Modulation (MFM)
encoding, 154
MONITOR installation
screen, 316
MONITOR program (PANDA
Systems), 315-316
monitors, 6
troubleshooting, 35-36
dark screen, 140

Morris, Robert, 58
Morris, Robert Jr., 58,
345-346
motherboard, 6
mouse
auto-pilot disasters, 89
clicking, 513
dragging, 516
moving files, 444-445
advanced options,
329-330
MSDOS.SYS file, 166,
199, 520
/MU switch, PCOPY
command, 432
Mutation Engine viruses,
342-343

N

/N switch
HOWBAD program, 335
PCOPY command, 432
/NA switch, PCOPY
command, 432
naming
devices, 168, 289-290
files, 112-113, 208
in directory entries,
175-176
misnaming, 97
viruses, 63-64
/ND switch, STOW
command, 500
Neff, Tom, 63
neutrons, 24
"new" hardware or software,
273-274
Newhouse, Eric, 63
nibbles, 13
/NL switch, MB
command, 410

No room for system
on destination disk
message, 210-211
NODEL program (PANDA
Systems), 305, 317-318
non-conductors, 25
Non-DOS disk error
reading/writing drive x
message, 209-210
Non-system disk or disk
error. Replace and
press any key when
ready message, 29-30, 65,
210, 241
Norton Utilities, 126
Calibrate, 200
Directory Sort (DS), 47
Disk Doctor, 188,
194-195, 200, 202-203,
205, 207, 209, 212
DISK EDIT, 268, 270
ERASE PROTECT, 195
IMAGE, 192
SAFE FORMAT and
UNFORMAT, 192
UNERASE, 190-191
Not ready error
reading/writing drive x
message, 210
/NP switch, PCOPY
command, 432
/NS switch, MB
command, 410
nucleus, atoms, 24
NUKELA virus, 63
NUL file, 180
numbering systems, 235-238
binary, 511
versus decimal, 12-14
hexadecimal, 13-14, 518
octal, 14
numeric keypad, 520
/NW switch, PCOPY
command, 432

0

/O switch
DIR command, 47
PCOPY command, 432-433
octal numbering system, 14
ASCII codes, 16-24
off-site backups, 128
Off/On switches, 150
Offset 00 (BOOT INDICA-
TOR), 260
Offset 00h (FILENAME
EXTENSION), 175-176
Offset 01 (STARTING
HEAD), 260-261
Offset 02 (STARTING
TRACK/SECTOR), 261
Offset 04 (PARTITION
TYPE), 262
Offset 05 (ENDING HEAD),
262-263
Offset 06 (ENDING SEC-
TOR/TRACK), 263-264
Offset 08 (STARTING
SECTOR FROM BEGIN-
NING), 265
Offset 0Bh (Attribute),
176-177
Offset 0C (TOTAL NUMBER
OF SECTORS), 265-266
Offset 0Ch (Reserved), 177
Offset 16h (File Time), 177
Offset 18h (File Date), 177
Offset 1Ah (Starting Cluster
Number), 177
Offset 1Ch (File Size), 178
ohms, 25
on-line services
DELPHI, exiting E-mail
service by back door, 90
PRODIGY, TSR
problems, 53
user groups and technical
support, 290

opening files, 179-180
operating systems, 520-521
DOS, see DOS
MegaBack program
requirements, 413
output, 521
overloading memory at
startup, 99
overwriting
FATs of floppy disks,
47-48
files, 55, 117, 195

P

/P switch
MONITOR program, 315
PCOPY command, 433
XCOPY command, 117
packing archive indexes,
495-496
PANDA Systems, 336
BOOTINFO program, 306
BROWSE program, 306,
310-311
DELALL program,
306, 319
DISKINFO program, 305,
311-312
DRHOOK program, 282,
287, 289, 305, 312-313
FINDPART program, 306,
319-320
installing disk
programs, 308
MONITOR program,
315-316
NODEL program, 305,
317-318
PARTINFO program, 306,
313-314
programs as shareware,
308-309

programs on-disk, 309
technical support, 336
WHEREIS program, 306,
314-315
PANDA93.LZH file, 307
parallel ports, 6, 521
parameters, 521
files as, 450
Split File, 434
parent directories, .. (Double
Dot) name, 230, 509
parity bit, 142
Parity Check message, 142
PARTINFO program (PANDA
Systems), 306, 313-314
partition tables, 247-249, 521
checking for mismatched
information with boot
sector and BIOS, 319-320
reconstructing, 255-267
recursive, causing endless
loops, 140-141
partitions, 169, 521
information about,
313-314
/PARTN switch, MIRROR
command, 243
PATH command, 145
Path not found message,
211
paths, 521
absolute, 509
full, viewing for
filenames, 179
search, 523
Patri-Soft Utilities
MegaBack program,
126-127, 306, 320-324,
363-416
PCOPY program, 306,
327-332, 417-453
Stowaway program, 306,
324-327, 455-507
PC Connection of Marlowe,
New Hampshire, 281

PC-Tools, 126
    Disk Fix program, 188,
        194-195, 200, 202-203,
        205, 209, 212
    Emergency Disk
        program, 207
    FORMAT and
        UNFORMAT
        programs, 192
    MIRROR program, 192
    UNDELETE program, 184,
        190-191, 195
PCOPY command, 423-436
PCOPY options screen, 329
PCOPY program (Patri-Soft
    Utilities), 306, 327-332
    command parameters,
        423-436
    copy-specification
        menus, 437-443
    copying files, 443-453
    disclaimer, 417-418
    features, 420-423
    license, 418
    PMOVE, 421
    registration, 418-420
    site licensing fees, 453
PCOPY93.LZH file, 307
PCs (personal computers)
    AT Class, saving and
        restoring setup informa-
        tion, 333-334
    booting, 240-241, 512
    environments, 8
    hardware, 5-6
    history, 3-4
    rebooting, 149, 522
    software, 6-8
    startup, 28-30
        troubleshooting,
            137-142
    synchronizing files
        between, 452
    transporting disks
        between, 451

Penticle chips, 28
performance, improving for
    batch files, 283-284
Peterson, A. Padgett, 60
pets, disasters caused by,
    94-95, 102
piracy, 91
planning for disasters, see
    disasters, planning for
PMOVE (PCOPY
    command), 421
ports, 6, 521
    Input/Output
        Address, 166
    parallel, 521
    serial, 523
power supply, 6
    troubleshooting, 40-41
Power-On Self-Test (POST),
    29, 239
    troubleshooting errors,
        141-142
precedence,
    COMMAND.COM,
    running programs, 144-145
primary DOS partitions, 169
PRINT SCREEN
    command, 36
PRN file, 180
process data, 5
processor interrupts, 519
processors, 521
PRODIGY on-line service,
    TSR problems, 53
program files
    COM/BIN versus EXE,
        284-286
    viruses in, 342
program infectors, 65-66
    direct versus indirect,
        66-67
    stealth techniques, 67
    see also viruses
programs, 5, 43, 521
    abnormal termination,
        guidelines, 186

anti-virus, 63, 68, 510
    behavior blockers, 70
    integrity checkers,
        69-70
    restoration programs,
        71-72
    scanners, 68-69
associated files, 510
backups, 123-124,
    126-127
BOMBSQAD, 63
bootstrap loader, 28-29
bugs, 232, 338
buying "new", 273-274
Check Disk (CHKDSK),
    217-231
CHK4BOMB, 63
CHKDIR, 307, 334-335
CMOS, 307, 333-334
COMMAND.COM,
    30-31, 102, 144-145,
    167-168, 514
conversion, 45-46
database, 44
DEBUG.COM
    (DEBUG.EXE), 232-234,
    242-243, 245-247,
    250-253, 267-270
DELBUT, 307, 334
documentation, 82-83
DOS-upgrade support,
    80-81
downloading, 62
dropper, 344
exiting, disasterous
    shortcuts, 89-90
FDISK, 250, 255-259
Fifth Generation's
    Fastback Plus, 126
HOWBAD, 307, 335
installing
    disasters caused by
        outsmart attempts,
        93-94
    planning for
        disasters, 81

rewriting
  AUTOEXEC.BAT file,
  51-52
rewriting CONFIG.SYS
  file, 48-51
latest technology, 277-279
LHARC, 307, 332-333
MIRROR, 243-244
Norton Utilities, 126
  Calibrate, 200
  Directory Sort (DS), 47
  Disk Doctor, 188,
    194-195, 200,
    202-203, 205, 207,
    209, 212
  DISK EDIT, 268, 270
  ERASE PROTECT, 195
  IMAGE, 192
  SAFE FORMAT and
    UNFORMAT, 192
  UNERASE, 190-191
PANDA Systems, 336
  as shareware, 308-309
  BOOTINFO, 188, 207,
    306, 309-310
  BROWSE, 306, 310-311
  DELALL, 306, 319
  DISKINFO, 305,
    311-312
  DRHOOK, 282, 287,
    289, 305, 312-313
  FINDPART, 306,
    319-320
  MONITOR, 315-316
  NODEL, 305, 317-318
  on disk, installing, 308
  on-disk, 309
  PARTINFO, 306,
    313-314
  technical support, 336
  WHEREIS, 46-47, 145,
    306, 314-315
Patri-Soft Utilities
  MegaBack, 126-127,
    306, 320-324,
    363-416, 417-453

PCOPY, 306, 327-332
Stowaway, 306,
  324-327, 455-507
PC-Tools, 126
  Disk Fix, 188, 194-195,
    200, 202-203, 205,
    209, 212
  Emergency Disk, 207
  FORMAT and
    UNFORMAT, 192
  MIRROR, 192
  UNDELETE, 184,
    190-191, 195
piracy, 91
product conversions,
  testing, 56
running
  under Windows, 54-55
  unknown/untested, 93
shareware, see shareware
spreadsheet, 44
stopped or locked,
  149-152
TSR unloaders, 53
TSRs (terminate-and-stay-
  resident), see TSRs
understanding before
  using, 92
uploading, 62
vaporware, 278-279
version upgrades, testing,
  55-56
viruses, see viruses
Weirdware, 279
wrong ones running,
  144-145
prompts, 521
protons, 24
PUBDOM93.LZH file, 308

Q-R

/QA switch, PCOPY
  command, 433

/R switch
  MB command, 410
  MONITOR program, 315
  PCOPY command, 433
  STOW command, 500
/RA switch, STOW
  command, 500
radio spectrum radiation,
  problems caused by, 94
RAM (random access
  memory), 27, 522
RAM disks, 522
  saving hard drives from
    batch files, 283-284
RAMDRIVE command,
  283-284
/RD switch, PCOPY
  command, 433
/RE switch, PCOPY
  command, 433
Read fault error reading
  drive x message, 211-212
Read the Book (RTB), 82
read-only attribute, 522
read-only files, 522
  removing
    designation, 197
  virus infections, 347
read/write heads, 522
  alignment, troubleshoot-
    ing, 146-148
  floppy disks, 155
  hard drives, 159-160
reading
  from files, 181-182
  to memory, 27
rebooting, 149, 522
records, 44
  boot, 209, 512
recovering
  data, planning for
    disasters
    assessing vulnerability,
      77-79
    determining levels of
      planning, 74-75

DOS-upgrade support, 80-81
hardware, 79
installing and using software, 81-82
management considerations, 75-76
program documentation, 82-83
site security preventive maintenance, 85-86
software, 79-80
storage media maintenance, 83-85
DOS Boot Sector
floppy disks, 242-243
hard disks, 243-246
files
deleted, 98-99, 182-185, 190
from deleted subdirectories, 191
virus-infected, 71-72
from disk write errors when archiving, 484-486
lost allocation units, 219-222
lost or damaged subdirectories, 193-194
warning labels for techniques, 215-216
recursive
batch files, 143-144
partition tables, 140-141
registers, 28
CS (Code Segment), 28-29
IP (Instruction Pointer), 28-29
registration, PCOPY program, 418-420
relational databases, 44
remote backups, 130-131

repair shops
finding, 280
sources of virus infection, 274-275
repairing
boot sectors, 239-267
FAT (File Allocation Table), 267-268
root directories, 268-269
subdirectories, 270
repartitioning hard disks, 258-267
RESTORE command, 114-115
Restore Processing command, MegaBack program, 389-398
restoring
archived files, 468-470, 486-492
backup files, 367, 378-379, 389-398
to lost hard drives, 398
backup indexes, 405-406
setup information, AT Class PCs, 333-334
virus-infected files, 71-72
retrieving files, DOS system, 170-172
reviews, believability, 277
RLL (Run Length Limited) encoding, 154
/RO switch, PCOPY command, 433
RoChenle, Mike, 343
ROM (read-only memory), 27, 522, 239
ROM-BIOS, 522
root directories, 523
repairing, 268-269
troubleshooting, 195
Rosenberger, Rob, 337
Ross, Ed, 335
RTB (Read the Book), 82
Run Length Limited (RLL) encoding, 154

S

/S switch
DIR command, 46, 145
FORMAT command, 211
MB command, 410
PCOPY command, 433
STOW command, 500-501
XCOPY command, 117
/SA switch, PCOPY command, 433-434
SAFE FORMAT (Norton Utilities), 192
salespeople, unknowledgable, buying from, 100-101, 275-276
saving
generation backup copies of files, 452
setup information, AT Class PCs, 333-334
scanners, 68-69
screens
Automatic File Selection, STOWAWAY program, 326
colors
MegaBack program, 407-408
Stowaway program, changing, 498
DRHOOK's Device Driver, 313
DRHOOK's DOS Memory Usage, 312
MONITOR installation, 316
PCOPY options, 329
Stowaway archiving, 328
troubleshooting dark, 140
scrolling, 523
endlessly repeating lines of text, 143-144
search paths, 523

searching for files,
46-47, 145
through all
subdirectories, 314-315
through multiple
directories, 450
Sector not found error
reading/writing drive x
message, 212
sectors, 48-49, 156, 523
Bad Sector mark, 174
boot, 30, 64, 512
Bios Parameter Block
(BPB) information,
309-310
causing endless
loops, 140
DOS Boot Sector,
239-240, 516
checking for mis-
matched information
with partition table,
319-320
MBR (Master Boot
Record), 239,
246-267, 519
viruses, 53, 60,
64-65, 67, 241-242,
253-255, 344
logical, 170
capacities, 170
security
assessing vulnerability,
78-79
site, preventive mainte-
nance, 85-86
Seek error reading/
writing drive x
message, 212
selecting files for backup,
369, 401-404
semantic data, 5
semiconductors, 26
serial ports, 6, 523

service
finding, 280
see also technical support
service calls, sources of virus
infection, 274-275
SFT (System File Table), 49
/SHA switch, PCOPY
command, 434
Shabeck, Tim, 75
shareware, 338
as sources of viruses, 343
PANDA Systems
programs, 308-309
Patri-Soft Utilities, 306
taking problems to ASP
(Association of
Shareware Profession-
als), 417
shells, 523
/SHN switch, PCOPY
command, 434
shrinkwrap safety, 273-274
/SHx switch, PCOPY
command, 434
signatures, virus, 68
silicon, 26
site
licensing fees, PCOPY
program, 453
security
assessing vulnerability,
78-79
preventive mainte-
nance, 85-86
sizes
files, 178
floppy disks, matching,
146-148
SMARTDRV command,
145-146
software, 6-8
assessing vulnerability, 77
planning for disasters,
79-80
see also programs

software interrupts, 519
Solomon, Dr. Alan, 353
sorting files in directory
listings, 47
source disks, 114
/SP switch, PCOPY
command, 434
spare parts, shopping list
for, 41-42
speakers, disasters caused
by, 101
/SPL switch, PCOPY
command, 434
split files
copying to multiple
floppy disks, 447
parameters, 434
spreadsheet programs, 44
/SS switch, PCOPY
command, 435
/ST switch, PCOPY
command, 435
stacks, 523
stamps, date and time, in
directory entries, 177
Starting MS-DOS
message, 190
startup
MegaBack program, 376
setting switches
automatically, 410
overloading memory, 99
PCs, 28-30
Stowaway program,
465-466
troubleshooting
bad boot sectors
causing endless
loops, 140
booting from hard
drives, 187-190
dark screen, 140
fan starts/nothing
happens, 138-139
not starting, 137-138

Power-On Self-Test
(POST) errors,
141-142
recursive partition
tables causing endless
loops, 140-141
TSRs, 52-53
stealth techniques, viruses,
67-68
stepper motors, 155
Stoned virus, 64
storage media, maintenance,
83-85
STOW command, 460,
465-466, 499-501
STOW93.LZH file, 308
Stowaway archiving
screen, 328
Stowaway program (Patri-
Soft Utilities), 306, 324-327
archive groups, 482-483
archive indexes
backing up, 503
building, 496-497
deleting, 497
for files, 473-474
for volumes, groups,
and sets, 474-475
packing, 495-496
archive sets, 473
multiple, 501-502
preparing, 475
archive volumes, 472-473
copying, 503-504
archiving files, 458-459,
466-468
expiration dates, 474
manually, 476-484
reasons, 457
command line param-
eters, 498-501
customizing, 460-465
deleting files
after archiving, 493
from archives, 494

disk write errors, recovering from, 484-486
display colors,
changing, 498
features, 458
help system, 504
installing, 459-460
manual, 456
menus, 475-476
preparing files for Auto
Restore, 493
restoring archived files,
468-470, 486-492
starting, 465-466
statistical summaries, 498
system requirements, 505
technical support,
506-507
troubleshooting, 505-506
verifying archived files,
494-495
warranty, 455-456
streaming tape backup
units, 127-128
style sheets, 44
subdirectories, 523
. (Dot) name, 230, 509
deleted, recovering files
from, 191
information about,
334-335
invalid entries, 228-231
lost or damaged, trouble-
shooting, 193-194
repairing, 270
SUBST command, 169
support
finding, 280
MegaBack program,
414-416
on-line services and user
groups, 290
PANDA programs on-
disk, 336
reviews, 277

Stowaway program,
506-507
trusting "knowledgable"
friends, 276
/SV switch
MB command, 410
STOW command, 501
swapping floppy disks,
overwriting FATs, 47-48
switches, 524
/4, PCOPY command, 424
/A
DIR command, 199
PCOPY command, 424
XCOPY command,
116-117
/AD, PCOPY
command, 424
/AF
MB command, 409
PCOPY command, 424
/AP, PCOPY
command, 424
/AZ, PCOPY
command, 424
/B
PCOPY command, 424
STOW command, 499
/BA
PCOPY command, 424
STOW command, 499
/BW, PCOPY
command, 425
/C, MB command, 409
/C2, PCOPY
command, 426
/C3, PCOPY
command, 426
/CD, PCOPY
command, 425
/CF, PCOPY
command, 426
/D
HOWBAD
program, 335

NODEL program, 317
PCOPY command,
426-427
STOW command, 499
/D-, PCOPY
command, 427
/D2, PCOPY
command, 427
/DC, PCOPY
command, 427
/DCA, PCOPY
command, 427
/DEL, STOW
command, 499
/DL, PCOPY
command, 427
/DO, PCOPY
command, 427
/DR, PCOPY
command, 427
/DS, PCOPY
command, 428
/DT, MIRROR
command, 184
/DX, PCOPY
command, 428
/DY, PCOPY
command, 428
/E, PCOPY
command, 428
/EQ, PCOPY command,
428-429
/EV
MB command, 409
STOW command, 500
/EX
PCOPY command,
429-430
STOW command, 500
/F
BACKUP
command, 115
CHKDSK command,
219-223, 228-230
MB command, 409

MONITOR
program, 316
PCOPY command,
430-431
STOW command, 500
/FI, PCOPY
command, 431
/FL, PCOPY
command, 431
/FO, PCOPY
command, 431
/ID
MB command,
380-381, 409-410
STOW command, 500
/IFA, PCOPY
command, 431
/IFP, PCOPY
command, 431
/L, PCOPY
command, 431
/LG, PCOPY
command, 432
/M
PCOPY command, 432
XCOPY command,
117
/ME, PCOPY
command, 432
/MU, PCOPY
command, 432
/N
HOWBAD program,
335
PCOPY command, 432
/NA, PCOPY
command, 432
/ND, STOW
command, 500
/NL, MB command, 410
/NP, PCOPY
command, 432
/NS, MB command, 410
/NW, PCOPY
command, 432

/O
DIR command, 47
PCOPY command,
432-433
Off/On, 150
/P
MONITOR program,
315
PCOPY command, 433
XCOPY command, 117
/PARTN, MIRROR
command, 243
/QA, PCOPY
command, 433
/R
MB command, 410
MONITOR program,
315
PCOPY command, 433
STOW command, 500
/RA, STOW
command, 500
/RD, PCOPY
command, 433
/RE, PCOPY
command, 433
/RO, PCOPY
command, 433
/S
DIR command, 46, 145
FORMAT command,
211
MB command, 410
PCOPY command, 433
STOW command,
500-501
XCOPY command, 117
/SA, PCOPY command,
433-434
/SHA, PCOPY
command, 434
/SHN, PCOPY
command, 434
/SHx, PCOPY
command, 434

/SP, PCOPY
    command, 434
/SPL, PCOPY
    command, 434
/SS, PCOPY
    command, 435
/ST, PCOPY
    command, 435
/SV
    MB command, 410
    STOW command, 501
/SZ, PCOPY
    command, 435
/T, PCOPY command,
    435-436
/TF, PCOPY
    command, 436
/TO, PCOPY
    command, 435
/U
    FORMAT command,
        192
    PCOPY command, 436
/V
    COPY command, 115
    MB command, 410
    MONITOR program,
        316
    PCOPY command, 436
/W, MONITOR
    program, 316
/WH, PCOPY
    command, 436
/WT, PCOPY
    command, 436
/X
    MONITOR program,
        316
    PCOPY command, 436
Symantec virus signature
    updates, 69
SYS command, 199-201
.SYS file extension, 524
system
    dates, stamps in directory
        entries, 177

files, 524
recovery boot disks,
    see boot disks
time, stamps in directory
    entries, 177
system attribute, 524
System File Table (SFT), 49
system units, 6
/SZ switch, PCOPY
    command, 435

T

/T switch, PCOPY
    command, 435-436
tables
    binary multiplication, 13
    FAT (File Allocation
        Table), see FAT
    Interrupt Vector
        Table, 286
    JFT (Job File Table), 49
    partition, see partition
        tables
    SFT (System File Table), 49
tape backup units, 127-128
tape backups, using
    MegaBack program
    with, 369
target disks, 114
    deleting files from, before
        copying files to, 450
technical support
    finding, 280
    MegaBack program (Patri-
        Soft Utilities), 414-416
    on-line services and user
        groups, 290
    PANDA programs on-
        disk, 336
    reviews, 277
    Stowaway program (Patri-
        Soft Utilities), 506-507

trusting "knowledgable"
    friends, 276
technology, latest, 277-279
telecommunications, 524
    backups using, 129-130
telephones, distinctive
    ringing, 131
temperature extremes,
    effects on magnetic media,
    83-84
Terminate-and-Stay-
    Resident programs,
    see TSRs
testing
    AUTOEXEC.BAT file
        for hanging system,
        189-190
    CONFIG.SYS file
        for hanging system,
        189-190
    product conversions, 56
    program version
        upgrades, 55-56
text
    browsing, 310-311
    endlessly repeating lines,
        143-144
/TF switch, PCOPY
    command, 436
theft, protecting against,
    85-86
Thompson, Ken, 58-59
time
    criteria for selecting files
        for copying, 444
    file stamps, in directory
        entries, 177
Tippett, Peter, 340
/TO switch, PCOPY
    command, 435
tower configurations, 6
tracks, 155, 524
    boot, 30
transistors, 26-27

Trojan horses, 60,
338-339, 524
  age of, 340
  Burleson (Donald)
    conviction, 344-345
  EGABTR, 63
  in boot infectors, 64-65
  Michelangelo, 64
  prevention guidelines,
    348-349
  Stoned, 64
  types of computers, 347
  versus viruses, 338-339
  see also viruses
troubleshooting
  abnormal program
    termination, 186
  allocation errors, 227-228
  boot sectors, 239-267
  endless loops, 140-141
  endlessly repeating lines
    of text, 143-144
  fan starts/nothing
    happens, 138-139
  FAT (File Allocation
    Table), 191-192, 267-268
  floppy disks, overwrit-
    ing, 47-48
  files
    cross-linked, 222-226
    deleted, 190-191
    missing, 145-146, 194
    overwriting, 195
  floppy disks
    formatting acciden-
      tally, 192
    transferring to other
      drives, 146-148
  floppy drives, 36-38
  hard disks, formatting
    accidentally, 192-193
  hard drives, 38-39
  installation, 48-52
  invalid subdirectory
    entries, 228-231

keysboards, 33-35
laptop/notebook
  computers, 41
lost allocation units,
  219-222
MegaBack program, 414
messages, 148
monitors, 35-36
planning for disasters,
  74-86
power supply, 40-41
Power-On Self-Test
  (POST) errors, 141-142
programs running under
  Windows, 54-55
root directories, 195,
  268-269
startup
  booting from hard
    drives, 187-190
  dark screen, 140
  not starting, 137-138
stopped or locked
  programs, 149-152
Stowaway program,
  505-506
subdirectories, 270
  lost or damaged,
    193-194
TSRs, 52-54
with "knowledgable"
  friends, 276
wrong programs running,
  144-145
TRUENAME command, 179
TSR unloaders, 53
TSRs (Terminate-and-
Stay-Resident programs),
286-289, 520
  displaying memory usage
    and associated interrupt
    vectors, 312-313
  loading/unloading, 52-53
  tweaking, 53-54

U

/U switch
  FORMAT command, 192
  PCOPY command, 436
U.S. government virus plant
  in Iraqi military computers
  during Gulf War, 346-347
UNDELETE program (PC-
  Tools), 184, 190-191, 195
UNDELETE command,
  184-185, 190-191, 195
undeleting, 524
  files, 182-185
UNERASE program, 190-191
UNFORMAT program
  (Norton Utilities), 192
UNFORMAT program
  (PC-Tools), 192
UNFORMAT command, 192
unformatting, 524
updating backup indexes to
  match hard drives, 408
upgrading
  DOS
    backwards compatibil-
      ity, 164-166
    support by data
      recovery utilities,
      80-81
    program versions, testing,
      55-56
uploading, 62
upper memory, 524-525
user
  groups, 290
  interface, 525
Utilities menu commands,
  MegaBack program,
  399-408
utility programs, 525
  see also programs

V

/V switch
    COPY command, 115
    MB command, 410
    MONITOR program, 316
    PCOPY command, 436
vaporware, 278-279
VDTs (Visual Display
    Terminal), 6
vendors
    flea markets, 281-282
    mail-order houses, 281
    of small-market software
        or hardware, 279
    support, checking about,
        100-101, 275-276
verifying
    archived files, 494-495
    backup volume data,
        404-405
Virus Security Institute
    (VSI), 60
viruses, 339, 525
    300bps subcarrier, 343
    age of, 340
    anti-virus, 68
        behavior blockers, 70
        foolproof protection,
            347
        integrity checkers,
            69-70
        preventive techniques,
            70-71
        programs, 315-316, 510
        scanners, 68-69
    backing up, 347
    boot sector, 53, 64-65
        in DOS Boot Sectors,
            241-242
        in Master Boot Records
            (MBRs), 253-255
        sources, 344
    BRAIN, 60

BSI (Boot Sector Infectors)
    infectors, 60
Burleson (Donald)
    conviction, 344-345
checking new software
    for, 56
companion, 61, 286
Core Wars, 58-59
data loss from, 341
defining, 59-62
direct infectors, 66-67
EGABTR, 63
Elk Cloner, 60-61
history, 62-63
humorous list of, 349-352
in data versus program
    files, 342
indirect infectors, 66-67
infection percentage,
    340-341
Internet Worm, 58
Jerusalem B, 66
list of, 353-362
MBR (Master Boot
    Record) infectors, 60
Michelangelo, 64, 71,
    107-108, 341-342
Morris (Robert Jr.)
    conviction, 345-346
Mutation Engine,
    342-343
naming, 63-64
NUKELA, 63
number documented on
    PCs, 341-342
number in existance, 341
possible symptoms,
    140-141
prevention
    guidelines, 348-349
    techniques, 70-71
program infectors, 65-66
read-only files,
    infecting, 347
signatures, 68

sources, 343
    repair shops, 274-275
stealth techniques, 67-68
Stoned, 64
symptomatic
    messages, 148
Trojan horses, 524
types of computers, 347
U.S. government plant
    in Iraqi military com-
    puters during Gulf War,
    346-347
undetectable, 342-343
versus Trojan horses,
    338-339
write-protected floppy
    disks, infecting, 348
written by hackers, 340
    see also Trojan horses
volts, 25
volumes
    archive, 472-473
        copying, 503-504
    backup, 380
        copying, 412
        indexes, 381
        preparing, 381-382
        rebuilding indexes
            from, 405-406
        sets, 380-381, 411
        verifying data, 404-405
von Neumann, John, 57
VSI (Virus Security
    Institute), 60
Vysottsky, Victor, 58

W

/W switch, MONITOR
    program, 316
warm boot, 149
warning labels for recovery
    techniques, 215-216

warranties
MegaBack program,
363-364
Stowaway program,
455-456
Weirdware, 279
/WH switch, PCOPY
command, 436
WHEREIS program (PANDA
Systems), 46-47, 145, 306,
314-315
wild card characters, 525
backups using file
extensions and, 112
Windows, running pro-
grams under, 54-55
windows, 525
wonks, 12
adopting, 280
WORM (Write Once, Read
Many) drives, 525
wormers, 339-340
worms, 60, 339, 525
defining, 61-62
InterNet, 58, 345-346
Morris (Robert Jr.)
conviction, 345-346
Write protect error
writing drive x message,
212-213
write-delayed caches, 526
write-protecting floppy
disks, 155, 526
virus infection, 348
writing
to files, 180-181
to memory, 27
/WT switch, PCOPY
command, 436

X-Z

/X switch
MONITOR program, 316
PCOPY command, 436
XCOPY command, 116-117

Your PC is stoned,
legalize marijuana
message, 148

Zbikowski, Mark, 285

The DR. PANDA UTILITIES

This special, half-price offer from **PANDA** Systems is available only to readers of *The Data Recovery Bible*. Among the most highly rated in the anti-virus industry, the **DR. PANDA UTILITIES** include:

- ➤ Automatic virus scanning at start-up to ensure a clean installation
- ➤ Complete line of generic detection and protection programs
- ➤ Finds and restores infected files
- ➤ Outwits even "Stealth" and "Mutation Engine" viruses
- ➤ Protects memory and critical system areas including boot sector
- ➤ Immediate restoration of infected boot sectors
- ➤ Complete audit trail of PC program use
- ➤ Professional testing utilities
- ➤ Complete on-disk documentation

The **DR. PANDA UTILITIES** provide the finest anti-virus protection available today. No other product automatically repels Boot Sector Viruses such as Michelangelo and Stoned.

The **DR. PANDA UTILITIES** can be installed to provide transparent, accurate identification and prevention for PC users from beginners to experts.

Send check or money order for $39.95 and this page to:

PANDA/ADS
14505 21st Avenue, Suite 228
Plymouth, MN 55447

Disk Contents

Disk Files

INSTALL	BAT	LHARC93	LZH	PCOPY93	LZH
HOWBAD	EXE	MBACK93	LZH	PUBDOM93	LZH
LHA	EXE	PANDA93	LZH	STOW93	LZH

MegaBack Utilities Unzips To

MEGABACK	DOC	REGISTER	DOC	ILINK	
MEGABACK	HLP	SITE	TXT	FILE_ID	DIZ
ORDER	FRM	OMBUDSMN	ASP	README	1ST
				MB	BAT

Stowaway

README	1ST	ILINK		VENDOR	DOC
STOW	EXE	SITE	TXT	STOW	BAT
STOWAWAY	DOC	FILE_ID	DIZ	STOSAWAY	DAT
STOW	HLP	DISCOUNT	TXT	STOWAWAY	LOG
ORDER	FRM	DESCRIBE	DOC	STOVOLIX	DAT
REGISTER	DOC	OMBUDSMN	ASP	STOFILIX	DAT
				STOGRPIX	DAT

Panda Utilities

LHA213	DOC	FINDPART	EXE	PCREADME	
HISTORY	ENG	BROWSE	COM	ORDER	FRM
LHA	HLP	CHKDIR	DOC	ILINK	
NODEL	EXE	CHKDIR	EXE	FILE_ID	DIZ
PARTINFO	EXE	CMOS	EXE	OMBUDSMN	ASP
DISKINFO	EXE	CMOS	PRN	PMOVE	BAT
BOOTINFO	EXE	CMOS	TXT	WHATS	NEW
MONITOR	EXE	DELBUT	DOC	MINSTALL	EXE
DRHOOK	EXE	DELBUT	COM	MBACK220	EXE
WHEREIS	EXE	PCOPY	EXE	SINSTALL	EXE
DELALL	EXE	PCOPY	DOC	STOW191	EXE
				LHA	EXE